THE RISE OF POPULIST NATIONALISM

THE RISE OF POPULIST NATIONALISM

Social Resentments and the Anti-Constitutionalist Turn in Hungary

Edited by

Margit Feischmidt
and
Balázs Majtényi

CEU PRESS

Central European University Press
Budapest–New York

Published in 2019 by
Central European University Press

Nádor utca 9, H-1051 Budapest, Hungary
Tel: +36-1-327-3138 or 327-3000
E-mail: ceupress@press.ceu.edu
Website: www.ceupress.com

224 West 57th Street, New York NY 10019, USA

Published in 2019 by arrangement with the Center of Social Sciences of the Hungarian Academy of Sciences.
Balázs Majtényi's research was supported by the Bolyai János Scholarship of the Hungarian Academy of Sciences.

The authors would like to thank Bálint Gárdos for the linguistic revision of the chapters.

ISBN 978-963-386-331-2 cloth

LIBRARY OF CONGRESS CATALOGING-IN-PUBLICATION DATA

Names: Feischmidt, Margit, editor. | Majtényi, Balázs, editor.
Title: The rise of populist nationalism : social resentments and the anti-constitutionalist turn in Hungary / edited by Margit Feischmidt and Balázs Majtenyi.
Description: Budapest ; New York : Central European University Press, 2019. | Includes bibliographical references and index.
Identifiers: LCCN 2019021325 (print) | LCCN 2019981599 (ebook) | ISBN 9789633863312 | ISBN 9789633863329 (ebook)
Subjects: LCSH: Constitutional history—Hungary. | Nationalism—Hungary. | Nationalism—Europe, Eastern. | Populism—Hungary. | Identity politics—Hungary. | Political culture—Hungary. | Post-communism—Hungary. | Hungary—Politics and government—1989– | Hungary—Social conditions—1989- | Constitutional law—Political aspects—Hungary.
Classification: LCC JN2067 .R57 2019 (print) | LCC JN2067 (ebook) | DDC 342.43902/9—dc23
LC record available at https://lccn.loc.gov/2019021325
LC ebook record available at https://lccn.loc.gov/2019981599

Printed in Hungary

Table of Contents

Introduction

MARGIT FEISCHMIDT and BALÁZS MAJTÉNYI

The authors of this book aim to understand the reasons behind and the meanings of public discourses that reframe politics in terms of nationhood and nationalism in post-socialist Eastern Europe, with a special emphasis on Hungary. The volume examines two arguments (our shorthand for which are shift and legacy) that offer concrete and contextual analyses of numerous theoretical questions related to the region by combining empirical and normative social science perspectives. Some authors focus on shifts in public law and political use of ethno-nationalism through the lens of constitutional law. Others study the social and political causes of this shift, i.e. the structural causes of the social demand for radical discourses on the nation. Ultimately, the volume attempts to explain populist nationalism—understood as the prioritization of the nation, historical argumentation and cultural particularism in the framing of public discourse in Hungary—as rooted in recent political, economic and social processes.

We focus primarily on Hungary, but we reflect upon the entire Central and Eastern European region and relate our findings to the scholarship on other semi-peripheral areas affected by similar processes of political and economic transition.[1] Furthermore, we acknowledge

---

1 L. Rudolf Tőkés, "Transitology: Global Dreams and Post-Communist Realities," *Central Europe Review* 10 (2000): accessed May 17, 2019, http://www.ce-review.org/00/10/tokes10.html.

that a number of phenomena we examine are not simply the results of the last financial crisis, the underdevelopment or the dependence of semi-peripheral societies, and that parallel phenomena are to be found not only in the South and East, but in the Western and Northern countries of Europe as well. The definitive paradigm in the international literature for interpreting the macro-processes in the region, transitology, as well as the literature on post-socialism, supposes a unidirectional process moving from dictatorship toward liberal democracy based on the free market. While reality never perfectly matches the model, it is fair to ask what exactly is being constructed in Hungary as it diverges from the visions of Western and Eastern liberals of a civic democracy in the Western mold.[2] This has become a central question for analysts. In this volume we focus on the shift that has moved discourses using unique collective identities, emphasizing a closed and homogeneous national-ethnic community and utilizing historical legitimacy, from the margins of public debate into the mainstream.[3]

The 'shift approach' is mostly adopted by the legal experts in the volume who emphasize that the Fundamental Law of Hungary is radically different from all previous Hungarian constitutions and other constitutions of EU member states, and is a quasi-mirror of the redefinition of the identity of the state. Kovács's chapter analyses the Fundamental Law through the concept of constitutional continuity, it argues that the Fundamental law and its amendments mean a disruption in Hungarian constitutional history. What makes the Hungarian case unique in the EU is that the Hungarian constitutional system diverges from the inclusive nature of the EU's legal system and although populist-exclusivist elements of political rhetoric are also present elsewhere in Europe—they have not become parts of constitutional law and have not transformed the political system. Through the lenses of political philosophy and constitutional law legal experts analyze the normative

---

[2] Tamás Csillag and Iván Szelényi, "Drifting from Liberal Democracy. Traditionalist/Neo-conservative Ideology of Managed Illiberal Democratic Capitalism in Post-communist Europe," *Intersections, East European Journal of Society and Politics* 1 (2015): 18–48.

[3] András Bozóki and Dániel Hegedűs, "An Externally Constrained Hybrid Regime: Hungary in the European Union," *Democratization* 7 (2017): 1173-1189.

statements and implications of discourses on identity. The authors in the second section take a sociological, socio-anthropological and political science approach by asking what role structural processes contribute to the strengthening of populism and nationalism.

The two sections of the volume taken together tackle the issues of the normative and social levels of identity politics, along with their mutual effects. We consider constitutions the most important documents for defining the identity of the state as well as the values that public authorities present to society as norms. The book focuses on the relation between constitution and society, namely how the popular perception of constitutional values can impact constitutional democracy and its institutions. Constitutional values refers to binding abstract ethical norms, which as ultimate goals determine the interpretations of constitutional documents.[4] Constitutional values as a symbolic code open the gate to going beyond the merely legalistic understanding of institutions.[5] If we want to explore the social and cultural underpinnings of institutions, we need to bring in the symbolic sphere.

This book tries to explore what people understand by constitutional values and why they are ready to defend or defeat those values. Some of those values are general, such as the ones emanating from the universal principles of human rights in modern societies. The other set of values can be explained on the one hand by a will to establish unique norms, and by a divergent political culture, on the other.

We make a distinction between inclusive and exclusive values. Inclusive constitutional values can integrate the interests of all members of the political community as they treat all members as morally equal and, as a result, they strengthen constitutional democracy. Exclusive constitutional values, on the contrary, protect only the ethnic, cultural, political, religious, and other identity elements of the dominant

---

[4] Dennis Davis, Alan Richter and Cheryl Saunders, "Introduction," in *An Inquiry into the Existence of Global Values: Through the Lens of Comparative Constitutional Law,* ed. Dennis Davis, Alan Richter and Cheryl Saunders (Oxford: Hart, 2015), 1–15; Pierre Schlag, "Values, 6 Yale," *Journal of Law & the Humanities* (1994): 219.

[5] Tomasz Warczok and Hanna Debska, "Sacred Law and Profane Politics: The Symbolic Construction of the Constitutional Tribunal," *Polish Sociological Review* 4 (2014): 461–474.

groups of the society. We share the argument that a critical mass of exclusive values leads to the fall of a constitutional democracy.[6] The move to the primacy of exclusive values in Hungarian public law is examined in the context of the legal system of the European Union, acknowledging that the liberal model of constitutional democracies (as supported by the EU) is based on human rights, the rule of law, equality before the law, and procedural values.

The legal studies chapters in the volume analyze and compare the 1989 Constitution of the Republic of Hungary with the 2011 Fundamental Law of Hungary from a comparative constitutional law perspective and a global and supranational constitutionalism perspective. The authors in these chapters answer the question of continuity/discontinuity between the two Hungarian constitutions by examining what internal and external limits are available against changes affecting the basic structure and essence of the constitution, and what (if anything) can limit the identity-building project vis-a-vis universal values in public law. Körtvélyesi's chapter presents through the cases of the US and Canada how politicians seek to maintain constitutional continuity when there is none in reality. Körtvélyesi argues that the opposite happened in the Hungarian case: there is a tension between the rhetoric of a revolutionary constitution making and the formal reliance on the validity of the 1989 Constitution.

Our book analyzes a process by which neutral (in the dominant universal and cultural sense) Hungarian constitutional identity moved toward one of cultural particularism, ethnically-based community and historical legitimacy. Among the effects of this process we primarily examine the ethnic nation concept *vis-à-vis* the egalitarian concept of people and political nation (which characterized the 1989 Constitution), and what kind of inequalities emerged between the majority and the ethnically defined minorities. Moreh's chapter, by looking at the case of external ethnic citizenship, analyzes Hungary's struggle to redefine its political community in a shift towards a re-ethnicization. According to Chronowski's chapter, because of the re-ethnicization of the constitutional use of the 'nation' it is not clear whether minori-

6 Zsolt Körtvélyesi and Balázs Majtényi, "Game of Values: The Threat of Exclusive Constitutional Identity, the EU and Hungary," *German Law Journal* 7 (2017): 1722.

ties fall under the same norms of political solidarity as the Hungarian majority. We ask how saturating the concept of the nation with emotions and values like fidelity, faith, and love affect inclusive values (e.g., equality, protection of human rights) and the realization or maintenance of liberal democracy that is predicated on such values. Does the constitutional reference to the will of the ethnic nation as a source of power point to a kind of past confirmation of the nation's will, or is the reference merely a part of the identity politics project supported by the majoritarian concept of democracy?

Our position is that the fact that the constitution follows the ethnic nation concept threatens the egalitarian nature of the state that is the principle that originally connected nation building and state building. Grounding social solidarity on ethnic origins leads to social exclusion, the stigmatization of peripheral groups, and the destruction of principles that make resistance to such processes possible. We focus on those constitutional provisions that criminalize homelessness, distribute social aid based on one's social usefulness, or that can be interpreted as legalizing self-defense or familism (limiting the concept of family). According to Chronowski's and Majtényi and Majtényi's chapters, penalizing homelessness or distributing social benefits on the basis of the "usefulness of one's activity to the community" by the constitution, combined with the re-ethnication of the political community lead to social exclusion and support the mainstreaming of prejudicial discourses.

The authors in the other section of the book, which analyzes social processes through empirical data, share the view that there is a new discourse at play, one which places questions of identity and cultural particularism in the center of public discourse and political struggles. The reasons behind this phenomenon are primarily structural: an economic restructuring whose roots are partly local and partly global that results in social conflicts.[7] Other reasons are more cultural: behind today's identity politics, based on exclusive values and communities, we find a tradition of thought that—in contrast to the universalist traditions of the Enlightenment—advertised a return to local communities

[7] Jens Rydgren, "The Sociology of the Radical Right," *Annual Review of Sociology* 33 (2007): 241–262.

and values.[8] The new primacy of questions of culture and identity in part emanate from changes in the political system; the changes' most important elements being the advance of the far-right and the crisis of the left. This is typified by the recent closing of the gap between the far-right and the moderate center, and the movement of previously extremist ideas into mainstream discourse.[9]

In interpreting the new nationalist identity politics, we critically examine the deprivation theory of sociology, which identifies new forms of nationalism and political particularisms as "the choice of losers."[10] We also consider the anti-modernist elements of identity politics, which support the dismantling of industry and lifestyles related to it and highlight the partial nature of modernization.[11] A third approach also seems applicable to Hungary: this approach emphasizes the strength of a two-directional class dynamic following a significant income gap which has appeared between the upper middle class that has successfully integrated itself into the hierarchy of the global market and the unsuccessful lower middle class.[12]

Another set of explanations, which are of particular importance for the empirical studies in this volume, resonate with supply theories.[13] These consider the question of what characterizes the public life context and political functions in which the various forms of collectivism

---

[8] Douglas R. Holmes, *Integral Europe: Fast-Capitalism, Multiculturalism, Neofascism* (Princeton: Princeton University Press, 2000).

[9] Margit Feischmidt and Peter Hervik, "Mainstreaming the Extreme," *Intersections. East European Journal of Society and Politics* 1(2015): 3–17.

[10] Terry Nichols Clark and Seymour Martin Lipset, *The Breakdown of Class Politics. A Debate on Post-Industrial Stratification* (Baltimore: Johns Hopkins University Press, 2001); Rydgren, "The Sociology," 241–262; Justin Gest, Reny Tyler and Jeremy Mayer, "Roots of the Radical Right: Nostalgic Deprivation in the United States and Britain," *Comparative Political Studies* 13 (2018): 1694–1719.

[11] Hans-Georg Betz, *Radical Right-Wing Populism in Western Europe* (London: MacMillan, 1994); Hans-Georg Betz and Carol Johnson, "Against the Current—Stemming the Tide: The Nostalgic Ideology of the Contemporary Radical Populist Right," *Journal of Political Ideologies* 3(2004): 311–327.

[12] Roger Eatwell, "Ten Theories of the Extreme Right," in *Right-Wing Extremism in the Twenty-First Century*, ed. P.H. Merkl and L. Weinberg (London: Frank Cass, 2003), 47–73.

[13] Rydgren, "The Sociology," 241–262.

and particularism are placed in opposition to individualism and universalism. The professionalization of, and the increasingly managerial approach to, politics that many scholars have described as a universal trend certainly contributes to the estrangement of blue collar workers from politics and representative bodies. Political entrepreneurs of the far-right then capitalize on these class-based grievances by centering their political language around notions of fairness.[14] Bartha and Tóth's chapter examines this process in the light of life-history interviews that indicate how the elite of Hungarian workers have embraced identity politics. They detect among elite skilled workers the rejection of liberal democracy and "the strong presence of a perceived 'threat' of the 'strangers', who violate 'established' social and moral norms." (Bartha and Tóth's chapter in this volume)

For decades now Hungarian society—in international comparisons—has been noted for its apathy ("passive mentality") and low levels of civic participation and activism. Oross, Róna and Szabó analyze this apathy of the young Hungarians based on their survey study and claim that the apathy can mainly be challenged by the extreme alternatives of the political spectrum. Recent studies have shown that interest in public life and the willingness to be politically active has grown in certain groups. As Molnár's chapter underlines, these groups, however, are not always committed to democratic values, i.e., growing civil society activism is strengthening antidemocratic processes as much as democracy itself. Molnár's chapter describes the process—through case studies analyzing specific organizations (the "Goyim Riders" biker club, the paramilitary organization Hungarian Guard, and foreign currency mortgage debtor groups)—how a part of the Hungarian civil society became "a hotbed of right wing radicalism." (Molnár's chapter in this volume)

The chapters in the volume examine political participation and civil society from various approaches. Some explore the civil society concept and the democratic vs. authoritarian political relationship on a theoretical level. Others consider the liberal principles of political participation in civil society in light of the results of quantitative and

[14] Jasper Muis and Tim Immerzeel, "Causes and Consequences of the Rise of Populist Radical Right Parties and Movements in Europe," *Current Sociology* 6 (2017): 457–477.

qualitative research. Political participation is particularly pertinent for youth groups, who, as recent research has shown, tend to be most attracted to the far right.

Our book places a particularly strong emphasis on the question of how the new forms of radicalism and nationalism affects those communities (and the members of such) that are situated in the center of nationalist discourse. This applies on the one hand to Hungarian diasporic communities that have emerged as the most important source of legitimacy for nationalist rhetoric. In their case, we explore how they re-express their national and minority identity in a space redefined by the spread of citizenship and the reevaluation of the nation. On the other hand, in two chapters Feischmidt and Majtényi and Majtényi examine the situation of the Roma in Hungary, who, due to the re-ethnicization of the nation concept have been squeezed out of the national community symbolically but who also suffer from race-based stigmatization and discrimination. Consequently, as Feischmidt shows, discursive forms of racialization became more and more powerful in everyday encounters as well.

In the empirical section of our volume's we explore and interpret the phenomenon whereby questions of culture, memory and identity move to the fore in public discourses. This discursive and ideological shift was first noticeable in the case of far right parties, but today it characterizes a wide swath of the political spectrum. It has become particularly enlivened through civil society activism, the subcultural activities of the youth and the services of the cultural industry, which have had as a goal the redefining and commodification of the nation.[15] New and old actors in public life have entered a competition to redefine and control the nation, and this is presented as a struggle undertaken for national culture and community, further legitimizing the process through a discourse on enemies threatening the above goals.

[15] Margit Feischmidt and Gergő Pulay, "Rocking the Nation. The Popular Culture of Neo-nationalism," *Nations and Nationalism* 2 (2017): 309–326.

BIBLIOGRAPHY

Bennett, W. Lance. "The Uncivic Culture: Communication, Identity, and the Rise of Lifestyle Politics." *Political Science and Politics* 4 (1988): 741–761.

Berezin, Mabel. *Illiberal Politics in Neoliberal Times: Culture, Security and Populism in the New Europe.* Cambridge: Cambridge University Press, 2009.

Betz, Hans-Georg. "Against the System: Radical Right-wing Populism's Challenge to Liberal Democracy." In *Movements of Exclusion: Radical Right-Wing Populism in the Western World,* edited by J. Rydgren, 311–327. New York: Nova Science, 2005.

Betz, Hans-Georg. *Radical Right-Wing Populism in Western Europe.* London: MacMillan, 1994.

Betz, Hans-Georg, and Carol Johnson. "Against the Current—Stemming the Tide: The Nostalgic Ideology of the Contemporary Radical Populist Right." *Journal of Political Ideologies* 3(2004): 311–327.

Bozóki, András, and Dániel Hegedűs. "An Externally Constrained Hybrid Regime: Hungary in the European Union." *Democratization* 7 (2017): 1173–1189.

Clark, Terry Nichols, and Seymour Martin Lipset. *The Breakdown of Class Politics. A Debate on Post-Industrial Stratification.* Baltimore: Johns Hopkins University Press, 2001.

Csillag, Tamás, and Iván Szelényi. "Drifting from Liberal Democracy. Traditionalist/Neo-conservative Ideology of Managed Illiberal Democratic Capitalism in Post-communist Europe." *Intersections. East European Journal of Society and Politics* 1 (2015): 18–48.

Davis, Dennis, Alan Richter and Cheryl Saunders. "Introduction." In *An Inquiry into the Existence of Global Values: Through the Lens of Comparative Constitutional Law,* edited by Dennis Davis, Alan Richter, and Cheryl Saunders, 1–15. Oxford: Hart, 2015.

Eatwell, Roger. "The Rebirth of the Extreme Right in Western Europe?" *Parliamentary Affairs* 3 (2000): 407–425.

Eatwell, Roger "Ten Theories of the Extreme Right." In *Right-Wing Extremism in the Twenty-First Century,* edited by P.H. Merkl and L. Weinberg, 47–73. London: Frank Cass, 2003.

Eatwell, Roger. "Charisma and the Revival of the European Extreme Right." In *Movements of Exclusion: Radical Right-Wing Populism in the Western World,* edited by J. Rydgren, 101–120. New York: Nova Science, 2005.

Evans, Jocelyn. "The Dynamics of Social Change in Radical Right-Wing Populist Party Support." *Comparative European Politics* 3 (2005): 76–101.

Feischmidt, Margit, and Peter Hervik. "Mainstreaming the Extreme." *Intersections East European Journal of Society and Politics* 1 (2015) 1: 3–17.

Feischmidt, Margit, and Gergő Pulay. "Rocking the Nation. The Popular Culture of Neo-nationalism." *Nations and Nationalism* 2 (2017): 309–326.

Gest, Justin, Reny Tyler, and Jeremy Mayer. "Roots of the Radical Right: Nostalgic Deprivation in the United States and Britain." *Comparative Po-*

litical Studies 13 (2018): 1–26. Accessed May 17, 2019. https://doi.org/10.1177/0010414017720705.

Holmes, Douglas R. *Integral Europe: Fast-Capitalism, Multiculturalism, Neofascism*. Princeton: Princeton University Press, 2000.

Inglehart, Ronald. *Modernization and Postmodernization. Cultural, Economic, and Political Change in 43 Societies*. Princeton: Princeton University Press, 1997.

Kalb, Don and Gábor Halmai, eds. *Headlines of Nation, Subtexts of Class: Working Class Populism and the Return of the Repressed in Neoliberal Europe*. New York: Berghahn, 2011.

Körtvélyesi, Zsolt, and Balázs Majtényi. "Game of Values: The Threat of Exclusive Constitutional Identity, the EU and Hungary." *German Law Journal* 7 (2017): 1721–1744.

Mouffe, Chantal. "The 'End of Politics' and the Challenge of Right-wing Populism." In *Populism and the Mirror of Democracy*, edited by F. Panizza, 50–71. London: Verso, 2005.

Muis, Jarson and Tim Immerzeel. "Causes and Consequences of the Rise of Populist Radical Right Parties and Movements in Europe." *Current Sociology* 6 (2017): 457–477.

Rydgren, Jens. "The Sociology of the Radical Right." *Annual Review of Sociology* 33 (2007): 241–262.

Rydgren, Jens. "Immigration Skeptics, Xenophobes, or Racists? Radical Right-wing Voting in Six West European Countries." *European Journal of Political Research* 47 (2008): 737–765.

Tőkés, L. Rudolf. "'Transitology': Global Dreams and Post-Communist Realities." *Central Europe Review* 10 (2000). Accessed May 17, 2019. http://www.ce-review.org/00/10/tokes10.html.

Schlag, Pierre. "Values, 6 Yale." *Journal of Law & the Humanities* 6 (1994) 2: 219–232.

Warczok, Tomasz, and Hanna Dębska. "Sacred Law and Profane Politics: The Symbolic Construction of the Constitutional Tribunal." *Polish Sociological Review* 4 (2014): 461–474.

Wilkin, Peter. "The Rise of 'Illiberal' Democracy: The Orbánization of Hungarian Political Culture." *Journal of World-Systems Research* 1 (2018): 5–42.

Constitutional Continuity Disrupted

KRISZTA KOVÁCS

Change attracts attention, continuity does not.[1] In 1989 a coordinated transition was underway in Hungary and the 1989 Constitution liberal democracy replaced communist authoritarianism. In 2010 the Fidesz-Christian Democratic coalition won the two-thirds majority of the seats in Parliament, which gave them the power to change the 1989 Constitution at will. One year into the term, the governing coalition adopted a range of constitutional amendments.[2] Shortly afterwards a wholesale constitutional review occurred, and the new constitution called the Fundamental Law was adopted with only the votes of the coalition's MPs. The parliamentary supermajority amended the Fundamental Law eight times[3] in the six years after coming to power in January 2012.

1 This is how J.W.F. Allison starts the book *The English Historical Constitution*. J.W.F. Allison, *The English Historical Constitution: Continuity, Change and European Effects* (Cambridge: Cambridge University Press, 2007), 1.

2 More on this see Kriszta Kovács and Gábor Attila Tóth, "Hungary's Constitutional Transformation," *European Constitutional Law Review* 7 (2011): 187ff. https://doi.org/10.1017/S1574019611200038.

3 There are seven amendments to the Fundamental Law, and the Transitional Provisions adopted on December 30, 2011 also contains substantive amendments to the Fundamental Law.

Several international organizations[4] and many scholars[5] criticized these constitutional developments and drew attention to the biased genesis of the Fundamental Law and the weak legitimacy of the document. This chapter does not focus on these matters, rather it concentrates on the topic of constitutional continuity and discontinuity: change in the constitution's main doctrines and its core institutions of central importance for ensuring the functioning of a liberal constitutional democracy.[6]

---

4 See e.g. UN Secretary General Ban Ki-Moon, Address at Hungarian Academy of Sciences organized by the Ministry for Foreign Affairs and the UN Association of Hungary, April 18, 2011.

Venice Commission, Opinion on the New Constitution of Hungary, Adopted by the Venice Commission at its 87th Plenary Session, June 17–18, 2011. Opinion no. 621/2011, CDL-AD(2011)01, Venice Commission, Opinion on the Fourth Amendment to the Fundamental Law of Hungary, Adopted by the Venice Commission at its 95th Plenary Session, June 14–15, 2013. Opinion 720/2013, CDL-AD(2013)012

European Commission Vice-President Viviane Reding, Hungary and the Rule of Law, Speech before the European Parliament outlining the European Commission's concerns about the Fourth Amendment, April 17, 2013.

5 See e.g. Miklós Bánkuti, Gábor Halmai and Kim Lane Scheppele, "Hungary's Illiberal Turn. Disabling the Constitution," *Journal of Democracy* 3 (July 2012): 138–146; András Bozóki, "Occupy the State. The Orban Regime in Hungary" *Debatte* 3 (2011) https://doi.org/10.1080/0965156X.2012.703415; György Dalos, Miklós Haraszti, György Konrád and László Rajk "The Decline of Democracy—the Rise of Dictatorship" *eurozine.hu*, January 2, 2012, https://www.eurozine.com/the-decline-of-democracy-the-rise-of-dictatorship-2/; István Deák, "Hungary: The Threat" *New York Review of Books* April 28, 2011; Gábor Halmai, "Towards an Illiberal Democracy. Hungary's New Constitution" *eurozine.hu*, January 25, 2012, https://www.eurozine.com/towards-an-illiberal-democracy/; Kriszta Kovács and Gábor Attila Tóth, "Hungary's Constitutional Transformation," 187; Jan-Werner Müller, "The Hungarian Tragedy" *Dissent* Spring (2011), 5-10; Jacques Rupnik, "Hungary's Illiberal Turn: How Things Went Wrong" *Journal of Democracy* 3 (July 2012): 132-37; Kristóf Szombati, "The Betrayed Republic. Hungary's New Constitution and the 'System of National Cooperation'" *www.cz.boell.org*, April 2011, https://cz.boell.org/en/2014/03/24/betrayed-republic-hungarys-new-constitution-and-system-national-cooperation; Gábor Attila Tóth, "Macht statt Recht. Deformation des Verfassungssystems in Ungarn" *Osteuropa* 4 (2013): 21–28.

6 When evaluating constitutional changes, the country's human rights situation is of major importance. However, this chapter does not focus on human rights issues. The main reason is that human rights violations occur in lib-

The chapter analyses the 2011 Fundamental Law with the help of the following two concepts: constitutional continuity and constitutional identity. It touches upon three different scholarly approaches concerning the continuity of the Hungarian constitutional system. First, it illustrates the idea that although certain minor infractions of constitutional continuity occurred, the Fundamental Law did not substantially change the underlying principles or the basic structure of the Hungarian State. Then, it turns to another view, which holds that the Fundamental Law more or less followed the path of the 1989 Constitution. However, the Fourth Amendment adopted in 2013 was a major unconstitutional infraction.

The chapter supports a third view, according to which the 2010–2011 constitutional amendments, together with the Fundamental Law and its subsequent amendments, ruptures the constitutional history of Hungary by substantially reshaping the previously existing constitutional framework and by launching a new identity. The commitment to the rule of law and the parliamentary democracy built upon the respect and protection of human rights and the social market economy was constitutive of the Hungarian regime between 1990 and 2010. The new regime is built upon the "rule by law" instead of the principle of the rule of law. Its main feature is the unity of powers instead of limited government based upon parliamentary democracy, and the system lacks the market economy guarantees.

---

eral constitutional democracies, too. These do not necessary lead to rupture in constitutional continuity. But the rupture certainly occurs when the core constitutional institutions and principles are not capable of governing a democratic society. For an in-depth analysis of the Fundamental Law's conception of human dignity, equality and civil liberties, see Part Three of the book *Constitution for a Disunited Nation: On Hungary's 2011 Fundamental Law,* ed. Gábor Attila Tóth (Budapest–New York: CEU Press, 2012). See also the so-called Sargentini report: Report on a proposal calling on the Council to determine, pursuant to Article 7(1) of the Treaty on European Union, the existence of a clear risk of a serious breach by Hungary of the values on which the Union is founded (2017/2131(INL)).

Constitutional Continuity and Identity Turn

For the purpose of the chapter, I differentiate between the continuity of a legal system and the continuity of a constitutional system. By legal continuity, I understand what Herbert Hart meant when he referred to continuity, which is "to be observed in every normal legal system, when one legislator succeeds another."[7] In this case, the legal regulations and the legal relationships (contracts, marriages, property relations, etc.) established thereby continue in force despite the demise of a system of government and the birth of a new one.

I use the notion of constitutional continuity in a substantive sense.[8] In this sense, the legal system and the basic structure of the state (the underlying constitutional principles and the system of constitutional organs) remains intact, despite the adoption of a constitutional amendment or even a new constitution. I should further clarify that under the notion of constitutional continuity I do not mean constitutional rigidity. A constitution should be open to alterations, if any such should be found necessary. However, these corrections by amendments should be strictly conformable to the underlying principles, which are foundational to the given legal and political order. This is how the persistence of the constitutional framework can be ensured.

The concept of constitutional identity may be of help when evaluating a given constitutional change: an amendment or even a new constitution. The constitutional identity is a contested and inarticulate concept, and there are different views on the exact meaning of the phrase.[9] Some scholars understand it as the identity of the people, the identity of

---

7 Herbert L. A. Hart, *The Concept of Law* (Sheffield: Clarendon, 1994), 51–61.

8 For a detailed analysis of formal validity of the constitutions, see the contribution of Zsolt Körtvélyesi in this volume. On the concept of constitutional continuity framed in a different language, see Renáta Uitz, *Constitutions, Courts and History. Historical Narratives in Constitutional Adjudication* (Budapest–New York: CEU Press, 2006).

9 More on the different conceptions see the Special Issue of the *German Law Journal* "Constitutional Identity in the Age of Global Migration" 7 (2017) 1587–1822.

the community.[10] Others suggest that constitutional identity embraces, among others, the identity of the community.[11] Rather than pursuing the idea of constitutions as reflections of communal identity or the identity of a people, and thus emphasizing a communitarian approach, I follow a different understanding that views constitutions as containing specific sets of core values and principles and as such can be identified and distinguished. I build on the thought that constitutional identity is located within the constitution.[12] Thus, the editors of this book are rightly of the position that constitutions are the most important documents in terms of the constitutional identity of the state.[13] But how can this identity be revealed?

First, in order to receive information on constitutional identity we should consider the whole set of constitutional values, principles and rules.[14] In other words, constitutional identity refers to the "constitutional essentials"[15] of a given constitutional order, which can be

---

[10] Michel Rosenfeld, "Constitutional Identity," in *The Oxford Handbook of Comparative Constitutional Law*, ed. Michel Rosenfeld and András Sajó (Oxford: Oxford University Press, 2012), 758.

[11] For instance, Anna Śledzińska-Simon offers a three dimensional model of constitutional identity based upon the "tripartite self" of the individual. Anna Śledzińska-Simon, "Constitutional identity in 3D: A Model of Individual, Relational, and Collective Self and its Application in Poland," *International Journal of Constitutional Law* 1, (2015): 124–155, 124. Anna Khvorostiankina views constitutional identity as a complex phenomenon, a combination of four interrelated meanings, including the identity of a constitution, of the people, of an actual political community and of a constitutional order. Anna Khvorostiankina, "'Constitutional Identity' in the Context of Post-Soviet Transformation. Europeanization and Regional Integration Processes (the Case of Armenia)," *Armenian Journal of Political Science* 1 (2017): 45–80.

[12] Michel Troper, "Behind the Constitution?," in *Constitutional Topography: Values and Constitutions*, ed. András Sajó and Renáta Uitz (The Hague: Eleven, 2011) 201–203.

[13] See the Introduction of this volume.

[14] José Luis Martí, "Two Different Ideas of Constitutional Identity: Identity of the Constitution v. Identity of the People," in *National Constitutional Identity and European Integration*, ed. Alejandro Saiz Arnaiz and Carina Alcoberro LLivina (Cambridge: Intersentia, 2013).

[15] John Rawls's well-known expression refers to the principles that structure the government and the basic rights and liberties, not including political issues that are matters of ordinary legislation. John Rawls, *Political Liberalism* (New York: Columbia University Press, 1993) 214, 227–29.

identified by the sets of norms–including the underlying principles, the system of constitutional organs and the basic liberties–providing information on the fundamental structure of the given state, that, when touched by constitutional change, would result in a modified constitutional identity.[16]

Second, the constitutional text, and the amendment procedures could be used as sources out of which we are able to determine the given state's constitutional identity.[17] Third, constitutional texts themselves have only limited potential for giving information on constitutional identity. The words of the constitution need to be interpreted, and socially embedded institutions, by interpreting and applying these words, could actually foster the constitutional identity. Constitutional identity is thus reaffirmed by experience,[18] and legislatures and courts are the institutions that have the authority to interpret the constitutional provisions.

The constitutional identity in this sense is a theoretical construct emerging from the text of the constitution, its interpretation, and its application.[19] In what follows, I compare the core institutions and doctrines of the 1989 Constitution and the 2011 Fundamental Law by examining the relevant constitutional provisions and their judicial application. I focus on the following question: is the Fundamental Law a symbol of constitutional continuity or does it signify a rupture in Hungarian constitutional history?

---

16 Kriszta Kovács, "Changing Constitutional Identity via Amendment," in *Constitutional Acceleration within the European Union and Beyond*, ed. Paul Blokker (London and New York: Routledge, 2018), 197–214.

17 Constance Grewe, "Methods of Identification of National Constitutional Identity" in *National Constitutional Identity and European Integration*, ed. Alejandro Saiz Arnaiz and Carina Alcoberro LLivina (Cambridge: Intersentia, 2013), 40ff.

18 Gary J. Jacobsohn, "The Formation of Constitutional Identities," in *Comparative Constitutional Law*, ed. Tom Ginsburg and Rosalind Dixon (Cheltenham: Edward Elgar Publishing, 2011), 131.

19 See Monika Polzin, "Constitutional Identity as a Constructed Reality and a Restless Soul," *German Law Journal* 7 (2017): 1595ff. http://www.germanlawjournal.com/volume-18-no-07.

Three Scholarly Approaches: Continuity, Rupture, or Something In-between?

Three different scholarly approaches concerning the continuity of the Hungarian constitutional system are present in the constitutional discourse.

First, there is the view that although certain minor infractions of constitutional continuity occurred (e.g. by allowing the retroactive law making), the Fundamental Law meant only a textual constitutional transformation and it did not substantially change the basic structure of the state, Hungary remained a democratic country under the rule of law. This view is represented among others by László Trócsányi, according to whom "the Fundamental Law should not be deemed a revolutionary constitution, since no changes were made in the structure of the state that would change the basic features of the country's administrative framework."[20] This standpoint emphasizes the constitutional continuity: parliamentary republic remained the form of government, and the control institutions, such as the Constitutional Court, though partially lost, also won certain powers. Similarly, András Jakab and Pál Sonnevend in one of their earlier articles argued for the continuity of the Fundamental Law with the 1989 Constitution and they asserted that the new constitution remained within the mainstream of European constitutionalism.[21] István Stumpf is also convinced that the Fundamental Law follows constitutional model of the continental Europe.[22]

A second view holds that "there is no tragic break between the old Constitution and the new one."[23] The Fundamental Law as it was

---

20 László Trócsányi, "The Creation of the Basic Law of Hungary," in *The Basic Law of Hungary: A First Commentary,* ed. Lóránt Csink, Balázs Schanda, and András Zs. Varga (Dublin: Clarus, 2012), 22.

21 András Jakab and Pál Sonnevend, "Continuity with Deficiencies: The New Basic Law of Hungary," *European Constitutional Law Review* 9 (2013): 102. https://doi.org/10.1017/S1574019612001058.

22 István Stumpf, "The Fundamental Law of Hungary," *Hungarian Review* 2 (2014): 43.

23 László Sólyom, "The Rise and Decline of Constitutional Culture in Hungary," in *Constitutional Crisis in the European Constitutional Area: Theory, Law and Politics in Hungary and Romania,* ed. Armin von Bogdandy and Pál Sonnevend (Oxford-Portland, OR: Hart, 2015), 20.

adopted in 2011, more or less followed the path of the 1989 Constitution and ensured that the functioning of the state shall be based on the principle of the division of powers and that the Constitutional Court shall be the supreme organ for the protection of the Fundamental Law. According to this view, however, the subsequent amendments, first and foremost the Fourth Amendment adopted in 2013, meant a major unconstitutional infraction.[24] It challenged a foundational principle thereby it was tantamount to a surreptitious introduction of a new constitution with a completely new identity. In the new system of government, Parliament is the supreme and constitutionally unlimited organ of state power. There is no constitutional body that can impose binding restraints on Parliament.[25] Parliamentary majority alone possesses final authority to introduce, change and interpret its own constitutional limits. The only real check on parliamentary sovereignty in the Hungarian system was the Constitutional Court, which can no longer serve as the supreme organ for the protection of the constitution. In order to substantiate this allegation, László Sólyom drew attention to the fact that nearly all of the provisions inserted into the Fundamental Law by the Fourth Amendment have been previously rendered unconstitutional by the Constitutional Court. [26] By overriding them, the parliamentary majority reserved the right to have the final and supreme authority on the Constitution's meaning. This gives the ruling majority the right to pass any law, in the form of a constitutional amendment, even if it is in direct opposition to the constitution's underlying principles. This pattern of "constitutionalization" of provisions of ordinary

[24] In their joint article, Pál Sonnevend, András Jakab and Lóránt Csink represent this view. See Pál Sonnevend, András Jakab and Lóránt Csink, "The Constitution as an Instrument of Everyday Party Politics: The Basic Law of Hungary," in *Constitutional Crisis in the European Constitutional Area: Theory, Law and Politics in Hungary and Romania,* ed. Armin von Bogdandy and Pál Sonnevend (Oxford-Portland, OR: Hart, 2015), 63.

[25] László Sólyom, "Ende der Gewaltentelung. Zur Änderungen des Grundgesetzes in Ungarn" *Osteuropa,* 4 (2013): 5-12.

[26] Kriszta Kovács, "Az Alkotmánybíróság többé nem az alkotmányvédelem legfőbb szerve" Sólyom László volt köztársasági elnökkel Kovács Kriszta beszélget, [The Constitutional Court is not the Guardian of the Constitution Anymore, Kriszta Kovács talks to László Sólyom] *Fundamentum* 1 (2013): 19–30.

law excludes the possibility of review by the Constitutional Court.[27] In addition, the Fourth Amendment, by repealing the previous case law of the Constitutional Court, erases en bloc the whole post 1989-constitutional history. To sum it up, while the Fundamental Law called for continuity with regard to the constitutional framework, the Fourth Amendment, by contrast, did not seek to link to the past two decades of constitutional democracy.

The starting point of the third view is that the 2010-2011 constitutional amendments, together with the Fundamental Law and its subsequent amendments meant a rupture in the Hungarian constitutional history.[28] The 1989 Constitution was capable of governing a democratic society. Although several constitutional amendments occurred during the two decades after the transition to democracy, these were mostly connected to larger pieces of legislation in order to create the harmony between the 1989 Constitution and the ordinary law. In addition, constitutional amendments empowered Hungary to join NATO and the European Union. Despite these constitutional changes, the basic structure of the state remained untouched until 2010.

Scholars approach this view differently and they describe the rupture in various ways. As Kim Scheppele noted, Fidesz has accomplished a constitutional revolution by legal means after a democratic election.[29] However, according to János Kis and Andrew Arató it was not a revolution, because, in Condorcet's sense, revolution is a radical, quick, and often violent change aiming at freedom, which presupposes the existence of despotism. But it was not even a counter-revolution, since both revolution and counter-revolution require ruptures of legality and legitimacy. János Kis wrote about a constitutional crisis and argued that the Fundamental Law removed Hungary from the

---

27 Opinion CDL-AD(2013)012 of the Venice Commission on the Fourth Amendment to the Fundamental Law of Hungary, para 81.

28 The edited volume *Constitution for a Disunited Nation: On Hungary's 2011 Fundamental Law*, ed. Gábor Attila Tóth (Budapest–New York: CEU Press, 2012) represents this view.

29 Kim Lane Scheppele, "Hungary's Constitutional Revolution," *The Conscience of a Liberal, The Blog of Paul Krugman*, December 18, 2011, http://krugman.blogs.nytimes.com/2011/12/19/hungarys-constitutional-revolution/.

family of liberal democracies.[30] In the view of Andrew Arató an illegitimate constitutional reform took place in Hungary, which reversed the revolutionary results of 1989.[31] Marco Dani adverted to the ill-conceived constitutional adventure, which could be studied and criticized as the most emblematical example of a broader trend: the decline of the idea of pluralist constitution.[32] István Pogány referred to the outcome of the "new constitutionalism" in Hungary as a "flawed constitution," which "represents a significant shift towards a more authoritarian political culture."[33] In accordance with this, András Bozóki and Dániel Hegedűs described the system as an "externally constrained hybrid regime," embedded in the common EU legal framework.[34]

Although these scholars apply varying labels to what happened in Hungary, they all agree that the 2010–2011 constitutional changes and the Fundamental Law substantially transformed the characteristics of Hungarian constitutionalism founded by the 1989 Constitution. In what follows I substantiate the statement that this flow of constitutional changes led to a rupture in constitutional continuity and launched a brave new regime in Hungary.

1989: Liberal Democracy

In 1989 the Constitution was adopted "with a view to promote a peaceful political transition to a rule of law state implementing a multi-party

---

[30] János Kis, "From the 1989 Constitution to the 2011 Fundamental Law," in *Constitution for a Disunited Nation: On Hungary's 2011 Fundamental Law*, ed. Gábor Attila Tóth (Budapest–New York: CEU Press, 2012), 2, 21.

[31] Andrew Arató, "Regime Change, Revolution, and Legitimacy," in *Constitution for a Disunited Nation: On Hungary's 2011 Fundamental Law*, ed. Gábor Attila Tóth (Budapest–New York: CEU Press, 2012), 35ff.

[32] Marco Dani, "The 'Partisan Constitution' and the Corrosion of European Constitutional Culture," *LEQS Paper* 68 (2013): 6. http://dx.doi.org/10.2139/ssrn.2348629.

[33] István Pogány, "The Crisis of Democracy in East Central Europe: The 'New Constitutionalism' in Hungary," *European Public Law* 19 (2013): 354, 367. http://www.kluwerlawonline.com/toc.php?pubcode=EURO.

[34] András Bozóki and Dániel Hegedűs, "An Externally Constrained Hybrid Regime: Hungary in the European Union," *Democratization* 7 (2018): 1173-1189. https://doi.org/10.1080/13510347.2018.1455664.

system, parliamentary democracy, and a social market economy"—as the preamble declared. Furthermore, the introductory part of the constitutional text asserted that Hungary is a republic and an independent, democratic state governed by the rule of law (Article 2). The commitment to the rule of law, parliamentary democracy built upon the respect and protection of human rights, and the social market economy was constitutive of the Hungarian regime. Hence, the 1989 Constitution had the potential to facilitate liberal democracy and to ensure the self-government of free and equal persons through law. The specific content of these underlying principles determined over time by the constitutional organs, first and foremost by the newly established Constitutional Court, through practice and interpretation.

THE RULE OF LAW

It is possible to describe the rule of law simply in formal terms, but it is also possible to argue that the rule of law is a substantive requirement.[35] The Constitutional Court opted for a formalistic understanding of the rule of law. It insisted that political intentions could only be implemented lawfully and within the framework of the Constitution—not vice versa, as before 1989, when the law was conceived of merely as a political tool. In the Court's phrasing in 1989 a "revolution under the rule of law" occurred. The revolutionary changes had been introduced by strictly keeping all constitutional guarantees, therefore the system change had to be considered to be of a morally higher value than the previous, similarly revolutionary changes, by respecting constitutional limitations it could not repeat crimes and injustices that revolutions usually understand to be justified and permissible.[36] This view led

[35] It is the case when someone argues that "there is more to the rule of law than constraint on power." For instance, Ronald Dworkin regards it as "the ideal of the rule by an accurate public conception of individual rights." Martin Krygier, "Rule of Law," in *The Oxford Handbook of Comparative Constitutional Law*, ed. Michel Rosenfeld and András Sajó (Oxford: Oxford University Press, 2012), 244.

[36] László Sólyom, "Introduction to the Decisions of the Constitutional Court of the Republic of Hungary," in *Constitutional Judiciary in a New Democracy: The Hungarian Constitutional Court*, ed. László Sólyom and Georg Brunner (Ann Arbor: Michigan University Press, 2000), 38–39.

the Court to conclude in decisions concerning retroactive justice that in cases of ex post facto criminal legislation the formal rule of law has priority over the demand for substantive justice. Therefore in Decision 11/1992 the Court struck down the law which would have retroactively extended the statute-of-limitations and allowed for the prosecution of perpetrators of murder and torture in the aftermath of the 1956 uprising against Soviet rule. The Court argued that the 1989 Constitution did not and could not confer a right for substantive justice.

The Court's concept of the rule of law went further than the conventional "rule-book" conception.[37] The case law confirmed that the rule of law was not a mere declaration; it had a fundamental value. The Court settled "legal certainty" as the core element of the rule of law, which required the unambiguity of legal norms but also the predictability of the operation of the legal institutions (Decision 9/1992). For this reason, procedural guarantees (such as the protection against retroactive laws, and the requirement of "reasonable time" before an adopted law comes into force) emerged as important features of the rule of law. In the Court's interpretation the rule of law also required public authorities to perform in accordance with the law, that is, within the organizational framework determined by law, according to the procedure prescribed by law, and within the limits regulated by law, accessible and predictable to citizens (Decision 56/1991). Connected to this, the Court considered the principle of separation of powers as an essential element of the rule of law and "the most important operational and organizational principle of the Hungarian State" (Decision 31/1990).

PARLIAMENTARY DEMOCRACY

In 1989 Hungary followed its own constitutional tradition concerning representative government as well as Western European solutions (first and foremost the German constitutional model) in establishing an adapted parliamentary system instead of importing a presidential architecture. The 1989 Constitution resembled the German Chancellor-led system with a strong prime minister. The prime minister-led govern-

[37] Martin Krygier, "Rule of Law," in *The Oxford Handbook of Comparative Constitutional Law*, ed. Michel Rosenfeld and András Sajó (Oxford: Oxford University Press, 2012), 242–246.

ment was politically responsible to the Parliament for its operation and was required to report regularly to the Parliament. In this constitutional model, the Parliament was the body in which the popular sovereignty of the people was exercised through elected representatives.

The 1989 Constitution introduced a consensual parliamentary democracy native to continental Europe. Since it assumed the presence of more than two parties in the Parliament and a coalition government, Hungary adopted a mixed electoral system with strong proportionate elements (with three tiers and combined two choices, one for the majoritarian and one for the proportional part). With this electoral system, 45.6 percent of the seats were allocated under the majoritarian part and 54.4 percent of the seats under the proportional system.[38] In order to govern the country properly, the system required a consensus of the coalition parties. The system was consensual in another sense, too. The model required that, at least in constitutional matters, governing parties involve not only their coalition partner, but also the opposition. Thereby, the coalition government was required to have an agreement with the opposition on the underlying principles and the basic structure of the state. The Constitution stipulated that more than thirty acts concerning some fundamental rights and regulating the functions and powers of basic constitutional organs (judiciary, Constitutional Court, ombuds-system, etc.) were subject to the two-thirds majority requirement.[39] As the Constitutional Court emphasized, the two-thirds majority was not only a formal requirement, but also the proof of a broad political consensus in Parliament (Decision 5/1990). The reason behind listing the two-thirds majority acts was that the government did not need to reshape the constitutional architecture or limit fundamental rights in order to govern the state properly.

In a parliamentary democracy, where the legislative and the executive powers are so intertwined, independent checks are of utmost

---

[38] Later it turned out that in this scheme, a party could secure two-thirds of the parliamentary seats with a little more than 50 percent of the votes.

[39] There were two categories of two-thirds laws: laws when the vote of two-thirds of the MPs present was necessary (for instance laws on fundamental rights, on the judiciary, the Constitutional Court, etc.) and laws when two-thirds majority of all the MPs were needed (in order to amend the constitution or to adopt the law on the national symbols).

importance. In Hungary, the judiciary served as one of the main constraints on the executive power. The Constitutional Court saw the judiciary as the power that should be "independent from the political determination of the other two branches and of its changes, and which in this sense permanent, continuous" (Decision 38/1993). In the Court's view, no other branch could be in a position to decisively influence the operation of the judiciary.

In addition to the judiciary, the ombuds-system served as a check on the executive power. The 1989 Constitution established an ombuds-system mainly with the competence to investigate maladministration from a constitutional point of view. It provided for the election of a parliamentary ombudsperson for fundamental rights, a specialized ombudsperson for the rights of national and ethnic minorities, and it foresaw the possibility of the election of other ombudspersons, if required by a law. In 1992 the Act on Data Protection provided for an ombudsperson, and in 2007 Parliament created the ombudsperson for future generations. There was no hierarchical relationship among the ombudspersons, they were all responsible only to Parliament. Their main functions were to investigate complaints in their respective fields and attempt to resolve them, usually through non-binding recommendations.[40]

However, in the Hungarian constitutional model, not only the administrative measures, but also parliamentary decisions, were subject to constitutional review. The 1989 Constitution established a Constitutional Court with the ability to review the constitutionality of ordinary laws. The Hungarian form of the judicial review was closer to the concentrated German and Austrian pattern than to the diffuse US judicial review. The Constitutional Court was institutionally separated from the ordinary court system. With respect to the competencies of the Constitutional Court, during the Roundtable talks it was agreed that its priorities should include the abstract review of all laws.[41] Accordingly, the abstract constitutional review of laws was

[40] See the annual reports of the ombudspersons in the Archive of the Office of the Commissioner for Fundamental Rights at http://www.ajbh.hu/en/web/ajbh-en/annual-reports-archiv.

[41] The democratic opposition had three demands concerning the Constitutional Court during the Roundtable talks. First, that the judges should be

standing at the center of the practice of the Court. The peculiarity of Hungarian constitutional adjudication was that anyone had the opportunity to initiate the posterior review of laws. There were no deadlines to be observed, nor was the applicant required to show any impact or other legally protected interest. In addition, all laws could be subject to constitutional review; there was no need to have a case or controversy behind (actio popularis). And since actio popularis existed, the Court had the possibility to play a key role in the revision of the entire legal system.

SOCIAL MARKET ECONOMY

The 1989 Constitution, as almost all modern constitutions of East Central Europe, spoke in the preamble of developing a "social market economy." The concept was imported from the German Social Market model, a model with strong welfare-state characteristics.[42] With reference to this, the 1989 Constitution contained a great number of social rights: the right to social security, to health, to work, to an income that corresponds to the performed work, to equal pay with those performing the same work, to rest, and to education.

Despite the presence of these rights in the 1989 Constitution the Constitutional Court interpreted them not as judicially enforceable rights, but as positive state obligations and policy goals (Decision 32/1991). While doing this, the Court usually referred to equality and the concept of "acquired rights" derived from the principle of rule of law. This was similar to the approach applied by the German Constitutional Court while interpreting the clause of "sozialer Rechtsstaat." Due to the Hungarian Court's narrow interpretation of social rights,

elected based upon a consensus, second, that everyone should have a standing before the Constitutional Court and third, that the Court should have the power to review the constitutionality of all laws and to annul the unconstitutional ones.

42 The term "social market economy" was chosen to disassociate the capitalism from its Anglo-American counterpart. János Kornai, "The System Paradigm Revisited," *Revue D'Études Comparatives Est-Ouest* 1-2 (2017): 244. http://dx.doi.org/10.1556/032.2016.66.4.1.

the presence of such rights, in the 1989 Constitution has not interfered with the free market reform.[43]

Culminating in Hungary's accession to the European Union in 2004, the democratic transition was widely judged a success, and Hungary joined the group of consolidated liberal democracies with a constitutionally guaranteed system of the rule of law, parliamentary democracy, and social market economy. However, a transition away from liberal democracy started in 2010.

2010: A Non-liberal State

A combination of domestic political scandals, collapsing state finances, and a global economic crisis that pushed Hungary into an IMF bailout made the electorate ready for a change in 2010. That year, the Fidesz–Christian Democratic coalition gained a supermajority of parliamentary seats, opening the way for a profound change of direction even though the parties did not campaign on a platform of constitutional reform. Subsequently, the ruling majority called its election victory "a successful revolution in the polling booth"[44] and replaced the 1989 liberal democratic constitution with a completely new one in 2011. The Fundamental Law became the symbol of the new regime. It does not acknowledge constitutional continuity with the previous liberal democratic regime. On the contrary, it breaks with the spirit that guided the 1989 Constitution. The Fundamental Law prefers the "rule by law"

[43] Herman Schwartz, "Do Economic and Social Rights Belong in a Constitution?" *The American University Journal of International Law and Policy* 4 (1995): 1243. Several judgments delivered by the Constitutional Court in 1995 meant an exception. It issued a series of decisions which blocked the immediate implementation of cuts in the system of child support, sick pay, maternity leave, and other social programs by invalidating several parts of the Economic Stabilization Act, the government's IMF-required austerity program which became generally known as the Bokros-package. The Court held that the government's failure to maintain at least a nominal level of social support violated fundamental rights. In addition, the speed with which these programs were modified violated the principle of legal certainty.

[44] 1/2010. (VI. 16.) OGY politikai nyilatkozata [Proclamation of the Parliament on the National Cooperation].

instead of the rule of law, the unity of powers instead of consensual parliamentary democracy and lacks the guarantees of the social market economy. The Prime Minister gave a name to this new regime. As an alternative to liberal democracy he offered the model of a non-liberal state. Non-liberal, because it explicitly challenges basic tenets of liberal constitutional democracy.

"(I)n 2010, and especially these days, we had to make a statement that, similarly to the statement I quoted for you earlier, was also categorized as blasphemy by the liberal world. We had to state that a democracy does not necessarily have to be liberal. Just because a state is not liberal, it can still be democracy. (…) We want to organize a work-based society that, as I have just mentioned, undertakes the odium of stating that it is not liberal in character. (…) we must break with liberal principles and methods of social organization, and in general with the liberal understanding of society. (…) the new state that we are constructing in Hungary is an illiberal state, a non-liberal state."[45]

THE "RULE BY LAW"

As shown above, one of the guiding principles of the two decades of liberal democracy was the rule of law, that no one, not even those who hold the most power, should be above the law. But as János Kornai rightly put, in Hungary the situation has changed, those in power are able to elevate any decision to the status of law quickly and without hindrance.[46] Under this new rule by law system, the law serves as a mere tool for the government that suppresses in a legalistic fashion.[47] The law has become instrumentalized, and brought in line with governmental decisions rather than constraining in advance how officials

---

[45] Prime Minister Viktor Orbán's Speech, July 26, 2014, Băile Tuşnad, (Tusnádfürdő) Romania, www.kormany.hu/en/the-prime-minister/the-prime-minister-s-speeches/prime-minister-viktor-orban-s-speech-at-the-25th-balvanyos-summer-free-university-and-student-camp.

[46] János Kornai, "Hungary's U-Turn," *Capitalism and Society* 1 Article 2. (2015): 4, https://ssrn.com/abstract=2629592.

[47] Brian Z. Tamanaha, "The Rule of Law for Everyone?" *Current Legal Problems* 55 (2002): 97-122, 101, http://dx.doi.org/10.2139/ssrn.312622.

operate. All the checks on law-making powers have been removed[48] up to and including constitutional amendments.

Already in 2010 numerous provisions that fell outside the regulatory scope of the Constitution have been incorporated into the Constitution, and the frequent constitutional amendments have made it difficult to follow and identify the Constitution's normative text in force. As the Constitutional Court put it, the amendments jeopardized the stability and the endurance of the Constitution as well as the principle of the rule of law (Decision 45/2012). For instance, constitutional amendments were adopted in order to make it possible to levy taxes with retroactive force. In 2010 Article 70/I(2) of the then 1989 Constitution was amended to provide constitutional cover for the 98 percent tax on public sector severance pay levied retroactively.[49] And although the Constitutional Court held the legislative provision unconstitutional in its Decisions 184/2010, the parliamentary supermajority amended Article 70/I(2) again to expressly allow retroactive taxation.[50] In its decision 37/2011 the Court again annulled the implementation of legislative provisions referring to the principle of human dignity. In the end, the parliamentary majority adopted a new law under which a 98 percent tax can be levied on severance payments made after January 1, 2010.

The adoption of the Fundamental Law in 2011 had further eroded the rule of law by introducing "the society's sense of justice" as one of its underlying principles. Article U of the Fundamental Law, dealing with the communist past, asserts that the society's sense of justice shall be ensured by making possible the retroactive prosecution of politically motivated crimes committed and not prosecuted during the communist regime. The provision should be read together with Article XXVIII(5) under which it is not against the principle of *nullum crimen sine lege* to prosecute or convict a person for an act, which, at the time when it was committed, was criminal according to the generally recognized rules of international law. In other words, the Fundamental Law

48 See, e.g., Miklós Bánkuti, Gábor Halmai and Kim Lane Scheppele, "From Separation of Powers to a Government Without Checks: Hungary's Old and New Constitutions," in *Constitution for a Disunited Nation*, 268.

49 More on this, see Kovács and Tóth, "Hungary's Constitutional Transformation," 192.

50 Kovács and Tóth, "Hungary's Constitutional Transformation," 193.

allows people to be prosecuted retroactively for the sake of "the society's sense of justice."

The rule of law concept of the 1989 Constitution and its interpretation given by the Constitutional Court includes the principle of legal certainty, the predictability of the operation of legal institutions and the ban on retroactive taxation and criminal legislation. Contrary to this, the Fundamental Law expressly authorizes retroactive law-making. Furthermore, as the Constitutional Court pointed out, it contains several provisions that fall outside the scope of subjects (from taxation to family policy) that should be regulated in a constitution (Decision 45/2012).

UNITY OF POWERS

The basic state structure seemingly remained the same in the Fundamental Law, but it is only a façade. The outward appearance of the system of constitutional organs was maintained to conceal a less creditable reality. One of the most essential characteristics of constitutionalism is popular sovereignty and the thereby limited governmental power's allocation and exercise of state power.[51] In a constitutional democracy the people's sovereign authority is ultimate and unlimited but the government is constitutionally limited and subordinate.[52]

The Fundamental Law is not able to function as a limit to governmental powers. Moreover, it does not even aim at limiting the government; rather, it aims at consolidating the power of the ruling parliamentary majority and restricts the competitive political process, (1) by cementing normal policy issues in two-thirds laws, (2) by stigmatizing the political rivals, (3) by changing the electoral rules and (4) by terminating the checks on governmental power.

---

[51] Louis Henkin, "A New Birth of Constitutionalism: Genetic Influences and Genetic Defects," in *Constitutionalism, Identity, Difference and Legitimacy: Theoretical Perspectives*, ed. Michel Rosenfeld (Durham: Duke University Press, 1994), 40-42.

[52] Wil Waluchow, "Constitutionalism," *The Stanford Encyclopedia of Philosophy* (Spring 2018 Edition), ed. Edward N. Zalta, https://plato.stanford.edu/archives/spr2018/entries/constitutionalism/.

(1) The Fundamental Law gives a special power of intervention in the domain of budgetary issues to the newly created Budget Council, the members of which are delegated by state leaders. The prior consent of the Budget Council is needed for the adoption of the budget law. If it is not given, and the budget is consequently not adopted by March 31 of the respective year, the Head of State may dissolve Parliament.[53] This solution splits the authority to adopt the budget between Parliament and the non-elected Budgetary Council. In a related development, the Fundamental Law requires that two-thirds laws regulate taxation, pension policy, and family issues.[54] With these provisions the Fundamental Law enshrines the constitution-maker parliamentary majority's political preferences concerning economic policy issues, makes political alteration difficult, and puts a heavy burden on future parliamentary majorities by constraining them in realizing their own economic, social, and family policy. As the Venice Commission summarized the situation: "The more policy issues are transferred beyond the powers of simple majority, the less significance will future elections have and the more possibilities does a two-thirds majority have of cementing its political preferences and the country's legal order."[55]

(2) One of the main functions of the constitutions of modern democracies is to outline and to facilitate the process of political competition and rotation in office. In this respect the Fundamental Law is deficient, since it stigmatizes one of the main political rivals of the ruling majority. For instance, Article U(1) of the Fundamental Law reads that political organizations having gained legal recognition during the democratic transition as legal successors of the Hungarian Socialist Workers' Party continue to share the responsibility of their predecessors as beneficiaries of their unlawfully accumulated assets. This means that the Hungarian Socialist Party remains responsible for the wrongdoings of its legal predecessor, the Hungarian Socialist Workers' Party. According to the Fundamental Law, this party is criminal in nature and its "leaders" are responsible for criminal offenses committed for

[53] Articles 3(3) and 44 of the Fundamental Law.

[54] Articles K, L, 38, and 40 of the Fundamental Law.

[55] CDL-AD(2011)016-e Opinion on the new Constitution of Hungary adopted by the Venice Commission at its 87th Plenary Session (Venice, June 17–18, 2011), para. 24.

political motives and left unprosecuted because of political motives. The provision thereby contains "collective responsibility" and does not hold former perpetrators responsible for concrete actions and through normal criminal procedures. The Venice Commission rightly points out that it attributes responsibility for the past by using general terms ("holders of power", "leaders") and vague criteria without any chance for an individual assessment.[56]

(3) A constitutional amendment reduced the number of MPs,[57] and essential changes occurred in the election system and procedure. First, the view of citizenship was tailored to the Fundamental Law's ethnocentric constitutional conception of citizenship.[58] Hungary allows preferential naturalization for ethnic Hungarians living beyond the borders by removing the requirement of residence in Hungary. The applicant has to prove (somehow) that s/he speaks some Hungarian and either s/he has to have at least one ancestor who was a Hungarian citizen, or s/he has to demonstrate the likelihood of origins from Hungary.[59] There is no time frame that would restrict the tracing of Hungarian ancestry. Therefore, this over-inclusive amendment paved the way for granting the right to vote for trans-border Hungarian citizens living outside of Hungary.[60] Second, Parliament significantly reshaped the boundaries of the electoral constituencies. The constituency

---

[56] Venice Commission 2013, On the Fourth Amendment of the Fundamental Law of Hungary, CDL-AD(2013)012, 720/213, Strasbourg June 17, 2013, 8.

[57] May 25, 2010 Amendment of the 1989 Constitution.

[58] Zsolt Körtvélyesi and Judit Tóth, "Naturalisation in Hungary: Exclusion by Ethnic Preference," *Open Citizenship* 1 (2011): 54–74.

[59] Article 4(3) of the Law on Hungarian Citizenship as amended by Law IVXL of 2010 on amendment of the Law on Hungarian Citizenship. More on this, see Monika Ganczer, "International Law and Dual Nationality of Hungarians Living Outside the Borders," *Acta Juridica Hungarica* 4 (2012): 316-333, http://dx.doi.org/10.1556/AJur.53.2012.4.4.

[60] Balázs Majtényi, Alíz Nagy, and Péter Kállai, "'Only Fidesz'—Minority Electoral Law in Hungary," *VerfBlog*, March 31, 2018, https://verfassungsblog.de/only-fidesz-electoral-law-in-hungary. Kriszta Kovács and Paul Blokker, "Unilateral Expansionism: Hungarian Citizenship and Franchise Politics and their Effects on the Hungarian-Romanian Relations," in *Good Neighbourliness in the European Legal Context*, ed. Dimitry Kochenov and Elena Basheska (Leiden: Brill/Nijhoff, 2015), 136–159.

boundaries were gerrymandered, creating large dragon-shaped districts to the advantage of the ruling party.[61] Third, Parliament retained a combined electoral system, but with two tiers, and modified the formula for the allocation of seats. With the new electoral system, 53.3 percent of the seats are allocated under the majoritarian part and 46.7 percent of the seats under the proportional part of the system. Last but not least, the new system does not compensate for lost votes, that is, votes for a single candidate who loses the district, but it prizes the winner ("winner-compensation"). It grants additional points on the party list to the party winning the constituency for multiple votes.[62] Consequently, the current electoral system is less proportional than the one used between 1990 and 2010.

(4) Under the 1989 Constitution, the judiciary, the ombuds-system and the Constitution Court were the institutions that served as important devices to check governmental power and to foster constitutionalism. The Fundamental Law, however, weakened the position of the courts by threatening the independence of the judiciary. It lowered the age limit for compulsory retirement from 70 to 62,[63] so the vast majority of senior judges had to leave the bench.[64] Also, a unique system of judicial administration—existing in no other European country—was introduced through the abolition of the previous structure of judicial self-governance and the creation of a centralized

---

[61] Gábor Attila Tóth, "Hungary," in *Constitutional Law of the EU Member States*, ed. Leonard Besselink et al. (Deventer: Kluwer, 2014), 797–798.

[62] Kim Lane Scheppele, "Hungary: An Election in Question. Part III: Compensating the Winners," *The Blog of Paul Krugman*, February 28, 2014, https://krugman.blogs.nytimes.com/2014/02/28/hungary-an-election-in-question-part-3/.

[63] Article 26(2) of the Fundamental Law.

[64] The Court of Justice of the EU held that premature judicial retirements were a violation of EU law on age discrimination (C-286/12), so Hungary paid compensation but was able to avoid restoring the most important judges to their prior posts and was able to keep all of the newly appointed judges. Kriszta Kovács and Kim Lane Scheppele, "The Fragility of an Independent Judiciary: Lessons from Hungary and Poland–and the European Union," *Communist and Post-Communist Studies* 3, (2018):189–200, https://www.sciencedirect.com/journal/communist-and-post-communist-studies/vol/51/issue/3.

National Judicial Office.[65] The president has the power to exercise the "central responsibilities of the administration of courts,"[66] and the president is, therefore, the "crucial decision-maker of practically every aspect of the organization of the judicial system."[67] The president has nearly complete discretionary power to appoint judges and court leaders, and to promote, demote, reassign, discipline and fire any judge. Given the system, judges cannot enjoy true autonomy and independence. In addition, the Seventh Amendment to the Fundamental Law introduced a new system of administrative courts.[68] These courts will decide, among others, on fundamental rights issues such as matters related to elections, asylum cases or the exercise of the right to peaceful assembly and freedom of information. The new system of administrative courts will start working in 2020 under the oversight of the Minister of Justice.[69]

Similarly, the previous ombuds-system does not remain intact. In the Fundamental Law the fundamental rights, data protection,[70] and minority affairs ombuds have been collapsed into one post headed by the person elected by the constitutional supermajority.

The new system of government affected the independence and the power of the Constitutional Court. First, the nomination rules

---

[65] Article 25(5) of the Fundamental Law.

[66] Article 25(5) of the Fundamental Law.

[67] This extensive power is criticized by the Opinion CDL-AD(2012)001 of the Venice Commission on the Legal Status and Remuneration of Judges and Act CLXI of 2011 on the Organisation and Administration of Courts of Hungary, paras 117–118. Similar concerns were raised by the UN Special Rapporteur on the independence of judges and lawyers on February 29, 2012 and on July 3, 2013, as well as by the Group of States against Corruption (GRECO) in its report adopted on March 27, 2015.

[68] Article 25(3) of the Fundamental Law.

[69] Hungarian Helsinki Committee, "Blurring the Boundaries: New Laws on Administrative Courts Undermine Judicial Independence," available at https://www.helsinki.hu/en/blurring-the-boundaries-new-laws-on-administrative-courts-undermine-judicial-independence/.

[70] The Court of Justice held that Hungary failed to fulfill its obligation to allow the ombudsman to serve their full term of office under Directive 95/46/EC (C-288/12). Hungary amended the rules on the appointment of the Commissioner, presented an apology and paid the agreed sum of compensation.

concerning the members of the Constitutional Court were changed. Previously the members had been nominated by a special committee consisting of one member of each parliamentary fraction and elected by a two-thirds majority of the plenum. Since 2010 the judges have been nominated by a parliamentary committee whose members are appointed from and by the parties according to their share of seats in Parliament.[71] As regards the election procedure, the president of the Court is no longer elected by his fellow justices for three years, but by parliamentary supermajority for twelve years, like every other member of the Court. Furthermore, by a constitutional amendment, the parliamentary majority enlarged the Court's membership from eleven to fifteen, so as to fill up the Court.[72] In addition to these structural changes, the competencies of the Court were restricted so that the Court can no longer review the constitutionality of certain financial laws. The Court may examine the constitutionality of laws related to the state budget, central taxes, stamp duties and contributions, custom duties, and central requirements related to local taxes only if the petition refers exclusively to the right to life and dignity, the protection of personal data, the freedom of thought, conscience and religion or the rights connected to the Hungarian citizenship.[73] But the Court may not assess these laws, for example, with regard to the principles of non-discrimination, rule of law, and the prevalence of the right to property. Furthermore, while the Fundamental Law retained the Constitutional Court on paper, the changes in its functioning were considerable in practice. The Fundamental Law abolished the actio popularis and shifted the focus of constitutional review from examining legislative and executive decisions to reviewing almost exclusively court decisions through the adoption of a modified form of the German constitutional complaint mechanism. Last but not least, since the Fourth Amendment to the Fundamental Law nullified the entire jurisprudence of the Constitutional Court from 1990-2011,[74] none of the decisions of the Court before the enactment of the Fundamental Law can be relied on

[71] July 5, 2010 Amendment of the 1989 Constitution.
[72] Law LXI of 2011 on the Amendment of the 1989 Constitution.
[73] November 16, 2010 Amendment of the 1989 Constitution.
[74] Point 5 of the Closing and Miscellaneous Provisions of the Fundamental Law.

as legal authority, including all of the Court's prior decisions on the rule of law, parliamentary democracy and market economy.

As a consequence of these significant institutional changes, the judiciary, the ombudssystem and the Constitutional Court can barely serve as independent checks on the governing majority.

MISSING MARKET ECONOMY GUARANTEES

One of the most important features of the 1989 Constitution was the heavy reliance on the socially committed market economy. In contrast, the Fundamental Law lacks the market economy guarantees. It does not take property rights seriously and it makes possible to waive protection of fundamental rights, citing the financial problems of the state. For instance, a private owner may only claim protection against state intervention if the national economic indicators are relatively favorable.[75] State interests enjoys priority, thereby the Fundamental Law gives constitutional rank to several financial issues (the budgetary procedure, provisions on national assets), but first and foremost it introduces a debt ceiling (50 percent of the GDP) and regulates the basic requirements –stability, transparency and sustainability– of fiscal policy.[76] In achieving the required public debt ratio and fiscal discipline, the primary responsibility rests on Parliament and the government. But in a quite uncommon way the Fundamental Law obliges the Constitutional Court, the judiciary and other state bodies to observe these principles in the course of their functioning.[77]

The justification given by the ruling majority for specifying in the constitution the desirable level of state debt and the obligations and prohibitions that prevail in situations where this is not achieved—competence cut of the Constitutional Court on budgetary matters and the prior consent of the Budget Council—was the financial problems of the state. The argument went that after the 2008 economic crisis the

[75] Article 37(4) of the Fundamental Law.
[76] Article 34(3) of the Fundamental Law. More on this, see Márton Varju, "Governance, Accountability, and the Market," in *Constitution for a Disunited Nation: On Hungary's 2011 Fundamental Law*, ed. Gábor Attila Tóth (Budapest–New York: CEU Press, 2012), 310.
[77] Article N of the Fundamental Law.

Hungarian governing majority needed more maneuverability, not limited by constitutional constraints, in order to manage the crisis, which hit Hungary hard, endangering the national currency and state solvency.

Hungary is still a capitalist system, where the dominance of private ownership and market coordination are present, but the ruling majority exerts a strong influence on the economy.[78] It is accurate to talk about cronyism and the private expropriation of state power by its practitioners to build up the new "national bourgeoisie."[79]

Conclusion

In this chapter I presented an argument according to which the Hungarian constitutional continuity was unimpaired by the Fundamental Law. I also demonstrated the view under which Fundamental Law called for continuity; only the Fourth Amendment broke with liberal constitutionalism represented by the 1989 Constitution. The chapter found convincing the third view under which the Hungarian constitutional continuity has been disrupted by the flow of constitutional amendments in 2010–2011 and by the adoption of the Fundamental Law.

The chapter examined the change introduced by the Fundamental Law and its subsequent amendments with the help of the concept of constitutional continuity. According to this concept, the constitutional continuity means that not only the legal system, but also the basic structure of the state remains intact despite the adoption of a constitutional amendment or even a new constitution. Applying this concept to the 2010-2011 Hungarian constitutional transformation the chapter concluded that the Fundamental Law, the most important document of the regime change, does not preserve the values and institutions that had been established soon after the 1989 democratic transition.

[78] For the characteristic features of the system see János Kornai, "The System Paradigm Revisited", 276ff.

[79] https://transparency.hu/en/news/hungary-bringing-up-the-rear-of-the-region-in-transparency-internationals-most-recent-world-corruption-ranking/.

It falls short of constitutional principles such as the rule of law, parliamentary democracy built upon the respect and protection of human rights, and the market economy. The Fundamental Law symbolizes the new rule by law regime with the unity of powers and the lacking market economy guarantees. A new identity has been founded by the Fundamental Law, an exclusionary identity that is built upon historical myths,[80] non-inclusive religious references,[81] and anti-egalitarian sentiments.[82] But that is another story and was told elsewhere.[83]

BIBLIOGRAPHY

Allison, J.W.F. *The English Historical Constitution Continuity: Change and European Effects*. Cambridge: Cambridge University Press, 2007.

Arató, Andrew. "Regime Change, Revolution, and Legitimacy." In *Constitution for a Disunited Nation: On Hungary's 2011 Fundamental Law*, edited by Gábor Attila Tóth, 35–57. Budapest–New York: CEU Press, 2012.

Bánkuti, Miklós, Gábor Halmai and Kim Lane Scheppele. "Hungary's Illiberal Turn. Disabling the Constitution." *Journal of Democracy* 3 (2012): 138–146.

Bozóki, András. "Occupy the State. The Orban Regime in Hungary." *Debatte* (2011). https://doi.org/10.1080/0965156X.2012.703415.

80 The Fundamental Law incorporates Hungary's historical constitution, the core ideas of which prefers a "mystic membership" to constitutional patriotism, and the ancient territory of the Hungarian Kingdom to the current borders of the state (National Avowal, Article R(3)).

81 See the National Avowal of the Fundamental Law. The Seventh Amendment to the Fundamental Law requires all state bodies to protect Christian culture.

82 Kriszta Kovács, "Equality: The Missing Link", in *Constitution for a Disunited Nation: On Hungary's 2011 Fundamental Law*, ed. Gábor Attila Tóth (Budapest–New York: CEU Press, 2012), 171–195.

83 See Zsolt Körtvélyesi and Balázs Majtényi, "Game of Values: The Threat of Exclusive Constitutional Identity, the EU and Hungary," *German Law Journal* 07 (2017), http://www.germanlawjournal.com/volume-18-no-07. 1721ff. and Kriszta Kovács, "The Rise of an Ethnocultural Constitutional Identity in the Jurisprudence of the East Central European Courts," *German Law Journal* 07 (2017): 1703ff, http://www.germanlawjournal.com/volume-18-no-07.

Bozóki, András and Dániel Hegedűs. "An Externally Constrained Hybrid Regime: Hungary in the European Union." *Democratization* 7 (2018):1173–1189. https://doi.org/10.1080/13510347.2018.1455664.

Dalos, György, Miklós Haraszti, György Konrád and László Rajk. "The Decline of Democracy—the Rise of Dictatorship." *eurozine.hu*, January 2, 2012, https://www.eurozine.com/the-decline-of-democracy-the-rise-of-dictatorship-2.

Dani, Marco. "The 'Partisan Constitution' and the corrosion of European constitutional culture." *LEQS Paper* 68 (2013). http://dx.doi.org/10.2139/ssrn.2348629.

Deák, István. "Hungary: The Threat" *New York Review of Books,* April 28, 2011.

Ganczer, Mónika. "International Law and Dual Nationality of Hungarians Living Outside the Borders." *Acta Juridica Hungarica* 4 (2012): 316–333. http://dx.doi.org/10.1556/AJur.53.2012.4.4.

Grewe, Constance. "Methods of Identification of National Constitutional Identity." In *National Constitutional Identity and European Integration*, edited by Alejandro Saiz Arnaiz and Carina Alcoberro LLivina, 37–48. Cambridge: Intersentia, 2013.

Halmai, Gábor. "Towards an Illiberal Democracy. Hungary's New Constitution" *eurozine.hu*, January 25, 2012. https://www.eurozine.com/towards-an-illiberal-democracy/.

Hart, Herbert L. A. *The Concept of Law*. Sheffield: Clarendon, 1994.

Henkin, Louis. "A New Birth of Constitutionalism: Genetic Influences and Genetic Defects." *Constitutionalism, Identity, Difference and Legitimacy: Theoretical Perspectives*, edited by Michel Rosenfeld. Durham: Duke University Press, 1994.

Jacobsohn, Gary J. "The Formation of Constitutional Identities." In *Comparative Constitutional Law*, edited by Tom Ginsburg and Rosalind Dixon, 129–142. Cheltenham: Edward Elgar Publishing, 2011.

Jakab, András, and Pál Sonnevend. "Continuity with Deficiencies: The New Basic Law of Hungary." *European Constitutional Law Review* 9 (2013): 102–138. https://doi.org/10.1017/S1574019612001058.

Kis, János. "From the 1989 Constitution to the 2011 Fundamental Law." In *Constitution for a Disunited Nation: On Hungary's 2011 Fundamental Law*, edited by Gábor Attila Tóth, 1–21. Budapest–New York: CEU Press, 2012.

Kornai, János. "Hungary's U-Turn." *Capitalism and Society* 1 (2015). https://ssrn.com/abstract=2629592.

Kornai, János. "The System Paradigm Revisited." *Revue D'Études Comparatives Est-Ouest* 1–2 (2017): 239–296. http://dx.doi.org/10.1556/032.2016.66.4.1.

Kovács, Kriszta and Gábor Attila Tóth. "Hungary's Constitutional Transformation." *European Constitutional Law Review* 7 (2011): 183–203. https://doi.org/10.1017/S1574019611200038.

Kovács, Kriszta. "Equality: The Missing Link." In *Constitution for a Disunited Nation: On Hungary's 2011 Fundamental Law*, edited by Gábor Attila Tóth, 171–195. Budapest–New York: CEU Press, 2012.

Kovács, Kriszta. "Az Alkotmánybíróság többé nem az alkotmányvédelem legfőbb szerve": Sólyom László volt köztársasági elnökkel Kovács Kriszta beszélget ["The Constitutional Court is Not the Guardian of the Constitution Anymore." Kriszta Kovács talks to László Sólyom]. *Fundamentum* 1 (2013): 19–30.

Kovács, Kriszta, and Paul Blokker. "Unilateral Expansionism: Hungarian Citizenship and Franchise Politics and their Effects on the Hungarian-Romanian Relations." In *Good Neighbourliness in the European Legal Context*, edited by Dimitry Kochenov and Elena Basheska, 136–159. Leiden: Brill/Nijhoff, 2015.

Kovács, Kriszta. "The Rise of an Ethnocultural Constitutional Identity in the Jurisprudence of the East Central European Courts." *German Law Journal* 7 (2017): 1703–1720. http://www.germanlawjournal.com/volume-18-no-07.

Kovács, Kriszta and Kim Lane Scheppele. "The Fragility of an Independent Judiciary: Lessons from Hungary and Poland–and the European Union." *Communist and Post-Communist Studies* 3 (2018):189–200. https://www.sciencedirect.com/journal/communist-and-post-communist-studies/vol/51/issue/3.

Körtvélyesi, Zsolt and Judit Tóth. "Naturalisation in Hungary: Exclusion by Ethnic Preference." *Open Citizenship* 1 (2011): 54–74.

Körtvélyesi, Zsolt and Balázs Majtényi. "Game of Values: The Threat of Exclusive Constitutional Identity, the EU and Hungary." *German Law Journal* 7 (2017): 1721–1744. http://www.germanlawjournal.com/volume-18-no-07.

Krygier, Martin. "Rule of Law" In *The Oxford Handbook of Comparative Constitutional Law*, edited by Michel Rosenfeld and András Sajó, 233–249. Oxford: Oxford University Press, 2012.

Khvorostiankina, Anna. "'Constitutional Identity' in the Context of Post-Soviet Transformation. Europeanization and Regional Integration Processes (the Case of Armenia)." *Armenian Journal of Political Science*, 1 (2017): 45–80.

Majtényi, Balázs, Alíz Nagy, and Péter Kállai. "'Only Fidesz'—Minority Electoral Law in Hungary." *VerfBlog*, March 31, 2018. https://verfassungsblog.de/only-fidesz-electoral-law-in-hungary/.

Martí, José Luis. "Two Different Ideas of Constitutional Identity: Identity of the Constitution v. Identity of the People." In *National Constitutional Identity and European Integration*, edited by Alejandro Saiz Arnaiz and Carina Alcoberro LLivina, 17–36. Cambridge: Intersentia, 2013.

Müller, Jan-Werner. "The Hungarian Tragedy." *Dissent*, Spring 2011, 5–10.

Pogány, István. "The Crisis of Democracy in East Central Europe: The 'New Constitutionalism' in Hungary." *European Public Law* 19 (2013): 341–368. http://www.kluwerlawonline.com/toc.php?pubcode=EURO.

Polzin, Monika. "Constitutional Identity as a Constructed Reality and a Restless Soul." *German Law Journal* 7 (2017): 1595–1615. http://www.germanlawjournal.com/volume-18-no-07.

Rawls, John. *Political Liberalism*. New York: Columbia University Press, 1993.

Rosenfeld, Michel. "Constitutional Identity." In *The Oxford Handbook of Comparative Constitutional Law*, edited by Michel Rosenfeld and András Sajó, 756–776. Oxford: Oxford University Press, 2012.

Rupnik, Jacques. "Hungary's Illiberal Turn: How Things Went Wrong." *Journal of Democracy* 3 (2012): 132–37.

Scheppele, Kim Lane. "Hungary's Constitutional Revolution." *The Conscience of a Liberal, The Blog of Paul Krugman*. December 18, 2011. http://krugman.blogs.nytimes.com/2011/12/19/hungarys-constitutional-revolution/.

Schwartz, Herman. "Do Economic and Social Rights Belong in a Constitution?" *The American University Journal of International Law and Policy* 4 (1995).

Śledzińska-Simon, Anna. "Constitutional Identity in 3D: A Model of Individual, Relational, and Collective Self and its Application in Poland." *International Journal of Constitutional Law* 1 (2015): 124–155. https://doi.org/10.1093/icon/mov007.

Sólyom, László. "Introduction to the Decisions of the Constitutional Court of the Republic of Hungary." In *Constitutional Judiciary in a New Democracy: The Hungarian Constitutional Court*, edited by László Sólyom and Georg Brunner, 1–65. Ann Arbor: Michigan University Press, 2000.

Sólyom, László. "Ende der Gewaltenteilung. Zur Änderungen des Grundgesetzes in Ungarn" *Osteuropa* 4 (2013): 5–12.

Sólyom, László. "The Rise and Decline of Constitutional Culture in Hungary." In *Constitutional Crisis in the European Constitutional Area: Theory, Law and Politics in Hungary and Romania*, edited by Armin von Bogdandy and Pál Sonnevend, 5–32. Oxford–Portland, OR: Hart, 2015.

Sonnevend, Pál, András Jakab, and Lóránt Csink. "The Constitution as an Instrument of Everyday Party Politics: The Basic Law of Hungary." In *Constitutional Crisis in the European Constitutional Area: Theory, Law and Politics in Hungary and Romania*, edited by Armin von Bogdandy and Pál Sonnevend, 33–110. Oxford–Portland, OR: Hart, 2015.

Szombati, Kristóf. "The Betrayed Republic. Hungary's New Constitution and the 'System of National Cooperation.'" *Heinrich Böll Stiftung* (April 2011). https://cz.boell.org/sites/default/files/uploads/2014/03/article_2_kristof_szombati.pdf.

Stumpf, István. "The Fundamental Law of Hungary." *Hungarian Review* 2 (2014): 43.

Tóth, Gábor Attila. "Hungary." In *Constitutional Law of the EU Member States*, edited by Leonard Besselink et al., 773–836. Deventer: Kluwer, 2014.

Tóth, Gábor Attila. "Macht statt Recht. Deformation des Verfassungssystems in Ungarn." *Osteuropa* 4 (2013): 21–28.

Tóth, Gábor Attila, ed. *Constitution for a Disunited Nation. On Hungary's 2011 Fundamental Law*. Budapest–New York: CEU Press, 2012.

Trócsányi, László. "The Creation of the Basic Law of Hungary." In *The Basic Law of Hungary: A First Commentary*, edited by Lóránt Csink, Balázs Schanda, and András Zs. Varga. Dublin: Clarus, 2012.

Troper, Michel. "Behind the Constitution?" In *Constitutional Topography: Values and Constitutions*, edited by András Sajó and Renáta Uitz. The Hague: Eleven, 2011.
Uitz, Renáta. *Constitutions, Courts and History. Historical Narratives in Constitutional Adjudication*. Budapest–New York: CEU Press, 2006.
Varju, Márton. "Governance, Accountability, and the Market." In *Constitution for a Disunited Nation: On Hungary's 2011 Fundamental Law*, edited by Gábor Attila Tóth, 301–331. Budapest–New York: CEU Press, 2012.
Waluchow, Wil. "Constitutionalism." *The Stanford Encyclopedia of Philosophy* (Spring 2018 Edition), edited by Edward N. Zalta, 2018.

Continuity, Discontinuity and Constitution-Making: A Comparative Account

ZSOLT KÖRTVÉLYESI

Introduction

As a symbolic marker of "break with the past," the FIDESZ government of 2010 set out to adopt a new constitution. This chapter looks at questions of shift and legacy through a seemingly technical element of this new Fundamental Law, the legal grounding rule that refers back to the 1949 Constitution. This legal continuity will be contrasted to the constitutional rhetoric of discontinuity, the Fundamental Law's declaration that the 1949 Constitution is null and void. The discussion below focuses on what is often termed "the identity of the legal system" in the literature,[1] and on the ambivalent relationship between the formal source of validity of the constitutional text (and of the legal system) and the expressed relationship between the old and the new legal regime; in other words, expressions of legality and legitimacy at a moment of constitutional shift.

Proponents of a new constitution often use constitutional arguments, making use of the legitimating force of the (internal) validity of law, that do not reflect the actual constitutional landscape and the relationship between the old and the new regime. This distorts the con-

---

[1] Joseph Raz, *The Concept of a Legal System* (Oxford: Clarendon Press, Second Edition, 1980), esp. chap. VIII; John Finnis, "Revolutions and Continuity of Law," in *Philosophy of Law: Collected Essays—Volume IV* (Oxford Scholarship Online, 2011), 407–434, accessed May 16, 2019, https://www.oxfordscholarship.com/view/10.1093/acprof:oso/9780199580088.001.0001/acprof-9780199580088-chapter-22.

stitutional reality in important respects, showing a false image about the very foundations of the new constitutional regime. Relying on the legitimating force of legal continuity, one can argue—as did many in the cases cited below—that the new regime relies on the constitutional foundations of the earlier regime, and whoever accepts the old regime with its rules on how to change elements of the constitutional framework should also more readily accept the new regime. Or, on the contrary, one could talk about a revolutionary change that denies the preceding constitutional framework while, in the background, maintaining constitutional continuity.[2] Rather than a mere call for honesty or a manifesto against camouflage,[3] this chapter puts these constitutional distortions into context in order to point to something larger, the relationship between law and politics.[4]

In the specific context of the Hungarian transition, this chapter presents a case study to demonstrate how the political rhetoric of discontinuity runs parallel to an underlying reality of continuity in the legal technical sense. This chapter argues that this endeavor gives important insight into the identity of the new regime. The Fundamental Law and the related government discourse downplays legal continuity as incidental or hidden, while it claims political disconti-

---

[2] This is not to say that proponents of a new constitutional regime or the text itself cannot make claims about the earlier regimes. New constitutions are adopted, at least partly, due to a perceived inadequacy of the old ones. But it is a different matter when these actors and texts make claims about the system's validity using legal, constitutional arguments.

[3] Although the text can also be read as such. The analysis should show the scope of constitutional argument, and where it should end; where constitutional lawyers should make it clear that they can no more say what is, but, at most, an opinion on what ought to be; where the legal system can coerce and use its own rule of validity to legitimize coercion, and where this power ends, opening up the question of legitimacy for political struggles. This implies honesty about what constitutional law (and constitutional lawyers or people using constitutional arguments) can do and how far it can go.

[4] The discussion nevertheless seeks to remain within the legal realm. Cf. Raz arguing that the "criterion of identity of legal systems is [...] determined not only by jurisprudential or legal considerations but by other considerations as well, considerations belonging to other social sciences," and adding that therefore he limits himself to questions that remain within the legal domain, "[n]ot wishing to trespass on other fields." Raz, *The Concept of a Legal System*, 188.

nuity with the recent past that includes not only the socialist legacy but also the "two turbulent decades of transition."[5]

The chapter follows a non-conventional approach in that it explores the questions arising from the legal and the political element in constitution-making, after a short theoretical sketch, through historical examples, and then applies these insights to the Hungarian case. The second part provides a summary of the theoretical arguments that are necessary to follow the later discussions, the third part presents emblematic cases of (successful and attempted) constitutional transitions, the fourth part assesses the Hungarian case, and the fifth part concludes.

My assumption is that the distortion of the formal validity of the constitution in political statements reveals something important about the foundational moment as well as about how the political elite behind the new constitution, and the regime marked by that text, thinks about the people and their relation to politics. This is the people with reference to whom the constitution is adopted, also marking, formally, the foundational moment of a regime. In Finnis' more explicit formulation: "the continuity and identity of a legal system is a function of the continuity and identity of the society."[6] The chapter concludes that the Fundamental Law of Hungary presents a mismatch in the sense that the political discourse and legitimacy arguments directly contradict the legal expression of this political will: the continued reliance on legality is traced back to the 1949 Constitution, which, among others, allows for the omission of the people from the process (but not the rhetoric) of constitution-making.

The Centrality of the Amending Rule and the Nature of Constituent Power

Those exercising the power of constitution-making always face a dilemma about continuity and discontinuity. While the two notions sound mutually exclusive, the examples will show that they can be and

[5] Parliament of Hungary, Political Declaration 1 of 2010 (June 16) of the Hungarian National Assembly on National Cooperation, adopted on June 14, 2010, official English translation available at http://www.nefmi.gov.hu/download.php?docID=2523, accessed May 14, 2019.

[6] Finnis, "Revolutions and Continuity of Law," 428.

are often played out simultaneously: politicians talk about one and do the other. On the one hand, legitimizing a constitution-making process always requires some opposition to, thus rupture with, the old constitution: the constitution-makers need to argue their case, why is change necessary and what was missing under the old regime? On the other hand, the examples might be read as demonstrations that most constitution-making procedures are marked by a fear of a complete rupture with the past.[7] Replacing the very foundations of the regime looks like a leap in the dark, raising, very directly, questions about popular legitimacy. The duality of continuity and discontinuity will present problems that reach well beyond the strictly constitutional realm, and will continue to plague the system while new "constitutional" moments will tilt the field towards discontinuity: the sense that the new constitutional regime rests on a mandate from the people, and not on surviving parts of the old regime the credentials of which have been questioned anyway.

The political force behind a new constitution is, at first sight, in a unique position because of its almost complete liberty to draw the basic structure of the emerging constitutional regime. On the other hand, this same moment marks the heightened vulnerability of this force. It cannot rely on a presumption of legitimacy, building on legal continuity, but confronts the need for legitimacy in a more direct way. This might explain why proponents might shy away from presenting changes as revolutionary or, in a twisted version, might maintain formal continuity while talking about a revolutionary shift. This double move of tying and untying is thus exemplary for what the system thinks about its own foundations, about its source of legitimacy, which could be read as an important element of the identity of the regime.

One might question the special role of founding moments. Bruce Ackerman talks about constitutional moments, when political decision-making challenges the existing constitutional framework by switching to a mode of "higher lawmaking."[8] Mark Tushnet disagrees on whether

---

[7] Hobbes affirms this fear when discussing the right of succession as an artificial eternity "without which, men that are governed by an Assembly, should return into the condition of Warre in every age." Thomas Hobbes, *Hobbes's Leviathan, reprinted from the edition of 1651* (Oxford: Clarendon Press, 1929), 149.

[8] Bruce Ackerman, *We The People, Volume 1: Foundations* (Cambridge, MA: Harvard University Press, 1991). See also: David A. Strauss, "The Irrele-

these are truly moments or should include changes through longer periods.[9] Both of these views suggest that comparably important constitutional changes can happen after the adoption, even outside the ordinary amending procedure. While this mitigates the importance of the one-off founding moment, the adoption of the constitution, its relevance and even centrality nevertheless remains. Constitutional founding moments do mark unique moments in the sense that the relationship between the legal foundations and the political necessarily reveals itself (even if this does not necessarily mean that the relationship between the two is also made clear in the dominant political discourse at the time). The contrast between continuity and discontinuity that I will look at is more readily available.

Normally, a revolutionary constitution-making means that there is no standard against which we can measure the legality of the constitution, only questions of legitimacy can be raised. The sanction flowing from "violating" (i.e. overwriting) the old, existing constitutional amending rule (or the one on adopting a completely new constitution) appears as a loss of legitimacy, a potential challenge for the new basic norm to rally public support. However, if the adoption of a constitution does not mark a formal break with the earlier order and grounds its own validity on this preceding framework, the legitimacy of the new constitution can also rely on the legality of the new constitution in light of the earlier constitution. In this case, the question of legality might also become a question of legitimacy, as the drafters of the new constitution can argue that there is a (formal, legal) continuity that should somehow make the new constitution more acceptable for the public.

A key element that can distinguish one constitutional change from the other is whether the formal rule of amending the constitution, or adopting a new one, changes or it remains the same, and whether the

---

vance of Constitutional Amendments," *Harvard Law Review* 5 (2001): 1457–1505.

[9] Mark Tushnet, "Constitutional Hardball," *John Marshall Law Review* 2 (2004): 532, 39n. On some of the problems of how to assess whether a constitutional moment has taken place, see Daniel Taylor Young, "How Do You Measure a Constitutional Moment? Using Algorithmic Topic Modeling to Evaluate Bruce Ackerman's Theory of Constitutional Change, Note," *Yale Law Journal* 7 (2013): 1990–2054.

new constitution "knows," in a procedural sense, about the old one. If the ultimate rule of recognition changes, this in itself might question arguments about constitutional continuity. The centrality of the amending clause[10] is explained by its ability to speak directly on the relationship between the old and the new constitutional framework and whether what we witness is stepping outside the earlier constitutional regime.[11] It is in this context that debates about the ability of the old constitution putting a constraint on the new one arise. There often is a tension between the content of the new and the old framework, but this might not create problems if the changes are truly revolutionary, in the formal sense, too. It is not hard to conclude that constitutional frameworks can be superseded by revolution, rebellion or turmoil. It is less obvious that pre-existing constitutional frameworks might fail to legitimize changes despite a discourse of constitutional continuity.

The topic presented here concerns what we could call the interface between law and politics beyond law, namely, the constituent power. The goal of this chapter is to assess legality arguments (and statements about constitutional continuity) in light of their impact on legitimacy. While I cannot explore here, in detail, the various accounts of the complex relationship between the wider political and the embedded legal realm, some basic observations and accounts have to be presented on

---

[10] Alf Ross also takes the amending rule as ultimate in the sense that it is "apolitical," as its change falls "outside the province of legal procedure." Alf Ross, *On Law and Justice* (Berkeley and Los Angeles: University of California Press, 1959): 81.

[11] E.g., for the European Union such a shift could be a move away from the present "constitutional amending rule," namely the national government based treaty changes, and a reliance on a different political process, either circumventing governments by a direct legitimation from the voters in the individual member states or completely detaching the process from the member states framework and grounding legitimacy in a direct and unified act of the European people, e.g., a Union-wide referendum. This would be the formal side of the substantial changes that Habermas urges. For his comparative account of the US foundational moment and the European prospects, see his lecture on "Transnationalizing Democracy: The Example of the European Union" at Boston College on May 8, 2014, http://frontrow.bc.edu/program/habermas/. In print: Jürgen Habermas, "European Citizens and European Peoples: The Problem of Transnationalizing Democracy," in *The Lure of Technocracy* (Malden, MA: Polity, 2015), 29–45.

how the two fields interrelate in the unique moment of adopting a new constitution.

The political and the legal could be rephrased in this context as the legitimacy and the legality arguments about the validity of a constitutional regime. The two elements of both of these pairs are strongly connected, and this is even more so at the founding moment of a new constitutional order. Legitimacy can be understood as answering a question of fact about empirical validity, social-political acceptance: whether people, in general, observe, or are in fact forced to observe legal rules emerging under that particular constitutional regime, or not. On the other hand, legality—in a somewhat simplified reading that is sufficient for our purposes here—can mean the possibility of legal enforcement through courts. As presented here, legality is an either-or question, whereas legitimacy is a question of shades. An action can be more or less legitimate, but can only be, in general, either legal (compelled or allowed by law) or illegal.

An important connection between legality and legitimacy is that, in an established rule of law regime, legality will confer presumed legitimacy on the actions of the state. This explains why proponents of a new constitution might be inclined to use arguments based on legal continuity. Looking at this question from the perspective of the law, the legal system has to rely, ultimately, on the wider political realm when claiming validity: it is a political decision to adopt a certain kind of constitution, and without the foundational decision, the legal system cannot come about. This link is a truism that all approaches share. There is a difference, however, in how various thinkers understand the nature of this link.

The classical formulation could be personified by Hans Kelsen presenting the legal system whose validity rests on a "basic norm" that itself cannot be validated by law. The source of the basic norm, whose validity is only presumed by law, can be traced back to "the first constitution."[12] This creates a link between law and its context, but,

[12] Hans Kelsen, *Introduction to the Problems of Legal Theory* (Oxford: Clarendon Press, 1934/2002), see especially Chapter V. Note, with David Dyzenhaus, "the oddness of a metaphor which says that a norm is both the foundation and the apex of a structure." David Dyzenhaus, *Legality and Legitimacy: Carl Schmitt, Hans Kelsen and Herman Heller in Weimar* (Oxford: Oxford University Press, 1997), 103, 4n, quoted by Martin Loughlin, *The Idea of Public Law* (Oxford: Oxford University Press, 2003), 99.

more importantly, it demarcates the two fields. Hart adds here that the basic norm (the "ultimate rule of recognition") is not simply assumed to be valid, it is more precise to say that this rule exists by way of its constant application as a valid rule, when dealing with law.[13] Just like it is (or, rather, it used to be) the case with the meter: the standard meter bar in Paris is not assumed to be precisely one meter, we accept it as being exactly one meter.[14] Internally, working inside of the law, we accept and apply the rule. While externally, it is a fact to be ascertained whether the rule (the basic norm and, ultimately, the entire legal system) has actual validity, in everyday practice.[15]

John Finnis is dissatisfied with both positions, when assessing the implications for constitutional continuity. According to him, Kelsen relies on a chain of past constitutions that cannot cope with (a) the time factor, i.e. that constitutions can have an effect under a succeeding constitution, too—or (b) the division of legal systems, e.g., in a process of decolonization. Hart's theory is then presented as one that is capable of dealing with these challenges, through the "rule of recognition," but at the price of making the hierarchical nature of law malleable.[16]

Another account of this relationship between law and politics can be attributed to Carl Schmitt. He challenges the nicely polished view of the legal system and argues that it is problematic on various accounts. For example, it omits the question of why people obey the law. Using Max Weber's categorization, in the absence of a charismatic and traditional legitimating source, the system can only rely on legal-rational justification. This is the motivation behind using and misusing arguments about legal validity, especially in the context of constitution-making. Schmitt offers a more precise formulation, which allows him to combine his and Weber's view: rather than accepting legality as a source of legitimacy itself, we can treat "the belief in

---

13 H.L.A. Hart, *The Concept of Law* (Oxford: Clarendon Press, 1994), 109.

14 Ibid. Note that right before the first publication of Hart's book, the meter bar was superseded by a more precise standard based on wavelength and later on the distance travelled by light.

15 Ibid., 110.

16 Finnis, "Revolutions and Continuity of Law," 414–421.

legality" as a form of legitimacy.[17] For Schmitt, the constituent power is not reduced to a one-time foundational moment after which we can understand law purified from direct political interference. For him, this political element continues to play an important role in maintaining the legal system. This widens the interface between law and politics.

Martin Loughlin describes the earlier accounts as normativist and decisionist approaches, respectively. Normativist accounts relegate the constituent power problem to politics, outside the scope of law, or even making, as Dyzenhaus argues, the very notion of constituent power superfluous, as in these theories the authority of law is derived from the inside, from the autonomy of a legal system and its qualities that help maintaining a political community.[18] In anti-positivist normativism, an appeal is instead made to the morality of law. Decisionism (Schmitt) acknowledges the open and indeterminate nature of law, due to its constant interaction with politics. Loughlin, however, contends that Schmitt fails to fully consider the shift from the rule of the prince to democracy, and remains attached to a closure that "can lead only to totalitarianism."[19] The relationist proposal maintains that "power and law are mutually constitutive and reciprocally dependent,"[20] and as such it is impossible to go back to the normativist or decisionist reduction that only considers one aspect of this relationship. It is in the legal framework that political power is realized and "the people" is constituted by the very foundational moment of the legal system. Yet, this moment does not bring about closure, and political struggle will con-

---

17 Carl Schmitt, *Legality and Legitimacy* (Durham: Duke University Press, 2004), 9. For a practical introduction to these issues, connecting it back to the US debate starting with Madison's concern about parchment barriers, see Eric A. Posner and Adrian Vermeule, "Demystifying Schmitt," In *The Oxford Handbook of Carl Schmitt,* ed. Jens Meierhenrich and Oliver Simons (Oxford: Oxford University Press, 2016), 612–626.

18 David Dyzenhaus, "Constitutionalism in an Old Key: Legality and Constituent Power," *Global Constitutionalism* 1 (2012): 233, cited by Martin Loughlin, "The Concept of Constituent Power," *European Journal of Political Theory* 13 (2014): 222.

19 Loughlin, "The Concept of Constituent Power," 228.

20 Loughlin, "The Concept of Constituent Power," 230–31, citing Herman Heller.

tinue over who is truly representing the people: "the space is crowded with the many who claim the authentic voice of constituent power."[21]

It is in this struggle that arguments about legal validity will appear. Once we acknowledge that this is a political struggle, we can grasp the stakes of the debate about continuity and discontinuity. John Finnis himself asserts that "there seems to be only one conclusion: the continuity and identity of a legal system is a function of the continuity and identity of the society."[22] It is striking in this light how the extralegal element, in many instances, is concealed from the view of the wider public, even though they are the same people that are the ultimate reference point, both in the legal and the wider political sense.

I will trace this issue through the case studies in the next section. My overview will be one-dimensional in the sense that I do not focus on every institutional and procedural aspect, or all substantive elements of the constitution. I am only interested in the statements about legality and constitutional continuity made in the debate surrounding the adoption of the constitution. This explains why I will not deal with rights-foundationalist or democratic-proceduralist accounts, or the dualist perspective offered by Bruce Ackerman.[23] I will not deal with "substantive" views that hold constitution-makers against substantive standards[24] that would make the comparative approach impossible within the limits of this chapter. Only in the Hungarian case will I map the debate in more detail. It is not the legitimacy of the new constitution per se that will be my central concern, but how legal validity argu-

---

21 Loughlin, "The Concept of Constituent Power," 233–34. Institutionalization marks the end of the "constituent power," that should remain outside of the instituted representational forms. Citing Claude Lefort, Loughlin argues that "legitimacy must be claimed in the name of the people, and the question of who represents the people remains the indeterminate question of modern politics. The function of constituent power is to keep that question open." Loughlin, "The Concept of Constituent Power," 234. Elsewhere Loughlin writes that "constituent power is the juristic expression of the democratic impetus. The concept expresses the tensions between democracy and law." Loughlin, *The Idea of Public Law,* 100.

22 Finnis, "Revolutions and Continuity of Law," 428.

23 Ackerman, *We The People, Volume 1: Foundations.*

24 See, e.g., Dworkin's standard using notions of equal respect and equal concern, Ronald Dworkin, *Justice for Hedgehogs* (Cambridge, MA: Belknap Press, 2011).

ments based on constitutional (dis)continuity, in particular, play into the legitimacy question, and how this relates to the role of the people. Accordingly, I will analyze the following issues: 1) How is the source of validity presented by the constitution-makers? 2) How does this relate to the formal source of validity (based on the internal logic of the legal system)? 3) What is the role of the people in both of these?

While it's impossible to provide a complete overview of the various instances where constitution-making mixes both continuity and discontinuity, and legitimacy and legality, I propose to embark on a journey by listing indicative constitutional moments to arrive at an understanding of the role of law and politics and the meaning of legal and political discourses on continuity and discontinuity, starting with the classic case of the adoption of the US Constitution.

Constitutional Shifts and their Representation: Cases

THE RATIFICATION OF THE US CONSTITUTION

James Madison in Federalist No. 40 claims that the Philadelphia Convention did nothing more than fulfil its constitutional mandate, contrary to what is widely held, and did not overstep that mandate.[25] Considering the primary goal of the Federalist Papers we can read this less as a strictly legal argument, although it is suggesting a legal continuity with the earlier framework based on the Articles of Confederation, and more as a political statement. Madison and his partners, after all, had a direct political goal: to persuade the voters to support ratification in their respective states. The Federalist Papers were written as political pamphlets (which does not, of course, belittle their importance or ingenuity).

However, the political argument is presented as a legitimacy argument based on constitutional continuity. We can then ask what makes others think that this might not be the case, and why Madison thinks he needs to argue for this interpretation. Let us first look at the amending rule that has a special significance from the point of view of

[25] The Federalist No. 40 (James Madison), arguing that the members of the Philadelphia Convention were, rightly, "deeply and unanimously convinced that such a reform as they have proposed was absolutely necessary to effect the purposes of their appointment."

the foundations of the system. Under the new regime, the constituent power is shared between Congress (and/or a Convention, proposing) and states (with legislatures or conventions, ratifying). Furthermore, no consensus among states is required, no single state can veto the process. Also, ratification is passed through state conventions instead of state legislatures, as the Articles of Confederation would have required: confirmation "by the legislatures of every State."[26]

This raises the issue whether the old sovereign can reclaim its right of amendment. Can the old *pouvoir constituant* be resurrected? Could a non-ratifying state—of which there was none, with the outlier Rhode Island ratifying in 1790—block the process, arguing that the Constitution is invalid under the Articles of Confederation? This question helps us consider how the political element is directly present in the constitutional shift. If we want to maintain that the Constitution is a valid text, we cannot rely on the Articles: they specified the mode of amending the foundational text of the "perpetual Union" that was disregarded. The Constitution can only be valid if it rests on a rule of recognition other than the old amending clause. This then takes us beyond the old framework, and contrary to how Madison presents his argument, hinting at an essential continuity, there is a foundational shift. Within the new framework we cannot raise questions about the validity of the old framework. Imagine a scenario where a state—like Rhode Island—or several states, continue to live under the Articles of Confederation. The ultimate fate of the two regimes will depend on the empirical validity of the two legal systems. This leads me to my second example.

THE DORR REBELLION: PARALLEL CONSTITUTIONS IN A COMMON FEDERAL FRAME

Hart describes an existing legal system as one where "the rules recognized as valid at the official level are generally obeyed." He describes cases where this does not materialize as "the pathology of legal systems," his first example being revolutions "where rival claims to govern are made from within the group."[27] This is exactly what happened in

26 *Articles of Confederation,* Article XIII.
27 Hart, *The Concept of Law,* 118.

1841–42 to Rhode Island, which had two constitutions:[28] the original one, a charter that survived from colonial times, without an amending clause,[29] and the new one, the 1841 Constitution.[30] The latter, called the "Freemen's Constitution," was initiated by a popular assembly and adopted by popular referendum followed by general elections. However, all of these proceedings were rejected by officials of the old regime, which was still in power.

The question raised by this unique situation was who are to speak in the name of the people of Rhode Island. The rebellion adopted its new constitution through extralegal means, from the point of view of the old regime. It sought to circumvent the undemocratic nature of the political system that excluded the majority of the population, including most of the white male adult population, not to speak about the others.[31] The "legal" regime (although "illegitimate", in the eyes of the rebels), based on the votes of the privileged minority, resisted all attempts to extend voting rights and end the excessive disenfranchisement. As a result of the parallel chain of events, two governors could claim authority.

---

[28] For a concise summary of the events, see the final judgment in *Luther v. Borden,* 48 U.S. 1, 35–38 (1849), involving a dispute between Martin Luther, a "rebel," and the regime of King (these are the real names, and we will see that both sides had also their dreams, like their later namesake).

[29] *Luther v. Borden,* 48 U.S. 1, 35 (1849).

[30] *Articles of a Constitution, adopted by the People's Convention, held October 4, 1841, and postponed to November 16, for final consideration,* Library of Congress, accessed on May 16, 2019, https://archive.org/download/articlesofconsti00rhod/articlesofconsti00rhod.pdf.

[31] On the two elections in more details: "At [the invalid] election a clear majority of all the adult males voted for the new frame of government. Not only this, but among those voting in favor was a clear majority of those duly registered as voters under the charter. ... The valid one received seven thousand votes; the invalid one nearly fourteen thousand. Yet the difference in validity lay in this: the seven thousand voted at a duly called election, and hence had authority to speak for the whole people; whereas the fourteen thousand voted at an irregular election, and hence spoke only for themselves." Roger S. Hoar, *Constitutional Conventions: Their Nature, Powers, and Limitations* (Boston: Little, Brown, and Company, 1917), 21–22, quoted by Akhil Reed Amar, "Guaranteeing a Republican Form of Government: The Central Meaning of Republican Government: Popular Sovereignty, Majority Rule, and the Denominator Problem," *University of Colorado Law Review* 65 (1994): 775.

From the perspective of validity, the old regime claimed authority based on strict legal validity, which can be traced back to their colonial charter. The supporters of the new constitutional system, on the other hand, could rely on increased democratic legitimacy (majority vote with wider participation), although they also made traditional legality claims (majority support from those entitled to vote under the existing regime). Now, can the legal system settle this dispute? The starting question should be which legal system we have in mind—we might reach opposing conclusions depending on how we start off. Based on the charter legal system, the new constitution cannot claim legal validity. If we, however, take the new state constitution as a starting point, it was adopted following its own rules, and should be able to determine the political structure of the state. It is clear that the legal validity argument defaults to circular reasoning or question begging. The question is which constitution should be valid, but we can only answer the question once we have selected our starting point, namely the constitutional regime (and with it, its basic norm) under which legal validity can be assessed. It is easy to conclude that law alone cannot resolve this dispute—unless we have a legal rule, a rule of recognition, above the two systems. In this particular case, the US federal system and its constitutional structure was available. Yet, even with that, the political element seemed to be decisive.

In *Luther v. Borden*[32] the Supreme Court of the United States was asked to settle the question of which constitutional system should be recognized and, as a result, if an official of the old system possessed the power to search a house. The judgment is in line with the opinion that these questions are primarily of a political nature. The Court confirmed that legal arguments should not determine the final outcome, it is a political question to be settled by political means, in this case the federal political branches.[33] To emphasize the role of politics even more, the federal court decision came too late to settle the

[32] *Luther v. Borden,* 48 U.S. 1 (1849).

[33] This seems to hold even for a strictly constitutional question of the guarantee of a republican form of government (Article IV Section 4 of the US Constitution). The Court held that it is Congress who could decide such controversies, not the courts (resting on some dubious arguments, involving practical hardship of evidence). *Luther v. Borden,* 48 U.S. 1, 42 (1849).

struggle between the two regimes, since brute force had already solved the problem.[34] By the time of the decision, there were no competing regimes any more, the forces of the old regime won the fight outside law, and the "rebellious" constitution became known as such, a (legal) dead end, an interesting episode of American constitutional history. Continuity rested with the old regime, and the alterations adopted followed that system. The state ultimately did adopt a new constitution in 1842, marking the end of the charter government.

Imagining an alternative scenario, it is possible to envisage two parallel, functioning court systems, issuing contradicting opinions on a case. In such a situation, the legal validity will rest on the validity of the respective legal systems, while the actual enforcement will decide which one can claim superiority in the practical sense. As the Rhode Island court at Governor Dorr's trial held, "if a government had been set up under what is called the people's constitution, and they had appointed judges to give effect to their proceedings, and deriving authority from such a source, such a court might have been addressed upon a question like this; but we are not that court."[35] The Supreme Court of the United States was also "not that court," and held that "it rested with the political power to decide whether the charter government had been displaced or not,"[36] and the courts should follow such determination.[37]

Even the otherwise dissenting Justice Woodbury concurred with this. *Luther v. Borden,* 48 U.S. 1, 51 (1849).

[34] To be more precise, it was brute force and the will of the majority: Dorr himself explains his retreat after the first defeats "that that a majority of the friends of the people's constitution disapprove of any further forcible measures for its support." Quoted by Justice Woodbury, diss. *Luther v. Borden,* 48 U.S. 1, 49 (1849).

[35] See Mr. Whipple's brief, for the defendants (i.e. the old regime), refers to p. 38 of the Rhode Island court opinion: *Luther v. Borden,* 48 U.S. 1, 26. (This part is usually omitted in the sources, but can be read at FindLaw: http://caselaw.lp.findlaw.com/scripts/getcase.pl?navby=CASE&court=US&vol=48&page=1).

[36] *Luther v. Borden,* 48 U.S. 1, 39 (1849). Furthermore: "Judicial power presupposes an established government capable of enacting laws and enforcing their execution, and of appointing judges to expound and administer them. The acceptance of the judicial office is a recognition of the authority of the government from which it is derived." Ibid., 40.

[37] This statement seems especially important for considering the post-Civil War Amendments, a case that I have no room to discuss here.

We can see that the law did not solve the ultimate validity question even where it was ultimate only on the level of a state that was embedded in a higher layer of constitutional law, federal constitutionalism (although, arguably, it could have solved or at least could have provided some basic guidelines). It is possible that international law could function in a similar way for all countries. This could allow us to rely on international legal procedures to decide competing claims of parallel constitutional structures.[38] Of course, this would raise further questions—which I cannot explore here[39]—and would only reinforce the political element, as opposed to legal assessment. We can, however, examine a case where a former colonial power and its legal structure could serve as an additional layer within which a fundamental constitutional change occurred. Seeking to further elaborate our view on the limits of law in assessing fundamental constitutional changes, I will now turn to the Canadian example.

THE REPATRIATION OF THE CANADIAN CONSTITUTION

Canada is usually seen as having gained independence from the British Crown, still with the Queen as a monarch, some time between 1916 and 1930.[40] Yet, even after that, it was not detached from Westminster in the legal sense—the constitutional system rested on the British North America Act, adopted by the British Parliament. This meant that all subsequent constitutional changes had to travel overseas for formal legal approval. After various attempts to fix this, it was in 1981 that the political situation seemed ripe for change and the frustration

---

[38] For Kelsen's thoughts on how international law could serve as the basic norm for all legal systems, see Kelsen, *Introduction to the Problems of Legal Theory*, 61–62.

[39] E.g., the literature on the right of self-determination deals with similar questions, including the recognition of the foundational moment, most recently concerning the Advisory Opinion of the International Court of Justice on the Kosovo Declaration of Independence (avoiding a legal judgment on its invalidity by placing it outside of the field where invalidity can be assessed): *Accordance with International Law of the Unilateral Declaration of Independence in Respect of Kosovo, Advisory Opinion, I.C.J. Reports 2010*, 403.

[40] Richard S. Kay, "The Creation of the Constitutions in Canada and in the United States," *Canada–United States Law Journal* 7 (1984): 147.

this situation caused on both sides of the Atlantic. There was widespread political agreement to initiate a process of constitutional "repatriation," yet, there was opposition from certain provinces, above all, from Québec, on what this process should look like. This was partly a result of the lack of rules on how to amend the constitutional framework that resulted in uncertainty around the role of the provinces. Despite the lack of directly guiding legal norms, there was "almost no explicit recognition that the matter could not be resolved by recourse to legal rules."[41]

But is such a strictly legal move possible? Can the constitutional system itself take care of the transfer of its own foundations? If we disregard for a moment the domestic debates around the proper role of the provinces, there seemed to be, at the time, a consensus about the basic steps of the process: (1) Canada adopts a text (with a strictly domestic amending clause) that (2) travels to Westminster, where it is adopted, (3) the new constitution is then promulgated, enters into effect, and, as a result, (4) Canada becomes capable of amending its own constitution. This implies that in step 2, the Queen in Parliament renounces the power to amend the Canadian Constitution (or any other legal norm of Canada). If this shift (or trick) works, then it is possible to change the constitutional foundations while we remain within the boundaries of the zone where strictly legal arguments about validity make sense.

Yet, this does not seem to hold as this description cannot account for the actual change, the fundamental shift, that is at the heart of the move. Hart describes this, using his terminology, as the shift of the ultimate rule of recognition.[42] Martin Loughlin also uses the post-colonial transition as an example that shows how non-relational accounts cannot make sense of the shift, especially since we usually believe that this is a one-way move, and Britain cannot reinstate sovereignty over

---

41 Ibid., 137.

42 Hart talks about a situation where "a new legal system emerges from the womb of an old one" and a "Caesarian operation," but I am not sure that the parallel holds if we focus on the importance of the ultimate rule of recognition that emerges, in the legal sense, fully independently from the old system. Hart, *The Concept of Law,* 120–21.

former colonies.[43] To examine this argument, let us consider another example from British history.

The British Parliament adopted a somewhat similar legal document concerning the status of Northern Ireland,[44] and a later event showed that the power that Westminster seemed to have given up could be revived, with reference to emergency.[45] Even if the parallel does not fit the Canadian case entirely, this example could serve as a thought experiment and show that something else, an additional element is required to irrevocably "repatriate" the constitution and break up these legal ties. This element can only come from outside of law. Repatriation can only be seen as final if we fully acknowledge what it was—the creation of a new basic norm. Once we consider this key element, we should also see that any other process, with or without giving veto power to each of the provinces (even without Westminster), could also have worked, provided that it has this extralegal element that we can call legitimacy. All we need to do is to make sure that the new regime is, in general, regarded by the population as worthy of their respect and obedience. This isn't a small task, on the contrary. Once we get rid of (false) legal stability arguments ("law alone can do it") and show the limits of constitutional law, we cannot rely on legal ceremonies alone or present the process as the inevitable and only solution to adopt a basic norm.

From this perspective, what actually happened in Canada, with the support of the federal government and most of the provinces (with the exception of Québec), the formal approval including Westminster and the Queen, seemed to be no more than a parade in legal robes to make sure that nobody challenges the process. If nobody notices that this is ultimately not a legal question, it will work. And the nationwide illusion worked, with illusionists hypnotizing with the language of constitutional law. Law was used for something that it cannot offer

43 Loughlin, *The Idea of Public Law*, 159.

44 The Indian Independence Act of 1947 could also be mentioned here. John Finnis uses this example. Finnis, "Revolutions and Continuity of Law," 414.

45 The example is cited in Kay, "The Creation of the Constitutions in Canada and in the United States," 140.

by itself. To reference Schmitt again, paraphrasing Weber, the belief in legality served as a source of legitimacy.[46]

To tame this evaluation, one could emphasize the role that law can play in extralegal processes. The legal framework can actually be decisive in the formation and articulation of political views. After all, the provinces and their leadership were all created based on legal rules. As Martin Loughlin notes, reflecting more generally on the enabling feature of the legal framework, "the establishment of a law-governed state is a means of generating political power."[47]

As in the previous case of constitutional shift in the US, courts became involved in Canada, too. The Supreme Court of Canada had to deal with complaints from provinces opposing the constitutional project. The divided court showed particular sensitivity to the fact that this delicate foundational question lies at the edge of law, and used the concept of "constitutional conventions" to explain that there are quasi-legal rules, not strictly binding or enforced by courts, but still part of the legal system.[48] This meant that the federal government, strictly speaking, could go ahead with a constitutional project without the consent of (all or most of) the provinces—i.e. no court would block this process—but it should not, because it would be in violation of a constitutional convention, requiring such an approval. Peter H. Russell presents this as the domestication of extralegal rules to fit the legal framework.[49] It is another question whether this is a successful attempt, considering that no enforcement is attached to an allegedly legal obligation. But even if we accept that it is, the decision shows the outer limits of law in prescribing how legitimacy can be assured for the fundamentally political procedure of defining who can change the constitution and how.

---

46 Schmitt, *Legality and Legitimacy*, 9.

47 Loughlin, *The Idea of Public Law*, 156.

48 *Reference re Amendment of Constitution of Canada,* [1981] S.C.J. No. 58, [1981] 1 S.C.R. 753 (S.C.C.).

49 Peter H. Russell, "The Patriation and Quebec Veto References: The Supreme Court Wrestles with the Political Part of the Constitution," *Supreme Court Law Review* 54 (2011): 69–76.

THE COMMON THREAD

We have seen that all legal systems presuppose an extralegal element upon which its validity ultimately rests. Be it a revolutionary change or a peaceful transition that seeks to maintain the façade of legality, law in itself can never account for the full scope of fundamental constitutional shifts. One should be skeptical about legal arguments when it comes to a fundamental shift in the constitutional structure, and take them as political arguments about legitimacy. Not that law cannot play a role, but it alone cannot account for the essence of the change, or if it can, the change is not truly fundamental. Law in the form of the existing framework legitimating the new regime was used in all of the cases presented above. The US Constitution was presented as a logical continuation of the Articles of Confederation despite the clear discontinuity between the two regimes. A similar pattern was followed in the Canadian case where proponents failed to make it clear that the desired transition cannot rest on constitutional continuity without allowing reversal, hence the crucial change occurred outside law. The Dorr Rebellion showed that law alone could not grapple with the question of competing constitutional regimes, even in the case of an all-encompassing federal framework being available. Courts declared themselves, for various reasons, incompetent to rule on the validity of the Dorr regime, holding that this is an extra-legal question to be resolved by politicians.

I will now turn to the Hungarian case that presents the same dilemma with a strange twist. This was not a case of arguments about continuity being used or misused, but arguments about discontinuity and revolutionary change. Arguments about discontinuity should be read here against the background of full formal continuity that not only omitted the inclusion of the people, but all political actors outside the governing party. The Hungarian case is certainly not unique in the confusion it displays regarding the role of law. It is also not unique in leaving out the people—which is but one source of legitimacy for a constitution, albeit a central one considering the references to popular sovereignty in the constitutional realm. The Hungarian case, rather, stands out as an example where strong rhetorical efforts to break with the immediate past (both with the twenty years of democracy and the state party regime preceding it) are combined with a seamless legal continuity in constitutional authorization.

The Hungarian Case

Hungary held its first democratic elections after the Soviet occupation, with Soviet soldiers still physically present, in 1990. Although this definitely marked the beginning of a new era, the democratic constitutional framework was already in place, formally adopted by the last communist parliament after having been negotiated by unelected opposition leaders, legitimated retroactively in light of the outcome of the first elections. The constitution was completely rewritten, article by article, and became an adequate framework for a democratic, multiparty, free market system, only its number remained the same, Act No. XX of 1949.[50] The preamble indicated, in line with the untouched numbering, that the modifications are adopted "until the adoption of the new constitution." The strength of the constitution was ambiguous, with the newly established Constitutional Court as a powerful guarantor, but matched with a weak rule for amendment, a mere two-third majority vote in the unicameral Parliament. As a result of the disproportionate electoral system, it was possible that the governing majority alone held this supermajority. This was the case already after the second free elections with a left-wing liberal coalition in 1994 (72% of the mandates with 50 and 73% of the votes in the two rounds, respectively), and later with a right-wing majority both in 2010 (68% of the mandates with 54% of the votes) and in 2018 (67% of the mandates with 45% of the votes).[51]

---

[50] The original 1949 Constitution was the translation of the Stalinist constitution. A widely held view was that there was only one clause that remained intact, the one on the capital of Hungary. Yet, even this clause was changed, as well as the title of the Act, as the "People's Republic of Hungary" in both cases read simply "Republic of Hungary" in the amended version.

[51] Rounded values based on data from the site of the National Election Office, valasztas.hu. Note that the rules changed before the 2014 elections making the system even more disproportionate (as the numbers clearly show—a fall of almost 10% in the votes received did not result in considerable fall in the ratio of mandates held), including the abolition of the second round. The results for the two rounds in 2010 are almost the same, hence only one number is indicated. The electoral system is more complicated than these numbers illustrate, as it combines the proportionate, list-based system (by parties or coalitions) and the district-based system (votes for local candidates).

While an amendment required a two-third majority vote, there was no rule for adopting a completely new constitution. This might not be a problem if we consider that the constitution cannot limit a new foundational moment anyway, for the reasons discussed earlier. On the other hand, if the new constitution is based on formal–constitutional continuity, the amending process might be used to rewrite the content, as it happened in 1989. It is hard to define what amounts to adopting a new constitution, as opposed to sweeping amendments, with the possible exception of amending the rules of adopting an amendment. Yet, the coalition of 1994–98 decided to adopt an amendment in 1995 establishing a rule that required a four-fifth vote for adopting the rules of procedure of constitution-making.[52] This concession, from the side of the majority, made sure that the opposition (four smaller right-wing parties at the time, including the now governing party) held veto power over the process. A text was drafted, but, for unclear reasons, it was turned down.

Although there were initiatives to adopt a new constitution, it was only after 2010 that the governing majority acted on this question, holding a supermajority on its own. As part of the process, this majority had to decide on the procedure. In contrast to the vote in 1995, they did not make concessions to the opposition; on the contrary, they formally annulled the 1995 rule.[53] Considering that the 1995 Act had a sunset clause, this might have been only a technical move, a reaction to the uncertainty around the validity of the rule. The sunset clause was activated at the end of the mandate of the 1994 Parliament, in 1998, but doubts were raised whether this should be read narrowly, only applying to the amending act, and not the amendment itself that was already incorporated into the constitution, which is a widely applied legal technique. Most likely in this case the rule itself

[52] *Act No. XLIV of 1995,* amending the Constitution. The new clause became Art. 24-5 of the Constitution.

[53] In a hidden way, in that an amendment concerning the election of constitutional judges (allowing the governing majority to sidestep the earlier practice of bipartisan parity) included a final clause, not mentioned in explanatory notes, on annulling Art. 24-5 of the Constitution that provided for the four fifth rule. *Bill T/189 of 7 June 2010, amending the Constitution,* http://www.parlament.hu/irom39/00189/00189.pdf.

ceased to be part of the constitution,[54] the governing majority in 2010 nevertheless moved to annul the clause, something akin to recognizing its validity. Furthermore, this meant that a four-fifth rule was overwritten with a two-third vote.[55]

This means that the governing majority, when it adopted the Fundamental Law of Hungary by a two-third majority in 2011, relied on the amending clause of the old constitution. With important changes elsewhere, many widely criticized inside and outside the country,[56] the amending clause remained the same. This means that the new text is based on formal–legal continuity at its foundations. Looking at other parts of the text, however, one might be puzzled about this strong element of continuity. There are two clauses in the Fundamental Law that speak to (dis)continuity directly: Article R(3) and Clause 5. I will now look into these briefly.

First, the intent of the framers was to include some reference to the "historical constitution." In principle, it could be possible that it was meant to have a symbolic force only, like it was a goal to have words

---

[54] For a contrary view, see, e.g., Andrew Arato, or Kim Lane Scheppele, in particular her response to the Hungarian Ambassador to the United States, posted in Paul Krugman's blog: Kim Lane Scheppele, "Hungarian Diplomatic Protest," *New York Times,* December 31, 2011, accessed May 16, 2019, http://krugman.blogs.nytimes.com/2011/12/31/hungarian-diplomatic-protest.

[55] This case raises interesting theoretical questions about the right threshold for annulling a rule that requires a 4/5 majority vote. While the annulment was adopted by a 2/3 majority, the original amendment was passed with consensus, without votes against or abstentions: 312 yes votes and 74 MPs absent, see the Minutes of the Parliament, Bill T/1042, vote at 17:19:02 on May 30, 1995, http://www.parlament.hu/szavaz/szavlist/55uh1902.htm.

[56] I cannot address the various criticisms, concerning both content and procedure, here. For critical accounts, see the contribution of Kriszta Kovács in this volume; or the opinion of the Venice Commission, "Opinion on the new Constitution of Hungary," June 17–18, 2011, accessed May 16, 2019, http://www.venice.coe.int/webforms/documents/default.aspx?pdffile=CDL-AD(2011)016-e; or Zoltán Fleck, Gábor Gadó, Gábor Halmai, Szabolcs Hegyi, Gábor Juhász, János Kis, Zsolt Körtvélyesi, Balázs Majtényi, and Gábor Attila Tóth, *Opinion on the Fundamental Law of Hungary, Amicus Brief to the Venice Commission,* ed. Andrew Arato, Gábor Halmai, and János Kis, June 2011, accessed May 16, 2019, https://sites.google.com/site/amicusbriefhungary/home/amicus-to-vc-english-final.pdf.

like "God," "Christianity," "Holy Crown" or "Carpathian basin" in the text, mostly in the preamble. Yet, Article R(3) is formulated as a call to the interpreter to read the text in conformity with the preamble and the "achievements of the historical constitution." This second notion sounds largely empty at this point, and it is hard to see how it can alter constitutional interpretation. The concept does not have an established meaning that could be applied to contemporary constitutional adjudication. Both the theory of the Holy Crown and the notion of the historical constitution were conceived under completely different historical circumstances, adapted to a monarchy, and it seems hard to bridge the gap between those times and today, after long decades of totalitarian as well as democratic regimes where the notion of the historical constitution was simply not relevant for developments in constitutional law. If the historical constitution is seen as embracing inherent limitations on power and the unity of the nation, or based on a more progressive interpretation (the equality of the former subjects), it is hard to see how such a vague notion can help us interpret the relevant clauses of the Fundamental Law that are already part of the text.[57] A possible definition that can make sense of the notion for constitutional adjudication today is to see the two-and-a-half decades' case law of the Constitutional Court as the "achievements of the historical constitution" maybe in addition to historical references that can serve as illustrations that certain constitutional principles are more than a century old in Hungarian public law thinking.[58]

---

57 For a more detailed overview, arguing for the incompatibility of the doctrine of the Holy Crown and of the historical constitution with present-day Hungarian and European constitutionalism, and that these are doomed to remain dead letter, see Zoltán Szente, "The Doctrine of the Holy Crown in the Hungarian Historical Constitution," *Journal on European History of Law* 1 (2013).

58 By way of illustration for the latter method, see the application of the "achievements of the historical constitution" to underline the importance of judicial independence in the decision No. 33/2012 (VII. 17.) of the Constitutional Court of Hungary, 74–80. The first reading, on the incorporation of the first two decades of the Constitutional Court, could be in line with the doctrine promoted by the first president of the Constitutional Court, László Sólyom, and known as the "invisible constitution." See the following section of the main text to see why this is an unappealing interpretation.

This leads me to the second clause of the Fundamental Law, which very directly speaks to the question of discontinuity. A rule that was inserted by the infamous Fourth Amendment[59] declares all earlier case law of the Constitutional Court invalid.[60] This definitely does not support the idea that the framers understand this body of law as part of the historical constitution that they want to see reflected in the interpretation of the text.

These clauses highlight the ambivalence of the Fundamental Law towards the country's constitutional past. On the one hand, they reject continuity with the directly available constitutional history, both in terms of rhetoric and as concrete technical rules, most importantly in the will to erase the more than two-decade long constitutional jurisprudence. The only relevant link is that the preamble refers to 1990 as the restoration of self-determination. Not even Act No. 1 of 1946, the "Small Constitution," an important reference to the 1989 Constitution,[61] is part of the canon of the Fundamental Law. Yet, the document builds up a narrative of organic development, historical continuity and events throughout the centuries that somehow culminate in the regime of the Fundamental Law. By the same move, the preamble creates a legal–political vacuum, declaring that Hungary was not sovereign from the 1944 German occupation to the first democratic elections in 1990, and also denying the validity of the 1949 constitu-

---

59 For a general overview, see Venice Commission, "Opinion on the Fourth Amendment to the Fundamental Law of Hungary," June 14-15, 2013, accessed May 16, 2019, http://www.venice.coe.int/webforms/documents/default.aspx?pdffile=CDL-AD(2013)012-e; and Miklós Bánkuti, Tamás Dombos, Gábor Halmai, András Hanák, Zsolt Körtvélyesi, Balázs Majtényi, László András Pap, Eszter Polgári, Orsolya Salát, Kim Lane Scheppele, Péter Sólyom, and Renáta Uitz, *Amicus Brief for the Venice Commission on the Fourth Amendment to the Fundamental Law of Hungary,* ed. Gábor Halmai and Kim Lane Scheppele, accessed May 16, 2019, https://sites.google.com/site/amicusbriefhungary/home/Amicus_Brief_Fourth_Amendment5.pdf.

60 Article 19-2 of the Fourth Amendment of the Fundamental Law of Hungary, amending Clause 5 of the Closing and Miscellaneous Provisions.

61 The "Small Constitution" can represent the aborted transition to democracy, and it created the institutional framework, a parliamentary system with a weak president, that was the basis of the framework established in 1989–90.

tion.[62] This time range includes the comprehensive rewriting of the 1949 constitution in 1989. Again, in virtue of Article R(3), the Fundamental Law should be interpreted in accordance with this preamble. While it is possible to argue that neither of the above contradictions is problematic,[63] it can be seen that there is a tension between the source of formal–legal validity of the text and the statements emphasizing discontinuity and denying the validity of the earlier framework. Had the majority taken seriously the discontinuity claim, they would have opened the question of how to adopt the new supreme law, it would have been less obvious why they were satisfied with the two-third rule.

If we contrast the making of the Fundamental Law with the 1989 process, the role of the people, as a point of reference but never actualized, seems similar. We see a switched asymmetry concerning both continuity (a) and representation (b).

a) The 1989 constitution was discontinuous with its predecessor in that it formed the basis of a truly revolutionary change, the transition from a one-party system to a multi-party democracy and capitalism. The Constitutional Court itself talked about a revolution, that itself should be assessed by strict rule of law standards. The text of the constitution still bore the year and number of the 1949 Stalinist constitution (No. XX of 1949) and the new preamble itself suggested that the constitution is transitional. The (revolutionary) content was ahead of the form that showed continuity. In contrast, the 2011 constitution, adopted on Monday of Easter and also dubbed the "Easter Constitution," clearly "skipped its Lent" and has been trying to show more than it actually is. According to its self-description and the surrounding political statements, it is the first and the final, true embodiment of a democratic and independent Hungary, a "granite strong" foundation for long coming decades, after the twenty years of troubled

62 On this and many other questions, providing an excellent summary and evaluation of the events, see János Kis, "Introduction. From the 1989 Constitution to the 2011 Fundamental Law," in *Constitution for a Disunited Nation: On Hungary's 2011 Fundamental Law,* ed. Gábor Attila Tóth (Budapest: CEU Press, 2011), 1–22.

63 Without addressing the convincing power of such arguments, one could claim that (1) the amending clause extends to the case of adopting a completely new text, with the four-fifth rule being invalid after 1998, and (2) the preamble uses a symbolic language, without direct legal relevance.

transition, marking the spiritual renewal of the nation.[64] According to the Prime Minister, the adoption of the Fundamental Law marks one of the finest moments of the history of the nation. This should be seen in contrast with the actual content that often repeats the substantial elements of the earlier constitutional text, and where it amends it, it is usually with the goal of rights restrictions, either through direct injection of restrictive clauses and less ambitious protection or through weakening independent institutional enforcement of these rights.

b) When it comes to participation through representation, the efforts of the state party system to include non-elected forces stands out as more inclusive than the drafting and adoption of the Fundamental Law that became a one-party constitution even though opposition forces were present in the Parliament. The Prime Minister himself contrasted the process of adopting the 1989 constitution to that of the Fundamental Law. According to this account, 1989–90 was a failure because of the lack of unity and a parliamentary majority, and this is why we sank into the mud of party bargains and compromises. Now, the 2011 process definitely lacked bargains and compromises and had the unity and parliamentary majority that allowed the emergence of the one-party constitution. It is clear how the driving vision of the Fundamental Law makes this an advantage—this allows for the clear expression of the will of the Hungarian nation, high above our heads, the people and the elected leaders. Paradoxically, this essentialist account likens the project to the Jacobin approach,[65] or even the 1949 Stalinist constitution where the selected few expressed the true will of the many, denying the legitimacy and reality of disagreement and making any compromise otherwise necessary for an inclusive constitution an ill instead of a virtue. We could contrast this to the statement of the rep-

---

64 See the Prime Minister's explanation: Viktor Orbán, *Kiállítás köszönti a hatálybalépést [Opening speech of the exhibition on the occasion of the entry into force of the Fundamental Law of Hungary]*, January 2, 2012, accessed May 16, 2019, http://www.miniszterelnok.hu/beszed/kiallitas_koszonti_a_hatalybadepest. I use this text as this is by the politician who personally developed the vision embodied in the new constitution and also explains the process of adoption.

65 Balázs Majtényi, "The Nation's Will as Trump in the Hungarian Fundamental Law," in *European Yearbook on Human Rights 2015*, ed. Benedek et al. (Vienna: Neuer Wissenschaftlicher Verlag, 2015), 252–253.

resentative of Fidesz from the debate of the 1995 compromise: "We have managed to put together an agreement that provides adequate guarantees to us that Hungary will get a constitution that is based on consensus. We will accordingly support the agreement."[66]

The politics of exclusion is present on other levels, too. Mirroring the Schmittian concept of the political decision on who the enemy is,[67] the Fundamental Law, as amended already in 2013 for the fourth time, declares that the largest opposition party, the Socialist Party, shares "the responsibility of their predecessors," i.e. the leaders of the one-party communist system. The document is based on exclusion from another perspective as well: the Fundamental Law speaks in the name of the ethnic Hungarian nation, with the minorities not being part of the "we," but mentioned as "part of the Hungarian political community" and "constituent parts of the State."[68]

This shows that the Fundamental Law departs in important respects from the representation of the "we the people" that usually marks the foundational moment. For the topic of this chapter, what is important is that the process of adoption and the related ideological view are both marked by a dishonesty about what is really going on the constitutional landscape. The framers tried to eat the cake and have it, too, by playing around continuity and discontinuity. The identity of

---

[66] Zoltán Trombitás, Speech of May 30, 1995, No. 58, *Minutes of the Parliament,* accessed May 16, 2019, http://www.parlament.hu/naplo35/088/0880032.htm.

[67] According to Schmitt's famous definition, the political is about defining who is a friend and who is an enemy. Carl Schmitt, *The Concept of the Political,* trans. George Schwab, (1932; Chicago: University of Chicago Press, 2007).

[68] The exclusion is clear from the full quote, speaking in the name of "us" while placing the nationalities outside of this: "the nationalities living with us form part of the Hungarian political community and are constituent parts of the State" (Preamble). For a detailed analysis of the ethnic component, see the contribution of Nóra Chronowski in this volume. As Martin Loughlin notes, citing Ulrich Preuss, "constituent power cannot be built on the foundation of ethnicity." See Ulrich Preuss, "The Exercise of Constituent Power in Central and Eastern Europe," in *The Paradox of Constitutionalism: Constituent Power and Constitutional Form,* eds. Martin Loughlin and Neil Walker (Oxford: Oxford University Press, 2007), cited in Loughlin, "The Concept of Constituent Power," 44n.

the Fundamental Law and the regime marked by this text relies on an argument of discontinuity, while it shies away from the consequences when it comes to the constitutional foundations.

Conclusion

The foundational moment plays an important role in the life of a constitutional regime. It speaks, often against the will of those involved, about the identity of the regime, its relationship to the people and to the pre-existing constitutional framework. Theoretical accounts agree that the shift of the ultimate rule of recognition, or basic norm, requires an extralegal input that cannot be understood within the limits of the previous regime.

Examining this shift in particular cases can reveal a mismatch between arguments and the underlying legal reality. In the case of the US Constitution, the formal break with the Articles of Confederation was coupled with arguments about continuity. The Dorr Rebellion could have used the federal framework, calling for recognition under the Guarantee Clause, but the US Supreme Court held that this is a non-justiciable clause to be applied by the political branches and not the courts. In Canada, the issue was the break away from this "outside" framework, in this case the formal power of the Westminster Parliament, with no possibility to reinstate this power, while maintaining the false image of full legal continuity where law can take care of the handing over of power.

It is against this background that the Hungarian case shows a reversed mismatch between formal–legal and political (dis)continuity. Here the legal continuity is buried under the rhetoric of a revolutionary change. The adoption of this allegedly revolutionary document, the text itself reveals this much, is based on the amending clause of the Act No. XX of 1949 (i.e. the earlier constitution) the two-third majority vote of the single house of the Parliament. Even the abortive attempt of 1994–98 had a more solid basis[69] than this, adopting

[69] It is worth quoting an opposition MP from 1995 who was member of the governing majority after 2010 and turned constitutional judge from government politician in 2012. László Salamon underlined, in 1995, that the

a rule for not simply amending the old constitution, but creating a new one, with a heightened threshold requiring a four-fifth majority giving veto power to the opposition. Yet, there would be no problem, from the point of the narrow matrix of legality and legitimacy, had the governing majority accepted the legal reality, i.e. that they exercised the amending power, instead of a revolutionary step. Dishonesty appears maybe as a logical consequence of the newspeak (or spin doctor's craft) of 2010, presenting the result of the general elections as a "revolution" the "revolution of the voting booth."[70] The image of the revolutionary constitution might be the reflection of this, a constitutional spin. If contrasted to the 1989–1990 changes, we see a double asymmetry in the representation of non-government forces (part of the process in 1989, but not in 2011, even though at this time they were parliamentary forces, which was not the case in 1989) as well as in continuity (1989–1990 brought revolutionary changes without constitutional fanfare; 2010–2011 brought revolutionary rhetoric without a match in constitutional law).

Discussing the identity and continuity of legal systems, Finnis argues that "the problem for the jurist is the same as the problem for the historian or for the good man wondering where his allegiance

Stalinist constitution was replaced in 1989–1990 by a democratic constitution based on the rule of law. He welcomed the move (the amendment establishing the four-fifth rule) that elevated the question of constitution-making above party politics and detached the process from "the momentary balance of political forces." László Salamon, speech of May 30, 1995, No. 28, *Minutes of the Parliament,* accessed May 16, 2019, http://www.parlament.hu/naplo35/088/0880028.htm. He also urged that the constitution, after getting the widest parliamentary support, should be put to a referendum. László Salamon, speech of May 30, 1995, No. 44, *Minutes of the Parliament,* accessed May 16, 2019, http://www.parlament.hu/naplo35/088/0880044.htm.

70 This is the expression consistently used by the Prime Minister and other government politicians, eventually elevated to the level of official politics, in the form of Political Declaration No. 1/2010. (VI. 16.) of the Parliament on National Cooperation: "In the spring of 2010 the Hungarian nation once again summoned its vitality and brought about another revolution in the voting booths." English translation available at: http://www.nefmi.gov.hu/english/political-declaration.

and his duty lie."[71] The drafters of the Fundamental Law wish to see a community where allegiance and (the newly emphasized side of constitutional) duty lie with the new regime, basing its legitimacy on the "revolution in the voting booths" of 2010, while rejecting Hungarian history between 1944 (but not before) and 1990 as well as the two post-1990 decades, presented only as a ("turbulent") prelude to the 2010 shift.[72] This hardly stands as a description of social and political reality and, as this chapter has documented, it directly contradicts the legal expression of this political will—the continued reliance on legality traced back to the 1949 Constitution. The rhetorical jump is not backed up by a direct reliance on an extralegal form of validation and, in particular, what many see as populist politics shied away from grounding its (legal) system on a direct expression of popular will to create a new beginning.

While examples from the other cases presented earlier can be seen as attempts to tame the fact of a revolutionary shift, the Hungarian case can be read as a constitutional bluff, saying more than what one has, inflating the scope of the change. Relying on established legal rules, however, proved helpful in minimizing challenges to the foundational act from the point of view of how "the people," in the name of whom the text is adopted, is present in the process.

BIBLIOGRAPHY

Ackerman, Bruce. *We The People, Volume 1: Foundations.* Cambridge, MA: Harvard University Press, 1991.

Amar, Akhil Reed. "Guaranteeing a Republican Form of Government: The Central Meaning of Republican Government: Popular Sovereignty, Majority Rule, and the Denominator Problem." *University of Colorado Law Review* 65 (1994): 749–86.

Bánkuti, Miklós, Tamás Dombos, Gábor Halmai, András Hanák, Zsolt Körtvélyesi, Balázs Majtényi, László András Pap, Eszter Polgári, Orsolya Salát, Kim Lane Scheppele, Péter Sólyom, and Renáta Uitz. *Amicus Brief for the Venice Commission on the Fourth Amendment to the Fundamental Law of Hungary,* edited by Gábor Halmai and Kim Lane Scheppele. Accessed May

[71] Finnis, "Revolutions and Continuity of Law," 434.

[72] Both quotes from the Political Declaration 1 of 2010.

16, 2019. https://sites.google.com/site/amicusbriefhungary/home/Amicus_Brief_Fourth_Amendment5.pdf.

Dworkin, Ronald. *Justice for Hedgehogs.* Cambridge, MA: Belknap Press, 2011.

Dyzenhaus, David. *Legality and Legitimacy: Carl Schmitt, Hans Kelsen and Herman Heller in Weimar.* Oxford: Oxford University Press, 1997.

Dyzenhaus, David. "Constitutionalism in an Old Key: Legality and Constituent Power." *Global Constitutionalism* 1 (2012): 229–260.

Finnis, John. "Revolutions and Continuity of Law." In *Philosophy of Law: Collected Essays—Volume IV.* Oxford: Oxford Scholarship Online, 2011. Accessed May 16, 2019. https://www.oxfordscholarship.com/view/10.1093/acprof:oso/9780199580088.001.0001/acprof-9780199580088-chapter-22.

Fleck, Zoltán, Gábor Gadó, Gábor Halmai, Szabolcs Hegyi, Gábor Juhász, János Kis, Zsolt Körtvélyesi, Balázs Majtényi, and Gábor Attila Tóth. *Opinion on the Fundamental Law of Hungary, Amicus Brief to the Venice Commission,* edited by Andrew Arato, Gábor Halmai, and János Kis, June 2011. Accessed May 16, 2019. https://sites.google.com/site/amicusbriefhungary/home/amicus-to-vc-english-final.pdf.

Habermas, Jürgen. "European Citizens and European Peoples: The Problem of Transnationalizing Democracy." In *The Lure of Technocracy,* 29–45. Malden, MA: Polity, 2015.

Hart, H.L.A. *The Concept of Law.* Oxford: Clarendon Press, 1994.

Hoar, Roger S. *Constitutional Conventions: Their Nature, Powers, and Limitations.* Boston: Little, Brown, and Company, 1917.

Hobbes, Thomas. *Hobbes's Leviathan, reprinted from the edition of 1651.* Oxford: Clarendon Press, 1929.

Kay, Richard S. "The Creation of the Constitutions in Canada and in the United States." *Canada–United States Law Journal* 7 (1984): 111–63.

Kelsen, Hans. *Introduction to the Problems of Legal Theory.* Oxford: Clarendon Press, 2002.

Kis, János. "Introduction. From the 1989 Constitution to the 2011 Fundamental Law." In *Constitution for a Disunited Nation: On Hungary's 2011 Fundamental Law,* edited by Gábor Attila Tóth, 1–22. Budapest–New York: CEU Press, 2011.

Loughlin, Martin. *The Idea of Public Law.* Oxford: Oxford University Press, 2003.

Loughlin, Martin. "The Concept of Constituent Power." *European Journal of Political Theory* 13 (2014): 218–37.

Majtényi, Balázs. "The Nation's Will as Trump in the Hungarian Fundamental Law." In *European Yearbook on Human Rights 2015,* edited by Wolfgang Benedek, Florence Benoît-Rohmer, and Matthias C. Kettemann, Benjamin Kneihs, and Manfred Nowak, 247–259. Vienna: Neuer Wissenschaftlicher Verlag, 2015.

Orbán, Viktor. "Kiállítás köszönti a hatálybalépést" ["Opening speech of the exhibition on the occasion of the entry into force of the Fundamental Law of Hungary"], January 2, 2012. Accessed on May 16, 2019. http://2010-2015.miniszterelnok.hu/beszed/kiallitas_koszonti_a_hatalybalepest.

Posner, Eric A. and Adrian Vermeule. "Demystifying Schmitt." In *The Oxford Handbook of Carl Schmitt,* edited by Jens Meierhenrich and Oliver Simons, 612–626. Oxford: Oxford University Press, 2016.

Preuss, Ulrich. "The Exercise of Constituent Power in Central and Eastern Europe." In *The Paradox of Constitutionalism: Constituent Power and Constitutional Form,* edited by Martin Loughlin and Neil Walker, 209–28. Oxford: Oxford University Press, 2007.

Raz, Joseph. *The Concept of a Legal System.* Oxford: Clarendon Press, Second Edition, 1980.

Ross, Alf. *On Law and Justice.* Berkeley and Los Angeles: University of California Press, 1959.

Russell, Peter H. "The Patriation and Quebec Veto References: The Supreme Court Wrestles with the Political Part of the Constitution." *Supreme Court Law Review* 54 (2011): 69–76.

Salamon, László. Speech of May 30, 1995, No. 28. *Minutes of the Parliament of the Republic of Hungary.* Accessed May 16, 2019. http://www.parlament.hu/naplo35/088/0880028.htm.

Salamon, László. Speech of May 30, 1995, No. 44. *Minutes of the Parliament of the Republic of Hungary.* Accessed May 16, 2019. http://www.parlament.hu/naplo35/088/0880044.htm.

Scheppele, Kim Lane. "Hungarian Diplomatic Protest." *New York Times,* December 31, 2011. Accessed May 16, 2019. http://krugman.blogs.nytimes.com/2011/12/31/hungarian-diplomatic-protest.

Schmitt, Carl. *Legality and Legitimacy.* Durham: Duke University Press, 2004.

Schmitt, Carl. *The Concept of the Political.* Chicago: University of Chicago Press, 2007 (1932).

Strauss, David A. "The Irrelevance of Constitutional Amendments." *Harvard Law Review* 114 (2001): 1457–1505.

Szente, Zoltán. "The Doctrine of the Holy Crown in the Hungarian Historical Constitution." *Journal on European History of Law* 4, no. 1 (2013): 109–15.

Trombitás, Zoltán. Speech of May 30, 1995, No. 58. *Minutes of the Parliament of the Republic of Hungary.* Accessed May 16, 2019. http://www.parlament.hu/naplo35/088/0880032.htm.

Tushnet, Mark. "Constitutional Hardball." *John Marshall Law Review* 37 (2004): 523–53.

Young, Daniel Taylor. "How Do You Measure a Constitutional Moment? Using Algorithmic Topic Modeling to Evaluate Bruce Ackerman's Theory of Constitutional Change, Note." *Yale Law Journal* 122 (2013): 1990–2054.

Accordance with International Law of the Unilateral Declaration of Independence in Respect of Kosovo, Advisory Opinion, I.C.J. Reports 2010.

Act No. XLIV of 1995, amending the Constitution of the Republic of Hungary.

Act No. CXXX of 2010 on lawmaking, Hungary.

Articles of a Constitution, adopted by the People's Convention, held October 4, 1841, and postponed to November 16, for final consideration, Library of Congress. https://archive.org/download/articlesofconsti00rhod/articlesofconsti00rhod.pdf.

Bill T/189 of June 7, 2010, amending the Constitution of the Republic of Hungary. http://www.parlament.hu/irom39/00189/00189.pdf.

Luther v. Borden, 48 U.S. 1, 35–38 (1849).

Minutes of the Parliament of the Republic of Hungary, Bill T/1042, vote at 17:19:02 on May 30, 1995. http://www.parlament.hu/szavaz/szavlist/55uh1902.htm.

Political Declaration No. 1/2010. (VI. 16.) of the Parliament of the Republic of Hungary on National Cooperation. English translation available at: http://www.nefmi.gov.hu/english/political-declaration.

Reference re: Amendment of Constitution of Canada, [1981] S.C.J. No. 58, [1981] 1 S.C.R. 753 (S.C.C.).

Venice Commission. "Opinion on the new Constitution of Hungary," June 17–18, 2011. Accessed May 16, 2019. http://www.venice.coe.int/webforms/documents/default.aspx?pdffile=CDL-AD(2011)016-e.

Venice Commission. "Opinion on the Fourth Amendment to the Fundamental Law of Hungary," June 14–15, 2013. Accessed May 16, 2019. http://www.venice.coe.int/webforms/documents/default.aspx?pdffile=CDL-AD(2013)012-e.

A Nation Torn Apart by its Constitution? Nationality and Ethnicity in the Context of the Hungarian Fundamental Law

NÓRA CHRONOWSKI

Introduction

Constitutions try to contribute to, and at the same time be evidence of, the constitutional identity of a given political community.[1] If constitution drafting is a discursive, democratic, representative and transparent process, it may help to close the gaps of the society, otherwise those gaps remain tenacious and anchored by the constitution.

In Hungary, a new constitution, the Fundamental Law of Hungary[2] (FL), was promulgated on April 25, 2011 and came into force on January 1, 2012. Its drafting rose to prominence in Europe and was severely criticized both by domestic experts and the Venice Commission. Before analyzing the text of the FL from the perspective of nation and ethnicity, it is worth recalling the main stages of Hungarian constitution-making. After the 2010 parliamentary elections, the political forces forming a parliamentary majority—possessing two-thirds of the seats—expressed their intention to create a new constitution. A parliamentary ad hoc committee, responsible for preparing the constitution, was set up in June, and started its work in September 2010. The composition of the committee reflected the parliamentary

---

1 Gary Jeffrey Jacobsohn, "Constitutional Identity," *The Review of Politics* 3 (2006): 361–397.

2 The official English translation of the Fundamental Law (consolidated version after the Fourth Amendment) is available at http://www.mfa.gov.hu/NR/rdonlyres/8204FB28-BF22–481A-9426-D2761D10EC7C/0/FUNDAMENTALLAWOFHUNGARYmostrecentversion01102013.pdf.

proportions of the party factions. During July and August, the committee invited expert teams from universities, research institutes, and representative organizations of the civil society to share their recommendations with the committee. Formally, all minority self-governments and the parliamentary commissioner for ethnic and national minority rights (special ombudsperson) were invited to send proposals. Finally, the special parliamentary commissioner and four—out of thirteen—minority self-governments (the Bulgarian, the German, the Croatian and the Ruthenian) submitted their recommendations. A common point was that they supported the elimination of the dual term (national and ethnic minorities) from the constitutional text and the introduction of a single term (nationalities), partly for historical reasons and partly for the better expression of the equality of national minorities. They also recommended the extension of individual minority rights by precise enumeration, strengthening the special commissioner's constitutional position, guaranteeing the status of minority self-governments, and finding the solution for parliamentary representation.[3] At this stage the expert and interest groups received no feedback from the parliamentary ad hoc committee, and their substantive participation was not provided for.

For a variety of reasons, the opposition left the preparatory committee, and then in December 2010 the concept, of the new constitution was endorsed only by the representatives of the ruling coalition in the ad hoc committee. Finally, on the basis of this concept no draft was elaborated, instead, the concept was put aside and all the parliamentary factions were given the chance to submit their own draft constitutions.

In early March 2011 two bills were lodged to the parliament, one of them by the governing party alliance and the other by an independent MP. They were discussed in parallel from March 21, and after 9 effective days of debate on April 18, 2011 the bill of the governing parties was endorsed with a two-third majority of the votes. No opposition MPs voted for the bill. This short summary clearly shows that

[3] András László Pap, "Észrevételek a nemzetiségek parlamenti képviseletének szabályozásához az Alaptörvényben, a választójogi törvényben és a nemzetiségek jogairól szóló törvényben," in vol. 1. of *Alkotmányozás Magyarországon 2010–2011,* ed. András Jakab and Tímea Drinóczi (Budapest–Pécs: Pázmány Press, 2013), 2–3.

the actual and effective constitution-making was really quick but not transparent at all. The general public had only five weeks to evaluate the text, and the scope of the actors with effective influence on the formulation of the draft remained secret. Academic institutions, expert organizations, civilians, minorities and other groups of the society had no role in the process, and the preparatory committee in the parliament was also just a part of the scenery. From the expressed proposals of the national and ethnic minorities the need for a parliamentary representation and the change of denomination, however, were taken into consideration. In return, the minorities lost their special, independent parliamentary commissioner[4] and the chance for better defined rights.

It is also interesting to look at the number of members of national and ethnic minorities, which increased from 313,832 to 555,507 between 2001 and 2011.[5] The reason for the difference may be the better advertisement of the census and the introduction of the minority electoral registration.[6] The actual number—based on the voluntary

---

[4] According to Minority Rights Group International: "Hungary was one of very few European states that has established a specialized Ombudsman for the protection of minorities. The Parliamentary Commissioner (Ombudsman) for the Rights of National and Ethnic Minorities was first elected in 1995 and was independent from both the judiciary and the executive power, reporting exclusively to parliament. The powers of this body were based on the former Hungarian Constitution of 1989 and it assumed an important function in the formulation of laws and policies regarding minority protection." http://www.minorityrights.org/?lid=5804.

[5] The data of the national census in 2001 and 2011. For a comparative table see Table 4.1. However, this data is criticized by experts for methodological problems of the survey and for measurement multiple ties.

[6] As Minority Rights Group International assessed: "Critics contended from the late 1990s that as the right to participate in minority self-government elections was open to all Hungarian citizens, i.e. it was based on the general right to vote at local elections, and did not depend on effective membership of a minority, many minority representatives were not from the relevant minority. The abuse of minority self-governments for political or other purposes was also addressed by modifying the system of minority elections. Article 70 of the former Constitution was amended in 2002 (entering into force in May 2004) so that only persons belonging to minorities can elect their self-governments and to stand as candidates in those elections. According to this legislation, those who decide to run in elections for minority self-governments are required to register with the head of the local election office and declare their

and anonymous confession of the residents—is more than 5 per cent of the total population. Since the data on belonging to a national or ethnic minority is sensitive and their confession is voluntary on the census questionnaire, almost 1.5 million people omitted the question. Thus, the number mentioned above is far from exact; other estimates—which are naturally not based on self-confession of those concerned—put just the proportion of the Roma minority at 5 to 10 percent of the total population. The regulation of national minority rights may directly affect approximately 10 percent of the population.[7] Neither the significant number of citizens, nor other groups of society were directly represented in the 2011 constitution making process in Hungary. The following examination focuses on the political and societal status of national and ethnic minorities, as it is reflected in the FL.[8]

Table 4.1. Number of nationalities—voluntary confession on censuses 1980–2011

	NUMBER			
	1980	1990	2001	2011
	TOTAL			
Hungarian	10,638,974	10,142 072	9,416 045	8,314 029
National and ethnic minorities				
Bulgarian	…	…	1,358	3,556
Gipsy (Romany, Bea)[8]	6,404	142,683	189,984	308,957

ethnic identity. However, the declared ethnic identity may not be questioned by the state organs." http://www.minorityrights.org/?lid=5804.

[7] András Magicz, "Re-regulation of National Minority Rights," in *Their Shield is the Law. The Ombudsman's Protection for Vulnerable Groups,* ed. Barnabás Hajas and Máté Szabó (Budapest: Office of the Commissioner for Fundamental Rights, 2013), 27.

[8] The significant change of number between 1980 and 1990 does not mean an exponential increase in the number of births in the Roma ethnic group, it just means that the number of voluntary confessions increased.

	NUMBER			
	1980	1990	2001	2011
	TOTAL			
Greek	...	...	2,509	3,916
Croatian	13,895	13,570	15,597	23,561
Polish	...	...	2,962	5,730
German	11,310	30,824	62,105	131,951
Armenian	...	...	620	3,293
Romanian	8,874	10,740	7,995	26,345
Ruthenian	...	...	1,098	3,323
Serbian	2,805	2,905	3,816	7,210
Slovakian	9,101	10,459	17,693	29,647
Slovenian	1,731	1,930	3,025	2,385
Ukrainian	...	...	5,070	5,633
National and ethnic minorities together	...	...	313,832	555,507
Arabic	...	...	1,396	4,537
Chinese	...	...	2,275	6,154
Russian	...	...	2,341	6,170
Vietnamese	...	...	958	3,019
Other	16,369	19,640	36,472	28,068
Did not wish to answer, no answer	–	–	570,537	1,455,883
Total	...	...	10,343,856	10,373,367
Population	10,709,463	10,374,823	10,198,315	9,937,628

Source: http://www.ksh.hu/nepszamlalas/tables_regional_00

Conceptualization of the Hungarian *People* and *Nation* in the Fundamental Law

It is problematic, from the perspective of the principle of democracy and popular sovereignty, that the FL does not clearly identify the political community to which it shall be applied, because the use of the concepts of political nation and cultural nation is inconsistent and controversial in the constitutional text. Article B of FL refers to the "people" as the source of public power,[9] and the preamble—at least according to its closing sentence—is written on behalf of the citizens.[10] Both statements are proofs of the political nation approach. At the same time, the opening sentence of the preamble, called the National avowal, puts the Hungarian nation in its centre, without defining who belongs to the nation, and the text of the preamble later also refers to the "intellectual and spiritual unity of our nation torn apart."[11] In the first part of the FL, under the title "Foundation," Article D uses the expression of "one single Hungarian nation."[12] This wording seems to support the cultural nation concept; i.e. the cultural and linguistic

[9] Article B(3)-(4) of the FL: "The source of public power is the people. The people shall exercise their power through their elected representatives or, in exceptional cases, directly."

[10] Closing sentence of the preamble: "We, the citizens of Hungary, are ready to found the order of our country upon the common endeavours of the nation."

[11] Preamble, opening sentence: "WE, THE MEMBERS OF THE HUNGARIAN NATION, at the beginning of the new millennium, with a sense of responsibility for every Hungarian, hereby proclaim the following: (…)"; Preamble, thesis 6–8: "We promise to preserve the intellectual and spiritual unity of our nation torn apart in the storms of the last century. We proclaim that the nationalities living with us form part of the Hungarian political community and are constituent part of the State. We commit to promoting and safeguarding our heritage, our unique language, Hungarian culture, the languages and cultures of nationalities living in Hungary, along with all man-made and natural assets of the Carpathian Basin."

[12] Article D of the FL: "Bearing in mind that there is one single Hungarian nation that belongs together, Hungary shall bear responsibility for the fate of Hungarians living beyond its borders, and shall facilitate the survival and development of their communities; it shall support their efforts to preserve their Hungarian identity, the assertion of their individual and collective rights, the establishment of their community self-governments, and their

belonging together irrespective of territorial unity, which became common—in sense of ethno-nation—in Central Eastern Europe during the 19th century.[13] From this perspective the recognition of the "nationalities living with us" shifts the emphasis to their difference (from the majority), or their secondary status.[14]

Under the constitutional theory, the term of (Hungarian) people refers to the political nation to which the national and ethnic minorities also belong. According to this concept, all the citizens living in a given territory belong to the nation, irrespective of their ethnic belonging, cultural diversity or different mother-tongue. This egalitarian nation concept is characteristic of common law countries and French constitutionalism, and its roots lie in the civil enlightenment. It is recognized by the FL as well, when it states that the "nationalities living with us form part of the Hungarian political community" and they "shall be constituent parts of the State" (see the preamble and Article XXIX).[15] However, the preamble of the FL makes a very clear grammatical distinction between the "nation" and the "minorities": the "nation" is "we," the minorities—living with "us"—are "they." This is a linguistically manifest exclusion of the minorities from the "we" (whatever that represents in this context), and this exclusion makes it necessary to reintegrate them at least into the state in Article XXIX and in the preamble—but not into the nation. It is problematic, because the preamble clearly puts the nation above the state.[16]

---

prosperity in their native lands, and shall promote their cooperation with each other and with Hungary."

13 Georg Brunner, *Nationality Problems and Minority Conflicts in Eastern Europe: Strategies for Europe,* (Gutersloh: Bertelsmann Foundation Publishers, 1996), 9–10; Csaba Pákozdi and Márton Sulyok, "The Birth of a 'New Nation'? Mapping Progressive Approaches to the Nation-concept Based on the Hungarian Fundamental Law," *Miskolc Journal of International Law* 2 (2011): 43–55; Herbert Küpper, "Paternalista kollektivizmus és liberális individualizmus között: az új magyar Alaptörvényben rögzített emberkép normatív alapjai," *Közjogi Szemle* 3 (2012): 8–11.

14 Balázs Majtényi, "The Nation's Will as Trump in the Hungarian Fundamental Law," *European Yearbook on Human Rights* (2015): 250.

15 Nóra Chronowski, "The New Hungarian Fundamental Law in the Light of the European Union's Normative Values," *Revue Est Europa* numéro spéciale 1 (2012): 135.

16 Küpper, "Ungarns Verfassung," 55–56.

Using the category of nation in a cultural sense has, on the one hand, a narrower, but on the other hand, a wider, meaning than the political nation. It has a narrower meaning because it comprises only those citizens who belong to the majority national-ethnic group of the country with the same culture, language, identity, historic fate perception, etc. At the same time it has a wider meaning as it identifies as belonging to the nation also those who live in other countries and are citizens of other states, but their language, culture and origin bind them to Hungary. These ethnic ties are underpinned by Article D on the responsibility for Hungarians living outside the borders, and Article G on the constitutional protection of the descent principle (*ius sanguinis*) in citizenship law—the combination of which supports the preferential naturalization of ethnic Hungarians living abroad without any effective territorial link to the country.[17]

Thus, because defining the "nation" is rather controversial,[18] under Hungarian constitutional law it would be better to use the term of "people" or "citizens." That also means that one can consider the (Hungarian) people as indispensable components of the state, as well as a community united by political solidarity.[19] From this perspective, it is extremely controversial that the FL specifies the subject of the constitution making power three ways. At the beginning of the preamble it refers to the "members of the Hungarian nation," but it is not clear whether it does so in a political or in a cultural sense.[20] At the end of the preamble, it speaks about citizens of Hungary, and then at the very end, in the postamble, it turns out that the FL was adopted by

[17] Zsolt Körtvélyesi, "Az 'egységes magyar nemzet' és az állampolgárság," *Fundamentum* 2 (2011): 49–50.

[18] András Jakab, "Defining the Borders of the Political Community: Constitutional Visions of the Nation," Manuscript, (2012): 43–44., accessed April 30, 2016. http://ssrn.com/abstract=2045648; Balázs Majtényi, "Alaptörvény a nemzet akaratából," *Állam- és Jogtudomány* 1 (2014): 80. According to Küpper, the FL applies the concept of ethno-nation. Herbert Küpper, "Paternalista kollektivizmus és liberális individualizmus között: az új magyar Alaptörvényben rögzített emberkép normatív alapjai," *Közjogi Szemle* 3 (2012): 9.

[19] József Petrétei, *Az alkotmányos demokrácia alapintézményei* (Budapest-Pécs: Dialóg Campus, 2009), 185–188.

[20] According to Körtvélyesi, the text of the preamble refers to the cultural nation. Zsolt Körtvélyesi, "From 'We the People' to 'We the Nation'," in *Constitution for a Disunited Nation,* ed. Gábor Attila Tóth, (Budapest: CEU Press, 2012), 113–114.

the members of Parliament elected in 2010. If the constituent was the Hungarian nation, which shares the public power with the nationalities living in Hungary, then the nationalities were not the subjects of the constituent power.[21] If the constitution making power is vested in the people in the sense of a political community, and the nationalities form part of this community, they must have been the subjects of the constituent power.

The unique solution of the FL differs from those constitutions of the Central-European region, which could also legitimately reflect the cultural nation context for historical reasons. For a short comparison it is enough to refer to the Constitutions of the Polish and Slovak Republics. The Polish Constitution of 1997 makes clear in its preamble and in Article 41 that the Polish Nation, as the bearer of the sovereignty, is composed of all equal citizens of the Republic.[22] Although the constitution refers to the Poles outside the borders and to the rights of ethnic minorities, the main principle is the political nation concept with minor cultural elements. In the Slovakian Republic, with its significant number of citizens belonging to a Hungarian national minority, the constitution defines Slovak people as all Slovak citizens, together with national and ethnic minorities who are subjects of the constituent power.[23]

---

[21] András László Pap, "Észrevételek a nemzetiségek parlamenti képviseletének szabályozásához," 434, 437; Majtényi, "Legislative Stupidities," 108.

[22] Polish Constitution of 1997, Preamble: "We, the Polish Nation - all citizens of the Republic, (...) Equal in rights and obligations towards the common good—Poland, (...) Bound in community with our compatriots dispersed throughout the world, (...) Hereby establish this Constitution of the Republic of Poland as the basic law for the State, based on respect for freedom and justice, cooperation between the public powers, social dialogue as well as on the principle of aiding in the strengthening the powers of citizens and their communities." Article 41: "Supreme power in the Republic of Poland shall be vested in the Nation." Article 35: "The Republic of Poland shall ensure Polish citizens belonging to national or ethnic minorities the freedom to maintain and develop their own language, to maintain customs and traditions, and to develop their own culture."

[23] "We, the Slovak People, Bearing in mind the political and cultural heritage of our predecessors, the experience gained through centuries of struggle for our national existence, and statehood, (...) Together with members of national minorities and ethnic groups living in the Slovak Republic, (...) we, the citizens of the Slovak Republic, have, herewith and by our representatives, adopted this Constitution" Preamble, Constitution of the Slovak Republic 1992.

Parliamentary Representation of Minorities (Nationalities) Under the FL

Article XXIX of the FL recognizes nationalities living in Hungary as "constituent parts of the State," and Article 2 prescribes that "Nationalities living in Hungary shall contribute to Parliament's work as defined by a cardinal act."

In 1992, before the adoption of the 1993 Act on Minority Rights, on the basis of the former Constitution, the Hungarian Constitutional Court declared that the legislature had created an unconstitutional situation with its failure to ensure minorities' representation. Whilst the Court accepted that parliamentary representation is not a precondition of the enforcement of the rights of nationalities, it stated that it would be the most effective means towards this end. The Act of 1993 on Minority Rights guaranteed political representation through local and nation-wide self-governments. To restrain ethno-business,[24] after a thorough academic and constitutional conversation, minority registration was introduced in 2005 on minority self-government elections. Registration is voluntary and based on self-determination, its baseline is the free choice on (national or ethnic) identity—thus, it cannot really prevent the abuse of minority rights.

After the 2010 parliamentary elections, the governing coalition almost immediately expressed a strong will for the introduction of minority representation in the parliament. The former Constitution (Act XX of 1949) was amended, and besides reducing the number of the seats in the parliament from 386 to 200 it was also prescribed that a maximum of 13 surplus mandates shall be guaranteed to minorities.[25] It was a strong political declaration of intents, but at the end of

[24] Before 2005 in the absence of minority electoral registration every citizen had the right to vote and stand as a candidate on minority self-governmental elections. As the minority self-governments received fiscal support from the central budget, some candidates decided to make a good use of the system without belonging to the national or ethnic minority they represented. See also Majtényi, "What Has Happened," 411–412.

[25] The former Constitution was amended on May 25, 2010, but the cited rule never came into force, and the FL finally repealed the former Constitution. Thus the amendment was just an adhoc demonstration of political will.

the day the FL adopted another solution. The shortcoming of the fixed number of minority mandates was clear—it suggested that the number of recognised minorities is constant and the recognition of a new minority would require a constitutional amendment as well. Thus, this construction was put aside during the constitution-making process. The final text of the FL does not guarantee parliamentary representation of the minorities explicitly, it just ensures a potential contribution to the work of the parliament. There are altogether 199 seats in the parliament (106 mandates for individual constituencies, 93 mandates for lists), and the nationalities may compete for preferential mandates during the general parliamentary elections. If a nationality list gets a preferential mandate, the number of party list mandates is accordingly reduced.

The representation of the nationalities now is guaranteed by the Acts on parliamentary elections (2011 and 2013),[26] and the new legal framework was applied first in April 2014. The ruling parties and their think-tanks assessed the new regulation a great success,[27] which remedies a twenty-year-old deficiency of the Hungarian political system. However, the new solution is not unambiguous and as it was endorsed during the legislative rush of the Hungarian parliament, the expert advises were not considered during the elaboration of the system. One of the core problems is who belongs to a nationality. The FL does not specify the notion of nationality or the conditions of being member of a national or ethnic group. Under the new Act on Nationalities (2011) a person belonging to a nationality shall not be necessarily a Hungarian citizen, but in respect of voting rights citizenship is a requirement.[28] Another—dogmatically and practically confusing—problem is that ethnic (nationality) representation is integrated into the political representative system of the unicameral parliament, disrupting its polit-

---

[26] Act CCIII of 2011 on the election of the members of National Assembly (Sections 7–18), and Act XXXVI of 2013 on electoral procedure (especially Sections 86–87, 255–257).

[27] See the commentary of the Századvég Foundation, http://szazadveg.hu/ld/s9y6w8p3m1m7q3m3w4d1_FH_2014_january.pdf.

[28] András László Pap, "Észrevételek a nemzetiségek parlamenti képviseletének szabályozásához," 428–429. See also Sections 1 and 170 of the Act CLXXIX of 2011 on the rights of nationalities.

ical character, but in turn, with the risk of politicization.[29] Any MP representing a nationality will necessarily be influenced by political party factions, and finally will represent mainstream political interest instead of specific minority interest. Furthermore, voters belonging to a nationality are forced to choose among their political or minority preferences. If they choose the nationality preference, they automatically exclude themselves from voting for party lists.

The Act on parliamentary election links both the active and the passive voting rights of nationalities to registration on the nationalities' electoral roll. When registering, a voter must explicitly state whether s/he wishes to vote in the election of MPs on party lists, i.e. refuses the possibility of the extension of nationality registration to parliamentary elections, and vice versa, s/he wishes to extend the nationality registration to the parliamentary elections. In the former case, s/he can vote for a party list, in the latter case, for a nationality list beside the single constituency candidate. By choosing the nationality-preference, the voter's potential to express political preference is reduced to the half of that of a non-nationality voter. The formal equality rule triumphs over the substantive one—every voter has two votes, but some of the voters initially have less chance to influence the political composition of the parliament.

Only the nation-wide nationality self-governments may set up nationality lists, thus other actors—e.g. minority associations or ethnic parties—have no influence on the composition of the lists, and cannot recommend candidates. In the 2014 and the 2018 parliamentary elections all nationalities successfully entered their lists. They cannot cooperate, joint nationality lists are prohibited.

The new electoral legislation provides nationalities with the opportunity to obtain preferential mandates. Under the preferential quota, one nationality mandate is guaranteed for the quarter of the votes cast necessary to gain a list mandate. The exact number always depends on participation, but taking into account the number of the members of nationalities and the nature of the new electoral system, estimates suggested long before the 2014 parliamentary elections that a preferential mandate can be obtained with approximately 20,000–24,000

29 Gábor Kurunczi, "A nemzetiségek parlamenti képviseletének kérdéséről," *Közjogi Szemle* 1 (2014): 58.

votes. The turn-outs justified the estimates, none of the nationalities had a chance for their own MPs in 2014, as the willingness of citizens to register as nationality voters was extremely low, and 22,022 was the limit of a nationality preferential mandate.[30] No more than one preferential mandate may be won from each nationality's list, but theoretically if more than 5 percent of all votes are cast for a nationality list, then other candidates may enter parliament from that list—but that is completely illusory considering that the total proportion of all nationalities together is approximately 5 percent of the inhabitants, according to the voluntary confessions. The Act states that if a nationality does not obtain a preferential mandate, it may send the top candidate on its list to parliament as a spokesperson, who is not a full MP, but participates in the work of parliament with consultative rights. In 2014 all of the nationalities delegated spokespersons to the National Assembly. This institution fits the unicameral political representation system of the Hungarian parliament better, although it does not offset the fact that those citizens who sacrificed their vote for a party list only have the possibility to elect a representative with a limited status.[31] Learning the lessons of the 2014 elections, in 2018 still only one nationality, the German list, obtained a preferential mandate, and the other nationalities delegated spokespersons to the parliament once again.

Table 3.2. Voters registered as members of a national minority
Number of voters in the nationalities' electoral (2014)

National minority	Total number of voters registered as members of a national minority	Registration is extended to the parliamentary elections 20 March 2014 – 6 April 2014	
Bulgarian	232	101	104
Greek	483	135	140
Croatian	3,727	1,535	1,623
Polish	711	130	133
German	23,543	13,749	15,209

[30] See tables 4.2 and 4.3.
[31] Gábor Kurunczi, "A nemzetiségek," 62.

National minority	Total number of voters registered as members of a national minority	Registration is extended to the parliamentary elections 20 March 2014 – 6 April 2014	
Armenian	455	186	184
Roma	25,498	18,150	14,271
Romanian	1,852	635	647
Ruthenian	993	599	611
Serbian	673	320	349
Slovakian	3,120	1,214	1,317
Slovenian	461	194	199
Ukrainian	544	453	502

Source: National Election Office, http://www.valasztas.hu/hu/ogyv2014/766/766_5_3.html

Table 3.3. Scores of nationalities on 2014 parliamentary elections

All votes cast for nationality and party lists			5,047,363
5% threshold			252,369
Limit of nationality preferential mandate			22,022
Number of nationality preferential mandate			0
Number of nationalities' spokespersons			13
List	Type of list	Votes	Proportion
German Nationality Self Government (MNOÖ)	Nationality	11,415	0.23 %
Hungarian Gipsy Party (MCP)	Party	8,810	0.17 %
Roma Nationality Self Government	Nationality	4,048	0.08 %
Croatian Nationality Self Government	Nationality	1,212	0.02 %
Slovakian List	Nationality	995	0.02 %
Romanian Nationality Self Government (ORÖ)	Nationality	463	0.01 %
Ruthenian Nationality Self Government (MROÖ)	Nationality	362	0.01 %
Ukrainian Nationality Self Government	Nationality	293	0.01 %

List	Type of list	Votes	Proportion
Serbian Nationality Self Government (SZOÖ)	Nationality	236	0.0 %
Slovenian Nationality Self Government	Nationality	134	0.0 %
Armenian Nationality Self Government	Nationality	110	0.0 %
Hungarian Greeks	Nationality	102	0.0 %
Polish Nationality Self Government	Nationality	99	0.0 %
Bulgarian Nationality Self Government	Nationality	74	0.0 %

Source: National Election Office, http://www.valasztas.hu/hu/ogyv2014/861/861_0_index.html

Table 3.4 – Scores of nationalities on 2018 parliamentary elections

Limit of nationality preferential mandate		23 831
Number of nationality preferential mandate		1
Number of nationalities' spokespersons		12
List	Number of voters	Votes
German Nationality Self Government	33,168	26,477
Roma Nationality Self Government	18,497	5,703
Croatian Nationality Self Government	2,278	1,743
Slovakian List	1,645	1,245
Romanian Nationality Self Government	798	428
Ruthenian Nationality Self Government	895	539
Ukrainian Nationality Self Government	556	270
Serbian Nationality Self Government (SZOÖ)	427	296
Slovenian Nationality Self Government	252	199
Armenian Nationality Self Government	268	159
Hungarian Greeks	239	159
Polish Nationality Self Government	264	210
Bulgarian Nationality Self Government	158	104

Source: National Election Office, http://www.valasztas.hu/orszagos-listak-eredmenye?p_p_id=ogylistaseredmenyadatlap_WAR_nvinvrportlet&p_p_lifecycle=0&p_p_state=normal&p_p_mode=view&p_p_col_id=column-2&p_p_col_pos=1&p_p_col_count=2&_ogylistaseredmenyadatlap_WAR_nvinvrportlet_tabId=tab2

Human Dignity, Equality and Solidarity—the Undermined Standards

During the Hungarian constitution-making in 2011 it occurred—and the Hungarian Government inquired from the Venice Commission—whether and to what extent it was necessary to incorporate the EU Charter of Fundamental Rights (hereafter: Charter) into the national constitution. The Venice Commission emphasized that "up-dating the scope of human rights protection and seeking to adequately reflect, in the new Constitution, the most recent developments in the field of human rights protection, as articulated in the EU Charter, is a legitimate aim and a signal of loyalty towards European values." However, the Commission also underlined that the incorporation of the Charter as a whole or of some parts of it could lead to legal complications, thus "it would be more advisable (…) to consider the EU Charter as a starting point or a point of reference and source of inspiration in drafting the human rights and fundamental freedoms chapter of the new Constitution."[32]

The adopted FL in its relevant chapter ("Freedom and Responsibility") incorporated some sentences of the Charter, but—compared to the Charter and especially after the Fourth Amendment of the FL in 2013—the content of the rights enumerated by the FL is less detailed and the text raises the possibility of wider limitation of rights. Furthermore, the context of the two bills of rights are completely different. It is worth referring also to the preamble of the FL, according to which "individual freedom can only be complete in cooperation with others." The Charter applies a completely different approach, and emphasizes in its preamble that the Union "places the individual at the heart of its activities." It raises the individuals' responsibility only in connection with the enjoyment of rights.[33] While the approach of the FL—taking

[32] European Commission for Democracy Through Law (Venice Commission) Opinion № 614/2011, Strasbourg, March 28, 2011, Opinion on Three Legal Questions Arising in the Process of Drafting the New Constitution of Hungary, Points 21, 25–28, 32.

[33] Charter Preamble: "Enjoyment of these rights entails responsibilities and duties with regard to other persons, to the human community and to future generations."

also into consideration the numerous basic obligations—is communitarian and nationalist, the Charter focuses on the philosophy of individual freedom and supports pluralism.[34]

The difference is not accidental. In the last decade the Hungarian society has become more and more closed, exclusive, and disunited. Discrimination, segregation, xenophobia, and hate speech have become parts of everyday life, with the support of political populism.[35] In the field of the most important human values, the FL legalized and reaffirmed unprecedented solutions based on unacceptable societal practice.

While most of the national and ethnic minorities are integrated into society, the target group of the above-mentioned phenomena is the Roma people. The facts are well known. As Minority Rights Group International reported "the marginalization of the Roma population increased. (...) Roma were among those most affected by Hungary's difficult transition period from socialism to a market-based economy and many lost their employment following economic decline and privatization of state industries. (...) Living conditions for Roma communities continue to be significantly worse than for the general population. Roma are significantly less educated and have below average income and life expectancy. The unemployment rate for Roma is estimated at 70 per cent, more than 10 times the national average, and most Roma live in extreme poverty. (...) Widespread discrimination against Roma continues in education, housing, penal institutions, employment and access to public institutions (...) especially Roma children suffer from stigmatization, exclusion and socio-economic disparities, notably related to housing, unemployment, access to health services, adoption and educational facilities because of their ethnic status."[36] The lowest point clearly came in 2008 and 2009: "According to media reports and information provided by the Hungarian Chief of Police and the European Roma Rights Centre (ERRC) and the Open Society Institute,

---

34 Also refers to this European Commission for Democracy Through Law (Venice Commission) Opinion № 621/2011, Strasbourg, June 20, 2011, Opinion on the New Constitution of Hungary, Point 57.

35 István György Tóth, *Bizalomhiány, normazavarok, igazságtalanságérzet és paternalizmus a magyar társadalom értékszerkezetében* (Budapest: TÁRKI, 2009), 13.

36 http://minorityrights.org/minorities/roma-8/.

since the beginning of 2008 there have been 15 incidents of Roma houses being firebombed with Molotov cocktails, and two attacks on Roma homes with hand grenades. During this time, at least five people of Roma origin have been murdered and more seriously injured in these and other incidents involving stabbings and beatings. (...) On 23 February 2009 a Roma father and his five-year-old son were shot dead in an attack on a family home in Tatárszentgyörgy, a village 40 miles south-east of Budapest, and two children were injured when the house was set on fire."[37]

Against this background, it is worth assessing how the FL reflects on the problems. Several of its provisions are deepening the gap between the Roma minority and the majority of society, either by sanctioning poverty, or having an anti-egalitarian character and implicitly addressing Roma people.[38]

The FL in its Article XV regulates the equality rights in order of the EU Charter, however without applying the latter's up-to-date solutions. Article XV lacks any mention of the prohibition of discrimination on the ground of sexual orientation,[39] genetic features, age,[40] ethnic origin, or membership of a national minority. Although the FL prohibits any discrimination on the grounds of race, color, and national origin, it does not take into consideration the special situation of ethnic and national minority groups in Hungary. An updated constitutional text should contain the legal consequences of the facts. In the context of the FL, "national origin" refers more to the majority nation,

---

[37] Ibid.

[38] Kriszta Kovács, "Equality: The Missing Link," in *Constitution for a Disunited Nation,* ed. Gábor Attila Tóth (Budapest: CEU Press, 2012), 186.

[39] See the Opinion № 621/2011 of Venice Commission, Points 76–80. It is important to note in this context that the Hungarian Act CXXV of 2003 on Equal Treatment and Promotion of Equal Opportunities forbids discrimination based on factors that include sexual orientation and sexual identity in the fields of employment, education, housing, health and access to goods and services.

[40] The prohibition of discrimination on the ground of age has an increasing significance in the case law of the CJEU, see e.g. C–144/04. *Werner Mangold v Rüdiger Helm*, Judgment of November 22, 2005 [ECR 2005, I–9981], or C-499/08. *Ingeniorforeningen i Danmark v Region Syddanmark*, Judgment of October 12, 2010.

and does not really apply to minorities.[41] Article XV(2) of the FL is an open-ended provision, thus during its interpretation the legislator, the courts of law and the Constitutional Court will be able to extend the grounds of non-discrimination, still it would have been reasonable to name expressly the mentioned grounds. The equality of men and women in Article XV(3) of the FL can be considered laconic compared to the Charter. The FL declares gender equality but does not specify it for employment, work, pay, marriage and family relations, although in practice discrimination appears in these relations most frequently. While Articles 25–26 of the Charter contain positive rights of the elderly and disabled people, the FL in Article XV(5) only promises the protection by the state in the form of special measures. It is worth mentioning that the Roma minority is not mentioned among the target groups of affirmative action.[42]

After the Fourth Amendment to the FL, Article XV(4) reads as follows in the official translation: "By means of separate measures, Hungary shall promote the achievement of equality of opportunity and social inclusion." The Hungarian text, however, applies the word "felzárkózás"—catching up, instead of "befogadás"—inclusion. The difference is revealing. The term"social catching up" created a constitutional basis for school segregation, the most affected by which are the Roma children.

As evidence, the Hungarian Supreme Court in April 2015 declared that segregation of the Roma in parochial schools is legal. The Chance for Children Foundation (CFCF), a Hungarian organization that campaigns for Roma education rights and was applicant in the case, reported: "Although the previous decisions by the Hungarian courts established on two instances that the school in Nyíregyháza segregates Roma children unlawfully, therefore this practice should be stopped, the Hungarian Supreme Court (Kúria) has taken a very different view on this case: it dismissed CFCF's claims."[43] Antecedents of the decision: "On 28 February 2014 the Court of Nyíregyháza delivered the first instance judgement. In 2007, as a result of

41 Chronowski, "The New Hungarian Fundamental Law," 130–131.

42 Kovács, "Equality," 193–194.

43 Chance for Children Foundation, The Nyíregyháza resegregation case, http://www.cfcf.hu/en/ny%C3%ADregyh%C3%A1za-resegregation-case.

CFCF's court action and extensive negotiations, Nyíregyháza closed its segregated school in the Guszev settlement and provided a free school bus for Roma children who were integrated to mainstream primary schools in the city center. Integration of children of the lower grades turned out to be successful, while for children of upper grades it was not. In 2011, the new mayor decided to have the school reopened as part of the Greek Catholic Church's primary school. He provided the school building for free and committed substantial local funds for extra financial help. (...) The Greek Catholic Church maintains a nursery, a primary and a secondary school in the city center which are considered elite schools. The Church has long been present in the settlement offering Roma missionary services. The segregated school was reopened in September 2011. Altogether 16 children of first grade enrolled to the "re-segregated" school."[44]

CFCF sued both the Church and the Hungarian state for introducing segregation. The Court of first instance established that "the Church segregated its pupils on a school level, and the municipality segregated Roma students by handing over the school building to the Church. The Court also noted that the religious education provided by the Church in the segregated school could not justify racial segregation. The Court pointed out that parents of the children enrolled at the Roma school did not choose the school because of the religious education it provided but because of its location and the fact that many Roma children were harassed in other schools. The Court prohibited the continuation of the illegal activity, therefore it banned the Church to launch new classes in the segregated school. The Court, however, dismissed CFCF's claim on termination of segregation by arguing that the Court could not order the closing down of the school completely because it would have violated the parent's right to freely choose education for their children and that it would have effected public law relationships which fall beyond the scope of civil litigation. The Court of second instance upheld the decision of the court of first instance. On April 22, 2015 the Supreme Court repealed the judgment of the court of first instance and dismissed the applicant's claims. The Supreme Court argued that the Greek Catholic Church has successfully justified the seg-

[44] Ibid.

regation by proving that it provided religious education and that parents have freely chosen the school and exercised their freedom of religion. (…) The Supreme Court took the position that the fact that the Greek Catholic Church conducted Roma pastoral care (pastoration) justified its decision to open a school in a Roma settlement and to maintain a Roma-only school, because it could not conduct Roma pastoral care in a school where the ethnic composition of the students was different."[45]

The case clearly illustrates that the FL is not a suitable legal norm to prevent segregation. The argumentation and logic of the Hungarian Supreme Court is reminiscent of the ancient judgment of the SCOTUS in *Plessy v. Fergusson* (1896) about "separate but equal" doctrine, which was overruled in the landmark *Brown v. Board of Education* (1954). In the meantime, the Hungarian government communicated that this judgement was the victory of the new "delicate segregation" policy.

At this point, it seems necessary to recall once more that the FL eliminated the dual definition of "national and ethnic minorities" and introduced—for historical reasons and upon the demands of some minorities—the word "nationalities" instead, which fails to reflect the fact that in Hungary, beside the national minorities, also recognizes two ethnic minorities—the Roma and the Ruthenian.[46] As to linguistic and cultural rights, any commitment for protection of minority languages can be found only in the preamble of the FL, while the protection of the Hungarian language—as official language—and sign language is a clear obligation for the state (see Article H of the FL). However, the FL contains in the chapter on fundamental rights also language rights of nationalities.[47] The former Constitution clearly asserted the

---

[45] Ibid.

[46] András László Pap, "Észrevételek a nemzetiségek parlamenti képviseletének szabályozásához," 95; András László Pap, *Democratic Decline in Hungary: Law and Society in an Illiberal Democracy* (London: Routledge, 2018): 95.

[47] "The Venice Commission finds regrettable that Art. H, which regulates the protection of Hungarian language as the official language of the country, does not include a constitutional guarantee for the protection of the languages of national minorities. It however notes that Article XXIX guarantees the right to the use of these languages by Hungary's 'nationalities' and understands this provision as implying also an obligation for the State to protect these languages and to support their preservation and development (see also the Preamble and Article Q of the Constitution)." Opinion № 621/2011 of Venice Commission, Point 45.

Hungarian state's obligation to ensure the fostering of the cultures of minorities, the use of their native language, etc. The FL uses the term "respect" in connection with the rights of nationalities, but avoids the use of terms "promote" or "protect" in Article XXIX. Furthermore, only the rights to express and preserve one's (minority) identity and the use of names in their native languages are formulated as individual rights, i.e. rights of persons belonging to nationalities. The other rights respected by the FL—such as the promotion of their own culture, the use of their native language, the education in their native language—seem to belong to minority communities.[48] The Fourth Amendment to the FL Article XXIX(3) has introduced the conditionality of recognition as a national minority on the level of constitution: "A cardinal Act may provide that recognition as a nationality shall be subject to a certain length of time of presence and to the initiative of a certain number of persons declaring to be members of the nationality concerned." As the Amicus Brief to the Venice Commission explains: "The amendment explicitly indicates that the recognition of a group as a nationality can be limited to those groups that have held national status already for a certain period of time, which appears to limit the ability of new groups to Hungary to claim such status. In addition, the recognition of a nationality may be made contingent on a minimum number of members of the nationality residing in Hungary, which limits the ability of smaller groups to claim nationality status. This may not sound terribly important, until one recognizes the rights that may not be claimed unless one is a member of a recognized nationality."[49]

By introducing the right to self-defense in the constitutional provisions (Article V), the boundaries of the individual and state responsibility become uncertain. The relationship between the new right and the monopoly of the state to enforce the constitution and the legislation as outlined in Article C(3) of FL remains an open question.[50] It

---

48 See also Opinion № 621/2011 of Venice Commission, Point 82.

49 Miklós Bánkuti et al. *Amicus Brief for the Venice Commission on the Fourth Amendment to the Fundamental Law of Hungary* (April 2013): 1–83, accessed May 10, 2018. http://fundamentum.hu/sites/default/files/amicus_brief_on_the_fourth_amendment.pdf, 56.

50 Article V of FL: "Every person shall have the right to repel any unlawful attack against his or her person or property, or one that poses a direct threat

can be presupposed that the former is an exception to the latter rule; however, this solution is rather unfortunate in case of a constitutional provision, because the constitutional text should be unambiguous, without exception rules. Furthermore, it is also open to debate what the relationship between the right to self-defense and the norm on justified defense in the Criminal Code is. Beyond the jurisprudential uniqueness, Article V clearly targets the Roma population, whose members are living in great poverty and in need they might commit petty offences against property.[51]

Among the rights guaranteeing free communication, the freedom to express one's opinion originally was formulated in the FL similarly to the former Constitution, but the Fourth Amendment to the FL introduced serious bans on speeches violating human dignity, the dignity of the Hungarian nation or minority groups.[52] This is the only point in the constitution where ethnicity became relevant, but the wording and the enumeration is still not in line with the non-discrimination rule of Article XV(2). Even the Venice Commission found that it contradicts European standards, because "the provisions on the dignity of communities are too vague and the specific protection of the 'dignity of the Hungarian nation' creates the risk that freedom of speech in Hungary could, in the future, be curtailed in order to protect Hungarian institutions and office holders."[53] The constitutional bans on free expression support the preservation of the disproportionate, impartial and controversial judicial practice in the field of hate-crimes that has been characterized by protecting the Hungarian majority against the Roma minority.[54]

---

to the same." Article C(3) of FL: "The State shall have the exclusive right to use coercion in order to enforce the Fundamental Law and legislation."

51 Kovács, "Equality," 190.

52 Article IX(5) of the FL: "The right to freedom of speech may not be exercised with the aim of violating the dignity of the Hungarian nation or of any national, ethnic, racial or religious community. Persons belonging to such communities shall be entitled to enforce their claims in court against the expression of an opinion which violates the community, invoking the violation of their human dignity, as provided for by an Act."

53 Opinion № 720/2013 of the Venice Commission, Point 141.

54 Lídia Balogh, Henriett Dinók and András László Pap, "A jog által láthatatlan? A gyűlölet-bűncselekmények szabályozási kérdései és gyakorlati problémái," *Fundamentum* 4 (2012): 95; Pap, "Democratic Decline," 119.

As to the value of social solidarity, social security does not appear as a fundamental right in the FL, but merely as something the state "shall strive" for, thus it only appears to be a state goal, which can be evaluated as a step backward in comparison with the former Constitution. In Article XIX(1) of FL among the titles to statutory subsidies (within the group of people in need) old age is not listed; it appears alone, separately from the categories of neediness, in paragraph (4). Social insurance does not appear as a constitutional institution, instead, in Article XIX(2) the expression "a system of social institutions and measures" is used as the means of achieving the defined state goal. Article XIX(3) also gives reason for concern both from the viewpoint of equal dignity and solidarity, as it contains the uncertain measure of "usefulness of activity to the community," which may be taken into account in deciding on the nature and extent of social aids.[55] It means that social support may be withheld in the absence of "useful activity," even if the person concerned is needy and the cause of the situation falls outside his or her own fault. The rule—again—reflects to the prejudices and stereotypes of the majority society that Roma people live on social subsidies and creates a constitutional basis for the government's community service programme.[56]

There is another strange constitutional rule, which contradicts the principle of dignity and targets one of the most vulnerable groups of society after the Fourth and Seventh Amendment, on criminalizing homelessness. Article XXII(3) of the FL read as follows after April 2013: "In order to protect public order, public security, public health and cultural values, an Act or a local government decree may with respect to a specific part of public space, provide that staying in public space as a habitual dwelling shall be illegal." In 2018 a general rule was introduced into the text of FL: "Using a public space as a habitual dwelling shall be prohibited." The amendments were reactions to the former decision of the Constitutional Court on the Misdemeanor Act,[57] in which the

---

55 Article XIX(3) of the FL: "The nature and extent of social measures may be determined by law in accordance with the usefulness to the community of the beneficiary's activity."

56 Kovács, "Equality," 191.

57 Decision № 38/2012. (XI. 14.) AB, see the press release here: http://www.mkab.hu/sajto/news/provisions-of-the-act-on-contraventions-criminalizing-people-living-at-public-areas-permanently-are-against-fundamental-law.

court stated that the punishment of unavoidable living in a public area fails to meet the requirement of the protection of human dignity. The Venice Commission criticized the constitutional rank of the regulation, because it aims to prevent the review by the Constitutional Court.

Conclusion

Although the FL seemingly, on the surface, recognizes the constitutional values of dignity, equality and solidarity, an in-depth analysis brings out the contradictions, the non-egalitarian and abusive messages. The FL is unsuitable for the integration of the political community and Hungarian society, it does not address the problem of ethnicity, and does not even try to close the gaps, or prevent segregation and discrimination. The hypocritical model of Hungarian nationality policy hides the problems and discrimination faced by the most numerous and segregated ethnic group in Hungary, the Roma. The adjective "ethnic" appears only once throughout the text and ethnicity questions are hidden in the historic term "nationality." In fact, this constitution was not created with the intention of uniting the political nation, and thus it is unable to fulfil the integrative function of a constitution.

BIBLIOGRAPHY

Balogh, Lídia, Henriett Dinók, and András László Pap. "A jog által láthatatlan? A gyűlölet-bűncselekmények szabályozási kérdései és gyakorlati problémái." *Fundamentum* 4 (2012): 91–98.

Bánkuti, Miklós, Tamás Dombos, Gábor Halmai, András Hanák, Zsolt Körtvélyesi, Balázs Majtényi, András László Pap, Eszter Polgári, Orsolya Salát, Kim Lane Scheppele, Péter Sólyom, and Renáta Uitz. *Amicus Brief for the Venice Commission on the Fourth Amendment to the Fundamental Law of Hungary*, edited by Gábor Halmai and Kim Lane Scheppele, (April 2013): 1–83. Accessed May 10, 2018. http://fundamentum.hu/sites/default/files/amicus_brief_on_the_fourth_amendment.pdf.

Brunner, Georg. *Nationality Problems and Minority Conflicts in Eastern Europe: Strategies for Europe*. Gutersloh: Bertelsmann Foundation Publishers, 1996.

Chronowski, Nóra. "The New Hungarian Fundamental Law in the Light of the European Union's Normative Values." *Revue Est Europa* numéro spéciale 1 (2012): 111–142.

Jacobsohn, Gary Jeffrey. "Constitutional Identity." *The Review of Politics* 3 (2006): 361–397.

Jakab, András. "Defining the Borders of the Political Community: Constitutional Visions of the Nation." Manuscript, (2012): 1–54. Accessed April 30, 2016. http://ssrn.com/abstract=2045648.

Kovács, Kriszta. "Equality: The Missing Link." In *Constitution for a Disunited Nation*, edited by Gábor Attila Tóth, 171–195. Budapest: CEU Press, 2012.

Körtvélyesi, Zsolt. "Az 'egységes magyar nemzet' és az állampolgárság." *Fundamentum* 2 (2011): 49–55.

Körtvélyesi, Zsolt. "From 'We the People' to 'We the Nation'." In *Constitution for a Disunited Nation*, edited by Gábor Attila Tóth, 111–140. Budapest: CEU Press, 2012.

Kurunczi, Gábor. "A nemzetiségek parlamenti képviseletének kérdéséről." *Közjogi Szemle* 1 (2014): 56–65.

Küpper, Herbert. "Ungarns Verfassung vom 25. April 2011. Einführung—Übersetzung—Materialien." Frankfurt-Main: Peter Lang Verlag, 2012.

Küpper, Herbert."Paternalista kollektivizmus és liberális individualizmus között: az új magyar Alaptörvényben rögzített emberkép normatív alapjai." *Közjogi Szemle* 3 (2012): 8–11.

Magicz, András. "Re-regulation of National Minority Rights." In *Their Shield is the Law. The Ombudsman's Protection for Vulnerable Groups*, edited by Barnabás Hajas and Máté Szabó, 27–30. Budapest: Office of the Commissioner for Fundamental Rights, 2013.

Majtényi, Balázs. "What Has Happened to Our Model Child? The Creation and the Evolution of the Hungarian Minority Act." *European Yearbook of Minority Issues* 6 (2005): 397–449.

Majtényi, Balázs. "Legislative Stupidities in the New Hungarian Constitution." *Peace Human Rights* 1 (2012): 105–110.

Majtényi, Balázs. "Alaptörvény a nemzet akaratából." *Állam- és Jogtudomány* 1 (2014): 77–97.

Majtényi, Balázs. "The Nation's Will as Trump in the Hungarian Fundamental Law." *European Yearbook on Human Rights* (2015): 247–259.

Pap, András László. "Észrevételek a kisebbségek parlamenti képviseletének szabályozásához az új alkotmányban." *Pázmány Law Working Papers* 27 (2011): 1–7.

Pap, András László. "Észrevételek a nemzetiségek parlamenti képviseletének szabályozásához az Alaptörvényben, a választójogi törvényben és a nemzetiségek jogairól szóló törvényben," *vol. 1. of Alkotmányozás Magyarországon 2010–2011*, edited by András Jakab and Tímea Drinóczi, 419–438. Budapest–Pécs: Pázmány Press, 2013.

Pap, András László. *Democratic Decline in Hungary: Law and Society in an Illiberal Democracy*. London: Routledge, 2018.

Pákozdi, Csaba, and Márton Sulyok. "The Birth of a 'New Nation'? Mapping progressive approaches to the nation-concept based on the Hungarian Fundamental Law." *Miskolc Journal of International Law* 2 (2011): 43–55.

Petrétei, József. *Az alkotmányos demokrácia alapintézményei*. Budapest–Pécs: Dialóg Campus, 2009.
Tóth, István György. *Bizalomhiány, normazavarok, igazságtalanságérzet és paternalizmus a magyar társadalom értékszerkezetében*. Budapest: TÁRKI, 2009.

Towards an Illiberal Extraterritorial Political Community? Hungary's "Simplified Naturalization" and Its Ramifications

CHRIS MOREH

Introduction

Hungary has had a long—and often compromised—history of dealing with the descendants of those citizens of the former Kingdom of Hungary who remained on lands annexed to neighboring countries after World War I. Following the Treaty of Trianon, Hungary lost two-thirds of its territory and population, including more than three million ethnic Hungarians. Reclaiming these lost territories and "reuniting" the "nation" became a central concern of interwar Hungarian politics, the aim of national reunification also shaping the political leadership's decisions during World War II. However, after the country's defeat on the side of the Axis and subsequent incorporation into the Eastern Bloc, irredentist agendas and ethnocultural conceptions of nationhood remained repressed for decades. These topics and claims could only re-emerge in the late 1980s, and Hungary's Constitution of 1989 included the stipulation that the "Republic of Hungary feels responsible for the fate of the Hungarians living outside its borders and promotes the maintenance of their relations to Hungary."[1]

[1] 6. § (3) of Act XXXI of 1989 amending the Constitution of 1949. Paragraph 6. § (1), on the other hand, rejected the possibility of any future territorial aggressions, claims and threats in the detriment of other countries' sovereignty. The original text of the Act is available in the EUDO-Citizenship database on National Citizenship Laws, http://eudo-citizenship.eu/databases/national-citizenship-laws.

While ethnic nationalism has seen a spectacular revival since the early years of postsocialism, the constitutional order, nevertheless, remained fundamentally reliant on a civic definition of nationhood, with the ethno-cultural principle creeping in merely as a "complementary element."[2] It is in this respect that the "simplified naturalization" introduced by the modification of the Citizenship Act in 2010[3] constitutes a significant shift in official identity and diaspora politics.[4] According to the new citizenship legislation, descendants of Hungarian citizens—or those who can "demonstrate the plausibility" of such descent—who can prove knowledge of the Hungarian language, may undergo a simplified procedure to acquire Hungarian citizenship, with the usual requirements of residence, subsistence, and a test of constitutional knowledge, all being waived.[5]

While the compatibility between ethnic preferentialism in citizenship legislation and liberal democratic norms has been hotly debated,[6] the significance of the 2010 amendment to the Act on Hungarian Citizenship is much broader. On the one hand, it is the closing act of a lengthier process of national "soul-searching" and party-political maneuvering which has dramatically shaped the current political land-

---

[2] Zoltán Kántor and Balázs Majtényi, "A 'kettős állampolgárság'—népszavazás, politikai vita, érvek," in *Romániai Magyar Évkönyv 2004/2005*, ed. Barna Bodó (Temesvár: Marineasa, 2005), 213–228.

[3] "Act XLIV of 2010 amending Act LV of 1993 regarding Hungarian citizenship." Available in both Hungarian and English translation at http://www.allampolgarsag.gov.hu/.

[4] Balázs Majtényi, "Etnikai származás és állampolgárság," *Jogi Iránytű* 1 (2011), accessed May 19, 2019, http://jog.tk.mta.hu/uploads/files/Jogi_Iranytu/Jogi_Iranytu_2011_1_Majtenyi_Balazs.pdf., Myra A. Waterbury, *Between State and Nation: Diaspora Politics and Kin-state Nationalism in Hungary* (1st ed.) (New York: Palgrave Macmillan, 2010).

[5] Judit Tóth. *UPDATE: Changes in the Hungarian Citizenship Law and adopted on 26 May 2010.* (San Domenico di Fiesole: EUI, EUDO Citizenship Observatory, July 13, 2010), accessed May 19, 2019, http://eudo-citizenship.eu/docs/CountryReports/recentChanges/Hungary.pdf.

[6] Costica Dumbrava, "External Citizenship in EU Countries." *Ethnic and Racial Studies* 13 (2014): 2340–2360; Kántor and Majtényi, "A 'kettős állampolgárság'; Mária M. Kovács, "The Politics of Dual Citizenship in Hungary," *Citizenship Studies* 4 (2006); Szabolcs Pogonyi, *Extra-Territorial Ethnic Politics, Discourses and Identities in Hungary* (Houndmills: Palgrave Macmillan, 2017); Waterbury, *Between State and Nation.*

scape. On the other hand, it is the starting point of a drastic institutional and ideological restructuring, in which the adoption of the new constitution and electoral reforms were initial steps in the direction of a self-described "illiberal democracy."[7] With that in mind, this essay aims to examine the internal logic of this broader ideological transformation by questioning the changed meaning of "political community" in the context of extraterritorial ethnic citizenship.

It had been argued by critics that "granting nonresident dual citizenship would have the practical effect of merging the Hungarian cultural nation and the political community."[8] This essay will question whether such a merger can be assumed to be that straightforward in practical terms, asking: what is it that shapes a community of extraterritorial citizens into an extraterritorial—or "transsovereign"[9]—*political* community? The first proposition to be made is that, at a minimum, *external* citizens become *political* citizens after being also granted voting rights supported by a basic extraterritorial electoral infrastructure—which was delivered by a set of Acts of Parliament during 2011 and 2013.[10] A further step would then be to consider the *active* nature of such political rights, that is, the electoral behavior of the newly enfranchised extraterritorial citizens. There is nothing genuinely new in either of these propositions or approaches.[11] But for these observed processes to begin making sense and to highlight the potentially far-reaching

[7] András L. Pap, *Democratic Decline in Hungary: Law and Society in an Illiberal Democracy* (Abindgon: Routledge, 2018).

[8] Waterbury, *Between State and Nation,* 124.

[9] Zsuzsa Csergő and James M. Goldgeier, "Nationalist Strategies and European Integration," in *The Hungarian Status Law: Nation Building and/or Minority Protection,* ed. Zoltán Kántor et al. (Sapporo: Slavic Research Center, Hokkaido University, 2004).

[10] The electoral law was first amended in December 2011 (Act CCIII of 2011 On the Elections of Members of Parliament), followed by changes to the law on electoral procedure, initially adopted in April 2013 (Act XXXVI of 2013 on electoral procedure) and subsequently revised in June and December by Act CCVII of 2013.

[11] Boldizsár Nagy, "Nationality as a Stigma: the Drawbacks of Nationality (What Do I Have To Do With Book-Burners?)," *Corvinus Journal of Sociology and Social Policy* 2 (2014); Pogonyi, *Extra-Territorial;* Levente Salat, "A könnyített honosítás látható és várható következményeiről. Válaszok a Magyar Kisebbség kérdéseire," *Magyar Kisebbség* 3–4/69–70 (2013).

challenges that they pose, one must move beyond the "liberal–republican" normative perspectives that usually drive academic analyses of the topic, and understand the confluence of the 2010 citizenship law, the subsequent changes in electoral legislation, and the constitutional reform from an "illiberal" standpoint.[12]

Secondly, these confluent processes together with the national soul-searching stretching throughout the 2000s have arguably resulted in reinterpreting the political community rather than simply extending it, as the assumed merger between the cultural nation and the body politic would suggest. Although liberal–republican normative analyses would deny any moral equivalence between the "de-ethnicizing" processes which have taken place in North-Western European countries with previously ethno-national citizenship models, and the "re-ethnicizing" processes in the South-Eastern part of the continent,[13] from

[12] I use "liberal–republican" and "illiberal" purely as heuristic constructs. The former is derived from Bauböck's differentiation between four general positions vis-à-vis the expansion of electoral rights beyond nation-state borders: *ethno-nationalism*, *traditional republicanism*, and two varieties of *liberalism*—reliant on the "all subjected to coercion" and "all affected interests" principles respectively—as well as a fifth principle of "stakeholder citizenship" that "combines insights from republican and liberal perspectives." See Rainer Bauböck, "Expansive Citizenship: Voting beyond Territory and Membership," *PS: Political Science and Politics* 4 (2005), 686; see also David Owen, "Resident Aliens, Non-resident Citizens and Voting Rights: Towards a Pluralist Theory of Transnational Political Equality and Modes of Political Belonging," in *Citizenship acquisition and national belonging: migration, membership and the liberal democratic state*, ed. Calder et al. (Basingstoke: Palgrave Macmillan, 2010). "Liberal–republican" refers to this wide pool of principles and combinations thereof, which most starkly contrast ethno-nationalist ones. On the other hand, "illiberal" is meant to denote the ambiguous self-described conception of ethno-national conservatism professed by the Fidesz–Christian Democratic government in power since 2010 (see Pap, *Democratic Decline*). It is not used as a slur, but as to describe a political outlook that, in the words of academic defenders of this version of illiberalism espouses "conservative, communitarian, nationalist, and Christian" values as a reaction to liberalism's perceived "failure to affirm the values that underpin family, community, and national life" (Frank Furedi, *Populism and the European Culture Wars: the Conflict of Values between Hungary and the EU* (London: Routledge, 2018), 116).

[13] Christian Joppke, "Citizenship between De- and Re-Ethnicization," *European Journal of Sociology* 3 (2003).

an "illiberal" perspective they could both be seen as equally involving what Benhabib[14] has described from a universalist perspective as democratic iterations: "complex processes of public argument, deliberation, and learning through which universalist right claims are contested and contextualized, invoked and revoked, throughout legal and political institutions as well as in the public sphere of liberal democracies."[15] Substitute "universalist" for "ethnic extraterritorial" and you have a good description of Hungarian debates on nation policy[16] since the democratic turn; replace "liberal" with "illiberal" and these iterations extend all the way to our present.

Before discussing these processes, I first briefly review the conceptual-normative tensions between de- and re-ethnicization of citizenship policies.

Transnational Citizenship Between *De*- and *Re*-ethnicization

Renegotiating the ethno-cultural and civic-territorial boundaries of the citizenry after these have become challenged by migratory movements and the intergenerational reproduction of otherness and transnational ties has been central to what we may call a contemporary debate over citizenship for three decades. Arguably, the debate started off as a reaction to Brubaker's[17] famous discussion contrasting the French legal tradition of *ius soli*—citizenship attribution based on place of birth—with Germany's *ius sanguinis*—citizenship based on descent (on blood)—and tracing their roots to divergent (civic or ethnic) patterns of nation-building. In this early discussion, citizenship was also considered as "membership in a large-scale republic that has

[14] Seyla Benhabib, *The Rights of Others: Aliens, Residents and Citizens* (Cambridge: Cambridge University Press, 2004).

[15] Ibid., 19.

[16] Zoltán Kántor, "Status Law and 'Nation Policy': Theoretical Aspects," in *The Hungarian Status Law: Nation Building and/or Minority Protection*, ed. Zoltán Kántor et al. (Sapporo: Slavic Research Center, Hokkaido University, 2004).

[17] Rogers Brubaker, *Citizenship and Nationhood in France and Germany* (Cambridge, MA and London: Harvard University Press, 1992).

boundaries roughly conforming to some partly pre-existing 'national' community."[18]

The revival of the civic/ethnic and the concomitant West/East divide—entailing also a progressive/regressive value judgement—has since been forcefully challenged on empirical grounds.[19] It has been argued that identifiable processes of de- and re-ethnicization effect a convergence between citizenship traditions,[20] although the inclusion of Central-Eastern Europe in the comparative analysis arguably reveals a trend of "legal divergence."[21] Citizenship scholars have also argued that states are not only causally constrained by their ideologies of nation-building, but immigration itself is central to redefining nationhood.[22] Moreover, in seeking to reconnect with the descendants of former citizens who had left the country at certain historical political-economic conjunctures, states are increasingly involved in what has been described as a "scramble for citizens,"[23] or more accurately, for the *right kind* of citizens. As Waterbury[24] has noted with a healthy

---

[18] Rogers M. Smith, "Citizenship and the Politics of People-Building," *Citizenship Studies* 1 (2001): 73; Yasemin N. Soysal, *Limits of Citizenship: Migrants and Postnational Membership in Europe* (Chicago, IL: University of Chicago Press, 1994).

[19] Rainer Bauböck and André Liebich, eds., *Is There (Still) an East-West Divide in the Conception of Citizenship in Europe?* (Fiesole: EUDO Citizenship Observatory, 2010); Oxana Shevel, "The Post-Communist Diaspora Laws: Beyond the 'Good Civic versus Bad Ethnic' Nationalism Dichotomy," *East European Politics & Societies*, 1 (2010); Stephen Shulman, "Challenging the Civic/Ethnic and West/East Dichotomies in the Study of Nationalism," *Comparative Political Studies* 5 (2002), Smith, "Citizenship"; Patrick Weil, "Access to Citizenship: A Comparison of Twenty-five Nationality Laws," in *Citizenship Today: Global Perspectives and Practices*, eds. Alexander T. Aleinikoff and Douglas Klusmeyer (Washington, DC: Brookings Institution, 2001).

[20] Joppke, "Citizenship Between"; Weil, "Access to Citizenship."

[21] Aleksandra Maatsch, *Ethnic Citizenship Regimes: Europeanization, Post-war Migration and Redressing Past Wrongs* (Houndmills, Basingstoke: Palgrave Macmillan, 2011).

[22] Christian Joppke, *Immigration and the Nation-state: The United States, Germany, and Great Britain* (Oxford: Oxford University Press, 1999).

[23] David Cook-Martín, *The Scramble for Citizens: Dual Nationality and State Competition for Immigrants* (Stanford, CA: Stanford University Press, 2013).

[24] Myra A. Waterbury, "Bridging the Divide: Towards a Comparative Framework for Understanding Kin State and Migrant-sending State Diaspora

sense of well-founded cynicism, "populations abroad represent a set of unique cultural, material and political resources for homeland state elites."[25] Underpinned by a worldwide trend towards increasing acceptance of dual citizenship[26] these processes raise important questions about the de-territorialization and fragmentation of citizenship.

Significantly less attention has been paid, however, to the "movement of borders over people" than to the movement of people over borders.[27] There is, in particular, a notorious imbalance in academic discussions of kin-states' engagement with kin-minorities, and migrant-sending states' engagement with emigrants, and their respective descendant living abroad, although in terms of structure and political dynamics the two cases present many similarities.[28] Transnationalism scholarship—as Pogonyi noted—has focused disproportionally on migrant communities' engagement with their countries of origin and the latter's diaspora politics, although the less studied "transborder" kin-communities are arguably "the paradigmatic examples of transnational engagement."[29] Rainer Bauböck's approach to political transnationalism is very useful for highlighting the basis of the commonalities between the two.[30] What is important from this perspective is not so much migrants' continued political orientation towards their origin countries, but "their increasing opportunities to combine external and internal status and affiliations."[31] In other words, the significance of *political* transnationalism lies in the actions

Politics," in *Diaspora and Transnationalism: Concepts, Theories and Methods*, eds. Rainer Bauböck and Thomas Faist (Amsterdam: Amsterdam University Press, 2010), 146.

25 See also Joppke, "Citizenship Between."

26 Maarten Vink, Gerard-Rene De Groot, and Ngo C. Luk, "MACIMIDE Global Expatriate Dual Citizenship Dataset," *Harvard Dataverse*, v3, 2015, accessed May 20, 2019, doi:10.7910/DVN/TTMZ08.

27 Rogers Brubaker, "Migration, Membership, and the Modern Nation-State: Internal and External Dimensions of the Politics of Belonging," *Journal of Interdisciplinary History* 1 (2010): 69.

28 Dumbrava, "External Citizenship"; Pogonyi, *Extra-Territorial;* Waterbury, "Bridging the Divide."

29 Pogonyi, *Extra-Territorial*, 81.

30 Rainer Bauböck, "Towards a Political Theory of Migrant Transnationalism," *International Migration Review* 3 (2003).

31 Ibid., 703.

taken by countries of origin that regulate external (or *extraterritorial*) legal categories of membership.

In his later analysis of political transnationalism, Bauböck[32] has directly touched upon these similarities when discussing "ethnizenship" and "denizenship" as two further transnational legal categories complementing "dual citizenship." The so-called denizens[33] can enjoy certain quasi-citizenship privileges based on residency in the territory of a destination country—*ius domicilii*—which mostly derive from universal, cosmopolitan, legal norms.[34] Ethnizenship, on the other hand, is somewhat the converse of denizenship, a form of "external quasi-citizenship" granted to co-ethnics living on the territory of another state.[35] Both denizenship and ethnizenship can count as first steps towards full membership; the former produces resident citizens with potentially different ethno-cultural heritage, while the latter creates extraterritorial non-resident citizens sharing the ethno-cultural heritage of the citizenship-granting nation-state, as in the case of Hungary.

In empirical terms, currently only six EU member states place any serious restrictions on the external acquisition of citizenship either at birth—through ius sanguinis—or by naturalisation. Half of the twenty-eight member countries—including Hungary—adopt an unqualified ius sanguinis, by which children of citizens automatically become citizens even if born abroad. Eighteen countries also allow for former citizens and their descendants to (re)acquire citizenship without residence requirements.[36] These legal empirical realities connect the various case-specific instances to rather similar outcomes in respect to the territoriality of contemporary citizenship. As the tragically late Kim Barry noted, "migration decouples citizenship and residence" to the effect that '[t]oday states are constituted increasingly by large numbers of resident noncitizens as well as nonresident, or external citizens—those

---

32 Rainer Bauböck, "Stakeholder Citizenship and Transnational Political Participation: A Normative Evaluation of External Voting," *Fordham Law Review* 5 (2007).

33 Tomas Hammar, *Democracy and the Nation State: Aliens, Denizens and Citizens in a World of International Migration* (Aldershot: Avebury, 1989).

34 Benhabib, *The Rights of Others*; Soysal, *Limits of Citizenship*.

35 Bauböck, "Stakeholder Citizenship."

36 Dumbrava, "External Citizenship."

who reside elsewhere.'[37] From the perspective of political transnationalism, external citizenship laws targeted at ethnic kin populations deliver similar effects regardless of whether their forbearers had once emigrated or not.

Yet they are rarely considered as remotely equivalent in respect to the ethics of membership. For example, in Benhabib's understanding, contemporary political membership requires balancing between "Westphalian" statist claims of sovereign self-determination and "post-Westphalian" adherence to universal human rights "through an *internal reconstruction* of these dual commitments."[38] It is accepted that "the boundaries of the political community, as defined by the nation-state system, are no longer adequate to regulate membership," and that through "reflexive acts of self-constitution … the boundaries of the demos can be readjusted."[39] However, as it follows from our earlier discussion, often more than two commitments need to be negotiated, such as a further one towards a "transsovereign" ethnic ideal increasingly asserted in many parts of the world.[40] But while the internally inclusive reconfiguration of the boundaries of the demos is celebrated, externally inclusive readjustments evoke scepticism. This dynamic is often shaped by political ideological differences across a left-right divide, as Joppke[41] explained in respect to the tension between de- and re-ethnicizing citizenship policies. However, both processes are arguably driven by similar "jurisgenerative politics," as will be discussed in respect to Hungary's extraterritorial citizenship law.

The Jurisgenerative Politics of Extraterritorial Citizenship in Hungary

In one of her casestudies examining democratic iterative processes in contexts where immigration had created the need to reconsider

---

37 Kim Barry, "Home and Away: The Construction of Citizenship in an Emigration Context," *New York University Law Review* 1 (2006): 17.

38 Benhabib, *The Rights of Others,* 2 (emphasis in the original).

39 Ibid., 1, 48.

40 Csergő and Goldgeier, "Nationalist Strategies."

41 Joppke, "Citizenship Between."

the rights of internal "others," Benhabib revisits Germany's decade-long struggle during the 1990s to de-ethnicize and redefine its *demos* through reforming the citizenship law.[42] The process involving "intense and soul-searching public debate" eventually led to radical transformations of German public consciousness in the 1990s.[43] Such democratic iterations, for Benhabib, necessarily involve a dimension of "jurisgenerative politics" reliant on "contestation around rights and legal institutions," and through which "others become hermeneutical partners with us by reappropriating and reinterpreting our institutions and cultural traditions."[44]

In a sense, similar processes have characterized the shaping of Hungary's extraterritorial citizenship, in a context where not immigration but the continued symbolic significance of the movement of borders across people had reinforced the need to consider the rights of external others. Arguably, "Hungarians living outside the borders"—especially those living on territories that used to be part of the Hungarian Kingdom—towards whom Hungary has declared a constitutional responsibility early on in its democratization process, as noted in the introduction, have served the double role of being simultaneously members of the nation's "ethical self" and representing its "sociological others" needing to become "hermeneutical partners" in a reappropriation and reinterpretation of the institutional and cultural vestiges of the socialist years. We can think here of the well-documented spread of a civic, political nation-state centered definition of nationhood during socialism, to which Guy Lázár's sociological studies from the 1970s–80s bear testimony.[45] Without attempting to review the entire iterative process that resulted in the Simplified Naturalization Act of 2010, I will highlight its fundamental structure.[46] As a whole, we can view it as

42 Benhabib, *The Rights of Others.*

43 Ibid., 208.

44 Ibid., 169.

45 Guy Lázár, "Kik tartoznak a nemzethez? Fiatalok a magyarság ismérveiről és a határokon túli magyarokról," *Magyar Kisebbség* 3–4/69–70 (2013). For an English summary of some of these findings, see Miklos Szabolcsi, "Ethnocentrism in Education: a Comparative Analysis of Problems in Eastern and Western Europe," *Prospects - Quarterly Review of Education* 2 (1989).

46 A detailed empirical analysis has already been undertaken in Waterbury, *Between State and Nation.*

Hungary's own soul-searching struggle to redefine its demos in a move towards a re-ethnicization rather than de-ethnicization.

FROM "OTHERS" TO ETHNIZENS TO CITIZENS

The alternating democratic governments have interpreted and held to the post-1989 constitutional responsibility for the fate of trans-border Hungarian communities in different ways, and during the prolonged process of European integration so-called "Hungarian–Hungarian relations" have been somewhat uneven, nationhood often becoming the terrain of "political competition."[47]

Proposals for an extraterritorial citizenship first surfaced in the early second half of the 1990s, being formulated by the World Federation of Hungarians (MVSZ), an originally irredentist global diaspora organization established in 1938 and reinstated in 1992 to "represent the entire Hungarian nation."[48] In 1998 the MVSZ publicly presented external citizenship as one of its main political goals,[49] the issue forcing political parties to express their stance right at the end of an electoral campaign following which the center-right Fidesz would form government.[50] As often mentioned by commentators, the party that will have become responsible for almost unilaterally implementing the cur-

[47] Zsuzsa Csergő and James M. Goldgeier, "Kin-State Activism in Hungary Romania, and Russia: The Politics of Ethnic Demography," in *Divided Nations and European Integration*, eds. Mabry et al. (Philadelphia: University of Pennsylvania Press, 2013), Nándor Bárdi, "Different Images of the Future of the Hungarian Communities in Neighbouring Countries, 1989–2012," *European Review* 4 (2013), Waterbury, *Between State and Nation.*

[48] See the available information on the Federation's website: www.mvsz.hu. It should be mentioned, however, that the idea of dual citizenship as a solution to the problems faced by trans-border Hungarians was put forward as early as 1992 by prominent liberal intellectuals such as György Konrád and László Végel (See György Szerbhorváth, "A mi utcánk," *Élet és Irodalom*, November 19, 2004, accessed May 20, 2019, https://kisebbsegkutato.tk.mta.hu/kettosallampolgarsag/publicisztika/pub_069.html, Sándor Balogh, Zsolt Németh and Károly Ravasz, "A kettős állampolgárságról: Kerekasztal-beszélgetés," *Vasárnapi Újság*, April 19, 1998, accessed May 20, 2019, http://www.gecse.eu/17.html).

[49] Waterbury, *Between State and Nation.*

[50] Balogh et al., "A kettős állampolgárságról."

rent preferential naturalization law had been rather split on the issue at that time. Nevertheless, as Benhabib reminds us in respect to jurisgenerative politics in general, "[p]olitical agents, caught in such public battles, very often enter the fray with a certain understanding of who they are and what they stand for; but the process itself frequently alters these self-understandings."[51]

Following its 1998 election victory Fidesz set out to map other avenues for resolving the so-called "Schengen problem" caused by Hungary's beginning of EU "accession talks" earlier than its neighbors. After lively debates, the government finally adopted in 2001 the so-called "Status Law" granting certain ethnizen rights to Hungarians living in neighboring countries.[52] A result of several compromises, the final version of the proposal represented little more than a "benefit law."[53]

It was during this period, between the first Fidesz government's accession to power and somewhat unexpected defeat in the 2002 general elections, that the jurisgenerative parameters of Hungarian identity politics were laid out. As pointed out by Kántor, designing a nation policy implied "the need to define, directly or indirectly, *who is Hungarian*,"[54] and this question would come to dominate all aspects of Hungarian domestic politics for the coming decade.

The topic of extraterritorial citizenship remained more or less tacitly on the agenda of right-wing groups dissatisfied with the compromises of the Status Law, and it was publicly raised again during summer 2003, when the MVSZ announced that it would begin collecting signatures for a petition proposing a referendum on the issue.

---

51 Benhabib, *The Rights of Others,* 209.

52 Officially "Act LXII of 2001 on Hungarians Living in Neighbouring Countries," adopted by Parliament on June 19, 2001. For a thorough analysis of the debates surrounding it, see Zoltán Kántor et al., eds. *The Hungarian Status Law: Nation Building and/or Minority Protection* (Sapporo: Hokkaido University, Slavic Research Center, 2004).

53 Osamu Ieda, "Post-communist Nation Building and the Status Law Syndrome in Hungary," in Kántor et al., *The Hungarian,* 11. Compromise had to be reached on three levels: first, domestically with the socialist and liberal opposition parties; second, at the intergovernmental level with neighboring countries whose legal citizens the proposal was aimed at; and thirdly, on the European level, with the Venice Commission being the major body involved.

54 Kántor, "Status Law," 105 (italics in the original).

While the proposition was received again with certain skepticism, from the safety of serving in opposition Fidesz eventually joined in on the cause. After the successful petition campaign a referendum was scheduled for December 2004, opening up the scene for a short political campaign that would clearly set the political right against the socialist-liberal ruling coalition which chose to instigate sentiments of welfare chauvinism to counter the symbolic nationalism of the conservatives.[55]

The process rekindled the previous debate, during which answers to the question of "who is Hungarian" had already gained contour along party fault-lines. This is well reflected in the words of George Schöpflin, a preeminent member of Fidesz's intellectual vanguard, in connection to the debates around the Status Law:

> in trying to find an acceptable political-cultural solution for the problem of the minority Hungarians, Budapest is at the same time struggling against one of the strongest of currents in Europe—the denial of the validity and legitimacy of ethnicity on the part of the hegemonic elites, not to mention their universalist allies in Hungary itself.[56]

The allegation of "universalism" echoes earlier accusations brought against left-wing and liberal political parties and individuals, of being "unnational," "antinational," or "cosmopolitan"—"the latter often a catchword for inauthentically Hungarian."[57] Falling short of being "authentically Hungarian" on political grounds would, of course, have no serious extra-rhetorical consequences, unless maybe the entire constitutional order is reconstructed on ethnocultural foundations, as it arguably happened in 2011–2012.

Eventually, the 2004 referendum was unsuccessful due to low turnout, even though the opposition had succeeded in tying the question on dual citizenship to a more mundane one about hospital privatization. The outcome induced a deep schism between trans-border Hungarians and the "mother-country" as well as further polarizing the political arena,

---

55 Kovács, "The Politics of Dual Citizenship."

56 György Schöpflin, "Citizenship and Ethnicity: The Hungarian Status Law," in Kántor et al., *The Hungarian*, 103.

57 Waterbury, *Between State and Nation,* 62.

and in fact the entire nation, along political-ideological divisions. What could be more telling in respect to both than the reaction of Transylvanian (Romanian) reverend Csaba Böjte to the outcome: "I think we all felt, even if we did not want to take notice of it, that our great family, nation is sick. The fifth of December has unraveled the healthy and the sick parts."[58] This assessment became officially shared by Fidesz, whose ensuing political strategy—not to say its entire political identity—was recast in opposition to its ideological enemy, the "antinational," "universalist," "sick" part of the Hungarian national and political community. Parallels between the politics of Fidesz and Schmittian conceptions of the political have already been explored in some depth in other studies.[59] It could also be argued that constructions of enmity along similar antagonisms are deeply rooted in the cultural history of Hungarian popular and populist movements, or that anti-populist movements and parties engage in such politics at least to a similar extent.[60] Yet, it is worth noting that it was the deliberative environment of the dual citizenship debates of the early 2000s which provided an arena for Fidesz to develop the maneuvers of rhetorical partisanship that would eventually propel it to victory in the 2010 "polling booth revolution."[61]

The political consequence of the failed referendum was, therefore, to tie the parties that had taken opposing stances on the question to their positions, dual citizenship becoming an election promise of the center-right opposition.[62] The promise was fulfilled following the 2010 elections, when, as result of a protracted democratic leadership crisis,

---

58 Csaba Böjte, "Jaj a népszavazás győzteseinek!," *Krónika*, December 10, 2004, accessed May 20, 2019, https://kisebbsegkutato.tk.mta.hu/kettosallampolgarsag/publicisztika/pub_221.html.

59 E.g. Márton Szabó, "Ellenfél és ellenség a politikában," *Politikatudományi Szemle*, 1 (2007).

60 Furedi, *Populism*, 128.

61 The post-election "Proclamation of National Cooperation" that was required to be displayed in most public buildings stated: "In spring 2010, the Hungarian nation gathered its strength once again, and brought about a successful revolution in the polling booth. Parliament declares that it recognizes and will respect this constitutional revolution," see *The Economist*, "Read the Large Print," *The Economist*, July 4, 2010, accessed May 20, 2019, http://www.economist.com/blogs/easternapproaches/2010/07/hungary.

62 Meanwhile, through *Act XLVI of 2005*, the socialist-liberal government eased access to citizenship for ethnic Hungarian migrants wishing to settle,

the center-right Fidesz–Christian Democratic People's Party alliance secured a two-third supermajority in the parliament. On May 26, two weeks after the official announcement of election results and three days prior to the new Prime Minister's oath of office, the amendment to the citizenship act was passed without any further consultations, although it should be noted that parliamentarians of all parties voted overwhelmingly in favor, and the new Socialist Party leadership later also officially distanced itself from the party's previous stance.[63]

The Simplified Naturalization Act has brought closure to the deeply divisive 2004 referendum, and, while it is unlikely to have also settled, once and for all, the definition of national identity or even the parameters of kin-state activism, it has certainly concluded Hungary's jurisgenerative moment. Its symbolic consummation was the ceremonial conferral in the Dome Hall of the Parliament of the half millionth new citizenship to Reverend Csaba Böjte on December 5, 2013—a date intended to redress "the shame caused by the national betrayal" of the failed referendum of nine years before.[64]

EXTERNAL CITIZENS AND POST-HOC DEMOCRATIC LEGITIMATION

Several factors have helped to solidify the democratic legitimacy of the law in the years following its adoption. First, from the legislators' perspective, the modified citizenship act is an unquestionable success. By May 2016 almost 801,000 people had applied for simplified naturalization, of which 762,000 already received citizenship,[65] and

eliminating the one-year residence requirement and waiving citizenship tests for certain applicants. See Kántor and Majtényi, *A "kettős állampolgárság."*

63 "Act XLIV of 2010, on the modification of Act LV of 1993 regarding Hungarian citizenship." The motion was passed with 344 supporting votes, three votes against, and 5 abstentions. On the process and timetable of government formation, see the Parliament's website: http://www.parlament.hu/fotitkar/alakulo/ciklusvalt.htm.

64 MTI, "Letette az állampolgársági esküt a félmilliomodik külhoni magyar," *MTI hírarchívum 1988–2015*, December 5, 2013, accessed May 20, 2019, http://archiv1988tol.mti.hu/Pages/HirSearch.aspx?Pmd=1.

65 Zoltán Kántor, "Két állampolgárság—két szavazat—két politikai közösség," Paper presented at the annual meeting of the Hungarian Society for Political Science, Esztergom, June 16, 2016.

an earlier aim of the government to confer one million citizenships based on the simplified naturalization procedure by 2018[66] was also reached on December 16, 2017.[67] Over 97 percent of all applicants are citizens of Romania, Serbia and Ukraine, neighboring countries with high number of Hungarian ethnic minority populations.[68] If we examine these applications alongside regional demographic, economic and political contextual factors, we find that 23 percent of those who would presumably satisfy the strictest elements of the eligibility criteria—based on self-declared knowledge of the Hungarian language—had already applied for preferential naturalization during the first three years (Table 5.1). This average is heavily reduced by the low application rate of Slovakian Hungarians—the second largest minority Hungarian group—who not only have less practical incentives to take up Hungarian citizenship, but also face the threat of losing their Slovak one, since Slovakia has imposed restrictions on dual citizenship in reaction to the Hungarian law.[69] In contrast, the greatest share of applicants is among Hungarians in Ukraine, where dual citizenship is also unrecognized, but its policing—at least in respect to Hungarians—is laxer. Pragmatic reasons could also be mentioned, and Table 5.1 highlights some macroeconomic and geopolitical differences that may add practical value to Hungarian citizenship should one choose to migrate, but we should be wary of drawing too strict causal connections between economic incentives and naturalization motivations. As

66 MTI, "Wetzel: 2018-ra egymillióan szerezhetnek magyar állampolgárságot," *MTI hírarchívum 1988–2015*, August 26, 2014, accessed May 20, 2019, http://archiv1988tol.mti.hu/Pages/HirSearch.aspx?Pmd=1.

67 MTI, "Nemzeti egység alakult ki a kettős állampolgárság kérdésében," *Origo.hu*, December 17, 2017, accessed May 20, 2019, http://www.origo.hu/itthon/20171217-nemzeti-minimum-alakult-ki-a-kettos-allampolgarsag-kerdeseben.html.

68 Kántor, *Két állampolgárság.*

69 Slovakia was the only country to take an adversarial stance and counter-actions (See Rainer Bauböck, ed. *Dual Citizenship for Transborder Minorities? How to Respond to the Hungarian-Slovak Tit-for-tat,* EUI Working Paper RSCAS 2010/75 (Florence: Robert Schuman Center for Advanced Studies, European University Institute, 2010), http://hdl.handle.net/1814/14625, Ágnes Töttős, "The Effects of an EU Member-State's Modified Citizenship Law: The Hungarian Example, With a Particular Focus on the Aspects of Free Movement," *Central and Eastern European Migration Review* 1 (2017)).

Table 5.1: Hungarians in neighboring countries and early simplified naturalisations (SN)

Country	Hungarian population ([E,L])	SN applications, by Citizenship (Sept. 2013)		GDP in 2011		EU	Dual citizen-ship allowed
		No.	As row % of ([L])	Per capita Intl$	As % of EU27 average		
Hungary	9,937,628a	–	–	22,737	67.9	Yes (2004)	Yes
Romania	1,227,623E 1,259,914L	330,970	26.3	17,363	51.9	Yes (2007)	Yes
Slovakia	458,467E 508,714L	1,707	0.3	25,560	76.4	Yes (2004)	No
Serbia	253,899E 243,146L	92,188	37.9	12,572	37.6	No	Yes
Ukraine	156,600 141,000c	64,030	45.4	8,295	24.8	No	No
Croatia	14,048E 10,231L	1,422	13.9	20,571	61.5	Yes (2013)	Yes

Sources:

Hungary: Census 2011 (http://www.ksh.hu/nepszamlalas/); Romania: Census 2011 (http://www.recensamantromania.ro/rezultate-2/); Slovakia: Census 2011 (http://slovak.statistics.sk/, direct link: http://ow.ly/LoOmm); Serbia: Vladimir Đurić et al., Etnokonfesionalni i Jezički Mozaik Srbije *(Belgrade: National Institute of Statistics, 2014); Ukraine: Census 2001 (http://2001.ukrcensus.gov.ua/eng/results/general/nationality/) and Balázs Kapitány, "Kárpát-medencei népszámlálási körkép,"* Demográfia 1 *(2013); Croatia: Census 2011 (http://www.dzs.hr/default_e.htm). On 'simplified naturalisations': http://allampolgarsag.gov.hu/*

Notes:

a: Total population, of which 1,623,599 declared themselves as members of ethno-national minority groups;

b: Slovakia amended its nationality law to limit dual citizenship as a response to Hungary's new citizenship legislation;

c: The planned 2010 Census has been postponed until 2020. Local researchers estimate the current Hungarian population of the Zakarpatska county to be at around 141,000;

E: "ethnicity";

L: mother-tongue or main language.

qualitative studies have shown, motivations are rarely monolithic, but almost always involve familial, sentimental, ethical and various prerogative reasons besides pragmatic ones.[70]

The public acceptance of the law has also consolidated. Domestic support for dual citizenship had already reached 65 percent by 2009,[71] and polls in 2012 have shown comparable levels of acceptance, despite significant differences based on party preferences.[72] Surveys of Hungarians in Romania have also registered a clear increase in 2013 compared to the previous year in both the level of approval of the law and intentions to apply.[73] At a press conference held in December 2017 in honor of the one-millionth simplified naturalization, Fidesz floor leader Gergely Gulyás declared that there is now almost complete "national unity" in support of external citizenship.[74]

New-old points of criticism emerged on four fronts. First, in respect to the law's ethno-cultural character, but in particular its internally exclusive nature when considered together with other changes to the naturalization law.[75] Second, its practical outcomes were seen by some as potentially undermining the political strength of transborder Hungarian communities.[76] Thirdly, the harshest criticisms concerned the extension of voting rights, which had not initially figured in the extraterritorial citizenship package.[77] All these points of contention relate, in one form or another, to the emergence of an ethno-cultural extraterritorial political community and the various interpretations given to such an entity. In the next sections I turn to the ethno-cultural and the political dimensions of extraterritoriality. What will become

---

70 Attila Z. Papp, "Kisebbségi identitáskonstrukciók a kettős magyar állampolgárság által," *Regio* 1 (2014), Pogonyi, *Extra-Territorial.*

71 Waterbury, *Between State and Nation,* 141.

72 Tamás Kiss and Gergő Barna, *Erdélyi magyarok a magyarországi és a romániai politikai térben* (Cluj-Napoca: Institutul Pentru Studierea Problemelor Minorităţilor Naţionale, 2013), 64.

73 Kiss and Barna, *Erdélyi magyarok.*

74 MTI, "Nemzeti egység."

75 Tóth, *UPDATE.*

76 Salat, "A könnyített honosítás", Levente Salat, "A politikai közösség kérdése a többség-kisebbség viszonyának a nézőpontjából," *Magyar Kisebbség* 3–4/61–62 (2011).

77 Nagy, "Nationality."

obvious is that the shaping of a new ideal of political community is an ongoing process which relies on broader legal transformations that complement the new Simplified Naturalization procedures. If the latter is the result of the democratic iterations discussed above, the new meaning of the political community is being forged through distinctively illiberal means.

The Ethno-cultural Contours of Extraterritorial Citizenship

The legislators' careful attempt to balance ethnic and civic principles in such a way that the law would be acceptable in the context of international legal norms did manage to create certain confusion among critics. On the one hand, some critics of the legislation highlighted the dangers behind the underlying non-ethnic requirements. Nagy, for instance, took exception at the fact that while "at the level of rhetoric, the leading slogan is national reunification across borders,"[78] the legislation carries "no ethnic preference in words, nor in the formal rules: language knowledge and imperial descent—these are the requirements."[79]

This assessment rekindled older fears about the potential democratic unbalancing consequences of extraterritorial citizenship. Kovács had earlier assessed that should the current conditions of the citizenship law materialize, then up to 5 million ethnic Hungarians from around the world could become citizens, slightly more than half the size of Hungary's resident population.[80] Similarly, Nagy proclaims that "if the seven million non-Hungarians [who had been citizens until] 1920 have at least fourteen million descendants today, then more people without any link to Hungarian ethnicity or culture are entitled to preferential naturalization than the whole present population (9.7 million) of Hungary."[81] Some countries already show such or similar characteristics, for example Ireland, with its actual external citizen population amounting to more than 80 per cent of the resident citi-

[78] Ibid., 60.
[79] Ibid., 39.
[80] Kovács, "The Politics of Dual Citizenship," 432.
[81] Nagy, "Nationality," 38–39.

zens, and a potential external citizenry at one point ten times greater than the residents.[82] Conversely, in countries like Moldova or Bosnia a majority of resident citizens are also actual or potential external citizens of neighboring states.[83]

Other critics were more circumspect of the official discursive attempts to mask the ethno-national character of the law. As Majtényi pointed out, while the terms set out in the text are not divorced from the civic conception of the nation, an ethno-cultural interpretation is projected on it by secondary guidance regarding its implementation.[84] Thus, underneath the non-ethnic appearances—which make it compatible with democratic civic norms—lies in fact an ethno-cultural preference that becomes obvious in the procedural guidance for caseworkers.

In realistic terms, the latter assessment is the better substantiated one. At the same time, this does not take away from the imperial undertone; would it have been possible from an international legal standpoint to extend citizenship collectively, thus circumventing the terms of the historical peace treaties—in other words, to unilaterally extend the ius sanguinis principle to those who had been citizens before 1920 and their descendants—the government may well have opted for it. The individual choice behind the current naturalization process and the ritual aspects attached to it are, however, significant both legally and sociologically. They are, I would argue, what first transforms the *cultural* nation into a *political* one in an illiberal sense, as I discuss later.

The most contentious aspects of the ethno-cultural characteristics of the citizenship law, however, become visible when considering other related legislation. In this respect Tóth has noted that besides the preferences granted to co-ethnics, "[t]he conditions for non-preferential

---

82 Willem Maas, "Extending Politics: Enfranchising Non-Resident European Citizens," paper presented at the 40th Annual Convention of the International Studies Association, Washington, DC, February 17, 1999, accessed May 20, 2019, http://www.yorku.ca/maas/Maas1999.pdf.

83 Szabolcs Pogonyi, Mária M. Kovács and Zsolt Körtvélyesi, *The Politics of External Kin-State Citizenship in East Central Europe* (EUI Working Paper RSCAS 2010/06. Florence: Robert Schuman Center for Advanced Studies, European University Institute, 2010), accessed May 20, 2019, http://hdl.handle.net/1814/19576.

84 Majtényi, "Etnikai származás."

naturalization contain a more restrictive public order requirement."[85] It is therefore argued that the external inclusivity of Simplified Naturalization has not been balanced out by similar internally inclusive measures, as is often the case when re-ethnicizing legislation is adopted.[86] For the emerging vision of "political community" this also means that it becomes further detached from territorial anchors and liberal–republican principles of democracy.

This critique is further enhanced when considering the changes to the citizenship legislation as part of the broader constitutional shift. On the highly symbolic date marking the first anniversary of the establishment of the 2010 Fidesz-Christian Democratic government, the ruling parties, backed with a parliamentary supermajority, signed into law the new Fundamental Law to replace the country's previous constitution[87]. As Pogonyi emphasizes, the new Fundamental Law's preamble "opens up the possibility of the interpretation that the constitution expresses the will and interest of ethnic Hungarians, whereas the minorities living in the country are only subjects of the Fundamental Law."[88] Furthermore, "the inclusion of the principle of ius sanguinis in the supreme law without mentioning other modes of acquisition has a clear symbolic message, which reinforces that Hungary is an ethnic nation."[89] From a liberal–republican viewpoint, the religious and ethnic preferentialism of the new constitution is clearly antiquated and anti-democratic. In an early assessment, the Venice Commission found that it failed to represent "the democratic will-formation of the country's citizens as a whole" and not only that "of the dominant ethnic group."[90]

From an illiberal point of view, however, it is the notion of "democratic will" itself which requires reinterpretation. In Frank Furedi's assessment, the "Fundamental Law does affirm values that are traditional and conservative. It is also explicitly illiberal. However, … it is not anti-democratic."[91] For Furedi, its democratic legitimacy emanates

---

85 Tóth, *UPDATE,* 1.
86 Joppke, "Citizenship."
87 Pogonyi, *Extra-Territorial,* 91.
88 Ibid., 92.
89 Ibid., 92.
90 Ibid., 93.
91 Furedi, *Populism*, 5.

from the "overwhelming democratic mandate" of the government that enacted it and the fact that it did not explicitly undermine the structure of government, the separation of powers or the protection of fundamental rights. While the latter may be true, just as the ethno-cultural dimensions of the Simplified Naturalization law only become explicit through the secondary procedural guidance concerning its implementation, the democracy-undermining consequences of the new illiberal constitutionalism may only materialize in conjunction with a variety of subsequent measures and practices[92]. But what is more important from the perspective of our current analysis, I would argue, is not the way in which legally sophisticated illiberals navigate the international liberal-democratic legal system,[93] but that the various illiberal measures together act to reconstitute the meaning of political community and the demos from which democratic legitimacy then derives. In this respect, of more import than the "overwhelming democratic mandate" that the Fidesz-Christian Democratic government had secured from domestic voters, is the ethical-symbolic mandate provided by the new peoples of the Fundamental Law, which includes the newly naturalized external citizens. This is undoubtedly a circular vision of normative authority, but one that attempts to solve the perennial "issue of normative foundation"[94] not through the linear logic on which the Western legal tradition is based, but through a symbolic logic that can "offer a meaningful sense of continuity to people's quest for identity"[95] across temporal and territorial limits.

The Political Dimensions of Extraterritorial Citizenship

While it may appear from the previous discussion that it is simply a case expanding the political community along ethno-cultural lines while simultaneously limiting its civic boundaries, two observations

---

[92] Pap, *Democratic Decline.*

[93] Gábor Halmai, "Legally Sophisticated Authoritarians: the Hungarian Lex CEU," *VerfBlog*, March 31, 2017, accessed May 20, 2019, http://verfassungsblog.de/legally-sophisticated-authoritarians-the-hungarian-lex-ceu.

[94] Furedi, *Populism*, 41.

[95] Ibid., 39.

could be made to further refine this perspective. On the one hand, as Salat[96] has argued, the Simplified Naturalization law has in effect passed on the responsibility for the future of Hungarian minorities onto them, and thus their position in respect to *any* political community—within the "triadic nexus" in which they exist[97]—will by and large depend on the degree to which they take advantage of the opportunities granted by the legislation. Based on early naturalization statistics and survey results showing a determined political reorientation among Romanian Hungarians towards Hungary,[98] he deems that the law has had the "gruesomely perverse" effect of undermining the development of sub-state Hungarian political communities in the neighboring countries.[99] Similar arguments regarding the possible effects of extraterritorial citizenship had already been made in theoretical terms,[100] and they are unquestionably valid from an institutional perspective, even if sociological differences between domestic-majority Hungarians and external-minority Hungarians may hinder the extent to which external citizens can fully "reorient" towards Hungary.[101] The role of individual choice in determining the substantive content of political community (a point stressed by Papp[102]) is also important in this respect. As Salat pointed out, for many the law may "carry the message that to be a good Hungarian one must exercise the right to reacquire Hungarian citizenship."[103] Those who do not exercise this right, on the other hand, will risk being excluded from the burgeoning political community, one which is partially open on ethno-cultural grounds, but which requires that members actively opt in as a fundamental political gesture.

---

96 Salat, "A könnyített honosítás."

97 Rogers Brubaker, *Nationalism Reframed: Nationhood and the National Question in the New Europe* (Cambridge: Cambridge University Press, 1996), Ch. 3.

98 Kiss and Barna, *Erdélyi magyarok.*

99 Salat, "A politikai közösség."

100 Rainer Bauböck, "The Trade-Off between Transnational Citizenship and Political Autonomy," in *Dual Citizenship in Global Perspective*, ed. Thomas Faist and Peter Kivisto (New York: Palgrave Macmillan, 2007).

101 Papp, "Kisebbségi identitáskonstrukciók."

102 Ibid.

103 Salat, "A könnyített honosítás," 189.

While the internally exclusive nature of the broader body of citizenship legislation may be said to create internal divisions between ethnic Hungarians and ethnic others, the practical effects of Simplified Naturalization can therefore also create external divisions. It is unlikely that all who consider themselves members of the ethnic and cultural nation will become citizens, and even though the naturalization target that the government had set itself has been achieved, it still represents less than half of those who may be eligible for naturalization (cf. Table 5.1). Thus, the previously existing discrepancy between the cultural and the political nation remains, while the future is now arguably less certain for those only belonging to the former.

A second dimension which refines the idea that the political community has been simply expanded along ethno-cultural lines emerges in respect to the extension of political rights to extraterritorial citizens. Extraterritorial enfranchisement had initially been explicitly rejected by Fidesz, and has remained for long one of the least popular benefits even among Fidesz supporters.[104] It had even been proposed that one former Fidesz minister's ruminations during the 2006 electoral campaign that the party could stay in power for twenty years should non-residential citizenship be granted to co-ethnics had cost them that election.[105]

Extraterritorial political rights remain controversial even from a restorative justice perspective, which is otherwise more accommodating of citizenship re-acquisition based on previously severed links with the granting state.[106] For Nagy the extension of voting rights has made it "obvious that the idea of a self-governing political community is no longer applicable to Hungary."[107] This assessment is based, on the one hand, on the assumption that external voters can significantly influence the outcome of democratic elections, which will then not affect them in their everyday lives but only those who live on the territory of the state (i.e. neither will they be subjects to domestic laws, nor will their material interests be affected). On the other hand, external ethnic citizens are assumed to have a more favorable attitude to the

[104] Kiss and Barna, *Erdélyi magyarok.*
[105] Pogonyi, *Extra-Territorial,* 94.
[106] Dumbrava, "External Citizenship."
[107] Nagy, "Nationality," 60.

ruling Fidesz-Christian Democrat coalition parties, due both to ideological and pragmatic reasons.

Empirical data on the political behavior of external citizens substantiates both assumptions. If we examine the outcome of the 2014 general elections, we find that out of approximately 350,000 external citizens of voting age with the right to vote 195,338 had registered on the voters' list, and 158,654 cast their votes; the final number of valid votes amounted to 128,429, with a staggering 95.5 percent cast in support of the incumbent Fidesz-KDNP coalition.[108] Although external voters could only vote for party lists, it has been shown that this vote had secured one extra seat in the 2014 Parliament for Fidesz, pushing it through the threshold required for a new absolute majority.[109] In the party's assessment, the 2014 general elections provided "the first opportunity in a century for the Hungarians living in the Carpathian Basin and elsewhere in the world to decide jointly on what kind of Parliament should be elected," and in this sense, the elections "were the joint celebration of Hungariandom."[110]

In Nagy's interpretation, the 2014 election results confirmed that external citizens have "become loyal voters of the power that acts to extend their opportunities."[111] It would be unseemly, however, to condemn any chunk of the electorate for choosing whom they feel best represents their interests—and again, polls among Hungarians in Romania have confirmed that only 6.8 percent of the respondents felt that Fidesz did not properly represent their interests, compared to over 30 percent for any other political party, including the more radical right.[112] The true meaning of these interests and their representation however, could hardly be comprehended from a liberal–republican perspective.

More important are the additional, internally limiting changes to the electoral legislations. As critics have noted, practicing polit-

108 Eszter Herner-Kovács, Gergely Illyés and Krisztián Rákóczi, "Külhoni szavazatok a 2014-es magyar országgyűlési választásokon," *Kisebbségkutatás* 2 (2014).

109 Pogonyi, *Extra-Territorial,* 105.

110 MTI, "Nemzeti egység."

111 Nagy, "Nationality", 60.

112 Kiss and Barna, *Erdélyi magyarok*, 26.

ical rights has effectively become more favorable to external citizens compared to domestic citizens who are temporarily abroad. The latter category covers all Hungarian migrants regardless of the time they have lived abroad as long as they retain a Hungarian permanent address, and who must vote in person at the diplomatic missions in their respective countries of residence, while external citizens have the option of postal voting.[113]

Although these limitations on postal voting were initially the outcome of pressure set by civil society actors to ensure electoral transparency,[114] in practical terms they do raise fears that the elected Parliament could become too closely shaped according to a party-political vision. Between 2011 and 2016 the number of Hungarian citizens residing long-term in one of the three major EU destination countries alone has increased by almost 207,000[115] and this rising outmigration is often perceived as an "exit" in Hirschmanian sense, in which economic reasons couple with disapproval of the dominant direction in Hungarian politics.[116] Thus, if this holds true, and the electoral system practically creates differential access to the exercise of political rights to groups of citizens with opposing ideological and party-political orientations, the danger is that a certain vision of politics could come to define the "political" nature of the "cultural nation."

This connects us back to the earlier discussion of the Schmittian character of Hungarian politics, and the political right's rhetorical contradistinction between the "national"—"healthy"—and the "antinational"—"sick"—segments of the nation. On the question of what a political community shaped by such highly polarized friend–

113 András Bozóki, *Access to Electoral Rights: Hungary*, EUI Working Paper RSCAS 2013/19. Florence: Robert Schuman Center for Advanced Studies, European University Institute, 2013, accessed May 20, 2019, http://hdl.handle.net/1814/29814, Nagy, "Nationality", Pogonyi, *Extra-Territorial.*

114 Bozóki, *Access,* 7.

115 Chris Moreh, "Az Egyesült Királyságba irányuló magyarországi elvándorlás a magyar és a brit migrációs rendszerek átalakulásának tükrében," *Ügyészségi Szemle* 3 (2017), 92.

116 Albert O. Hirschman, *Exit, Voice, and Loyalty: Responses to Decline in Firms, Organizations, and States* (Cambridge, MA: Harvard University Press, 1970).

enemy distinctions may look like, I believe we can accept Szabó's opinion that such political tactic:

> defines the political community as a *moral* community, that is to say, as such a democratic community, whose members are bound together by shared ethical principles, or at least that the person or organization that fails to obey these norms excludes herself from the political community.[117]

In this interpretation, the emerging 'illiberal democratic' political community is defined to a lesser extent by ethno-cultural criteria, and more by moral and ideological principles. At its extreme, if such a political community could ever materialize, it would be an extraterritorial ethical community based on conservative Christian values, or ad absurdum a party-political community that manages to raise barriers to the democratic inclusion of those who have self-excluded through non-adherence to the community's ethics.

In order to grasp the nature of the emerging extraterritorial political community we must understand it through an illiberal lens and in the spirit of the broader constitutional changes. As proposed earlier, these changes together effected a rewriting of the dominant national narrative; not the inclusion of external citizens *within* or in relation to a territorially defined political community, but rather the reconstitution of the political community itself *through* extraterritorial citizenship. Thus, when Act CCIII of 2011 on the Elections of Members of Parliament secures voting rights to external citizens in stating "that Hungarian citizens living beyond the borders of Hungary shall be a part of the political community," it is understandable that "readers versed in political philosophy," like Nagy,[118] would feel puzzled.

The "political community" invoked, however, is not the one that Nagy would take for granted, but one emanating from the new moral and constitutional order. For this reason, Nagy's ensuing question that "If the Hungarians living beyond the borders are 'part of the political community,' then what makes it political?" is both essential and

[117] Szabó, "Ellenfél és ellenség," 16 (emphasis in the original).
[118] Nagy, "Nationality," 37.

unanswerable on a liberal–republican platform. It is essential, because inquiring about political community means inquiring about the *political* nature of a community rather than merely about what shapes collectives into communities subjected to or engaged in political activity.[119] What makes it political from an illiberal viewpoint, is an assumed common ethical vision of the future, and a sense of historical duty to work together towards achieving an essentially immaterial goal—in other words, the same ethical-symbolic arch connecting past, present and future generations that appears in the National Avowal of the new Fundamental Law.[120] Such an understanding of political duty is hard to interpret from a liberal–republican perspective because it replicates very closely the constitutive ideals of modern conservatism, which sprang precisely from the rejection of the republican contractarianism of the French revolution.[121] For an illiberal conservative, "the Burkean celebration of tradition regards [the values of the past] as providing the moral foundation for political order."[122]

Similarly, the electoral weight of external citizens discussed earlier is also justified through certain communitarian standards based on the "kinship principle" famously formulated by Michael Walzer. This principle sees states more "like families rather than clubs, for it is a feature of families that their members are morally connected to people they have not chosen, who live outside the household."[123] In this sense, the Hungarian political family is seen as one in which some family mem-

---

[119] Cf. Adrian Little, *The Politics of Community: Theory and Practice* (Edinburgh: Edinburgh University Press, 2002).

[120] Balázs Majtényi, "The Nation's Will as Trump in the Hungarian Fundamental Law," in *European Yearbook on Human Rights 2015*, ed. Benedek et al. (Vienna: Neuer Wissenschaftlicher Verlag, 2015), 251.

[121] Most notably, in a famous passage in Edmund Burke, *Reflections on the French Revolution & Other Essays* (London: J. M. Dent & Son, 1910), 93. I also surmise that the substitution of the term "covenant"/"contract" with that of "alliance" in the Fourth Amendment to the Fundamental Law was done in a presumably unconscious drive to realign it with a Burkean meaning (of contract as partnership), rather than to intentionally provide it with a religious-transcendent analogy (but cf. Majtényi's analysis in this volume).

[122] Furedi, *Populism*, 117.

[123] Michael Walzer, *Spheres of Justice: A Defence of Pluralism and Equality* (New York: Basic Books, 1983), 41.

bers living outside the household are given a strong say in how the household should be organized.

The question, then, is why a polity within the core institutional frameworks of the current international legal order should apply such an ideologically specific definition of itself. It is unquestionably a definition that "invokes the image of a country/people/nation, which is based on tribal, blood-based and historical fantasies,"[124] and illiberals may not even dispute this. Yet, they may argue that its anachronism consists not so much in being outdated, but instead, in being *ahead* of its time. The broader concerns raised by the processes analyzed in this essay, therefore, are to do not with Hungary's domestic political developments, but with changes in the international political system in which it is embedded.

Conclusions: a Crisis of Territoriality or a Crisis of Liberal Imagination?

I began this essay by arguing that while normative distinctions between de-ethnicizing legal reforms and re-ethnicizing ones may be legitimate on liberal–republican grounds, they are likely to hinder our understanding of developments such as Hungary's extraterritorial citizenship law. By reference to concepts devised by Benhabib[125] to describe processes whereby immigration countries such as Germany have redefined their demoi to include their "internal other" by de-ethnicizing their citizenship laws, the essay attempted to highlight some of the procedural and symbolic similarities with the case of Hungary, where similarly lengthy public debates and "national soul-searching" have enabled the legal and political inclusion of the country's external co-ethnics. The parallel with the Benhabibian narrative has also aided the argument that the extraterritorial extension of political rights did not merely expand the political community, but has sought to radically redefine it in line with an illiberal ethnical vision.

---

[124] Nagy, "Nationality," 37.
[125] Benhabib, *The Rights of Others.*

Through a critical discussion of the ethno-cultural characteristics and the political dimensions of extraterritorial citizenship, this essay has highlighted how Hungary's preferential citizenship law must be understood as intimately related to broader constitutional changes. The combined effect of these changes, the essay argued, is to substantially shift the meaning of political community away from one grounded in liberal–republican frames of meaning and towards one structured around illiberal ethical values.

Nevertheless, the idea of an extraterritorial political community raises several issues in addition to those commonly envisaged by theorists of post-nationalization. Benhabib herself did not fail to highlight that "*territoriality* has become an anachronistic delimitation of material functions and cultural identities," but imagined future post-national developments to be in the direction of a neo-Kantian "cosmopolitan federalism."[126] Other theorists had a much starker view of imagined extra-territorial futures. Bauböck, for instance, has detailed a dystopian vision of hypermigration, in which internationally mobile populations would outnumber the immobile, with the effect that the whole process would "undermine the very structure of territorial citizenship."[127] In Bauböck's assessment,

> the major difference to the contemporary world would not be a devastating increase of cultural diversity, but a loss of heterogeneity within these non-territorial polities, whose members would be self-selected to be similar to each other in their interests, identities and ideologies.[128]

Such a scenario, however unlikely it is in respect to our near future, is not only pulled closer to reality by increasing levels of global mobility, but also, as argued before, by increasing levels of interest by polities in expanding membership to include persons with specific characteristics.

---

126 Ibid., 5.

127 Rainer Bauböck, "Temporary Migrants, Partial Citizenship and Hypermigration," *Critical Review of International Social and Political Philosophy* 5 (2011), 689.

128 Ibid., 686.

Also, in Bauböck's opinion, such a world would be governed by a libertarian or semi-authoritarian system at a global level.

In similar vein, we may inquire about possible future developments in the international political system that would be normatively more accommodating of the illiberal extraterritorial community discussed in reference to Hungary. One could build, for instance, on the renewed interest in the idea of "neomedievalism" having even been applied directly in reference to the Hungarian Status Law.[129] The concept has broadened considerably since Hedley Bull's[130] original sparse statements, Falk[131] already identifying "three neomedieval discourses," of which the third—relating to "the recovery of the sacred"[132] —has now expanded to also loosely encompass political theories such as those proposed by new "radical traditionalists" like Alexander Dugin in Russia or Alain de Benoist in France—and actively engaged with in Hungary by radical-right elites (see Jobbik founder and once leader Gábor Vona's[133] own ruminations)—and which, while remaining outside mainstream academic political philosophy, have an equal, if not greater, opportunity to influence the future of global geopolitics due to their often unsettling proximity to power.[134]

A future international system in general agreement with such views would rely on civilizational groupings organized around a "non-imperialistic" empire whose administration would transcend democratic party-political mechanisms. This is the vision for Europe painted more than half a century ago by Julius Evola—a main intellectual source for new traditionalists—when he theorized about "an empire in

---

129 Stephen Deets, "The Hungarian Status Law and the Specter of Neo-medievalism in Europe," *Ethnopolitics* 2–3 (2008).

130 Hedley Bull, *The Anarchical Society: a Study of Order in World Politics* (London: Macmillan, 1977).

131 Richard Falk, "A 'New Medievalism'?" in *Contending Images of World Politics*, eds. Greg Fry and Jacinta O'Hagan (London: Macmillan, 2000), 108.

132 Ibid., 112.

133 Gábor Vona, "Some Thoughts on the Creation of Intellectual Eurasianism," *Journal of Eurasian Affairs* 1 (2014).

134 For similar conclusions drawn from a different analysis regarding Hungarian political discourse, see also Chris Moreh, "The Asianization of National Fantasies in Hungary: A Critical Analysis of Political Discourse," *International Journal of Cultural Studies* 3 (2016).

a true and organic sense" which "was previously displayed in the European medieval world."[135] "In this world," Evola continues,

> individual States have the character of partial organic units, gravitating around ... a principle of unity, authority, and sovereignty of a different nature from that which is proper to each particular State. But the principle of the Empire can have such a dignity only by transcending the political sphere in the strict sense, founding and legitimizing itself with an idea, a tradition, and a power that is also spiritual.[136]

Discussing extreme imaginary worlds is, in my opinion, not unjustified. It enables us to look beyond the liberal democratic principles that dominate our thinking, and may also remind us of the fact that historically radical global political restructuring occurred during relatively short periods of turmoil, but on the back of long-term technological and economic processes. Discussing them in relation to changes such as those taking place in Hungarian citizenship law has a more modest justification, serving to show how they may indeed fit better in such imaginary worlds, and highlighting both the possibilities and dangers involved.

BIBLIOGRAPHY

Balogh, Sándor, Zsolt Németh, and Károly Ravasz. "A kettős állampolgárságról: Kerekasztal-beszélgetés." *Vasárnapi Újság*, April 19, 1998. Accessed May 20, 2019. http://www.gecse.eu/17.html.

Bárdi, Nándor. "Different Images of the Future of the Hungarian Communities in Neighbouring Countries, 1989–2012." *European Review 4* (2013): 530–552.

Barry, Kim. "Home and away: The Construction of Citizenship in an Emigration Context." *New York University Law Review* 1 (2006): 11–59.

Bauböck, Rainer. "Towards a Political Theory of Migrant Transnationalism." *International Migration Review* 3 (2003): 700–723.

Bauböck, Rainer. "Expansive Citizenship: Voting beyond Territory and Membership." *PS: Political Science and Politics* 4 (2005): 683–687.

[135] Julius Evola, *Men Among the Ruins: Post-war Reflections of a Radical Traditionalist* (Rochester, VT: Inner Traditions, 2002), 277.

[136] Ibid., 277.

Bauböck, Rainer. "Stakeholder Citizenship and Transnational Political Participation: A Normative Evaluation of External Voting." *Fordham Law Review* 5 (2007): 2393–2447.

Bauböck, Rainer. "The Trade-Off between Transnational Citizenship and Political Autonomy." In *Dual Citizenship in Global Perspective*, edited by Thomas Faist and Peter Kivisto, 69–91. New York: Palgrave Macmillan, 2007.

Bauböck, Rainer. "Temporary Migrants, Partial Citizenship and Hypermigration." *Critical Review of International Social and Political Philosophy* 5 (2011): 665–693.

Bauböck, Rainer, ed. *Dual Citizenship for Transborder Minorities? How to Respond to the Hungarian-Slovak Tit-for-tat*. EUI Working Paper RSCAS 2010/75. Florence: Robert Schuman Center for Advanced Studies, European University Institute, 2010. http://hdl.handle.net/1814/14625.

Bauböck, Rainer, and André Liebich, eds. *Is There (Still) an East-West Divide in the Conception of Citizenship in Europe?* Fiesole: EUDO Citizenship Observatory, 2010.

Benhabib, Seyla. *The Rights of Others: Aliens, Residents and Citizens*. Cambridge: Cambridge University Press, 2004.

Böjte, Csaba. "Jaj a népszavazás győzteseinek!" *Krónika*. December 10, 2004. Accessed May 20, 2019. https://kisebbsegkutato.tk.mta.hu/kettosallampolgarsag/publicisztika/pub_221.html.

Bozóki, András. *Access to Electoral Rights: Hungary*. EUI Working Paper RSCAS 2013/19. Florence: Robert Schuman Center for Advanced Studies, European University Institute, 2013. Accessed May 20, 2019. http://hdl.handle.net/1814/29814.

Brubaker, Rogers. *Citizenship and Nationhood in France and Germany*. Cambridge, MA and London: Harvard University Press, 1992.

Brubaker, Rogers. *Nationalism Reframed: Nationhood and the National Question in the New Europe*. Cambridge: Cambridge University Press, 1996.

Brubaker, Rogers. "Migration, Membership, and the Modern Nation-State: Internal and External Dimensions of the Politics of Belonging." *Journal of Interdisciplinary History* 1 (2010): 61–78.

Bull, Hedley. *The Anarchical Society: A Study of Order in World Politics*. London: Macmillan, 1977.

Burke, Edmund. *Reflections on the French Revolution & Other Essays*. London: J. M. Dent & Son, 1910.

Cook-Martín, David. *The Scramble for Citizens: Dual Nationality and State Competition for Immigrants*. Stanford: Stanford University Press, 2013.

Csergő, Zsuzsa, and James M. Goldgeier. "Nationalist Strategies and European Integration." In *The Hungarian Status Law: Nation Building and/or Minority Protection*, edited by Zoltán Kántor, Balázs Majtényi, Osamu Ieda, Balázs Vizi, and Iván Halász, 270–302. Sapporo: Slavic Research Center, Hokkaido University, 2004.

Csergő, Zsuzsa, and James M. Goldgeier. "Kin-State Activism in Hungary Romania, and Russia: The Politics of Ethnic Demography." In *Divided Nations and European Integration*, ed. Tristan J. Mabry, John McGarry, Margaret

Moore, and Brendan O'Leary, 89–126. Philadelphia: University of Pennsylvania Press, 2013.

Deets, Stephen. "The Hungarian Status Law and the Specter of Neo-medievalism in Europe." *Ethnopolitics* 2–3 (2008): 195–215.

Đurić, Vladimir, Darko Tanasković, Dragan Vukmirović, and Petar Lađević. *Etnokonfesionalni i Jezički Mozaik Srbije.* Belgrade: National Institute of Statistics, 2014.

Dumbrava, Costica. "External Citizenship in EU Countries." *Ethnic and Racial Studies* 13 (2014): 2340–2360.

Evola, Julius. *Men Among the Ruins: Post-war Reflections of a Radical Traditionalist.* Rochester, VT: Inner Traditions, 2002.

Falk, Richard. "A 'New Medievalism'?" In *Contending Images of World Politics*, edited by Greg Fry, and Jacinta O'Hagan, 106–116. London: Macmillan, 2000.

Furedi, Frank. *Populism and the European Culture Wars: The Conflict of Values between Hungary and the EU.* London: Routledge, 2018.

Halmai, Gábor. "Legally Sophisticated Authoritarians: the Hungarian Lex CEU." *VerfBlog*, March 31, 2017. Accessed May 20, 2019. http://verfassungsblog.de/legally-sophisticated-authoritarians-the-hungarian-lex-ceu.

Hammar, Tomas. *Democracy and the Nation State: Aliens, Denizens and Citizens in a World of International Migration.* Aldershot: Avebury, 1989.

Herner-Kovács, Eszter, Gergely Illyés, and Krisztián Rákóczi. "Külhoni szavazatok a 2014-es magyar országgyűlési választásokon." *Kisebbségkutatás* 2 (2014): 7–19.

Hirschman, Albert O. *Exit, Voice, and Loyalty: Responses to Decline in Firms, Organizations, and States.* Cambridge, MA: Harvard University Press, 1970.

Ieda, Osamu, "Post-communist Nation Building and the Status Law Syndrome in Hungary." In *The Hungarian Status Law: Nation Building and/or Minority Protection*, edited by Zoltán Kántor, Balázs Majtényi, Osamu Ieda, Balázs Vizi, and Iván Halász, 3–57. Sapporo: Slavic Research Center, Hokkaido University, 2004.

Joppke, Christian. *Immigration and the Nation-state: The United States, Germany, and Great Britain.* Oxford: Oxford University Press, 1999.

Joppke, Christian. "Citizenship between De- and Re-Ethnicization." *European Journal of Sociology*, 3 (2003): 429–458.

Kántor, Zoltán. "Status Law and 'Nation Policy': Theoretical Aspects." In *The Hungarian Status Law: Nation Building and/or Minority Protection*, edited by Zoltán Kántor, Balázs Majtényi, Osamu Ieda, Balázs Vizi, and Iván Halász, 105–119. Sapporo: Slavic Research Center, Hokkaido University, 2004.

Kántor, Zoltán. "Két állampolgárság—két szavazat—két politikai közösség." Paper presented at the annual meeting of the Hungarian Society for Political Science, Esztergom, June 16, 2016.

Kántor, Zoltán, and Balázs Majtényi, "A 'kettős állampolgárság'—népszavazás, politikai vita, érvek." In *Romániai Magyar Évkönyv 2004/2005*, edited by Barna Bodó, 213–228. Timişoara: Marineasa, 2005.

Kántor, Zoltán, Balázs Majtényi, Osamu Ieda, Balázs Vizi, and Iván Halász, eds. *The Hungarian Status Law: Nation Building and/or Minority Protection*. Sapporo: Hokkaido University, Slavic Research Center, 2004.

Kapitány, Balázs. "Kárpát-medencei népszámlálási körkép." *Demográfia* 1 (2013): 25–64.

Kiss, Tamás, and Gergő Barna. *Erdélyi magyarok a magyarországi és a romániai politikai térben*. Cluj-Napoca: Institutul Pentru Studierea Problemelor Minorităţilor Naţionale, 2013.

Kovács, Mária M. "The Politics of Dual Citizenship in Hungary." *Citizenship Studies* 4 (2006): 431–451.

Lázár, Guy. "Kik tartoznak a nemzethez? Fiatalok a magyarság ismérveiről és a határokon túli magyarokról." *Magyar Kisebbség* 3–4/69–70 (2013): 301–319.

Little, Adrian. *The Politics of Community: Theory and Practice*. Edinburgh: Edinburgh University Press, 2002.

Maas, Willem. "Extending Politics: Enfranchising Non-Resident European Citizens." Paper presented at the 40th Annual Convention of the International Studies Association, Washington, DC, February 17, 1999. Accessed May 20, 2019. http://www.yorku.ca/maas/Maas1999.pdf.

Maatsch, Aleksandra. *Ethnic Citizenship Regimes: Europeanization, Post-war Migration and Redressing Past Wrongs*. Houndmills, Basingstoke: Palgrave Macmillan, 2011.

Majtényi, Balázs. "Etnikai származás és állampolgárság." *Jogi Iránytű*, 1 (2011). Accessed May 19, 2019. http://jog.tk.mta.hu/uploads/files/Jogi_Iranytu/Jogi_Iranytu_2011_1_Majtenyi_Balazs.pdf.

Majtényi, Balázs. "The Nation's Will as Trump in the Hungarian Fundamental Law." *In European Yearbook on Human Rights 2015*, edited by Wolfgang Benedek, Florence Benoît-Rohmer, and Matthias C. Kettemann, Benjamin Kneihs, and Manfred Nowak, 247–259. Vienna: Neuer Wissenschaftlicher Verlag, 2015.

Moreh, Chris. "The Asianization of National Fantasies in Hungary: A Critical Analysis of Political Discourse." *International Journal of Cultural Studies*, 3 (2016): 341–353.

Moreh, Chris. "Az Egyesült Királyságba irányuló magyarországi elvándorlás a magyar és a brit migrációs rendszerek átalakulásának tükrében." *Ügyészségi Szemle*, 3 (2017): 86–101.

MTI. "Letette az állampolgársági esküt a félmilliomodik külhoni magyar." *MTI hírarchívum 1988–2015*, December 5, 2013. Accessed May 20, 2019. http://archiv1988tol.mti.hu/Pages/HirSearch.aspx?Pmd=1.

MTI. "Wetzel: 2018-ra egymillióan szerezhetnek magyar állampolgárságot." *MTI hírarchívum 1988–2015*, August 26, 2014. Accessed May 20, 2019. http://archiv1988tol.mti.hu/Pages/HirSearch.aspx?Pmd=1.

MTI. "Nemzeti egység alakult ki a kettős állampolgárság kérdésében." *Origo.hu*, December 17, 2017. Accessed May 20, 2019. http://www.origo.hu/itthon/20171217-nemzeti-minimum-alakult-ki-a-kettos-allampolgarsag-kerdeseben.html.

Nagy, Boldizsár. "Nationality as a Stigma: the Drawbacks of Nationality (What Do I Have To Do With Book-Burners?)." *Corvinus Journal of Sociology and Social Policy* 2 (2014): 31–64.

Owen, David. "Resident Aliens, Non-resident Citizens and Voting Rights: Towards a Pluralist Theory of Transnational Political Equality and Modes of Political Belonging." In *Citizenship Acquisition and National Belonging: Migration, Membership and the Liberal Democratic State*, edited by Gideon Calder, Phillip Cole and Jonathan Seglow, 52–73. Basingstoke: Palgrave Macmillan, 2010.

Pap, András L. *Democratic Decline in Hungary: Law and Society in an Illiberal Democracy*. Abindgon: Routledge, 2018.

Papp, Attila Z. "Kisebbségi identitáskonstrukciók a kettős magyar állampolgárság által." *Regio* 1 (2014): 118–155.

Pogonyi, Szabolcs. *Extra-Territorial Ethnic Politics, Discourses and Identities in Hungary*. Houndmills: Palgrave Macmillan, 2017.

Pogonyi, Szabolcs, Mária M. Kovács, and Zsolt Körtvélyesi. *The Politics of External Kin-State Citizenship in East Central Europe*. EUI Working Paper RSCAS 2010/06. Florence: Robert Schuman Center for Advanced Studies, European University Institute, 2010. Accessed May 20, 2019. http://hdl.handle.net/1814/19576.

Salat, Levente. "A politikai közösség kérdése a többség-kisebbség viszonyának a nézőpontjából." *Magyar Kisebbség* 3–4/61–62 (2011): 159–190.

Salat, Levente. "A könnyített honosítás látható és várható következményeiről. Válaszok a Magyar Kisebbség kérdéseire." *Magyar Kisebbség*, 3–4/69–70 (2013): 226–240.

Schöpflin, György. "Citizenship and Ethnicity: The Hungarian Status Law." In *The Hungarian Status Law: Nation Building and/or Minority Protection,* edited by Zoltán Kántor, Balázs Majtényi, Osamu Ieda, Balázs Vizi, and Iván Halász, 87–104. Sapporo: Slavic Research Center, Hokkaido University, 2004.

Shevel, Oxana. "The Post-Communist Diaspora Laws: Beyond the 'Good Civic versus Bad Ethnic' Nationalism Dichotomy." *East European Politics & Societies*, 1 (2010): 159–187.

Shulman, Stephen. "Challenging the Civic/Ethnic and West/East Dichotomies in the Study of Nationalism." *Comparative Political Studies*, 5 (2002): 554–585.

Smith, Rogers M. "Citizenship and the Politics of People-Building." *Citizenship Studies*, 1 (2001): 73–96.

Soysal, Yasemin N. *Limits of Citizenship: Migrants and Postnational Membership in Europe*. Chicago, IL: University of Chicago Press, 1994.

Szabó, Márton. "Ellenfél és ellenség a politikában." *Politikatudományi Szemle*, 1 (2007): 9–20.

Szabolcsi, Miklos. "Ethnocentrism in Education: a Comparative Analysis of Problems in Eastern and Western Europe." *Prospects - Quarterly Review of Education*, 2 (1989): 149–164.

Szerbhorváth, György. "A mi utcánk." *Élet és Irodalom*, November 19, 2004. Accessed May 20, 2019. https://kisebbsegkutato.tk.mta.hu/kettosallampolgarsag/publicisztika/pub_069.html.

The Economist. "Read the Large Print." *The Economist*, July 4, 2010. Accessed May 20, 2019. http://www.economist.com/blogs/easternapproaches/2010/07/hungary.

Tóth, Judit. *UPDATE: Changes in the Hungarian Citizenship Law and adopted on 26 May 2010.* (San Domenico di Fiesole: EUI, EUDO Citizenship Observatory, July 13, 2010) Accessed May 19, 2019. http://eudo-citizenship.eu/docs/CountryReports/recentChanges/Hungary.pdf.

Töttős, Ágnes. "The Effects of an EU Member-State's Modified Citizenship Law: The Hungarian Example, With a Particular Focus on the Aspects of Free Movement." *Central and Eastern European Migration Review* 1 (2017): 65–74.

Vink, Maarten, Gerard-Rene De Groot, and Ngo C. Luk. "MACIMIDE Global Expatriate Dual Citizenship Dataset," *Harvard Dataverse*, v3, 2015. Accessed May 20, 2019. doi:10.7910/DVN/TTMZ08.

Vona, Gábor. "Some Thoughts on the Creation of Intellectual Eurasianism." *Journal of Eurasian Affairs* 1 (2014): 13–16.

Walzer, Michael. *Spheres of Justice: A Defence of Pluralism and Equality*. New York: Basic Books, 1983.

Waterbury, Myra A. *Between State and Nation: Diaspora Politics and Kin-state Nationalism in Hungary* (1st ed.). New York: Palgrave Macmillan, 2010.

Waterbury, Myra A. "Bridging the Divide: Towards a Comparative Framework for Understanding Kin State and Migrant-sending State Diaspora Politics." In *Diaspora and Transnationalism: Concepts, Theories and Methods*, edited by Rainer Bauböck, and Thomas Faist, 131–149. Amsterdam: Amsterdam University Press, 2010.

Weil, Patrick. "Access to Citizenship: A Comparison of Twenty-five Nationality Laws." In *Citizenship Today: Global Perspectives and Practices*, edited by Alexander T. Aleinikoff and Douglas Klusmeyer, 17–35. Washington, DC: Brookings Institution, 2001.

Shift in the Hungarian Roma Policy

BALÁZS MAJTÉNYI and GYÖRGY MAJTÉNYI[1]

Introduction

This chapter analyzes the Roma policies of Hungary after the regime change of 1989, highlights the dysfunctions of liberal democracy in the period from 1989 to 2010 and shows how the anti-egalitarian character of the Hungarian National Cooperation System after 2010 reinforces the continuous and growing exclusion of the Hungarian Roma.

The first part of the chapter underlines how the exclusive interpretation of the nation as a social category leads to the exclusion of the Roma. The exclusive interpretation is partly rooted in Hungarian history: the majority population has been historically constructed as a social (upper) class in comparison to the low social status associated with the Roma minority.

The second part of the chapter focuses on the situation of the Roma within Hungarian society after the democratic transition in 1989. It underlines that in spite of the transition to constitutional democracy after 1989, which institutionalized an egalitarian concept of the political nation and established democratic institutions and minority rights, the exclusion of the Roma remained continuous in Hungarian society. In fact, their situation deteriorated: they increasingly became subject to poverty, unemployment, rising segregation and

[1] This research was supported by the Bolyai János Scholarship of the Hungarian Academy of Sciences. György Majtényi's research was supported by the National Scholarship Programme of the Slovak Republic.

racial violence. This implies besides the dysfunctions of the minority rights that the social policy of liberal democracy failed, which in turn was one of the causes behind the fall of Hungarian liberal democracy after 2010.

The Hungarian state did little after 1989 to change the social status of the Roma within Hungarian society, most of them living in poverty (although the majority of the poor are not Roma), while constructing the image of an efficient social and minority policy, and the concept of a benign state which treats the Roma minority as a privileged group within the social policy system.[2] Quite counterproductively, the dysfunctions of the system strengthened prejudice and discrimination on behalf of the majority population against the Roma, widely considered as a privileged group of social policy.

With this historical background in mind, the last part of the chapter examines the effects of the illiberal turn of Hungary after 2010 regarding the Roma minority. The political discourse after 2010 has institutionalized an exclusive concept of the nation and dismantled the democratic institutions of the Constitution of 1989. It has increasingly built the identity of the state on the exclusive community of ethnic Hungarians, corresponding to and perhaps laying the ground for the rising segregation and racial violence in society at large. The chapter argues that after the authoritarian turn of the political system post-colonial theory[3] is adaptable to the recent situation of the Hungarian Roma, it considers post-colonialism as the fundamental logic of functioning of the new regime which meant (among others) the segregation and exclusion of the poor and the minority communities.

Post-colonial theory holds that post-colonization, also as a narrative, creates the institutions and infrastructure that maintains social

---

[2] Mónika Mária Váradi, "Szegénység, kirekesztettség" [Poverty, exclusion], in *Közösségtanulmány. Módszertani jegyzet* [Community studies. A metholodogical handbook], ed. Éva Kovács (Budapest: Néprajzi Múzeum—Pécsi Tudományegyetem BTK Kommunikáció- és Médiatudományi Tanszék, 2007), 69–87.

[3] Edward W. Said, *Orientalism* (Vintage Books, New York, 1978); Aijaz Ahmad, "Post-Colonialism: What's in a Name?" in *Late Imperial Culture*, ed. Roman de la Campa and, E. Ann Kaplan, and Michael Sprinker (London: Verso, 1995); Epifanio San Juan, *Beyond Postcolonial Theory* (New York: St. Martins Press, 1998).

exclusion. According to the theory, post-colonialism is an oppressive and controlling technique emerging in discursive practice through which, for example, the subjugation and oppression of excluded groups in modern societies can be described.[4] In our interpretation, state institutions not only created unique dependence systems within the Hungarian National Cooperation Regime; the functioning and the discourses they created[5] made it nearly impossible for those living in poverty—among them, the Roma—to express and present their individual and collective experiences to the public.

Until the regime change mainly the term Gypsy (cigány) was used in discourses, also by policy documents and scientific researches in Hungary, later the term was increasingly replaced by Roma. Before the regime change the term Gypsy most often referred, at least partly, to a social group constructed and described from the outside. Recently, the Roma category—which was adopted originally by Roma communities to declare their ethnic or national identity—has also been used in discourses related to wider social groups that are regarded as Gypsy/Roma by the majority. Of course, these words/categories always take on different connotations in different texts, and their meanings cannot be clearly and indisputably circumscribed, not even in the given contexts. Furthermore, there are interactions between these two categorizations, for example, the experience of social exclusion against persons and groups regarded as Gypsy/Roma can strengthen the sense of community among the excluded groups and the common national minority identity of the Hungarian Roma. In this chapter, we usually use the word Roma, as the generally accepted term to describe a national minority identity. We retain the original wording (Roma/Gypsy or "Gypsy") where we deem it important for contextualization.

---

[4] For more on this issue related to East Central European history, see: Natasha Kovacevic, *Narrating Post/Communism: Colonial Discourse and Europe's Borderline Civilization* (London: Routledge, 2008); Christina Sandru, *Worlds Apart? A Postcolonial Reading of Post-1945 EastCentral European Culture* (Cambridge: Cambridge Scholars Publishing, 2012).

[5] In this study, by power discourses we mean those strategic, linguistic and conceptual efforts of the contemporary power/ruling system which, in the interest of its own legitimacy, were used to create the public sphere of the time and which tried to exclude or eradicate those social actors, phenomena and experiences that weakened this legitimacy.

Nation as a Social Class?

Unified Hungarian history—like other national histories—is obviously a construction, a post hoc creation that is an important part of Hungarian national identity. The construction of national identity can be based in pre-modern times when belonging to a nation was restricted to a small group of a society.[6]

In the Middle Ages, the majority of people living in the territory of Hungary probably spoke Hungarian, but this does not mean that they were Hungarians in the sense of a modern concept of the nation. To be Hungarian primarily meant occupying a social position. In the Middle Ages, Hungarians were the king's subjects, and social differences distinguished the Magyars (Hungarians) from the Magyar-speaking Seklers. Later sources reveal considerably more about the Magyars, which primarily implied a social position, an exceptional feudal class, and membership in the noble nation.[7] This concept of the Hungarian nation is clearly not the same as the modern egalitarian concept of nationhood.[8] After the appearance of nationalism, theoretically everyone could belong to the nation regardless of their social position, and the residents of the country—no matter what they thought—became members of a political nation through a construction of public law. This undoubtedly contributed to making society more egalitarian.[9]

---

[6] Cf. Anthony D. Smith, *Ethno-Symbolism and Nationalism: A Cultural Approach* (New York: Routledge, 2009).

[7] Jenő Szűcs, *Nemzet és történelem. Tanulmányok* [Nation and history. Studies] (Budapest: Gondolat, 1974); Benedek Varga, "Political humanism and the corporate theory of state: Nation, patria and virtue in Hungarian political thought of the sixteenth century," in *Whose Love of Which Country? Composite States and Patriotic Discourses in Early-Modern Central Europe*, eds. Balázs Trencsényi and Márton Zászkaliczky (Leiden—Boston: Brill, 2010), 283–314.

[8] Balázs Majtényi, *A nemzetállam új ruhája. Multikulturalizmus Magyarországon* [The new cloth of nation state: Multiculturalism in Hungary] (Budapest: Gondolat, 2007).

[9] Ernest Gellner, "The Coming of Nationalism and its Interpretation: The Myths of Nation and Class," in *Mapping the Nation*, ed. Gopal Balakrishnan (London: Verso, 1996), 98–132.

The anti-egalitarian social category interpretation of the premodern Magyars did not entirely disappear, given that over time it remained the basis of prejudice toward and exclusion of various minorities (e.g., Jews, Roma/Gypsies) and remains so to this day. According to Antal Örkény and György Csepeli, Hungarian identity as tied to social position was imposed on other groups. Identity is not just a question of "who am I?", but also one of "who am I not?". As such, it can be related to prejudices toward differently situated social groups in majority society in an explicit fashion. In the case of Jews, the basis of differentiation was success and wealth, while in the case of Roma the reason for differentiation was failure and poverty.[10] The transformation of identifying membership in a social group into belonging to the majority or minority resulted in the birth of Gypsy or Roma as a social category distinguished from the Hungarian majority within society, and thus formed the history of the Roma issue.

István Bibó, a definitive figure in 20th century Hungarian political thought, wrote the following about the failure of the assimilation of Hungarian Jews: "Hungarian society, from the very beginning, assimilated or offered the opportunity to assimilate on dishonorable, disrespectful terms,"[11] given that the adoption of the Hungarian language or self-identification as a Hungarian did not result in the majority acknowledging one as a Hungarian.[12] We feel that Bibó's observations pertain to the Roma as well—the Hungarian majority obstructed the masses of self-defined Hungarian, socially marginalized, and Hungarian-speaking Roma from the opportunity to blend in.

The second half of the 20th century saw the expression and awareness (in the circles of majority power, science and the general population) of Roma being a significant constituent "group" in our society, and

---

10 György Csepeli and Antal Örkény, "The Making of a Minority: Competing Claims of Definitions of Being Roma in Contemporary Hungarian Society," *Central European Political Science Review* 17 (2016): 150–179.

11 István Bibó, "Zsidókérdés Magyarországon 1944 után," [The Jewish question in Hungary after 1944] in *Válogatott tanulmányok* II [Selected studies II], ed. István Bibó (Budapest: Bibó István örökösei, 1990), 746.

12 Writing about 1944, he emphasized the collective responsibility of Hungarian society for the annihilation of the Jews, and encouraged that social memory treat the Holocaust as a crime committed against members of the Hungarian nation, i.e., against itself.

their numbers were rapidly growing. There is another explanation for the emergence of a mass Roma population of several hundred thousand—beyond demographic or event history (e.g., immigration)—whereby the representatives of the state presented the difference between majority and minority, Hungarians and Roma, on a national level. The border separating the two groups was drawn with such visibility that everyone could see it clearly. Differences and contrasts that previously existed on the local level now appeared at the level of the entire society and were given a new dimension. This constructed community of a unified Roma people was connected by researchers and state officials to various social phenomena like poverty or low levels of education.[13]

By assimilation we mean not only the linguistic and cultural melding, but similarly to Rogers Brubaker, a phenomenon that necessitates the social acceptance of a group, and which thus cannot be realized through the marginalization and exclusion of a group.[14] Typically, lacking social acknowledgment in contemporary Hungary, those Roma who have been successful in the labor world are challenged when trying to assimilate. Margit Feischmidt brings up the example of micro-villages in southwestern Hungary and describes how economic success of the Roma does not guarantee their social acknowledgment.[15]

All questions concerning the integration of Hungarian Roma can be examined within the national history, and these questions are—among other things—about the relations between members of the political community. As the example of the Hungarian Roma, and that of the persons and groups regarded as Roma/Gypsy show, the continuing existence and recreation of historical social categories can be a barrier to inclusion.

---

[13] See for details: Balázs Majtényi and György Majtényi, *A Contemporary History of Exclusion. The Roma Issue in Hungary from 1945 to 2015* (CEU Press: Budapest—New York, 2016).

[14] Rogers Brubaker, "The Return of Assimilation? Changing Perspectives on Immigration and its Sequels in France, Germany, and the United States," *Ethnic and Racial Studies* 4(2001): 531–548.

[15] Margit Feischmidt, "Kényszerek és illeszkedések. Gazdasági és szimbolikus stratégiák aprófalvakban élő romák életében" [Economic and symbolic strategies of Romani people living in Hungarian villages], *Szociológiai Szemle* 2 (2012): 54–84.

The Roma as an Underclass?

During state socialism power discourses disintegrated the phenomenon of poverty in the public sphere of the time, which meant that the poor and poverty could not be brought up in public forums for some time. The Hungarian state, when it did deal with the real situation of the poor, tended to wrap its interventions in the cloak of "Gypsy policy," primarily "slum eradication," given that poverty officially did not exist in "socialism." The problems of poverty were often described as "the Gypsy issue" in public. As such, this term was used as a social category labelling an underclass social status and at the same time also related to the choice of minority identity.

The first representative sociological study in 1971 estimated the Roma/Gypsy population to be 320,000.[16] The study led by István Kemény used the opinion of the majority society as a basis: the project considered those people who were labelled as such by their non-Roma environment to be Gypsy.[17] Given that Roma origin was always a stigma in the eyes of the public opinion, this was the only designation of all possible definitions upon which a "national representative study" could be executed. However, this definition suggested that the relationship of Roma to the majority population and their "separateness" was defined not by culture, the existence of a Roma nation/minority status

---

16 István Kemény, "A magyarországi cigány lakosság" [The Hungarian Gypsy population], *Valóság* 1 (1974): 63–72.

17 István Kemény, "A magyarországi cigányok helyzete" [The status of the Gypsies of Hungary] in *Beszámoló a magyarországi cigányok helyzetével foglalkozó 1971-ben végzett kutatásról* [Report on research carried out in 1971 on the situation of Gypsies in Hungary], ed. István Kemény (Budapest: MTA Szociológiai Kutató Intézete, 1976), 7–67.; The 1993–1994 national representative Gypsy study was based on the same principles. Gábor Havas and István Kemény, "A magyarországi romákról" [On the Hungarian Roma], *Szociológiai Szemle* 3 (1995): 3–20. The Szelényi-Treiman study empirically confirmed that the number of Gypsies in Hungary was much lower when measurement was based on self-proclamation of ethnic identity and higher when the environment (in this case the interviewer) was able to categorize the subjects. Iván Szelényi and Donald J. Treiman, *Social Stratification in Eastern Europe after 1989. General Population Survey* (Los Angeles: UCLA, Department of Sociology, 1993).

or an identity choice, but by the exclusionary behavior of the members of the majority society.[18] The researchers asked social workers, village teachers, council employees, police, and from time to time neighbors to point out those in the given settlement they considered Gypsies. They also estimated that two-thirds of the Roma population still lived in "Gypsy settlements," with more than two-thirds of them in pise or mud-brick shacks. Forty-four percent of their homes did not have electricity, while only eight percent of homes had running water.

After the regime change, between 1993 and 2003, representative Roma/Gypsy studies employed methods similar to that of the 1971 project. Their approach can be summarized as follows: "...we had the research goal of examining the social position of people deemed Gypsy by their surroundings in that well-known social stratum in which those who do not view themselves as Gypsy but as members of the majority society firmly and clearly differentiate themselves from people they consider to be Gypsy."[19] Based on the 1993 representative sociological study and school statistics, the number of people deemed Gypsy by the non-Roma environment at the beginning of the 1990s was about 455,000.[20] Ten years later, in 2003, sociological studies estimated this number to be 550,000–570,000.

Data from the census of 1990 indicated that only 143,000 Roma lived in Hungary. The 2001 census showed 190,000 people who claimed Roma/Gypsy identity (among others).[21] The census of 2011 showed that the number of those who identifying themselves as Roma/

[18] István Kemény expressed the following in his summarizing work: "...we cannot speak of a Gypsy culture or subculture, but of the subculture of the lower strata, within which the lifestyle groups of Gypsies provide various colours." Kemény, "A magyarországi cigányok helyzete," ["The status of the Gypsies of Hungary,"] 42. For more detail on the issue see: Péter Szuhay, *A magyarországi cigányok kultúrája: etnikus kultúra vagy a szegénység kultúrája* [The culture of the Gypsies in Hungary: an ethnic culture or the culture of poverty] (Budapest: Panoráma, 1999).

[19] Gábor Kertesi and Gábor Kézdy, *A cigány népesség Magyarországon. Dokumentáció és adattár* [The Gypsy population in Hungary: Documentation and statistics]. (Budapest: Socio-typo, 1998), 15.

[20] Ibid., 96; István Kemény, Béla Janky and Gabriella Lengyel, *A magyarországi cigányság, 1971–2003.* [The Gypsies of Hungary, 1971–2003] (Budapest: Gondolat, 2004), 42.

[21] Kemény, Janky and Lengyel, *A magyarországi cigányság, 1971–2003*, 42.

Gypsy (among other categories) grew to 315,000. This number, which reflected multiple identities, despite showing considerable growth, was still far below the numbers based on categorizations of the majority.[22]

The 1990s saw a vigorous debate over the Roma/Gypsy concept used—partly through necessity—in sociological research. The question was over which ascription to use: the self-ascription of interviewees, the external majority definition, the immediate environment, the opinion of the interviewer, or some combination of the above. The debate was not primarily about who is Roma, but the nature and difficulty of social science categorization. The sociological approaches were based on the realization that in Hungary the majority category could be seen as a "social fact," given that social actions and masses of attitudes had a defining effect.[23] It was this phenomenon that the above-mentioned representative sociological studies were reflecting to. The dominant discourse that has constructed the Roma from the viewpoint of the majority and that has determined scientific discourse, too.

Theoretically, in any case when we attempt to answer the question of who may be a member of a given minority or ethnic group, the primary aspect and starting point should be the individual's free choice, or whether the individual ascribes himself/herself as belonging to the minority or wishes to assimilate. In Hungary, however, the adoption of Roma identity, much like assimilation, has long been made difficult by an environment of prejudice and discrimination. For this reason, many feel that when we speak of the Roma, we must use sociological data as a foundation. The use of the results of such research does not mean that the methods of sociological classification are beyond criticism. We must mention that this approach to categorization is not typical in the

---

22 "Census of 2011," Központi Statisztikai Hivatal [Hungarian Central Statistical Office], accessed May 10, 2019, http://www.ksh.hu/nepszamlalas/nemzetisegi_adatok.

23 Naturally, the Gypsies/Roma, or the category of those people who were "deemed Gypsy by the majority" is also a construction. The border separating the two groups is plastic and crossable. Typically, even when sociologists use self-ascription of the individual as a starting point, they still incorporate the majority definition. For an analysis of the sociological approaches see: Csaba Dupcsik, *Megnevezés, meghatározás, megszámlálhatóság.* [Denomination, definition, countability,] 2011, accessed April 8, 2019, http://www.ideaintezet.hu/sites/default/files/Megnevezes_IDEA.pdf.

cases of other minorities. We assume that there would be widespread dismay in Hungary if sizing up the German minority in Hungary, or drafting policies toward it designated the community members based on residential or visible markers in the eyes of the majority.

The generalization of the starting point of these sociological researches—who were labelled as Roma/Gypsy by the majority society—and using it in policy and legal documents can serve to justify the daily practices of differentiation and can reinforce several stereotypes about the Roma as seen in circles of the majority. It makes free identity choice impossible and obstructs the path to assimilation. That is why the general use of the above categorization (that is based on the opinion of the majority) can strengthen the above-mentioned anti-egalitarian concept of the nation as a social category.

Roma Policy after the Regime Change

After the 1989 regime change the Hungarian liberal democracy used the political concept of nation and recognized national identity as an individual choice. The Constitution of 1989[24] declared and defined the parliamentarian republic, the separation of powers, and ensured guarantees of human rights. Thus, in theory, the individual became free to choose assimilation or the acceptance of minority status, free of coercion.

In the spirit of the 1989 Constitution, the Hungarian Constitutional Court exercised a moral reading[25] of the Constitution, putting the right to human dignity on the top of the hierarchy of human rights and connecting it with equality when "the right to equal dignity con-

---

24 Act XXXI of 1989 was formally a constitution amendment since it copied the structural form of Act XX of 1949.

25 "Most contemporary constitutions declare individual rights against the government in very broad and abstract language ... The moral reading proposes that we all—judges, lawyers, citizens—interpret and apply these abstract clauses on the understanding that they invoke moral principles about political decency and justice." Ronald Dworkin, *The Moral Reading of the Constitution*, accessed April 1, 2019, www.nybooks.com/articles/archives/1996/mar/21/the-moral-reading-of-the-constitution.

stituted the basis of the most important decisions."[26] The moral concept behind human rights is based on personal autonomy, freedom and equality. The Court underlined that everybody must be treated as a person with equal dignity.[27] The Constitutional Court elaborated the general equality rule "according to which the law should treat every person with equal respect."[28] This required that all members of society must have equal human rights. Furthermore, the 1989 Constitution recognized national and ethnic minorities as sub-political communities within the political community, and committed themselves to the model of multiculturalism in the area of minority rights.

Democratic governments with divergent political commitments have consistently faced the question of whether the state should transform its Roma policy into a minority policy, or treat the situation of the Roma as a social (and minority) issue. As a result, the fundamental principles of such policies were never obvious. In Hungary following the regime change, the mixing of various concepts and policies, along with the lack of political support and political will to carry them out, has led to dysfunction and incomprehension in many cases. State legal protection and interest representation organizations were forced to primarily deal with social disadvantages that weighed on the community. In practice, being Roma remained a social position in the post-socialist world. Discrimination, poverty or segregation have all become determining factors in contemporary society as well.

THE LACK OF EFFECTIVE SOCIAL INCLUSION POLICY

The social care system was shaky during the state socialist times, too. However, in the 1990s as the system totally collapsed, many found themselves in hopeless conditions, which brought to surface a series of social problems that were hidden before (e.g., poverty, exclusion, unem-

---

[26] László Sólyom, "The Role of Constitutional Courts in the Transition to Democracy with Special Reference to Hungary," *International Sociology* 1 (2003): 133–161.

[27] The Constitutional Court's understanding of equality was based on Dworkin's theory of equality of resources. Ronald Dworkin, *Taking Rights Seriously* (Cambridge, MA: Harvard University Press, 1977).

[28] Hungarian Constitutional Court Decision 9/1990. (IV. 25.)

ployment, homelessness), as well as ethnic tensions. Characteristically, statistical analyses showed that after 1989, among the Roma populations in all of the former state socialist countries in East-Central Europe, labor force exclusion was suffered the worst by those in Hungary, given that it was there that their proportion among the unemployed was highest.[29] In the eyes of those who were "falling behind," "failure" and a social position of disadvantage took on an ethnic meaning, and could be interpreted as a result of being a member of the minority.

To take just one example, school and residential segregation of Roma has increased significantly after 1989. In the field of school segregation, research shows that between 1993 and 2003 the number of Roma children deemed mentally challenged and thus sent to a special school or class increased: a 2003 study indicated that twenty percent of Roma children attended such schools or classes.[30] In Hungary today there are 180 segregated schools and 3,000 segregated classrooms.[31] Primary school surveys conducted in 2000 and 2004 showed a steady increase in school segregation.[32] In 2002 the socialist-liberal govern-

29 János Ladányi, "Romaügyek pedig nincsenek!" [There are no Roma affairs], *Egyenlítő* 1(2003): 21–26.

30 Béla Janky, "A cigány családok jövedelmi helyzete" [The income status of Gypsy families], in *Társadalmi riport* [Social report], ed. Tamás Kolosi and István György Tóth and György Vukovich (Budapest: TÁRKI, 2004), 402.

31 Emília Molnár and Csaba Dupcsik, *Country Report on Education: Hungary, 2008,* 17–18, accessed April 8, 2019, http://www.romaeducationfund.hu/sites/default/files/documents/edumigrom_background_paper_hungary_educ.pdf.

32 Gábor Havas and István Kemény and Ilona Liskó, "Cigány gyerekek az általános iskolában" [Gypsy children in primary school], (Budapest: Oktatáskutató Intézet Új Mandátum Könyvkiadó, 2002); Gábor Havas and Ilona Liskó, *Szegregáció a roma tanulók általános iskolai oktatásában* [Segregation of Roma students in primary schools] (Budapest: Felsőoktatási. Kutatóintézet, 2005); Judit Lannert, *A társadalmi kirekesztődés folyamata az oktatásban* [Process of social exclusion in education], KSH, A szegénység és a társadalmi kirekesztődés folyamata, tanulmányok, 2004; Gábor Kertesi and Gábor Kézdi, "Általános iskolai szegregáció. Okok és következmények" [Primary school segregation. Causes and consequences], in *A társadalom peremén.* [The fringes of society], ed. Gábor Kertesi: (Budapest: Osiris Kiadó, 2005), 377–387; Gábor Kertesi and Gábor Kézdi, "Általános iskolai szegregáció Magyarországon az ezredforduló után" [Primary school segregation in Hungray after 2000] *Közgazdasági Szemle*11(2009): 959–1000.

ment launched a new equality and integration policy in the field of education. The program attempted to reduce inequalities in education that were afflicting not only the Roma but wider groups as well. As part of the policy, the Ministry of Education promoted the integration of children with multiple disadvantages, and limited the possibility of child selection at school admission. A survey, based in microsociological investigations, conducted before the government change in 2010 suggested that this policy was already showing some results,[33] even if it did not lead to systemic changes.

The democratic system approached the social integration of the Roma community, using the new motto of "the improvement of the social situation of the Gypsy population." These integration programs, however, brought only superficial results. The main state branch overseeing the allocation of public funds, the State Audit Office, estimated that between 1996 and 2006 governments spent 120 billion forints on integration. From 2002 these amounts spiked, thanks to accessing European Union funds. However, despite domestic and international publicity, these programs should not be seen as gigantic in scale. Their extent is characterized by the fact that this is half of the amount that the state spends in one year on maintaining fields, woods, fisheries and hunting grounds. The State Railways Company receives 190 billion forints per year from the budget.[34] Independent of the amount spent, difficulties cropped up: according to the State Audit Office—which in Hungary is the Parliament's main body for supervising financial and economic governance—the proportion of funds that actually reached the supposed beneficiaries could not be estimated. The Hungarian state also did not access all of the available European funds in this field.

---

33 Gábor Kézdi and Éva Surányi, "A Successful School Integration Program. Roma Education Fund," accessed April 8, 2019, https://www.romaeducationfund.hu/sites/default/files/publications/a_succesful_school_integration_kezdi_suranyi.pdf; Gábor Havas and János Zolnay, *Az integrációs oktatáspolitika hatásvizsgálata Kutatási beszámoló* [Impact evaluation of the educational integration policy] (Budapest: Európai Összehasonlító Kisebbségkutatásokért Közalapítvány, 2010).

34 Summary evaluation study on the rate and efficiency of aid used since the change of regime for the improvement of the situation and advancement of the Roma in Hungary. State Audit Office, Institute for Development and Methodology, 2008.

DYSFUNCTIONS OF MINORITY RIGHTS

Following the 1993 Minority Act, establishing minority self-governments, a theoretical possibility opened for the Roma/Gypsies in Hungary to represent their interests in accordance with corporate or participatory democracy—with elected, publicly empowered organizations—in the life of the democratic state. However, minority self-governments became subject to the whims of municipal governments on the local level. At the national level, the government in power—when it found it necessary—easily managed to ensure that loyal (to those in power) minority bodies could be established.

The 1993 version of the minority law was bleeding from numerous wounds already, but its most obvious flaw was the fact that voting rights were not restricted to members of minorities until 2005. One cannot speak of minority self-government when it is the authorities who decide who the minority representatives will be, or when the entire population can take part in their election. Although the minority law attempted to ensure Roma representation in the state sphere, in reality the right to delegate representatives was transferred from the hands of the state to the hands of the "majority." Based on the number of votes cast at earlier elections, it can be safely claimed that a significant number of citizens who were not members of any minority voted for minority candidates: at the first election 1,777,299 people, at the second 2,657,722 people cast their votes for a minority candidate. As such, the rights of minorities as defined by the Constitution were violated, given that it was not they who established their minority self-governments. In some municipalities, this election system resulted in the forming of certain groups opposed to the minority group. A typical example took place during the minority elections in 2002. The citizens of Jászladány voted out the members of the minority government who were protesting against segregated education. They were able to do so because the mayor's wife and supporters were voted into the minority self-government by means of the "majority votes." A questionnaire and interview research project conducted between 2000–2002 showed that Roma minority self-governments—diverging from the identity politics and cultural mandates set out for them in the law—were basically working to solve social problems and to raise the level of education for the young Roma. On the one hand, this indicated that the minority self-government system was not functioning in accordance with its original mandate, and on the other hand it became clear that the operation of the state and municipal social system was ineffective, to say the least.

The Minority Act was amended in 2005, and the system of registering minority voters was established. But this amendment and the later modifications of the minority regulation were not able to change the unfavorable situation of the minority self-governmental elections, and could not exclude the possibility of persons who don't belong to a minority participating in local minority elections. The basic question remained: how can Roma politics and its organizations be protected from the "majority" on the local level, or from politics-at-large on the national level?

A turn against the official policies of earlier periods—which did not acknowledge the minority status of the Roma—probably played a role in recognizing the Roma minority. The securing of minority status represented (or could have meant) a kind of compensation for historical disadvantages, but it did not solve the social and economic problems. However, only a few years passed before it became clear that the new period did not bring an essential change in the relationship between the Roma/Gypsy minority and the "majority." Having recognized this, the state interpreted and reinterpreted its Roma/Gypsy policy from time to time. As a result, the unresolved question of assimilation cropped up again and again.

The developing liberal democracy seemed to provide space for minority self-organization. However, it became clear that social practice that imagined national communities had split society into constructed groups based on power viewpoints—into Roma/Gypsies and Hungarians or non-Roma/Gypsies, who were, according to identity construction based on exclusion, Hungarians. The Roma/Gypsies were excluded from the nation and a basic fault line was drawn in Hungarian society.

ANTIGYPSYISM IN HUNGARY AND VIOLENCE AGAINST THE ROMA

"Gypsy organizations must distance themselves from criminals," said Prime Minister Gyula Horn to an audience of Roma politicians in

1997.[35] Urban legend has it that someone in the back row retorted: "We expect the same of the Hungarian government."

The stereotype of "Gypsy crime" in Hungary was—at least in part—created and maintained by the institutional system of law enforcement. After the regime change the so-called "Gypsy lines" ceased within the police forces, although they continued to use "Gypsy background" as a unique marker in investigations. The national Chief of Police apparently put an end to this practice with an inner order in November 1996. Researchers—taking a stand against well-known prejudices—had proved in the 1980s that crime statistics are not affected by ethnic affiliation, but that certain criminal acts are related to social situation. This seemingly did not influence public opinion, and neither did the speeches of politicians. In Hungary it appears that it is only the Roma ethnic affiliation that sparks interest in crime news.

Under state socialism thoughts that were openly hateful and racist could hardly be expressed publicly. However, because the past was never faced, social attitudes and patterns of behavior that carried these were preserved. They survived the regime change and then gained in strength. Sadly, extremist and racist principles soon escaped the political quarantine that the democratic regime-changing powers had shut them in. In the history of the liberal democracy the visible advance of the minority-hating extreme right wing is tied to the success of the Hungarian Truth and Way Party (MIÉP) in the 1998 parliamentary elections.[36] This extreme right radical party was formed by István Csurka, who had been expelled from the Hungarian Democratic Forum in 1993. In 1999, mostly university students established a radical organization called the Right-Wing Youth Community, or Jobbik. In 2003 the organization became a political party, and it soon grew to challenge MIÉP. Among the various extreme rightist organizations, the increasingly radical Jobbik slowly established a leading role. The party's 2007 Gábor Bethlen Program contained a demand to use the armed forces to combat "Gypsy crime," which was supplemented by the idea of establishing gendarmeries. This became a central element

[35] *Köznapi események krónikája 1997* [Chronics of everyday events—1997] (Budapest: Magyar Helsinki Bizottság—Roma Sajtóközpont, 1998).

[36] MIÉP garnered 5.5% of the popular vote in the 1998 parliamentary elections.

of the radical party's rhetoric: "The establishment of an organizational unit within the police to prevent and investigate Gypsy crime in crisis-stricken counties."[37] (The Royal Hungarian Gendarmes was a law enforcement arm organized on military principles in the age of the Dual Monarchy and the Horthy era: in 1944 it played an active role in capturing Hungarian Jews.)

The Jobbik barge was soon home to paramilitary organizations based on violence against minorities. These first became visible on the political stage on August 25, 2007, with the establishment of the Hungarian Guard Tradition-Keeping and Cultural Association and the related paramilitary Hungarian Guard Movement, both with organizational ties to Jobbik. Only the former of the two organizations was a legal entity, and as such the movement could not be sued in court. The president of the association was Gábor Vona, whom the association named Chief Captain of the Guard. Jobbik's former founding president joined by two other founding members released a statement following the establishment of the Guard, calling the paramilitary organization "an unmeasurable and unacceptable source of risk" and left the party.[38] The uniformed Guard members did not make a secret of the fact that they organized to fulfill state law enforcement roles, and they developed an inner hierarchy typical of armed forces, based on ranks. The movement initiated thousands of members in various locations. To instil fear, the Guard held marches in settlements populated by Roma. For example, in December 2007 the Guard marched in Tatárszentgyörgy to support "rural public security", but in fact to threaten the local Roma: the organizers used this framework to step up against "Gypsy crime."

---

[37] Gábor Bethlen program point 9. Order is the soul of all things. The full text of the program is available at: http://www.jobbik.hu/rovatok/bethlen_gabor_program/bethlen_gabor_program.

[38] "Lemondott a Jobbik három alapítója a Magyar Gárda miatt" [Three Jobbik founders quit because of Hungarian Guard] accessed May 10, 2019, https://index.hu/belfold/hirek/345594. For a summary of events surrounding the Hungarian Guard: Attila B. Hidvégi, "Gárdaszellem" [Garda's spirit], in *Cigánynak lenni Magyarországon. Jelentés 2007* [A Roma's life in Hungary. Report 2007], ed. Erika Törzsök, Ildi Paskó and János Zolnay (Budapest: Európai Összehasonlító Kisebbségkutatások Közalapítvány, 2008).

With the strengthening of the extreme right and the increasingly serious ethnic conflict, the country was shocked by a series of murders targeting the Roma.[39] The judgement in the current court case holds that four men held an armed robbery in Besenyszög, fired shots on the refugee camp in Debrecen, and attacked Roma persons with arms and Molotov cocktails in nine settlements: on July 21, 2008 in Galgagyörk, August 8 in Pirics, September 5 in Nyíradony, September 29 in Tarnabod, November 3 in Nagycsécs, December 15 in Alsózsolca, then February 23, 2009 in Tatárszentgyörgy, April 22 in Tiszalök, and August 3 in Kisléta. The attacks in Kisléta and Tiszalök resulted in one death each, while those in Nagycsécs and Tatárszentgyörgy resulted in two deaths each. As an effect of the attacks, the Roma felt threatened. During this period Roma "patrol groups" were established in several settlements.[40] The residents of small villages were right in thinking that they could not rely on the protection of the state. In the Tatárszentgyörgy attack in 2009, a 27-year old father and his 5-year old son were shot by racist serial murderers while trying to escape their burning home. (The Guard had marched in the town in 2007.) The effectiveness of the work of the doctor, the firefighters and the police that arrived on the scene is illustrated by a statement released by the Pest County Police District after the attack, which held that "the initial opinion of the firefighting investigators is that an electric short caused the fire in which two lives were lost."[41] The series of murders of Roma/Gypsies, the tangible spread of racism and the ineffectiveness of the legal protection provided by the state once again led non-governmental organizations to broaden their activities to include the legal protection of the Roma minority.

---

39 Anita Danka, "Rossz helyen lenni rossz időben, avagy mit üzennek a gyűlölet-bűncselekmények?" [Wrong times, wrong place: what is the message of hate crimes?], *Föld-rész* 3–4 (2009): 92.

40 "A romák tovább járőröznek" [The Roma continue to patrol], *FigyelőNet*, accessed April 25, 2019, http://www.fn.hu/baleset_bunugy/;20090825/romak_tovabb_jaroroznek.

41 Report on the circumstances of the double murder in Tatárszentgyörgy on February 23, 2009, and the ensuing investigation. European Roma Rights Center, Legal Protection Office for National and Ethnic Minorities, Hungarian Civil Liberties Union joint report. http://www.nwki.hu/attachments/487_TSZ_Jelentes.pdf. 8.

On July 2, 2009 the court established that the operation of the Guard was illegal and demanded it to be disbanded. The court's decision stated that the association's organizational unit encompasses the Hungarian Guard and as such the sentence extends to both organizations.[42] The concrete reason for disbanding was the Guard's 2007 meeting in Tatárszentgyörgy, an inciting event that used the terms "Gypsy crime" and "Gypsy terror." The legal disbanding did not bring the expected results, as shortly after the decision—on July 25, 2009—a membership similar to that of the Guard formed the New Hungarian Guard Movement, which in its founding statement proclaimed that "given that New Hungarian Guard Movement is a long name," they would continue using the name Hungarian Guard.[43] On August 22, 2009 at the first initiation event of the New Hungarian Guard, 620 members were sworn in, and a "gendarmes squadron" was established. Jobbik has been holding mandates in the Hungarian Parliament since 2010, and by today it has become the strongest opposition partly due to their politically popular antigypsyism.[44]

Roma Policy of the National Cooperation System

In May 2010 the National Assembly of the Republic of Hungary accepted the government program of the Fidesz-KDNP party alliance that obtained more than two-thirds of the seats in the parliamentary

[42] On July 2, 2009, the appeal court confirmed the decision of the lower court: during deliberation it referred to the European Convention on Human Rights (Rome Convention) Article 5 (right to freedom and security) as well as the International Convention on the Elimination of all form of Racial Discrimination (ICERD) Article 4, point b) (banning organizations agitating for racial separation). Court of Budapest. Decision no. 5.Pf.20.738/2009/7. Full text available at http://www.itelotabla.hu/fileadmin/fajlok/fovaros/2009/mg_itelet090716.doc.

[43] Founding statement: http://magyargarda.hu/alapito_nyilatkozat.

[44] Gergely Karácsony and Dániel Róna, "A JOBBIK titka, A szélsőjobb magyarorszagi megerősödésének lehetséges okairól" [Of the secret of the JOBBIK, possible causes of the strengthening of the rights extremists in Hungary], *Politikatudományi Szemle* 1 (2010): 31–63.

election.[45] Shortly thereafter, in June 2010, the National Assembly approved the Declaration on National Cooperation as a political document, which stated that "a new social contract was laid down during the April general elections through which the Hungarians decided to create a new system: the National Cooperation System."[46] The Hungarian Parliament passed Hungary's new constitution, the Fundamental Law on April 18, 2011, which entered into force on January 1, 2012 and superseded the Constitution of 1989.

The new constitution is not facing the past, the contemporary history of Hungary.[47] As János Kis stated, "The Fundamental Law only recognizes the (pre-1944) glorious pages of Hungarian history, but does not acknowledge the acts and failures that give cause for self-criticism. It only holds to account the—reputed or genuine—injuries to the Hungarian people by foreign powers, and does not wish to acknowl-

[45] See Gábor Halmai, "An Illiberal Constitutional System in the Middle of Europe," in *European Yearbook of Human Rights,* ed. Benedek Wolfgang et al. (Cambridge—Antwerp—Chicago –Vienna: Intersentia, 2014), 512.

[46] "Political Declaration 1 of 2010 (16 June 2010) of the Hungarian National Assembly on National Cooperation," accessed December 20, 2015, http://www.kulugyminiszterium.hu/NR/rdonlyres/1EC78EE5-8A4B-499C-9BE5-E5FD5DC2C0A1/0/Political_Declaration.pdf.

[47] In the interwar period Miklós Horthy, a former Austro-Hungarian admiral, ruled Hungary as Regent from March 1st, 1920 until October 16th, 1944. Hungary was formally a—restricted—parliamentary democracy, but autocratic tendencies gradually strengthened as a result of Nazi influence and the Great Depression. Hungary joined the Axis Powers in World War II, and took part in the War on their side. However, on March 19, 1944 German troops occupied Hungary, and on October 15, 1944 the Regent was replaced by a puppet Nazi government. Following the fall of Nazi Germany, Soviet troops occupied Hungary, and after a short democratic period the country fell under a state socialist regime by adopting the totalitarian state model of the Soviet Union. This was the beginning of a more than four decade-long state socialist dictatorship (1948–1989/1990) that can be divided from the viewpoint of political history into two different periods named after the party-leaders: the Rákosi-era (1949–1956), and the Kádár-era, which followed the suppression of the 1956 revolution (1957–1989). Mátyás Rákosi was the General Secretary of the Hungarian Working People's Party between 1948–1953 and János Kádár ruled the country as first secretary of the Hungarian Socialist Workers' Party between 1956–1988. State socialism ended with Hungary's peaceful revolution of 1989, i.e., with the regime change.

edge the wrongs committed by the Hungarian state against its own citizens and other peoples."[48]

The Preamble of the Fundamental Law of Hungary introduced an ethnic (cultural) concept of the nation.[49] It stated the following, "We promise to preserve the intellectual and spiritual unity of our nation torn apart in the storms of the last century."[50] As János Kis points out, "The Fundamental Law defines it as a community, the binding fabric of which is 'intellectual and spiritual': not political, but cultural. There is no place in this community for the national minorities living within the territory of the Hungarian state."[51]

As Michel Rosenfeld mentions, constitutional identity and national identity "originate[d] in the late eighteenth century and both are identities constructed and projected by imagined communities."[52] Constitutional identity must remain distinct from the cultural nation; only in this way can the moral equality of all members of the political community be ensured. In spite of this, as Nóra Chronowski's chapter underlines, since the Fundamental Law uses the concept of an ethnic nation, the ethnicity-based form of national identity defines the constitutional identity of Hungary. The Constitution itself makes a distinction between "we, the Hungarian nation" (ethnic nation) and "the people who live among us."[53] The primary role of the ethnic nation can also endanger the egalitarian character of the state, which once linked

[48] "Opinion on the Fundamental Law of Hungary," ed. Andrew Arato et al., accessed April 8, 2019, http://lapa.princeton.edu/hosteddocs/amicus-to-vc-english-final.pdf., 10.

[49] *Opinion on Hungary's New Constitutional Order: Amicus Brief to the Venice Commission on the Transitional Provisions of the Fundamental Law and the Key Cardinal Laws*, ed. Gábor Halmai et al., accessed January 1, 2015, available both in English and Hungarian at https://sites.google.com/site/amicusbriefhungary, 7. or Zsolt Körtvélyesi, "From 'We the People' to 'We the Nation,'" in *Constitution for a Disunited Nation Hungary's New Fundamental Law*, ed. Gábor Attila Tóth (Budapest: CEU Press, 2012).

[50] NATIONAL AVOWAL (Fundamental Law).

[51] See Opinion on Hungary's New Constitutional Order: Amicus Brief to the Venice Commission on the Transitional Provisions of the Fundamental Law and the Key Cardinal Laws, supra note 34, at 7.

[52] Michel Rosenfeld, *The Identity of the Political Subjects (Selfhood, Citizenship, Culture and Community* (New York: Routledge, 2010), 12.

[53] For more on this topic see Nóra Chronowski's chapter in this volume.

together nation- and state-building.[54] If the Constitution does not regard all citizens as equal, it allows for potential limitations on human rights, especially regarding the rights of minorities.

As we will analyze it later, the Fundamental Law has provisions that are explicitly against the Roma and support the mainstreaming of prejudicial discourses.[55] For instance Article V ensures the following:[56] "Everyone shall have the right to repel any unlawful attack against his or her person or property, or one that poses a direct threat to the same, as provided for by an Act." The article is denounced for protecting the ethnic Hungarian middle class from the socially excluded (among whom Roma are overrepresented), and it strengthens the stereotype of "Gypsy crime" and the antigypsyism in the Hungarian society and raises it on the constitutional level. As Kriszta Kovács points out, "this article is about a right to self-defense in a state of nature described by Hobbes, and not a basic right in a constitutional state."[57]

Under democratic rule of law with human rights, law-makers cannot act against the moral equality of citizens and must exhibit equal attention to and respect toward each member of the political community. Use of the ethnic concept of nation as a definitive element of the constitutional identity of state as happened in the Hungarian Fundamental Law, without regard for the principle of equality, such as when only the members of a particular social class (nobility, workers, members of a caste, etc.) may belong, naturally also does not fulfill this demand.[58]

The equality of the members in a political community draws a clear borderline between paternalistic, anti-egalitarian regimes and democratic, egalitarian ones. Hungary based its new identity in its new

[54] On the possible conflict of state and nation building in Central and Eastern Europe: Zsuzsa Csergő and James M. Goldgeier: "Kin-State Activism in Hungary, Romania, and Russia, The Politics of Ethnic Demography," in *Divided Nations and European Integration,* ed. Tristan James Mabry, John McGarry, Margaret Moore and Brendan O'Leary (Philadelphia: University of Pennsylvania Press, 2013), 89–126.

[55] Kovács, "Equality: The Missing Link," 190.

[56] Ibid., 190.

[57] Ibid., 190.

[58] For more on this topic see Chronowski's chapter in this volume.

Constitution on the anti-egalitarian legacy of the past, including an anti-egalitarian view of the nation and the history of the exclusion of minorities.

A NEW SOCIAL POLICY

In accordance with the antiegalitarian character of the Fundamental Law, the institutional system of social aid is being dismantled and the barrier that was constructed after the regime change to obstruct exclusion and segregation in education is broken through.

Passages of the Fundamental Law also foreshadow and/or demand social processes that will lead to the exclusion of the Roma. The Fourth Amendment of the Fundamental Law has Article XV Paragraph 4 using the term "catching up" alongside equality of opportunity, the term "catching up" by the government, entailing a concept whereby the efforts of the individual are necessary for success.[59] This makes it possible to limit those rights who do not make enough efforts to improve their peripheral social situation according to the present Hungarian government which seems to totally ignore the phenomenon of social exclusion.

As part of the right to work, Article XII of the Fundamental Law stipulates the obligation to work according to one's abilities and possibilities: "Everyone shall be obliged to contribute to the enrichment of the community through his or her work, in accordance with his or her abilities and possibilities." This provision has the potential to be directed against the Roma community, which is the biggest minority in Hungary, most afflicted by unfavorable social conditions and widespread prejudices. The sentence above removes those fundamental rights that guarantee the prevention of the introduction of measures that could bind the provision of unemployment aid to work or to an activity deemed socially useful.[60]

The government has put aside the model of the welfare state to create a new "workfare society" in accordance with the new constitu-

59 "Balog Zoltán beszéde—Felzárkózás-politika a XXI. században," accessed April 8, 2019 http://www.balogzoltan.hu/balog-zoltan-beszede-felzarkozas-politika-a-xxi-szazadban.

60 Arató, Halmai and Kis, "Opinion," 16.

tional framework.[61] This approach has a negative effect on those living in dire poverty, especially the Roma/Gypsies.[62] Article XIX of the Constitution limits the rights of the unemployed, who are entitled to social aid only if the jobless person experiences "unemployment for reasons outside of his or her control." Paragraph 3 of the same Article states that "The nature and extent of social measures may be determined in an Act in accordance with the usefulness to the community of the beneficiary's activity." In the name of the workfare society, 2011 saw the passing of a workfare program entitled the National Work Plan (which was later renamed the Hungarian Work Plan). The rationale for the program was the mistaken and prejudiced idea that unemployment is caused not by external circumstances but by a situation whereby it is more advantageous for an individual to live off social aid and perhaps work in the black market on the side. As such, it is assumed that the only people who do not work are those who do not want to. Those excluded from the labor market are forced to take on work that will not result in their returning to the labor market (e.g., removing ragweed, mowing grass, cleaning parks and tidying woods). Should they not do so, they will be denied the minimal benefits.

The "public-purpose" program that practically forces people into physical labor and the laws that support it bear a resemblance to both state socialism and the dictatorial heritage from before World War II. We can witness the state socialist desire to reach full employment resurfacing, when the treatment of employment as a social problem becomes secondary. Further, the attempt to tie social rights to work is reminiscent of authoritarian times. At the same time, there are differences: the social benefits system constructed under state socialism, one of the functions of which was to increase dependence on the state—as we have explained above—has been radically dismantled. It appears that there was a need to put the poor in a submissive position, and that the real goal of what passes for social policy is to make the creation of a majority possible in the long term. Winning over the middle class happens by

[61] The term workfare society ("munkaalapú társadalom") is used in the speech of Viktor Orbán on July 26, 2014 in Băile Tuşnad (Tusnádfürdő).

[62] Dorottya Szikra, "Democracy and Welfare in Hard Times: The Social Policy of the Orbán Government in Hungary Between 2010 and 2014," *Journal of European Social Policy* 24(2014): 486–500.

riding anti-Roma and anti-poor sentiments existing in society through the separation, the discpline and exclusion of disadvantaged and minority groups strengthens the definition of the nation as a social class. It is easy to draw a line from the present to the heritage of the pre-WWII authoritarian Horthy regime, given that the current program received the same name as the National Work Plan passed in 1932 under Prime Minister Gyula Gömbös, a well-known racist. That plan also subjugated the interests of the individual to those of the nation and sought to offer support to the poor in return for work.

The forced labor nature of the workfare system[63] is articulated in the legal regulation (Act CVI/2011) where, following the principle of aid for work, it is stated that those who do not take part in the workfare program for at least thirty days in the given year can be excluded from social benefits. Those who do not send their children to school and do not keep their homes and gardens in order are to be excluded from workfare, which pays significantly less than minimum wage. Besides this, the government lowered the mandatory education age from 18 to 16, and dismantled the system for retraining and adult training, making success in the labor market even more difficult, and further weakening the chances of the poor to study, find meaningful employment, and have equality of opportunity in general.[64] Recent times have seen attempts by lawmakers to dismantle legal obstacles to segregation. The law on public education was modified in 2014, allowing the Minister to authorize separated education for Roma children in certain cases.[65]

In April 2015 the Hungarian Supreme Court decided that the educational segregation of Roma children living in dire poverty, under the guise of religious education, was legal. The Court's decision reversed the progress of a decade of successful desegregation litigation in Hungary. The specific case had been pushed by the Equal

[63] Balázs Berkovits, "A közmunka mint fegyelmezés" [Workfare as a disciplining tool], accessed April 8, 2019, http://szuveren.hu/tarsadalom/a-kozmunka-mint-fegyelmezes.

[64] Dorottya Szikra, "Produktív szociálpolitika" [Productive social policy], accessed April 8, 2019, http://szuveren.hu/tarsadalom/produktiv-szocialpolitika.

[65] Act 2014/CV on the amendment of the Public Education Act under paragraph (§ 25 (5) of Art.Z).

Chance for Children Foundation (CFCF) as an anti-segregation case that affected the Roma living in the Huszár district of the city of Nyíregyháza, which is a Roma settlement. Responding to pressure from CFCF, the municipal authority had once shut the school down, in 2007. But the school reopened in 2011 as a Greek Catholic institution. Minister of Human Resources Zoltán Balog, whose portfolio includes education and is himself a Calvinist pastor, has consistently taken the side of the pro-segregation school.

After 2010 in Hungary—as we stressed in the Introduction—one can observe a process whereby extreme right-wing discourses on Roma minority have become increasingly mainstream, given that an ever wider swath of society relates to these proclamations.[66] Constitutional provisions also contribute to a violent climate and are an indirect form of discrimination against socially marginalized groups. This is especially dangerous in the current time of open ethnic conflict, when paramilitary groups "patrol" the Roma areas of small settlements, or when extremist movements incite for action and vigilantism against "Gypsy crime."

This was all observable in an incident after 2010, one reflecting the ever more open ethnic conflict at the local level. Between March 1 and March 15, 2011 the streets of Gyöngyöspata (a town of 2,500 in Northeast Hungary) were patrolled by members of the Better Future Civic Association,[67] the Outlaw Platoon and the Defense Force paramilitary groups, all in military-styled outfits.[68] The clothing of the Defense Force closely resembled the uniform of the Hungarian Guard, consisting of a white shirt, black vest, boots and outer layer with a coat of arms with Árpád stripes.[69] (The flag with Árpád stripes was a medi-

---

[66] See e.g. Zsuzsanna Vidra and Jon Fox, "Mainstreaming of Racist Anti-Roma Discourses in the Media in Hungary," *Journal of Immigrant & Refugee Studies* 12 (2014): 437–455.

[67] The association was founded by 11 former members of the disbanded Hungarian Guard; the president was Békés County President of the New Hungarian Guard.

[68] Report of the Parliamentary Commissioner on the rights of national and ethnic minorities on the events in Gyöngyöspata in March of 2011 and the danger of similar phenomena, accessed November 11, 2015, http://www.kisebbsegiombudsman.hu/data/files/203198066.pdf.

[69] Ibid., 9.

eval flag of Árpádházi dynasty in Hungary. In modern Hungarian history, before and during World War II it also became a symbol of extremist right-wing movements.) The patrolling plan was reported to the police ahead of time, who acknowledged it. At the same time the extreme right-wing Jobbik party held a party function on March 6, against "Gypsy terror," in which local residents appeared alongside party sympathizers from across the country. The aim of the event, when it was announced, was the following: "We are demonstrating at the request of the residents of Gyöngyöspata who are terrorized by the strata of the local Roma population living off of crime… we demand the investigation and sanctioning of illegal acts."[70] (The village has a long history of segregation. In 2014 the Chance for Children Foundation successfully sued the municipal council—with a Jobbik majority—the local school, and the maintaining state institution, given that the local Demeter Nekcsei Elementary School had been illegally segregating Roma children based on their heritage between 2004 and 2012.) Parliament responded to the events by modifying the Criminal Code,[71] although after the conflict only Roma were taken into custody. Referring to the situation in Gyöngyöspata, the former mayor resigned and a member of Jobbik took over as mayor following a by-election. The Jobbik mayor led the town from 2011 to 2014, which in 2014 elected a new mayor, a candidate of the FIDESZ-KDNP governing coalition. At the local level it is apparent that the Roma—non-Roma differentiation not only signifies simple social hierarchy and subject-superordinate relations, but unequivocal power relations as well, which are connected to the phenomenon of exclusion and its maintenance with any tools necessary.

The Shift

At the time of the regime change of 1989–90 there was a consensus among democratic parties that the previous state socialist system could be left behind only by the creation of the democratic rule of law, and

[70] Ibid., 14.

[71] Tóth, *Constitution for a Disunited Nation.*

the implementation of market economy, where individual initiative and responsibility, and not the will of the majority or state would drive things forward. After 2010, the concept of the egalitarian democratic rule of law guaranteeing human rights has been replaced with an anti-egalitarian vision of illiberal democracy, which adopts labor, municipal and educational segregation and builds an increasing number of obstacles to the integration of the Roma minority.

This situation is reminiscent of underclass societies and in many ways of one-time colonial societies that were split in two ("world cut in two"). The latter parallel is illustrated by a quote exemplifying the world of a former colony cut in two:[72] "The dividing line, the frontiers are shown by barracks and police stations. In the colonies it is the policeman and the soldier who are the official, instituted go-betweens, the spokesmen of the settler and his rule of oppression."[73] If we replace settler with majority Hungarian, and barracks with villages, then the division into two and the metaphor of frontier become applicable to describe the social relationship between the non-Roma and Roma of Hungary. To the excluded residents of slums (defined as Roma) the state stands for nothing more than an institution of oppression. If this really is the world that has been built, then it can no longer be described through terms of equality and the rule of law, given that this kind of society is based on extreme exclusion and on the complete rejection of integration. Beyond the denial of equality and the rule of law, total segregation and thinking in terms of exclusive racial and ethnic categorization bear with them the risk of ethnic conflict. This means that those put into the categories of the socially excluded can turn against the "majority." Hungarian Prime Minister Viktor Orbán in one of his speeches given during the refugee crisis drew a parallel between the Roma and Islamic refugees. The Prime Minister underlined that Hungary could not handle another unintegrated group like the Roma. The speech was based on the differentiation between us/them, and forced the clash of civilization paradigm on the Roma issue.[74]

---

[72] Frantz Fanon, *The Wretched of the Earth* (New York: Grove Press, 1963), 38.

[73] Ibid.

[74] "Orbán: We shouldn't be Expected to Live with Many Muslims https://refugeecrisisinhungary.wordpress.com/2015/09/09/orban-we-shouldnt-be-

If the minority group is labelled the Other, then the minority group itself will view the majority as the Other, one that, thanks to real differentiation, appears to truly exist and be truly unified.[75]

Oppressive and controlling patterns as laid out in stories of colonization are familiar to those who have observed how European societies have subjugated and oppressed the Roma.[76] The current system in Hungary is colonial in the sense that the subjugation based on difference is a state that cannot be changed. [77] The social practice whereby social and cultural differences between the majority and minority are organized in a hierarchical system and interpreted as such has been institutionalized by today. The new Hungarian National Cooperation System builds its identities on the historical legacy of the premodern (anti-egalitarian) concept of nation (nation as a class), and the social exclusion of the Hungarian Roma (ethnicity as underclass). In the daily practice of state institutions this means the division of citizens into those who have the right to state support and those who do not:

---

expected-to-live-with-many-muslims/. Jenő Setét, a prominent Hungarian Roma rights activist, reflected on the Prime Minister's speech with the following speech: "Hungarian politics keeps harping on about the burden of 800 thousand Gypsies living here, which is why we can't accommodate the refugees. But this is not true. There isn't a single thing the refugees have taken away from me… There is something the refugees and Hungarian Gypsies do have in common. That is the mistreatment of both groups. I am here to refute those words of Viktor Orbán and all the other Hungarian politicians, when they use us as ammunition to shoot at Europe… There was power that meant only to rule over people, and considered them objects. Then people vested themselves with civil rights." See "We belong here! Hungarian Activists Fight Back in Refugee Crisis," accessed November 11, 2015, http://bright-green.org/2015/09/15/we-belong-here-hungarian-activists-fight-back-in-refugee-crisis/.

[75] Karl Schmidt, *The Concept of the Political* (Chicago: University of Chicago Press, 2007), 28–9.

[76] Angéla Kóczé and Nidhi Trehan, "Postcolonial Racism and Social Justice: The Struggle for the Soul of the Romani Civil Rights Movement in the 'New Europe,'" in *Racism, Post-colonialism, Europe,* ed. G. Huggan (Liverpool: Liverpool University Press, 2009), 50–77.

[77] Walter Mignolo See, "Delinking: the Rhetoric of Modernity, the Logic of Coloniality, and the Grammar of De-coloniality," *Cultural Studies* 2 (2007): 449–514.

those who are "worthy" and those who are "unworthy."[78] Loyalty structures that are tied to the practice of exclusion have developed.

Conclusion

This chapter has underlined the continuity of the exclusive view of the nation as a social category in Hungarian society through historical periods and its effects on the status of the Hungarian Roma. It has pointed out the discrepancy between the ambitions of liberal democracy (1989–2010) and those of the National Cooperation System (2010–): the latter clearly dropped the unachieved egalitarian objectives of the former system.

In Hungary, in the years from 1990 to 2010 social inequalities not only escalated, but became ethnicized. Discrimination, poverty and segregation were all determining, or even constitutive factors of the "liberal democracy" itself. The constitutional shift of 2010 was partly rooted in the failure of the alternating conservative and left-wing liberal governments to implement effective social inclusion policies. It is significant to underline that the Hungarian antiegalitarian turn was successful at least partly because it followed also the social preferences of dominant voting groups.

Since 2010 Hungary has been constructing illiberal democratic institutions in which state policies and the attitudes of the representatives of the state are increasingly similar to those of the dictatorial past. According to our interpretations, the independent state institutions that could have protected the human rights of the socially excluded Roma stopped functioning after the public law shift. The rising segregation and the lack of functioning national human rights institutions draw a clear borderline between the majority and the socially excluded minority. The political system has become post-colonial in the sense that it treats exclusion, the hierarchical relationship

---

78 Herbert J Gans, "Über die positiven Funktionen der unwürdigen Armen. Zur Bedeutung der 'underclass' in den USA," in *Armut im modernen Wohlfahrtsstaat. Sonderheft 32 der Kölner Zeitschrift für Soziologie und Sozialpsychologie*, ed. Stephan Leibfried and Wolfgang Voges (Hg.), (Opladen: Westdeutscher Verlag.S., 1992), 48–62.

between majority and minority, and subject status as its unchangeable foundation, which for the most part was connected to the operational practice of state institutions. At the same time, the power discourses hide the individual and collective experiences of poverty and minority situation.

Exclusion today has become part of the daily practice of the state and municipal authorities. Discourses that consolidate legitimacy continue to maintain the image of a unified majority and separated minority, divided and antagonized. The state has returned to historic times, even though the kind of majority Hungarian history and the Hungarian nation they wish to see again never existed in reality, and could never be real and just, it is merely a reference point for whoever happens to be in power. The governing party alliance, by legalizing their story-like view of history, limiting fundamental rights, dismantling institutions of legal protection and making their functioning impossible, has closed a chapter in the history of the Roma in Hungary, when the liberal democratic state policies at least attempted to institutionalize an egalitarian concept of the nation.

BIBLIOGRAPHY

Ahmad, Aijaz. "Post-Colonialism: What's in a Name?" In *Late Imperial Culture,* edited by Roman de la Campa, Ann E. Kaplan, and Michael Sprinker, 135–146. London: Verso, 1995.

Beck, Ulrich. *Die Erfindung des Politischen: Zu einer Theorie reflexiver Modernisierung*. Frankfurt-Main: Suhrkamp Verlag, 1993.

Berkovits, Balázs. "A közmunka mint fegyelmezés" [Workfare as a disciplining tool]. Accessed April 8, 2019. http://szuveren.hu/tarsadalom/a-kozmunka-mint-fegyelmezes.

Bibó, István. "Zsidókérdés Magyarországon 1944 után" [The Jewish question in Hungary after 1944]. In *Válogatott tanulmányok* II [Selected studies II], István Bibó, 621–809. Budapest: Magvető, 1990.

Blanchard, Olivier Jean, Kenneth A. Froot, and Jeffrey D. Sachs. *The Transition in Eastern Europe*. Chicago: University of Chicago Press, 1994.

Brubaker, Rogers. "The Return of Assimilation? Changing Perspectives on Immigration and its Sequels in France, Germany, and the United States." *Ethnic and Racial Studies* 4 (2001): 531–548.

Csepeli, György, and Antal Örkény. "The Making of a Minority: Competing claims of Definitions of Being Roma in Contemporary Hungarian Society." *Central European Political Science Review* 17 (2016): 150–179.

Csergő, Zsuzsa, and James M. Goldgeier. "Kin-State Activism in Hungary, Romania, and Russia: The Politics of Ethnic Demography." In *Divided Nations and European Integration,* edited by Tristan James Mabry, John McGarry, Margaret Moore, and Brendan O'Leary, 89–126. Philadelphia: University of Pennsylvania Press, 2013.

Fanon, Frantz. *The Wretched of the Earth.* New York: Grove Press, 1963.

Feischmidt, Margit. "Kényszerek és illeszkedések. Gazdasági és szimbolikus stratégiák aprófalvakban élő romák életében" [Economic and symbolic strategies of Romani people living in Hungarian villages]. *Szociológiai Szemle* 2 (2012): 54–84.

Gans, Herbert J. "Über die positiven Funktionen der unwürdigen Armen. Zur Bedeutung der 'underclass' in den USA." In *Armut im modernen Wohlfahrtsstaat. Sonderheft 32 der Kölner Zeitschrift für Soziologie und Sozialpsychologie,* edited by Stephan Leibfried, and Wolfgang Voges, 48–62. Opladen: Westdeutscher Verlag.S., 1992.

Gellner, Ernest. "The Coming of Nationalism and its Interpretation: the Myths of Nation and Class." In *Mapping the Nation,* edited by Gopal Balakrishnan, 98–132. London: Verso, 1996.

"Governmental attacks against Hungarian NGO sphere." Accessed November 13, 2019. http://tasz.hu/files/tasz/imce/timeline_of_gov_attacks_against_hungarian_ngos_20140921.pdf.

Halmai, Gábor. "An Illiberal Constitutional System in the Middle of Europe." In *European Yearbook of Human Rights,* edited by Benedek Wolfgang, Florence Benoît-Rohmer, Wolfram Karl, Matthias C. Kettemann, and Manfred Nowak, 497–514. Cambridge–Antwerp–Chicago–Vienna: Intersentia, 2014.

Hankiss, Elemér. *East European Alternatives.* New York: Oxford University Press, 1990.

Kállai, Ernő. *Helyi cigány kisebbségi önkormányzatok Magyarországon* [Local Gypsy selfgovernments in Hungary]. Budapest: MTA Etnikai-nemzetiségi Kisebbségkutató Intézet—Gondolat Kiadói Kör, 2005.

Karácsony, Gergely, and Dániel Róna. "A JOBBIK titka, A szélsőjobb magyarorszagi megerősödésének lehetséges okairól" [Of the secret of the JOBBIK, possible causes of the strengthening of the rights extremists in Hungary]. *Politikatudományi Szemle* 1 (2010): 31–63.

Kemény, István. "Előszó" [Introduction]. In *A romák/cigányok és a láthatatlan gazdaság.* [The Roma/Gypsies and the invisible economy], edited by István Kemény, 28–29. Budapest: Osiris—MTA Kisebbségkutató Műhely, 2000.

Kemény, István. "A magyarországi cigányok helyzete" [The status of the Gypsies of Hungary]. In *Beszámoló a magyarországi cigányok helyzetével foglalkozó 1971-ben végzett kutatásról* [Report on research carried out in 1971 on the situation of Gypsies in Hungary], edited by István Kemény, 7–67. Budapest: MTA Szociológiai Kutató Intézete, 1976.

Kemény, István. "Tennivalók a cigányok/romák ügyében" [Some Proposals on the Gypsy / Roma Question]. In *A cigányok Magyarországon* [Gypsies in

Hungary], edited by István Kemény, 251–252. Budapest: Magyar Tudományos Akadémia, 1999.

"Kerényi György interjúja Kaltenbach Jenő kisebbségi ombudsmannal." [An interview with Jenő Kaltenbach, parliamentary commissioner for minority rights, by György Kerényi]. *Fundamentum* 2 (2000): 35–42.

Kis, János. "Between Reform and Revolution." *East European Politics and Societies* 12 (1998): 300–83.

Kisebbségek Magyarországon, 1999 [Minorites in Hungary, 1999], edited by Mária Zayzon Demeter. Budapest: Nemzeti és Etnikai Kisebbségi Hivatal, 2000.

Kóczé, Angéla, and Nidhi Trehan. "Postcolonial Racism and Social Justice: The Struggle for the Soul of the Romani Civil Rights Movement in the 'New Europe.'" In *Racism, Post-colonialism, Europe,* edited by G. Huggan, 50–77. Liverpool: Liverpool University Press, 2009.

Kovacevic, Natasha. *Narrating Post/Communism: Colonial Discourse and Europe's Borderline Civilization.* London: Routledge, 2008.

Körtvélyesi, Zsolt. "*From 'We the People' to 'We the Nation.'*" In *Constitution for a Disunited Nation: Hungary's New Fundamental Law,* edited by Gábor Attila Tóth, 111-–140. Budapest: CEU Press, 2012.

Kovács, Kriszta. "Equality: The Missing Link." In *Constitution for a Disunited Nation. On Hungary's 2011 Fundamental Law,* edited by Tóth Gábor Attila, 171–196. Budapest: CEU Press, 2012.

Ladányi, János. "Romaügyek pedig nincsenek!" [There are no Roma affairs]. *Egyenlítő* 1 (2003): 21–26.

Ladányi, János, and Iván Szelényi. *Patterns of Exclusion: Constructing Gypsy Ethnicity and the Making of an Underclass in Transitional Societies of Europe.* New York: Columbia University Press, 2006.

Ladányi, János, and Iván Szelényi. *A kirekesztettség változó formái* [The changing forms of exclusion]. Budapest: Napvilág, 2004.

Majtényi, Balázs, and György Majtényi. *A Contemporary History of Exclusion. The Roma issue in Hungary from 1945 to 2015.* Budapest: CEU Press, 2016.

Majtényi, Balázs. *A nemzetállam új ruhája. Multikulturalizmus Magyarországon* [The new cloth of nation state: Multiculturalism in Hungary]. Budapest: Gondolat, 2007.

Majtényi, Balázs. "What Has Happened to Our Model Child? The Creation and Evolution of the Hungarian Minority Act." *European Yearbook of Minority Issues* 5 (2006): 397–419.

Messing, Vera. "Egymásnak kiszolgáltatva. Inter-etnikus konfliktusok és a média." [At the Mercy of Each Other. Interethnic Conflicts and the Media]. In *Kisebbségek kisebbsége. A magyarországi cigányok emberi és politikai jogai* [Minority among the minorities: Human and political rights of Roma in Hungary], edited by Mária Neményi and Júlia Szalai, 316–353. Budapest: Új Mandátum Kiadó, 2005.

Mignolo, Walter. "Delinking: the Rhetoric of Modernity, the Logic of Coloniality, and the Grammar of De-coloniality." *Cultural Studies* 2 (2007): 449–514.

Miklósi, Zoltán. "Demokrácia: liberális, alkotmányos és egyéb" (Democracy: Liberal, constitutional and other"). Accessed January 13, 2019. http://szuveren.hu/politika/demokracia-liberalis-alkotmanyos-es-egyeb.

Molnár, Emilia, and Kai A. Schafft. "A helyi roma/cigány kisebbségi önkormányzatok tevékenysége és céljai Magyarországon 2000–2001-ben" [The activities and goals of local roma/gypsy minority self-governments in Hungary in 2000 and 2001]. *Szociológiai Szemle* 1 (2003): 79–99.

Opinion on Hungary's New Constitutional Order: Amicus Brief to the Venice Commission on the Transitional Provisions of the Fundamental Law and the Key Cardinal Laws. Edited by Gábor Halmai, Kim Lane Scheppele, Miklós Bánkuti, Tamás Dombos, Zoltán Fleck Gábor Halmai, Krisztina Rozgonyi, Balázs Majtényi, László Majtényi, Eszter Polgári, Bernadette Somody, and Renáta Uitz. Accessed January 1, 2019. https://sites.google.com/site/amicusbriefhungary.

Rosenfeld, Michel. *The Identity of the Political Subjects (Selfhood, Citizenship, Culture and Community).* New York: Routledge, 2010.

Said, Edward W. *Orientalism.* New York: Vintage Books, 1978.

San Juan, Epifanio. *Beyond Postcolonial Theory.* New York: St. Martins Press, 1998.

Sandru, Cristina. *Worlds Apart? A Postcolonial Reading of Post-1945 East-Central European Culture.* Cambridge: Cambridge Scholars Publishing, 2012.

Schmidt, Karl. *The Concept of the Political.* Chicago: University of Chicago Press, 2007.

Ştefănescu, Bogdan. *Postcommunism/Postcolonialism: Siblings of Subalternity,* Bucharest: Editura Universităţii din Bucureşti, 2012.

Szikra, Dorottya. "Democracy and Welfare in Hard Times: The Social Policy of the Orbán Government in Hungary between 2010 and 2014." *Journal of European Social Policy* 24 (2014): 486–500.

Szikra, Dorottya. *Produktív szociálpolitika* [Productive social policy]. Accessed April 8, 2019, http://szuveren.hu/tarsadalom/produktiv-szocialpolitika.

Szűcs, Jenő. *Nemzet és történelem. Tanulmányok* [Nation and history. Essays]. Budapest: Gondolat, 1974.

Szuhay, Péter. *A magyarországi cigányok kultúrája: etnikus kultúra vagy a szegénység kultúrája* [The culture of the gypsies in Hungary: an ethnic culture or the culture of poverty]. Budapest: Panoráma, 43–44.

Smith, Anthony D. *Ethno-Symbolism and Nationalism: A Cultural Approach.* New York: Routledge, 2009.

Timmer, Alexandra. "Report State-of-the-art Literature Review Human Rights, Democracy and the Rule of Law." Accessed November 12, 2015. http://www.fp7-frame.eu/wp-content/materiale/reports/01-Deliverable-3.1.pdf.

Varga, Benedek. "Political Humanism and the Corporate Theory of State: Nation, Patria and Virtue in Hungarian Political Thought of the Sixteenth Century." In *Whose Love of Which Country? Composite States and Patriotic Discourses in Early-Modern Central Europe,* edited by Balázs Trencsényi and Márton Zászkaliczky, 283–314. Leiden–Boston: Brill, 2010.

Váradi, Mónika Mária. "Szegénység, kirekesztettség" [Poverty, exclusion]. In *Közösségtanulmány. Módszertani jegyzet* [Community studies. A metholodogical handbook], edited by Éva Kovács, 69–87. Budapest: Néprajzi Múzeum – Pécsi Tudományegyetem BTK Kommunikáció- és Médiatudományi Tanszék, 2007.

Vidra, Zsuzsanna, and Jon Fox. "Mainstreaming of Racist Anti-Roma Discourses in the Media in Hungary." *Journal of Immigrant & Refugee Studies* 4 (2014): 437–455.

New Forms of Nationalism and the Discursive Construction of the Gypsy Other

MARGIT FEISCHMIDT

Introduction

This chapter is part of a larger project which aims to increase understanding of the re-emergence of nationalism in Hungary in rather new forms. New nationalism[1] can be comprehended in relation to the successful establishment of the populist far right, as well as to the increasing demand for issues of identity and culture in fields outside politics, such as civic and leisure activities, media, cultural consumption, and everyday discourses. Nevertheless, as this chapter claims, everyday discourses of belonging and exclusion signalled long before the appearance of far-right alternatives that the reconstruction of solidarity is framed in ethno-racial terms, and moreover, is focused on the othering of the Roma by the ethnic majority of rural Hungary. My investigation applies a social-anthropological perspective in the analysis of nationalism and reveals the discourses as well as the social relations which have generated the demand for this discourse and an increasing responsiveness towards identity politics and national mythologies in Hungarian society.

Concepts, symbols of sameness and othering are strongly interconnected both in politics and everyday discourses.[2] Thus, discur-

---

1 Andre Gingrich and Marcus Banks, *Neo-Nationalism in Europe and Beyond. Perspectives from Social Anthropology* (London: Berghahn Books, 2006).

2 Ruth Wodak, Rudolf de Cillia, Martin Reisigl and Karin Liebhart, *The Discursive Construction of National Identity* (Edinburgh: Edinburgh University Press, 1999).

sive approaches interpret nationalism as a discourse of homogenization and classification which is able to create a category of "us" only through and in strong connection to the construction of a category of "them"—or in other words, as Verdery states, the nationalization of sameness requires the ethnicization of otherness.[3] In the present paper, everyday discourses are analyzed which produce the othering of the "Gypsy" category, along with their impact on the image and discursive reproduction of "Hungarianness." Furthermore, I examine the process of othering from the perspective of the Roma, with the aim of describing what forms of minority self-representation are connected to discursively imposed "Gypsy" otherness in Hungary. Additionally, this implies exploring what opportunities are left for those categorized as "Gypsies" to identify with the unmarked majority; that is, with "Hungarianness."

This paper examines the local variations within the discourse of Gypsy othering by looking at their structural relations and semantic precedents and, most importantly, at how the practice of Gypsy othering is connected to the discourses defining "Hungarianness." The analysis focuses on how identification with the category of "Hungarian" acquires meaning—through the domestication of official, institutional rites, and the nation-building discourse of local organizations (political parties, the media)—in ethnically divided local communities, where a significant part of the population is of Roma background or identifies as such.

The data analyzed herein were collected using two methods: participant observation and focus groups interviews. The data originate from villages where a significant part of the population is of Roma background, and in two cases forms a majority. One of the villages is located in Somogy County, another in Szabolcs-Szatmár County, near the Ukrainian border, while the third is found in Borsod County, in the vicinity of a former industrial center (accordingly, I use the names of the counties to replace the names of the villages). In all three locations focus-group interviews were conducted with Roma and non-Roma par-

[3] Verdery, Katherine, "Ethnicity, Nationalism and State-making: Ethnic Groups and Boundaries: Past and Future," in *The Anthropology of Ethnicity: Beyond "Ethnic Groups and Boundaries,"* edited by Hans Vermeulen and Cora Govers (Amsterdam: Het Spinhuis, 1994), 33-58.

ticipants (a total of six focus-group interviews). Additional individual interviews and observations were also carried out and the research also made use of related secondary literature and media sources.

The common characteristic of the three villages in the study is the fact that the general structural transformation which brought hardship to the majority of villages in Hungary had a particularly negative impact on the former, economically, demographically, and politically. In Somogy, former peasant inhabitants have migrated away, leaving behind an impoverished, post-industrial population. In Szatmár, locals were formerly employed in the industrial center, but the 1990s saw the start of return to agriculture. The Borsod village is dominated by the struggle between two parts of the population: those villagers who were dismissed from jobs in the industrial sector, who then found no success in agriculture, and the inhabitants of the "ghetto," who are even more excluded from the job market and who repeatedly transgress previously established internal boundaries.

There have also been significant changes within the Roma communities in all three villages: Somogy has had a Roma mayor for a number of years and, thanks to this, a group of middle-aged Roma men have acquired a leading role in the village, overshadowing that of the elderly peasants and the recently settled, former industrial workers. In Szatmár, one part of the Roma population has gained access to certain economic opportunities, while their communal life and system of values has been transformed through the influence of a neoprotestant church, while the other part still lives in squalor. Borsod is the location of the largest post-industrial Roma "ghetto" in Hungary; a positive shift in the lives of the inhabitants was brought about by various church-related and civil initiatives, with the majoritarian population having been unprepared for these changes.

The three villages examined in this study are equally characterized by the transformation of local social relations, which in each case has overturned the social order regulating the relationship between Roma and non-Roma villagers. This local order of interethnic cohabitation was unjust and unequal, yet it remained unchallenged and unchanged for a very long time to the extent of effectively resisting the equalizing policies of the state-socialist era. Silence was maintained through the practices which separated the everyday life of Roma and non-Roma villagers, and through the physical segregation of housing, work, and school. Present-day conflicts are caused by the fact that the silence that regulates Roma–Hungarian coexistence has been subverted by various intersecting socioeconomic and political processes. Based on the findings in the three villages, the study identified three structural processes which are linked directly or indirectly with the changing relations between Roma and non-Roma.

The first is a process of deprivation. In all three locations, there are many individuals who ended up living in the village due to the selective and segregational mechanisms within broader Hungarian society—they are the victims of a general economic and social transformation, mainly after having lost their jobs in the industrial or agricultural section. Thus, these individuals, seen either as "Hungarian" or "Gypsy," find themselves in a similar state of deprivation—nonetheless, they manifest different types of reactions. Ethnic Hungarians, who see themselves as being superior and of higher status, are thus particularly motivated to use all available symbolic tools in order to differentiate themselves from the "Gypsies"—in spite of their living in near identical social conditions. That is, acute feelings of uncertainty and vulnerability drive the disenfranchised members of the majority to create an inferior category for the less fortunate, in opposition to which they can perceive their own social position as being superior, secure, and dignified.

Another significant process is manifested through endeavors towards the restoration of social status. More specifically, the ethnic Hungarians react similarly in relation to their perception of the upward mobility of the Roma, as exemplified through improvements in the education and the position of the latter on the job market and, most importantly, the increase in their social emancipation. These changes threaten, in their view, the deep and structurally embedded order.

The third process is related to the devaluation of local cultures in general, and more specifically, of the rural life-form, together with all its traditional values. This phenomenon is seen as a serious problem on the one hand by the elderly villagers who represent continuity (although their number is quite small), and on the other hand by those who have reconstructed their livelihoods on the basis of farming, and now wish to create symbolic legitimacy for this strategy. The attempt to restore the traditional rural values associated with an idealized image of peasant life frequently clashes with the values of the locals who do not fit into this image. Put differently, it is exactly these practices of restitution (e.g. religious or heritage programs) which construct the difference[4].

Voicing Problems by Blaming "the Gypsies"

The participants of the focus group interviews were not asked directly about the Roma, but rather they were given the opportunity to speak about the most important problems in the lives of their villages. However, we soon realized how discussions about social problems and local tensions became ethnicized,[5] as shown in the following quote:

> I think that the biggest problem with our village is the increasing poverty. Our problem comes from the fact that those who were poor have got even poorer, and as a consequence, we have to allocate 570 million forints for social aid each year. Another consequence of poverty is that the better-off Hungarian children who wish to be educated all leave the region, and only the poor people stay here, most of them Roma, who practically live on welfare. As a result, there is a lot of stealing, a lot of damage everywhere—there are days when they just vandalize and destroy. The losses caused by stealing are huge; metal and firewood simply disappear. They destroy with no reason at all.[6]

[4] Margit Feischmidt and Kristóf Szombaty, "Understanding the Rise of the Far Right from a Local Perspective: Structural and Cultural Conditions of Ethno-traditionalist Inclusion and Racial Exclusion in Rural Hungary." *Identitites,* (2017): 3, 313-333.

[5] We followed the same methodological strategy a few years earlier when researching the everyday manifestations of ethnicity and nationalism within the context of Romanian–Hungarian relations in Kolozsvár/Cluj Napoca (Brubaker et al., *Nationalist Politics and Everyday Ethnicity*). While in that particular case the analysis revealed that ethnic differences have no significance in terms of discussions about what the participants considered real problems, in the case of the villages we studied we observed the opposite: the "Gypsy question" trumped everything else.

[6] INT Borsod Majority.

The most diverse set of problems, ranging from the consequences of migration, the depopulation of the villages, the difficulties of living off the land and from farming, the hardships of rural life, the disintegration of civil and religious organizations, etc., do not appear on their own as topics of local public thinking. Each of these problems is framed by a one-track process that involves reducing complexity to one single cause: the presence of the "Gypsies." According to the local narrative, the "Gypsies" are a demographic threat. Demographic decline and the flight of the middle class are mutually enforcing processes, having as the central issue the "Gypsy school" in the geographical center of the village. This is treated as an intrusive element not only by villagers, but also by the pedagogical staff who work there:

> Because out of three hundred children, two hundred and eighty are Roma. They are unmanageable and ill-mannered... I don't want to overstate the case, but it is a daily problem with them that they get into fights, and we have to employ four people in the school to maintain some kind of order. But this is simply impossible, because if twenty children are in a line they start a fight in a blink of an eye, and then the kids run home, they bring their parents, two or three of them, they bring the neighbors, to show us how things should be done, and they ask, why don't we teachers do our jobs, why isn't the principle doing something, why aren't we protecting their children? As I said, four people are not enough, we should designate a guardian angel to each kid, and we'll see [what happens] from then on. The problem here, the fundamental problem, is with their upbringing.[7]

The Roma are invoked as the cause of problems, even in connection with farming, issues concerning the uncultivated lands around the village, and the decline in grape and fruit production. In such cases, the related discussions become lively: every participant has an opinion about the topic of the Roma who, according to the them, loot and spend irrationally, who have unkempt children, and who not only avoid honest work but are unwilling to change anything about their way of

[7] INT Borsod Majority.

life. No debates took shape on these occasions—rather, the villagers took the events as an opportunity to share a set of stories and examples which complemented each other, having their roots in a common worldview and attitude.

Other significant topics were the depopulation of the villages, disused houses being occupied by the Roma, and small offences against private property also attributed to the Roma. Stealing is systematically associated with "Gypsies," while the victims are always identified as "Hungarians." Feelings of fear and frustration are mainly exhibited by elderly people and by newcomers—people who have lost their existence owing to the local industrial decline.

The dynamics of the discourse on "Gypsies" within the focus group interviews were defined by the attempts of participants to exceed each other in voicing even more deprecating and disdainful remarks. At the beginning of the discussions some participants tried to differentiate and point out the nuances—after a while, however, positive examples were all forgotten, and as the discussion advanced from one topic to the other (work, school, and the household) only the negative statements remained, increasing the level of collective contempt. The most common discursive elements of the interviews were related to forms of deviation and reveal how the perceived disruption of moral order is being ethnicized.

However, there is another set of problems which stem from those who harm order in another way: this involves the successful Roma. Through their ambition and success, they break out of the limits of the established order.

The discourse about the Roma in one of the villages is built around the categories of "decent Gypsy" vs. "not decent Gypsy." It also includes a temporal distinction, which associates "decent Gypsies" with the past, and "not decent Gypsies" with the present. Such historical narratives involve attempts to preserve the social and economic institutions that previously guaranteed the superiority of "Hungarians," and maintain the memory of the social order which regulated everyday inter-ethnic relations within these limits. The image of the "Gypsies in the past" was also recalled by the Roma we interviewed, who explained how the practice of "giving in" or "offering yourself" to the "Hungarians" represented the only opportunity to be respected by them. Furthermore, the "Gypsies of the past" had another key characteristic: they were entirely invisible in the public spaces of the village, "they were *not in* the village" and no one was interested in knowing "what they were doing, *out there*." This meant that, in spite of the Roma working as servants in the houses of the peasants, and as day-laborers on their lands, one did not have to think of them. One of the interviewees reflected on this system of relations through the story of her mother:

> Folks in the old days were even willing to go and clean someone's toilet. If today you told someone, "look, I've got this nice little job for you, come over and empty the cesspit," well, that someone would jump at you. They'd want to beat you up, it's that much of an insult. Also, in the past the Gypsies who worked for the Hungarians didn't get any money. Take for example my mother… She went to this Hungarian woman, to work for her, we waited all day, and then in the evening she brought home this "*sóder*." They cut the meat off the pig's shoulders, leaving just the bones, and that's what she was able to bring home, that's what she got for her work. Today, everyone works for cash. If the Hungarian says, here's 2000 forints, go and spray my cucumbers, the Gypsy asks for 3000. Gypsies don't act like servants anymore, you understand, they dictate.[8]

The quoted passage illustrates why majority discourses require the idealization of the past: because in the present, Roma do not act like they did "in the old days." According to this line of thought, the image of the "decent" and subservient Gypsy is the alter ego of the "not decent" Gypsy, who "does not know their place," and who repeatedly challenges and subverts the pact involving the power relations made with the "original Gypsies." In the opinion of the Hungarian villagers, the "not decent Gypsies" are those who are "not afraid of anything," who think they are entitled "to do far too much," and who "got too smart for their own good."[9]

[8] Thanks to Sándor Borbély for undertaking this interview.

[9] These statements are taken from the second group interview conducted on August 6, 2008.

There is a similar tendency in the Roma community of the Borsod village, especially in terms of a desire to subvert the prescribed expectation of invisibility. It has arisen due to the dissemination of ideas which have led to the questioning of the previous pact about the proper social hierarchy, and because it "boosts the self-confidence of the Gypsies."

In this part of the paper, I have outlined how the category of the "Gypsy" is instrumentalized for the purpose of defining and labelling various problems within the local context of social relations. In the following section, I examine how the process of ethnic differentiation, connected to the dissolution of the social order, has influenced the articulation of the identity of a group that sees itself as being superior, and the restoration of a communal system of values which offers a sense of security.

Readjusting the Order Framed in Ethnic Terms

The participants of the focus-group interviews who called themselves "Magyars" spoke of the lack of a Hungarian national consciousness. They believe that one reason for this is the general indifference and apolitical attitude of the Hungarians, with one of the interviewees complaining that he is accosted if he puts a flag on his house on a national holiday. Another reason is that the national holidays are "ruined" by local Gypsies—here shifting the discussion from Hungarian identity to the otherness of the Roma, as a much more familiar topic of conversation. National holidays have been made impossible ever since the Roma became the majority at the school, because—according to a local teacher—the Roma children do not know how to behave:

> I am so ashamed when I think about our 6 October commemoration… you were also there! So this little show has been prepared with so much love by my colleagues for years, and it was such an honor and reward for the children to be able to go out on the stage and perform and take part in the whole commemoration. But today we can't even select any of the children to go and take part in the show, and to recite a poem about the memory of the Hungarian revolution, for example. I mean, the appearance of these children… they can't even stand still… and what did they

> do during the anthem! How many arms should a teacher have to control them, that behaviour, I don't know. The anthem is in the fourth year curriculum, but I'm unable to teach it to them. They don't want to learn the Gypsy anthem either. Not even that.[10]

The same group became increasingly more motivated to talk when the conversation moved to the topic of Hungarian minorities in neighboring countries. The discourse about "authentic Hungarians" was articulated in the following way:

> I will tell you honestly; the real Hungarians are those who declared their Hungarianness even under oppression and persecution, and not the ones living in the country, in Hungary, that is. (...)
> Nowadays, the real Hungarians are living in the Szeklerland. Anyone who lives in this country, even if they try to revive a Hungarian consciousness within themselves or in the people around them, they will never be able to revive the kind of consciousness that the Szeklers have. Because there the Romanian oppression—that is, first the Soviet oppression, and then the Romanians took over, and persecuted the Hungarians (...) but they always preserved the knowledge that they were Hungarians and that they needed to stick together. That they could not allow the Romanians to break them up. Well, it [the breaking up of unity] happened here![11]

Trips to Transylvania and conversations with Transylvanian Hungarians can also take on the role of experiencing what "authentic Hungarianness" is like.

In Somogy the topic of "Hungarianness" was approached and articulated in a similar way but from a very personal perspective. Two women in the group, originally from Romania, and more specifically, from Szeklerland, gave voice to grievances experienced while migrating for work and then attempting to settle down in Hungary. In the end,

[10] INT Borsod Majority.
[11] INT Borsod Majority.

the complaint about a lack of acceptance turned into an articulation of Hungarianness. The experiences of unacknowledged national belonging and the struggle for recognition—recurring themes of ethnic migrant narratives—are directly related to the practice of naming or at least hinting at those who are seen as being responsible for this—there Romanians, here the Roma—, and who thus become the enemies of "Hungarians":

> It is very hard for me, because I come from a city with a population of twenty-two thousand. Compared to the standard of living I had, that is, my husband and I had there, well, this here for us is ... mud. As opposed to being up there, on the high shelves, now we are down in the mud. Our community, friends, relatives, everyone is back home, here we're only in touch with M. I hear it in the village: the Romanians this, the Romanians that, but I feel that I am as Hungarian as they are. Even though I can speak Romanian just as well as Hungarian, my name is Hungarian, and the names of my children are also Hungarian—but this is what we get... we'll survive.[12]

During the group interview in Somogy, the two women from Transylvania were the only ones who declared a personal emotional connection to their Hungarianness.

The other opinion leader in the group was a woman originally from Western Hungary and the owner of the local store, she spoke to the group about her son, now living abroad, who consciously assumed his "Hungarianness" by wearing "ancient Hungarian clothing." In the context of the discussion, she felt that the only way to keep up with the "fought-for" Hungarian identity of the Transylvanians was by making reference to the books of Albert Wass. As her example illustrates, the overly "natural" and indistinct national identity of the majority is measured against the idealized cases of those who had "fought" for their Hungarianness.

The study observed that in the interview with the group of women in Somogy the topic of Hungarian identity was dominated by a com-

[12] INT Somogy Majority.

petitive discourse and no critical stance could develop. Participants were able to join in the competitive conversation in three ways: the first and simplest was to assume the position of a cross-border minority Hungarian, and to refer to a "fought-for Hungarianness"; the second path was the invocation of kinship ties to the Hungarian extreme right-wing subculture; and the third possibility was to demonstrate knowledge of nationalistic literature.

These tendencies could only have been balanced out by state institutions, but these have been eliminated and the state has withdrawn from the villages. As a consequence, majoritarian residents of the village are involved in legitimizing another discourse, namely that of historicizing nationalism, which constructs all of its positive references by way of appropriating the cross-border Hungarian minorities and the "detached territories." A suggestive example of the re-evaluation of historical traditions was the charity ball organized at the time of our fieldwork in Szatmár. The official goal of the ball was to raise money for the renovation of the local Calvinist church, but the unspoken function of the event was to be an exclusively "Hungarian festivity" to compete with the village day festival which was "taken over by the Gypsies." Being the initiative of the women from the local presbytery, the "charity ball" on August 9, 2008 was an occasion for the meeting of "Hungarian" Calvinist families who had either originated from, or were in some way connected to the village. Given that the local Roma are also christened Calvinists, there had to be a discourse explaining why they were excluded from the festivity:

> The Gypsies have a party every week and so far they've never invited any Hungarians… We don't belong together.
> No week passes by without a Gypsy party. They bring those plates full of sandwiches. No Hungarian ever showed up there.[13]

In relation to the two "admissible" Roma families which were brought up as positive examples, the villagers exercise more covert forms of exclusion that nonetheless reproduce the oldest and most essentialist type of distinction: the dichotomy of clean/unclean or higher/lower

[13] INT Szatmár Majority.

work. The women from these two families, although they were taking part in the general preparations for the festivity, were not included in the cooking process, unlike the rest of the villagers. Conversely, they were charged with the cleaning up of the interior of the church, a two-day task that was supervised by the caretaker, with the assistance of day-laborers from Ukraine (who, unlike the Roma women, were paid). Thus, the particular role played by each family in the preparations for the festivity reinforced their position in the local struggle for social status.

The openly articulated need for someone to "show the Gypsies where they belong" is shared in the other two villages as well. Participants in Somogy opined that the *Magyar Gárda* (Hungarian Guard) would be able to "restore order." In Borsod, the group exhibited strong emotions—a mixture of disgust, anger, and fear—in support of a statement by one of their fellow villagers, who proposed two options for the Hungarians in the village who feel threatened by the Roma: one is to flee the village, the other to stay and fight. Those opting to fight see the roots of the conflict in the incompatibility of the two cultures, "we try to fight, two different cultures." The belief in the existence of such essential differences was present in the local mentality, it was the main factor which made the message of the extreme right-wing party so appealing to the villagers.

In the spring of 2010, news of the first of the public meetings that were to be held in the Borsod village by the young far right party, Jobbik was received with dread by the Roma community. Nonetheless, the meeting was not cancelled, but on the contrary, was held with a full house in the village cultural center. The Roma reacted to the right-wing mobilization with a demonstration that took the shape of a Holocaust commemoration. The event was portrayed by the media—in accordance with the intentions of the organizers—as the largest anti-racist demonstration of the year organized outside of Budapest. In Borsod the most trenchant conflicts occurred in the early 2010s, but they have tended to reappear periodically. In most cases, they are centered on the local school, which is maintained by a foundation and a small Buddhist church with the mission of supporting the tutoring of local undereducated Roma. Jobbik MP, Zsolt Endrésik, had the following to say about this institution in one of his parliamentary speeches: "Has anybody outside of SZDSZ ever heard of this Jai Bhim

Network? Of Buddhist Gypsies who Holocaust-march together with the Jews?"[14] As a consequence, the school is kept under constant control—a practice which is repeatedly initiated by the extreme right-wing party, and executed by the institutions of state administration.

In this section I have tried to describe those structural processes which subvert in a direct or indirect way the pact of invisibility that applies to the "Gypsy ghetto" in the village, and which challenge the hierarchical order between the Roma and non-Roma inhabitants. Tension is highest when external actors appear in the local context, and the emancipating Roma are joined by international organizations or churches who employ a human-rights discourse. This is experienced by the local majority population as a threat, and they react to it through discourses and political activity which promise the symbolic restoration of an earlier social order. Through this analysis I have shown on the one hand how the topic of the Roma has become the main focus of local discourses on loss, on uncertainty, and on the dissolution of social order. On the other hand, I have presented how the category of "Hungarianness" is being used in the attempted restoration of a sense of order and self-worth through the adoption of a historicizing nationalist discourse.

[14] "In recent years there has been significant expansion of [the number of] educational institutions in Borsod country, more specifically, in the region of Ózd, by the so-called Ambedkar Gymnasium, run by the allegedly Buddhist church called Jai Bhim Network. Their presence and expansion is due to the catastrophic economic circumstances of the region which forces local governments to abandon state educational institutions, and practically to hand them over to anyone who is willing to take charge of them. Has anybody outside of the SZDSZ ever heard of this Jai Bhim Network? Of Buddhist Gypsies who Holocaust-march together with the Jews? Especially in Borsod? They advertise themselves as being committed to educating Gypsy children, preparing them for jobs and getting them diplomas. The reality, however, in a nutshell, is the following: the Ambedkar is only a gymnasium by name, and does nothing that would even resemble the activity of an educational institute. What goes on there, that is labelled as teaching, is in fact just clowning around." http://www.dalit.hu/a-jobbik-felszolalasa-a-parlamentben-buddhista-ciganyok-akik-holokauszt-menetelnek-zsido-vezetokkel-plane-borsodban/.

Gypsy's Othering Experienced by Roma People

In this part of the paper I examine how the villagers who are identified as Gypsy perceive the majority framing of the dissolution of social order as a "Gypsy problem." Furthermore, I shed light on the experiences which are connected to Gypsy othering, and investigate what possible opportunities these inhabitants have to emancipate their collective and ethnic identity from the denigrating and stigmatizing discourse of the majority. In closing, the analysis will focus on how the process of Gypsy othering and its perception by minority inhabitants affects the chances of those who are seen as or identify as Roma in adhering to the category of Hungarian.

In the focus-group interview with Roma participants, I asked them to describe "what it is like to be Gypsy." Naturally, I am aware that this is a loaded question, and the answers to it were strongly predetermined by the fact that it had been posed by a researcher belonging to the majority, and that as such it would not produce an insider account of "Gypsyness," but a discourse which exhibited a reaction to the relationship with non-Roma outsiders. I am also aware that such direct questions should be avoided if one is interested in understanding the nuances of identity construction. However, focus-group interviews do not allow for such examination. What they do represent is a means of analyzing the discourses and anti-discourses which make up the public speech of the villagers.

The Roma focus groups in Somogy were defined by a debate about whether, compared to the situation in the past—when it was hopelessly shameful to be identified as Roma—anything had actually changed or improved in past decades. Those who made the case for positive change related arguments based on personal experiences of upward social mobility. One of the proponents of this view was the mayor of the village, who repeatedly recalled that in his childhood he had to walk barefoot, but that today he has his own house in a neighboring village.

The counter-position was held by a young man who strongly opposed the arguments of the mayor throughout the discussion, and who described the deterioration of the situation of the Roma. He stated that it was difficult to talk about the human rights of those who have been laid off and who suffer systematic discrimination, and much harder to claim that their situation has improved and that they should be proud:

> Now, if we look at the conditions, in the communist period, when we didn't go to school, welfare aid was there—of course, our parents had to work eight hours per day for it, but there were jobs. My dad worked, my mom worked. Today we don't even have the opportunity. In those days, I came all the way to the village, and Mr. Laci Kocsis, the district police officer, would ask me: 'hey kid, what are you doing here?' 'Well, I am on leave, Mr. Laci.' 'What do you mean?' 'I have to work.' I am not saying that the Roma got paid large sums for the unskilled work and construction work they did, but at least they could work every day. Children could see that their dads and their moms went to work every day. And both of them got a salary. In today's world... nowadays you, or I, or the other guy, has some sort of a job, at most one person in a family, but there are cases where none of the parents are employed. They only get welfare aid and child benefit. They are not better off in any way![15]

The interview with the Roma men in Somogy revealed that the key element in their collective self-identification is labor. Such talk about work in the presence of the researcher was also prompted by the need for recognition: they wished to refute the stereotypical image of the Roma as people who avoid work and live off others. Roma interviewees in Szatmár talked about their work in the present, since—in spite of them having been laid off from their original place of employment—in recent years most families have acquired a notable income from farming and doing the same work as all the other, non-Roma villagers:

> Ten years ago, the Gypsies, they were oppressed here. But the Gypsies showed that, yes, they can rise from the depths. Parents took their children to school and now everyone has about ninety-nine percent of a middle-school education. (...) In our family

[15] INT Somogy Minority.

> alone I can name three Gypsy relatives who have a college degree. And thanks to this, we get a bit of recognition from the population, they appreciate us because of our work, and we can say that, just as our parents laid the foundations for us to stay here, we are doing the same, trying to lay the foundations here for our children and grandchildren.[16]

The need for recognition through work is emphasized by the enumeration of achievements—their education, their degrees, their employment—which the participants see as constituting the basis for gaining respect and esteem in "Hungarian" society. The underlying assumption here is that work makes everyone equal and this prompted one of the interviewees to nostalgically recall a time when, in his opinion, this situation was closer to reality:

> We are not Gypsy. Or at least that is how we feel. We do not speak the Gypsy language any more. This is why we are Hungarian Gypsies. (...) Gypsy people are always like this. If they are being appreciated, they commit themselves. This whole difference, it was not created by the Gypsies, it was done by the law, by regulations, by decrees, and by those greedy people who always want more... (...) But when they take it away from me, they should not say to me that I am Gypsy.[17]

Such discursive strategies which were aimed at diminishing social and cultural differences were widely shared in the group. None of the participants argued for the need for Gypsy/Roma traditions. The older generation in the Somogy and the Szatmár group discussion shared a consensus about a wish to follow an assimilationist strategy, yet at the same time they showed that they understood that the feasibility of such a strategy had diminished due to the structural inequalities they faced in the job market.

The discourses of identity construction for the young Roma we interviewed were however, significantly different. The experience

[16] INT Szatmár Minority.
[17] INT Szatmár Minority.

which they commonly share is systematic discrimination, activated in various situations in relation to their socially marked skin color:[18]

> Now, that is offensive. They treat us like we're all the same, and then everybody is afraid of the Gypsies. That's what I hate the most, when they're afraid of me. I really hate it when people are scared of me. And if I go to some other place, I can benefit from the fact that I don't look like a Gypsy. But when they find out, everybody looks at me differently. Well, not everybody, but most people. This is why it is better for us, as Béci said, to be among Gypsies. Because that would never happen here.[19]

The interviewees articulated two everyday strategies through which they can react against Gypsy othering: the practices of hiding and isolation, or retreat into the familiar company of those with similar experiences. Conversely, the younger generation of Roma consider that the act of openly "being Gypsy" involves engaging in behavior which is seen as different from and even opposed to the norms of the majority. The consensus among the young Roma participants judges such behavior as unacceptable, demonstrating a strong need to adhere to the majority image of the Roma:

> B: They should know how to behave. Because there are some Gypsies who just don't know how to behave. We go to a place, and they start to dance and sing in Gypsy, well, I really hate that. I just can't stand that. Let's say, we go to a group of people, and they're Hungarians. But these Gypsies don't know the limits. It's so annoying that they don't know the limits. And then the Hungarians will despise them for the Gypsy singing

---

18 The most remarkable description of markers which are inscribed into the body and the skin, and thus are unavoidable and unalterable, was given by Franz Fanon in his essay entitled "Fact of Blackness" published originally in 1952 in his *Black Skin, White Mask.* There are striking similarities between the quoted passages from the interviews with the Roma participants and the insights in Fanon's biographical essay. I am grateful to Attila Melegh who confirmed for me the plausibility of this comparative perspective.

19 INT Szatmár Minority.

and the dancing. I can't stand that, because then I am lumped together with them, they generalize, and they see me as being like them, although I am not. And I really hate it when that happens.

Zs1: We also don't like it if, in a place which is full of Hungarians, they go in and start acting "Gypsyish." But in other places, they can go ahead and do it.

B: Yes, in other places, where there aren't any Hungarians... I mean, in the company of Gypsies... I am ready to bring out the guitar and we can dance.

F.M.: You use such interesting words, such as "acting Gypsyish." What does it mean?

Zs: Misbehaving.

B: When they start singing in Gypsy, and they stare at people, like "booo, to hell with you, may cancer eat your guts," and they start quarreling with people.[20]

While the phenomenon of "acting Gypsyish" can be seen as a performative practice which "brings to life" the stigmatized image that the majority has of Gypsies, another type of everyday behavior—called being "very Gypsy" by the young participants—represents the conscious over-communication and exhibition of identity (in the sense of Goffman's "showing off"). According to the interviewees, there are two ways to behave "very Gypsy": either by accepting the role of the subaltern, or by overcoming it through subversive gestures. The most effective tool for engaging in the latter option is music—through "Gypsy music" the Roma youth can attach a positive experience to their identity. Sport can also have a similar function. To the question who they support at the Olympics, the unanimous reply of participants was "the Brazilians." One of them talked in detail about Brazilian football, emphasizing that the reason for identifying with them comes from a shared sense of "blackness." The discourse of the young participants helped carve out a new ethnicity that connected similar elements from geographically and culturally distant contexts, and which focused on skin color:

[20] INT Szatmár Minority.

Zs: Very Gypsy? It is also about appearance. If someone is very Gypsy, then they're like Mari. She can't even speak. A person who is very Gypsy can't even speak, in any given situation, only like: "it's alright you, boy..." For example, I mean that they can't even speak normally to teachers, or any other person. They always do this silliness, they always think of crazy stuff... Actually, I am also talking about myself here... I often feel that I am very Gypsy and I enjoy it. I often enjoy being very Gypsy.

B: Sometimes I do too, if I am in that kind of a situation. I just release everything from inside.

F.M.: Can you tell me about some of these situations...

B: For example, when we play basketball we put Gypsy music on our phones, we start to sing, we dance, we party, and that's it...

Zs: Or, for example, when we are in a place where there is a mixed crowd, with Gypsies and Hungarians, and there is disco music playing, like Tiesto, for instance, and a bunch of us who are a bit sillier by nature, we start to do the Gypsy rhythm to Tiesto, and we start Gypsy dancing. And that is so awesome.[21]

Writing about how elements of African-American and colonial culture appear in the everyday life of Roma communities, Cili Kovai describes the phenomenon in the following way:

"In the houses of the Roma settlement the walls are covered with posters of black rap stars, with 50 Cent and Tupac Shakur staring down on us defiantly. The youth from the settlement call themselves 'gettósok' [people of the ghetto] which in their eyes is a positive label of 'coolness.' Thus, it seems that the African-American analogies work in several social scenarios in relation to the Roma. (...) Through this analogy the Roma youth are simultaneously making the Roma identity livable for themselves, but also searching for ways to escape from being Roma."[22]

---

21 INT Szatmár Minority.

22 Cecília Kovai, "Hidden Potential in 'Naming Gypsy': The Transformation of Gypsy Hungarian Distinction," in *The Gypsy "Menace." Populism and the New Anti-Gypsy Politics,* ed. Michael Stewart (London: Hurst & Company, 2012), 42.

Kovai[23] states that the kinship network within the Roma settlement makes it possible for the otherwise stigmatized Roma identity to be lived out in an intimate, closed, familiar, and safe environment. However, on the basis of the precedents, the assimilationist strategy followed by the parents of respondents, and the rupture in the transmission of traditional culture, in the locations of my research I saw a much stronger tendency to re-evaluate the categories of Roma/Gypsy not through the rehabilitation of the local, "given" Roma identity, but through the construction of a new ethnic identity. This new ethnicity is, on the one hand, inherently political (it that is that it meant to be a political answer to everyday racism), and on the other hand, it uses mediatized cultural symbols and images of transnational and urban "zones of freedom."

In all three villages there are examples of the organized social action of the Roma community. In Somogy the local minority self-government assembled a group of middle-aged Roma men, who at first collaborated only with the purpose of organizing various programs, but then became official members of the self-government committee. In Szatmár there is also a minority self-government, yet it has a significantly smaller impact than the all-Roma Free Christian congregation. For this group, composed of elderly and middle-aged members, instead of the usual shame associated with being Roma, the experience of religious communion, the adopted language of the church, and the promise of redemption and Christian brotherhood provide a real opportunity for living with a sense of dignity:

> We're not ashamed of being Gypsy (...) I give thanks to Our Lord Jesus Christ, because He does not discriminate between his followers. He does not see you as Gypsy, or Hungarian, or Greek, or Jew. Jesus loves everyone in equal measure. I believe that he loves us even today, and I believe that He lives within us through His love, and that we live in Him. And the fact that we are Gypsy, here, in our community, since it is true that there is always strength in numbers, when the precious spirit of the Lord dwells in us, like it did tonight, glory be Thy name, then the love

[23] Ibid., 281–295.

> of God lives within us. And so we are not ashamed to openly admit to the fact that we are Gypsy. Just like we are not ashamed to accept Jesus Christ.[24]

The Holocaust commemoration organized in Borsod was similar to the more well-known event, the March of Life. This illustrates how the actors and the cultural toolkit involved in the emancipatory struggle of the Roma in the village are not local, but are to a large extent transnational. This is the reason why the event was seen as alien by the local majority community, and provoked the opposition of the local elite who felt that now, besides their usual struggles with the Roma community, they are faced with an international response which uses the minority group against them.

In this part of the study I have described how the self-identification of the Roma is to a great extent influenced by the majority discourse which constructs and imposes the category of the "Gypsy" as the image of an Other, signifying social problems. I also showed how the Roma relate to this constructed image, and what few alternatives they have to create and embody a non-subordinated Roma identity that is independent of the hegemonic discourse. Slightly differing from similar research, our focus-group interviews revealed the existence of a common social identity which is counter to the usual majority-minority opposition, and is founded on the importance of and access to labor. In this given context, labor is the source of a common identity rooted in social practice. It remains a question, nonetheless, whether this shared experience can be connected to the idea of political and class-based communities.

In the following section I focus on this question, and on the related problem of how the practice of othering and structurally defined social distance determine the chances of those marked as "Gypsy" being part of an unmarked broader national community, meaning being "Hungarian." I explore the possibilities for connecting and living the two identities: both ethnic (Gypsy) and national (Hungarian). Furthermore, I examine how the relation to national culture and loyalty towards the state is formed in these local contexts, and how

---

24 INT Szatmár Minority.

this changes due to the transformation of the structural and discursive changes presented above.

"They Took Away our Hungarianness"

In each focus-group interview with Roma participants, I also asked participants to describe what it means to be Hungarian, and to live in Hungary. In the case of Roma respondents the most common reaction was that of surprise, since, as they reported, it is unusual for them to think of themselves as Hungarian. After some further inquiry on my part, most of the responses pointed towards a general identification with the country. However, while those belonging to the older and middle-aged generation mostly expressed positive emotions in relation to this identification, those of the younger generation typically had a negative attitude. All participants agreed, however, that the country probably means much more to "Hungarians" than it does to the Roma living inside the borders.

The only scenario in which the participants could imagine being identified as Hungarian was if they went abroad, but none of the interviewees had had such an experience. Inside the country, it appears that the majority discourse has been so effective at stressing the differences that any identification with Hungarianness has lost its meaning and its content. This shift has its roots primarily in the local conflicts and the unequal relations which have segregated "Hungarian" and "Gypsy" villagers. It has additionally been deepened through the activity of the local institutions of minority self-government, since these have replaced a previous strategy of hiding with the differentiation of a minority discourse:

> I'll tell you the truth, you know, we, as Roma, as Gypsy, well… I'm not saying that we are not proud to be Hungarian. Of course we are! If God made it possible for me to be in a better financial situation so that I could travel to another part of the world, I would proudly declare that I was a Hungarian citizen. Or that I was a Gypsy from Hungary. But what can I say? I think the Roma do not really feel it important to stress that, you know, "I am Hungarian" or something like that, because of this devel-

> opment in the country… In my opinion the whole thing has developed ever since they started attacking the Minority Self-Government politically, and then the Gypsy Minority Self-Government was formed. And I think that the consequence of this political situation is that now every year there is renewed conflict between Gypsies and Hungarians.[25]

According to the Roma interviewees, the differences are caused by the discriminatory behavior of the majority, as most commonly identified on the job market. However, some of the respondents pointed out that they also encounter practices of social differentiation which are not rooted in economic interests, and which form an even deeper and wider cleavage based on visible markers or phenotypical traits. In this dichotomy, Hungarians are white and the Roma are black. In spite of the actually existing variety of colors of skin, such a black-and-white analogy builds differentiation on biological grounds, and—in contrast to cultural traits—renders it unchangeable and unbridgeable.

Nonetheless, some of the older participants in the group discussion actually do want to think of themselves as Hungarians. However, even they seem to remember a time when such an identification was stronger and more honest. In past years they have felt that they have been deprived of the opportunity to openly express their national belonging in the way that the members of the ethnic majority can.[26]

> I was proud that I could be Hungarian, but I am not proud anymore. Because of two reasons. Although I wasn't crazy about it, I could wear the [Hungarian national] rosette, since it was a sign of pride. But thanks to Fidesz, who have appropriated it, now I am ashamed to wear the rosette. If I put it on, it

25 INT Somogy Minority.

26 This is similar to the phenomenon of how the identities of African-Europeans and African-Americans are subjected to majority representations, as described by Frantz Fanon, *Black Skin, White Masks: New Interdisciplinary Essays* (2006; Manchester: Manchester University Press, 1952) or, in the case of Jews, according to Sartre's analysis. For further research on this, see András Kovács, A *Másik szeme. Zsidók és antiszemiták a háború utáni Magyarországon* (The Eye of the Other. Jews and Antisemites in Post-War Hungary). (Budapest: Gondolat Kiadó, 2008).

> would mean that I am a supporter of Fidesz! If I wear the sign of Greater Hungary, they also look at me strangely. In the past it did not mean what it does today. It was appropriated by Jobbik; they added the white-and-red stripes, and it doesn't belong to Jobbik. I have friends who are actually afraid of wearing this symbol, because if a non-Gypsy or someone who is not part of Jobbik sees it, they will know that you are also not a member of Jobbik, and they will beat you up. The other thing is that I was always proud to be Hungarian. Once I went to the kebab fast-food place, and because I have a lisp and I don't talk properly, the guy there asked me what country I was from. They were quite amazed at this kebab place in Budapest that I was Hungarian. When I think about it, I realize that if a supporter of Jobbik had heard me, he would have laughed at me. Another thing is, I think, that we are a hundred times more Hungarian than the members of Jobbik who think of themselves as true Hungarians! Because it is us who are preserving the Hungarian and Vlach Gypsy culture that was created here in Hungary. (…) It would be good to be Hungarian if it didn't mean what it does today, that only those are Hungarians who are autochthonous, who are true natives, and who have no other kind of ethnic blood in their veins. But I ask them this: throughout the history of Hungary, didn't all kinds of nationalities settle here from every direction? Is there such a thing as a pure Hungarian? One that is racially pure?[27]

Associating the causes of social conflict with the Roma—that is, reducing a complex set of phenomena to the single idea of ethnic opposition, and identifying the victims as Hungarians—induces a tendency to "racial psychosis," as Aladár Horváth put it. The author states in an interview that:

"…those exiled into the Gypsy category are deprived of the opportunity to think of themselves as Hungarians. In many villages if the number of burglaries rises, the police simply go out to the Gypsy settlement and beat the inhabitants senseless. If the local police officer writes in his report about the 'Magyars' using the capital 'M,'

[27] INT Somogy Minority.

and wants to pit them against the Gypsies, then we are dealing with a 'racial psychosis.' We have been denied the right to see ourselves as Hungarians, because they took away our Hungarianness. In the old 'commie' era we were raised to assimilate to this country, and in return we were promised equality with the 'gadjos.' The Gypsies really believed that they could be equal to the others. But today the Gypsies find themselves on a downward slide and think of themselves as tenth-rate citizens."[28]

The phenomenon of dual identification which, as many have noted, is characteristic of minorities in Hungary, has specific features in the case of the Roma. Namely, that for them an identification with Hungarianness also means adherence to the negative image which has been created about the Roma by the perceptions of the majority. Aladár Horváth writes that:

"...we, the Roma, also have an identity defined by the majority population which reflects the way they see us and how they differentiate us as a community. (...) Based on this second or outer part of our double identity, we consider ourselves equal members of a nation which is not entirely convinced that we all belong together. Yet we see ourselves through their eyes. The problem comes from the fact that this outer element of our double identity contains quite a lot of negative prejudice against us. That is, we identify with the negative opinions which were formed about us by the majority population in two ways: we accept them, and then our collective self-image will be defined by self-reproach. Or we rebel against it [them], in which case we end up being in constant struggle with this outer [external] part of our identity."[29]

Conclusion

Based on ethnographic research and focus-group interviews conducted in three Hungarian villages, the main claim of the current study is that

[28] http://magyarnarancs.hu/belpol/elvettek_a_magyarsagunkat_-_horvath_aladar_polgarjogi_vezeto_a_roma-magyar_konfliktusokrol-72666 (last download May 13, 2019).

[29] http://www.commmunity.eu/2011/09/29/magyar-nemzet-roma-nemzet/ (last download May 13, 2019).

everyday nationalism is reproduced in discourses of othering and propelled by the social disenfranchisement of non-Romani inhabitants of rural Hungary. A complex variety of social problems, losses, and conflicts are framed by an ethnicizing discourse. The blaming of Roma is triggered by the losses the peasants and workers have suffered due to structural transformations in post-socialist Hungary, the loss of employment, and of the social security in general which characterized their daily lives during late socialism. This social order was only partially equalizing, but in large part hid an ethnic hierarchy which has been challenged in the recent past by Roma villagers, either through by their individual social mobility or by their communal activity.

Douglas Holmes[30] claims that the success of extreme right-wing rhetoric in the marginal villages of the European Union was brought about by the framing of social problems within a new, "integrationist" discourse that became appealing for a peasant population that had grown disenchanted by integration policies and globalization. This statement can be applied to Hungary with certain modifications. The experience of disenfranchisement and the lack of local communities and national institutions that work on a local level explains the lack of positive discourses of belonging. In our research, there was no discourse about Hungarianness connected to everyday life, and only very little connected to festivities or commemorations. In spite of this, Hungarian identity was not perceived in the local context as being that of the unmarked civic. It was codified through the forceful, all-encompassing, and re-framing discourse about the Roma that acquired meaning only in reference to Hungarian–Roma relations as defined by this discourse. Similar to the power relations between racially marked subalterns and unmarked dominant groups (as Stuart Hall conceptualized it), or the dichotomy of the colonized East and the colonizing West (as described by Edward Said), Hungarian–Roma relations can also be understood as emerging though a discursive regime defined by symmetrical counter-concepts. Depending on the given context, "Gypsy" can be a culturally, morally, and (more frequently) racially marked category of the subaltern that has "Hungarian" as

30 Douglas Homes, *Integral Europe. Fast Capitalism, Multiculturalism, Neofascism* (Princeton: Princeton University Press, 2000).

its unmarked conceptual antithesis, and which constructs the idea of "Hungarianness" as a superior and hegemonic position of power. Following the logic of this linguistic practice, the "natural" distinction within such a discourse creates two identical epistemological categories for "Gypsy" and "Hungarian," even though the latter remains unmarked and is mentioned quite rarely. In other words, the discursive construction of "Gypsyness" through racial characteristics consequently implies the racial definition of "Hungarianness."

This leads me to one of the most significant conclusions of the study: due to the fear caused by weakened social positions and the overall framing of social problems within the "Gypsy question," all attempts at collective self-definition adopt a language of exclusion which is built on a proposition of fundamental and essentialist differences. That is, the meaning of "Hungarianness" in the three ethnically mixed villages is defined through a racist logic, fueled by the structural contradictions of local society.[31] Racism, in a universal sense, is understood to be the result of structural circumstances that emerge because of conflicts over scarce resources, institutional and everyday forms of distinction, segregation within the job market, unequal access to power and prestige, and restrictions on inter-group contact[32]. Furthermore, it is commonly accepted that racism increases when the consequences of social and economic crises affect the power relations between various groups. Verena Stolcke has identified a new form of racism—cultural racism—which can be seen as a response to the social problems caused by recession and economic uncertainty (such as unemployment, housing shortages, a high crime-rate, and the deterioration of social services).[33] My claim here is the following: the case of three Hungarian villages proves that welfare chauvinism is a key factor in the emergence of a rhetoric which constructs opposition between a threatened nation and a threatening minority, and in general attempts to restore a world-

[31] This is the reason why such villages have become so important in terms of both extreme right-wing political mobilization and media attention (as the example of Gyöngyöspata shows).

[32] John Rex, *Race Relations in Sociological Theory* (London: Weidenfeld and Nicholson, 1971).

[33] Verena Stolcke, "Talking Culture: New Boundaries, New Rhetorics of Exclusion in Europe," *Current Anthropology* 36, no. 1 (1995): 1–13.

view in which everything and everyone returns to their prescribed position, as determined by the former hierarchy.

This statement also explains why individuals who are seen as Roma cannot identify with the category of "Hungarian," this is because they sense that this form of identity has been discursively re-framed to mean the opposite of "Gypsy." The promise of traditional liberal Hungarian nationalism in relation to the Roma minority was that through the processes of "social integration" and "social inclusion" the latter would became part of the nation—the reward for social mobility would be equal membership in the national community. The reality, however, is that the gradual disappearance of social differences was accompanied not by a decrease in symbolic distance but, on the contrary, a significant increase. Discursive forms of distinction are becoming more essentialist and more powerful. Social mobility in the short term has not brought about the promised inclusion of the Roma into the national community, but triggered a nationalist discourse which excludes even emancipated and socially accomplished members of the Roma minority.

BIBLIOGRAPHY

Brubaker, Rogers, Margit Feischmidt, Jon Fox, and Liana Grancea. *Nationalist Politics and Everyday Ethnicity in a Transylvanian Town.* Princeton, NJ: Princeton University Press, 2006.

Fanon, Frantz. *Black Skin, White Masks: New Interdisciplinary Essays*. Manchester University Press, (1952) 2006.

Feischmidt, Margit and Kristóf Szombati. "Understanding the Rise of the Far Right from a Local Perspective: Structural and Cultural Conditions of Ethno-traditionalist Inclusion and Racial Exclusion in Rural Hungary." *Identitites,* 3 (2017): 313–333.

Fox, Jon, and Cynthia-Ildriss Miller. "Everyday Nationhood." *Ethnicities* 4 (2008): 536–563.

Gingrich, Andre, and Marcus Banks. *Neo-Nationalism in Europe and Beyond. Perspectives from Social Anthropology.* New York: Berghahn Books, 2006.

Holmes, Douglas. *Integral Europe. Fast-capitalism, Multiculturalism, Neofascism.* Princeton: Princeton University Press, 2000.

Kovai, Cecília. "Hidden Potential in 'Naming Gypsy': The Transformation of Gypsy Hungarian Distinction." In *The Gypsy "Menace". Populism and the New Anti-Gypsy Politics,* edited by Michael Stewart, 281–295. London: Hurst, 2012.

Kovács, András. *A Másik szeme. Zsidók és antiszemiták a háború utáni Magyarországon.* (The Eye of the Other. Jews and Antisemites in Post-War Hungary). Budapest: Gondolat, 2008.

Kalb, Don, and Gábor Halmai, eds. *Headlines of Nation, Subtexts of Class. Working Class Populism and the Return of the Repressed in Neoliberal Europe.* New York: Berghahn, 2011.

Rex, John. *Race Relations in Sociological Theory.* London: Weidenfeld and Nicholson, 1971.

Stewart, Michael. "Populism, Roma and the European Politics of Cultural Difference." In *The Gypsy "Menace": Populism and the New Anti-Gypsy Politics*, edited by Michael Stewart, 3-23. London: Hurst, 2012.

Stolcke, Verena. "Talking Culture: New Boundaries, New Rhetorics of Exclusion in Europe," *Current Anthropology* 36, no. 1 (1995): 1–13.

Verdery, Katherine. "Ethnicity, Nationalism and State-making: Ethnic Groups and Boundaries: Past and Future." In: *The Anthropology of Ethnicity: Beyond "Ethnic Groups and Boundaries,"* edited by Hans Vermeulen and Cora Govers, 33–58. Amsterdam: Het Spinhuis, 1994.

Wodak, Ruth, Rudolf de Cillia, Martin Reisigl, and Karin Liebhart. *The Discursive Construction of National Identity*. Edinburgh: Edinburgh University Press, 1999.

Wodak, Ruth, Majid KhosraviNik, and Brigitte Mral, eds. *Right Wing Populism in Europe. Politics and Discourse.* London: Bloomsbury, 2013.

Zolnay, János. "Abusive Language and Discriminatory Measures in Hungarian Legal Policy." In *The Gypsy "Menace": Populism and the New Anti-Gypsy Politics*, edited by Michel Stewart, 25–42. London: Hurst, 2012.

Civil Society and the Right-wing Radicalization of the Public Sphere in Hungary[1]

VIRÁG MOLNÁR

Introduction

The massive nationalist-populist shift of Hungarian politics and public discourse has proceeded steadily since at least the 2009 European parliamentary elections that launched the far right political party, Jobbik[2] ("Movement for a Better Hungary") on its path to become the second largest political force in the country. Political analysts as well as academic commentators have repeatedly pointed to the existence of a weak civil society—a legacy of nearly half-a-century of communist rule—as an important reason for the continuing democracy deficit of postsocialist countries.

The well-known French historian and political theorist, Jacques Rupnik, for instance, accused Central and Eastern European (CEE) countries of "backsliding" from the liberal democratic project. He has argued that even though the CEE countries' achievement of EU membership was meant to signal the conclusion of the post-authoritarian transition process, it has actually revealed that institutional convergence has proved insufficient in re-democratizing the postsocialist world. He offers a culturalist explanation, tracing the setbacks to the

---

1 This chapter is a revised and extended version of V. Molnár, "Civil Society, Radicalism and the Rediscovery of Mythic Nationalism," *Nations and Nationalism* 1 (2017): 165–85.

2 Jobbik's name is a play on words, meaning both "better" and "more to the right."

failure of the democratic consolidation to capture the "habits of the heart" and thus transform civic culture—"without which," he argues, "the legitimacy and stability of democratic institutions will always remain doubtful."[3]

The growing influence of the radical right in Eastern as well as Western Europe is indeed truly alarming. Within this context, it is especially puzzling how Hungary, initially probably the most staunchly liberal of all the post-socialist transition countries, has come to spearhead a right-wing populist backlash. I suggest that by shifting the focus from political parties and formal democratic institutions to broader patterns of political participation in the realm of societal self-organization, the so-called "third domain," or civil society, we can gain important sociological insights into these developments. Moreover, this chapter argues against the conventional wisdom that sees the lack of civil society activism as the ultimate cause behind the nationalist-populist turn. It demonstrates that civil society has been quite vibrant in the post-1989 period. However, rather than working exclusively toward strengthening and complementing liberal political institutions, it has also provided fertile soil to the spread of right-wing populism, radicalism and xenophobia. In fact, I contend that civil society organizations have been instrumental in turning right-wing radicalism into a significant political force.

The following analysis builds on in-depth case studies of specific organizations, including the "Goyim Riders" biker club, the Hungarian Guard paramilitary organization, and foreign currency mortgage debtor groups to offer insight into the workings of "uncivil" society in post-millennium Hungary. The chapter focuses on the Hungarian experience because the populist backlash has been especially deep-seated in this country, producing the most successful far-right parliamentary party in the region. The paper also has general implications for understanding the recent rise of radical populism across Central and Eastern Europe, underscoring that 20 years after the fall of communism, post-socialist countries have reached yet another turning point that few would have anticipated at the time of the velvet revolutions.

---

[3] Jacques Rupnik, "From Democracy Fatigue to Populist Backlash," *Journal of Democracy* 4 (2007): 19.

The Civil Society and Democracy Link

Civil society is a widely used but analytically somewhat slippery term. Most broadly defined, it denotes processes of societal self-organization.[4] It is seen as constitutive of democracy, and its health is considered vital to ensuring the legitimacy of democratic political institutions.[5] Civic associations, popular movements, and various other organized publics are understood to make up a relatively autonomous public sphere that mediates modern social life between the state and the market as well as between the state and individuals. Civil society is thus conceptualized as a social and communicative space in which democratic practices and values evolve in the context of reasoned deliberation.[6] In the case of political transitions from authoritarianism to democracy, civil society has been identified as essential both in mounting an initial challenge to authoritarian rule (e.g., in Eastern Europe or South Africa) as well as in ensuring that formal democracy is fully translated into substantive democracy in the post-authoritarian democratization process.[7]

Precisely how civil society contributes to democracy has been the subject of ongoing debate with some positions more dominant than others but with no signs of an emerging consensus. In an essay on post-transition South Africa, the political sociologist Patrick Heller[8] distinguished three theoretical strands that conceptualize the nature of the link between civil society and democracy, especially in a post-tran-

---

[4] John A. Hall, "The Nature of Civil Society." *Society* May/June (1998): 32-41.

[5] Jürgen Habermas, *The Structural Transformation of the Public Sphere: An Inquiry into a Category of Bourgeois Society* (Cambridge, MA: MIT Press, 1989), Robert Putnam with Robert Leonardi and Raffaella Y. Nanetti, *Making Democracy Work: Civic Traditions in Modern Italy* (Princeton: Princeton University Press, 1993).

[6] Craig J. Calhoun, *Habermas and the Public Sphere* (Cambridge, MA: MIT press, 1992), Habermas, *The Structural Transformation,* Mabel Berezin, "Politics and Culture: A Less Fissured Terrain." *Annual Review of Sociology* 23 (1997a): 361–83.

[7] Peter Heller, "Civil Society and Democracy in Post-Transition South Africa," Unpublished manuscript.

[8] Ibid.

sition context. In the following I use this basic classification scheme as a starting point but rework and extend its categories in my analysis.

The first, liberal perspective sees civic associations as intrinsically beneficial for democracy and society.[9] According to this view, societal self-organization "allows for co-operation with the state whilst enabling individuation."[10] Civil society organizations generally pursue progressive causes and constitute a field of voluntary collective action and civic associationalism, providing a healthy balance to social life between state and market control. In many ways, and despite some gradually growing criticism, the liberal perspective remains the dominant understanding of the impact of civil society on democracy.

The second perspective grows out of the social movement literature, arguing that in the post-authoritarian period civil society contracts in response to the emergence of formal democratic institutions and the "professionalization" of political activity.[11] This perspective underscores the importance of pre-transition civil society in effectively mobilizing support in service of the regime change. But it contends that as the transition to democracy opens up new incentives and formal channels to engage the state, grassroots civic participation progressively wanes. This position in fact perfectly dovetails with Jacques Rupnik's diagnosis of the reasons behind the populist backlash in Central and Eastern Europe, as he states that the democratic setbacks arise from the fact that constitutionalism (and economic liberalization) took precedence over citizenship and participation.[12] At the same time, this argument closely resonates with the more general Gramscian interpretation that sees civil society as organized implicitly by the state and ruled by consent through hegemony.[13] Namely, political power in post-transition countries becomes consolidated and centralized not only

[9] Jean Cohen and Andrew Arato, *Civil Society and Political Theory* (Cambridge, MA: MIT Press, 1992), Hall, "The Nature."

[10] Hall, "The Nature," 32.

[11] Patricia L. Hipsher, "Democratic Transitions as Protest Cycles: Social Movement Dynamics in Democratizing Latin America," in *The Social Movement Society*, ed. Sidney Tarrow and David Meyer (New York: Rowan and Littlefield, 1998), 152–172.

[12] Rupnik, "From Democracy," 19.

[13] Antonio Gramsci, *Selections from the Prison Notebooks* (New York: International Publishers, 1971).

in the state apparatus but is also diffused more broadly across society through the media, religious and cultural organizations, trade unions and kinship networks, narrowing the gap between "political society" and "civil society."

The third perspective includes a group of scholars who voice skepticism about the liberal view that associational life is, by default, beneficial for democracy.[14] Key proponents of this minority approach focus primarily on inter-war Europe and show through a series of detailed historical case studies how a vibrant associational life contributed decisively to the rise of fascism in Germany, Hungary and Italy. Sheri Berman (1997), for instance, argues that a strong civil society in Weimar Germany, which arose from Germans' frustrations with the repeated breakdowns of political parties and the national government, facilitated Hitler's ascent to power. Similarly, Dylan Riley[15] compares Italy with Spain and Romania to show that strong civic associations in north-central Italy provided crucial organizational resources to the fascist movement. His work extends earlier research that shows how preexisting civic associations were coopted by Mussolini's fascist regime.[16] For Hungary, the historian Mária Kovács[17] describes how the professional and civic associations of the classic liberal free professions (doctors, engineers, lawyers) became a hotbed for illiberal ideas during the 1930s, revealing that the right-wing radicalism of civil society actually surpassed the democratic deficit of inter-war parliamentary politics. These studies all critique neo-Tocquevillean theories and Robert Putnam's social capital thesis by demonstrating that under conditions of weak political institutionalization, high levels of associationalism can

---

[14] Ariel Armony, *The Dubious Link: Civic Engagement and Democratization* (Stanford: Stanford University Press, 2004).

[15] Dylan Riley, "Civic Associations and Authoritarian Regimes in Interwar Europe: Italy and Spain in Comparative Perspective," *American Sociological Review* 2 (2005): 288–310, Dylan Riley, *The Civic Foundations of Fascism in Europe: Italy, Spain, and Romania, 1870-1945* (Baltimore: JHU Press, 2010).

[16] Mabel Berezin, *Making the Fascist Self: The Political Culture of Interwar Italy* (Ithaca, NY: Cornell University Press, 1997b).

[17] Mária Kovács, *Liberal Professions and Illiberal Politics: Hungary from the Habsburgs to the Holocaust* (New York: Woodrow Wilson Center and Oxford University Press, 1994).

actually lead to social fragmentation, political radicalization and the triumph of illiberal politics.

Unsurprisingly, my research falls in line with the skeptical approach. But I also argue that the weakness of political institutions is not the only condition under which civil society can contribute to undermining the democratic qualities of a political regime. The case of right-wing radical populism[18] in contemporary Hungary and Eastern Europe is interesting because its emergence takes place in a period of highly stable democratic political institutions. Europe in the 1930s still suffered from the devastation of the war, from the effects of sweeping peace treaties that radically redrew national borders and triggered the migration of large populations, not to mention the botched communist revolutions, and the Great Depression that together accounted for a feeble and volatile political situation across the continent. But the political transitions of 1989 were unique in their peacefulness and their meticulous attention to democratic constitutionalism. Moreover, the nearly unconditional commitment to European Union membership created an external monitoring process that was meant to ensure the deepening of post-authoritarian democratization while reintegrating the CEE region into a prosperous and stable Europe. In other words, the post-1989 political context couldn't have been more markedly different from that of the 1930s with respect to the solidity of democratic political institutions.

The growing appeal of right-wing populism and its diffusion via civil society have to do with a more nuanced crisis of political legitimacy in post-socialist CEE that began to transpire around the turn of the millennium and has been growing in vigor ever since, gaining fresh impetus in the aftermath of the 2008 financial crisis. This political legitimacy crisis feeds on a re-evaluation of the transition as inherently flawed, reflecting merely a political compromise between the pre-1989 democratic opposition and the ex-communist elite. The former was allowed to implement the political project of democratic liberalization while the latter was allowed to benefit from radical economic

[18] I use a broad definition of populism understood as "democratic illiberalism" (see Takis S. Pappas, "Populist Democracies: Post-Authoritarian Greece and Post-Communist Hungary," *Government and Opposition* 1 (2014): 1-23.)

liberalization, convert its political privileges into economic capital, and be spared from lustration.[19] This largely explains why contemporary right-wing populist rhetoric revolves around three leitmotifs: anti-communism, anti-corruption, and anti-capitalism.[20]

Civil Society and Everyday Nationalism

Broadening the definition of civil society to include "uncivil" publics that can promote non-democratic and illiberal politics helps to open up conceptual space in the civil society literature in two important ways. First, it allows for a better understanding of the intricate connections between nationalism and the public sphere.[21] There is growing empirical research in a variety of geopolitical contexts that spotlights the importance of this relationship. Peter Stamatov,[22] for instance, draws attention to the significance of ethnonational mobilization in reconstituting the public sphere in postcommunist Bulgaria through the emerging coalition of local elites and popular groups and the creation of a new political language. In a related vein, Chris Hann has demonstrated how ideas of democracy and civil society were exploited by nationalist organizations during the post-1989 transition.[23] Nevertheless, national mobilization in the public sphere is not confined to

19 The Czech and Germany trajectories deviate from this general pattern somewhat, as these two countries implemented some form of decommunization in the 1990s.

20 There is variation among CEE countries in the extent to which these three themes are seen as closely interrelated. In Hungary, for instance, anti-corruption rhetoric is intimately linked with the need for decommunization whereas in Poland the anti-corruption and anti-communist motifs are not as closely intertwined. Anti-capitalism comes in many guises including anti-austerity, anti-globalization, anti-colonization, anti-EU, and even anti-Semitic rhetoric and sentiments.

21 Peter Stamatov, "The Making of a 'Bad' Public: Ethnonational Mobilization in Post-communist Bulgaria," *Theory and Society* 29 (2000): 549–572.

22 Ibid.

23 Chris Hann, "Nationalism and Civil Society in Central Europe: From Ruritania to the Carpathian Euroregion," *in The State of the Nation: Ernest Gellner and the Theory of Nationalism*, ed. J. A. Hal, (Cambridge: Cambridge University Press, 1998) 243–257.

Eastern Europe. In Spain, civic associations contributed significantly to the spread of Basque terrorism.[24]

There is mounting evidence though that since the turn of the millennium in many post-socialist countries and in Hungary in particular civil society has emerged as the main arena in which the symbolic repertoire of a new nationalism is articulated.[25] As the cultural anthropologist Margit Feischmidt[26] suggests, it is not the state that plays the decisive role in recasting Hungarian nationalism but civic actors, far right political groups and their media outlets backed by a vigorous industry that has turned nationalist identity politics into a profitable business. In the case of Hungary this is actually not a historical singularity because in the Reform era in the second half of the nineteenth century civic associations (reading clubs, ballroom societies, private literary salons, etc.) also played a crucial part in Hungarian independence efforts and the nation state building project.[27]

Second, the more expansive definition draws attention to civil society as an important domain in which the construction of everyday nationhood[28] can be empirically captured. Civil society offers key insights into the formation of political culture(s) understood as "the matrix of meanings embodied in expressive symbols, practices, and beliefs that

---

24 David D. Laitin, "National Revivals and Violence," *European Journal of Sociology* 36 (1995): 3–43.

25 *Nemzet a mindennapokban. Az újnacionalizmus populáris kultúrája*, ed. Margit Feischmidt et al. (Budapest: L'Harmattan, 2014), Balázs Trencsényi, "Beyond Liminality? The Kulturkampf of the Early 2000s in East Central Europe." *Boundary 2* 41 (2014): 135–152.

26 Margit Feischmidt "Nemzetdiskurzusok a mindennapokban és a nacionalizmus populáris kultúrája," in *Nemzet a mindennapokban. Az újnacionalizmus populáris kultúrája*, ed. Margit Feischmidt et al. (Budapest: L'Harmattan, 2014), 7–51.

27 Robert Nemes, "The Politics of the Dance Floor: Culture and Civil Society in Nineteenth-century Hungary," *Slavic Review* 60 (2001): 802–823, Robert Nemes, *The Once and Future Budapest* (DeKalb: Northern Illinois University Press, 2005).

28 Rogers M. Brubaker et al. *Nationalist Politics and Everyday Ethnicity in a Transylvanian Town* (Princeton, NJ: Princeton University Press, 2006), Tim Edensor, *National Identity, Popular Culture and Everyday Life* (Oxford: Berg, 2002), Jon E. Fox and Cynthia Miller-Idriss, "Everyday Nationhood," *Ethnicities* 8 (2008): 536–563.

constitute ordinary politics in a bounded collectivity."[29] Thereby, the empirically grounded study of civil society can serve as an analytical strategy to address the conceptual shift in nationalism research that increasingly locates the national in everyday practices and in the realm of popular culture rather than exclusively in elite and official discourses.[30] The research agenda of everyday nationhood focuses especially on four ways through which the nation is produced and reproduced in everyday life: "talking the nation" (i.e., understanding the discursive construction of the nation through routine talk in interaction); "choosing the nation"; "performing the nation"; and "consuming the nation."[31] In this paper I show that civic associations provide an excellent organizational context where these processes and practices can be empirically explored.

Moreover, by triangulating civil society, everyday nationalism and political culture I will approach contemporary right-wing radicalism not as a codified political ideology but as a more fluid subculture where expressive symbols, material objects, rituals, everyday consumption and lifestyle patterns are essential carriers of political convictions and group membership. This analytical move echoes another trend in the broader literature that favors the notion of publics over civil society in capturing the dynamics of the public sphere. Increasing reliance on the category of publics has been motivated in large part by research on non-Western societies including Japan and the postcolonial world.[32] Scholars studying

---

[29] Jeffrey C. Goldfarb, *Reinventing Political Culture: The Power of Culture Versus the Culture of Power* (Cambridge, UK: Polity, 2012), Mabel Berezin, "Politics and Culture: A Less Fissured Terrain," *Annual Review of Sociology* 23 (1997a): 364.

[30] Brubaker et al., *Nationalist Politics,* Edensor, *National Identity,* Feischmidt et al. *Nemzet a mindennapokban,* Fox and Miller-Idriss, "Everyday Nationhood," *Headlines of Nation, Subtexts of Class: Working Class Populism and the Return of the Repressed in Neoliberal Europe*, ed. Don Kalb and Gábor Halmai (New York: Berghahn Books, 2011).

[31] Fox and Miller-Idriss, "Everyday Nationhood," 537.

[32] Partha Chatterjee, *Politics of the Governed: Reflections on Popular Politics in Most of the World* (New York: Columbia University Press, 2004); *Civil Society and the Political Imagination in Africa: Critical Perspectives,* ed. Comaroff, John L. and Jean Comaroff (Chicago: University of Chicago Press, 1999); Eiko Ikegami, "A Sociological Theory of Publics: Identity and Culture as Emergent Properties in Networks," *Social Research* 4 (2000): 990–1029; Eiko Ikegami, *Bonds of Civility. Aesthetic Networks and the Political Origins of Japanese Culture* (Cambridge, UK: Cambridge University Press, 2005).

these societies have argued that the notion of civil society imposed a "pedagogical vision of public life," derived from the canons of European social theory and extrapolated from the European historical experience, which was in conflict with existing forms of public participation in non-Western contexts.[33] A reconstituted notion of publics, however, helps to eschew the strong normative implications of the civil society concept.[34] In this chapter, I continue to use the term civil society but de-normativize it by incorporating not only "civil" but also all sorts of publics, regardless of their value orientations, in its definitional scope.

Before turning to a closer examination of the landscape of radical nationalist civic associations, I would like to offer some historical background to how the place of the political has changed in Hungary in the 2000s, and how the boundaries between political and civil society—or, in other words, the state and the public sphere—have been reconfigured in the wake of a mounting political legitimacy crisis around the reassessment of the transition

Civil Society and the Crisis of Political Legitimacy in Post-Millennium Hungary

There are two important turning points in capturing the role of civil society in the rise of right-wing radicalism in Hungary, which coincided with the general parliamentary elections of 2002 and 2006. Whilst many commentators attribute the soaring popularity of illiberal politics to the most recent economic crisis and the near complete financial meltdown of the Hungarian state in the fall of 2009, the re-emergence of right-wing radicalism in fact goes back as far as the turn of the millennium. While the economic crisis has clearly contributed to the appeal of political radicalism, it was not its main trigger. By the arrival of the Great Recession right-wing radicalism was already in full swing; it was a significant, though not yet a parliamentary, political force.

In 2002 the conservative Fidesz (Young Democrats) lost the parliamentary elections to the Socialists while also failing to force the res-

[33] Francis Cody, "Publics and Politics," *Annual Review of Anthropology* 40 (2011): 37–52.

[34] Ikegami, "A Sociological Theory."

ignation of the new Socialist Prime Minister who became embroiled in a political scandal about his past as a communist informant shortly after his inauguration. Confronted with these electoral defeats, Viktor Orbán, the leader of Fidesz, decided to return politics to the masses. He founded the so-called Civic Circles (Polgári Körök) movement, encouraging his political supporters to set up local chapters to continue regular informal discussions about the future of Hungary, claiming that such honest dialogue premised on true political representation will become obsolete in the parliament, now that the ex-communists had returned to power.

Civic Circles quickly cropped up across the country and became organized into a loose national network. Circles were set up even among the Hungarian diaspora in the US. While vigorous at the beginning, the activism of Civic Circles faded over the next couple of years. Orbán's initiative, nevertheless, reminded Hungarians of one of the important lessons of 1989, namely that political activity does not have to be confined to the parliament. Jobbik, which was founded in 1999 as a youth organization of right-wing Christian university students, also became solidified in this process of "rediscovering" civic associationalism sparked by the Civic Circles movement.

Fidesz's attempt to start the Civic Circles network to extend the reach of politics beyond the parliament offers two important lessons for understanding the changing relationship between parliamentary politics and civil society in post-1989 Hungary. First, despite gradually fizzling out, the initiative was a reminder of the potential of civil society as a domain of political and social activism. Second, it showed that civic associations that are used merely as fodder for political parties and are treated instrumentally to extend their political influence would not be viable over the long run. Civic Circles quickly became empty vessels for Fidesz's political propaganda and dwindled. However, many civic organizations that were founded as a result of this effort to redraw the boundaries of the political but were not the product of Fidesz's post-election astroturfing strategy have actually continued to grow in earnest.[35] It is, therefore, important to underscore that Jobbik emerged separately from and remained independent of the Fidesz-led Civic Circles movement, becoming a political party in 2003.

[35] Trencsényi, "Beyond Liminality?"

The second, and even more decisive, turning point came in 2006 after the infamous speech of the re-elected Socialist Prime Minister, Ferenc Gyurcsány, delivered at an internal Socialist Party event, was leaked to the media. The speech revealed that the Socialists consistently lied about the state of the Hungarian economy (most crucially, about the level of the budget deficit) during the 2006 parliamentary election campaign.

The incident and the severity of the public's reaction, which led to street riots in Budapest during the fall of 2006, turned Hungary into a laughing stock of international news media. It was also probably the first and only time that Hungary made it into Jon Stewart's Daily Show. Foreign press coverage ruthlessly mocked the naiveté of Hungarians who were seemingly unaware that politicians in parliamentary democracies also lied through their teeth in order to get reelected. Despite the obvious pathetic overtones of the situation, the incident generated grave and irreversible consequences for Hungarian political democracy. The Socialists' desperate efforts to repair the damage and the opposition's counter-efforts to exploit it turned political populism and demagoguery into the dominant language of politics on the left as much as on the right, setting the tone of Hungarian political culture at large.[36] As a result, Hungary was increasingly morphing into a "populist democracy"; namely, a pluralist political system in which both the party in office as well as the major opposition party are characterized by strong populism.[37]

The ensuing street riots in the fall of 2006, besides representing the all-time nadir of post-1989 politics, proved to be crucial in facilitating the rise of the radical right. On the one hand, the sheer incompetence of the police in handling the riots as well as real and alleged incidents of police brutality against the rioters further eroded the legitimacy of the Socialist government. It also immediately revived the image of the police, all too familiar from the communist era, as an instrument of political repression rather than as a guarantor of law and order. On the other hand, and more importantly, the riots brought together a number of disconnected radical civic groups that were hitherto largely unaware of each other's existence. The riots brought them

36 Palonen, "Political Polarisation."
37 Pappas, "Populist Democracies."

visibility as well as opportunity to connect with other like-minded loose groupings and organizations. Simultaneously, the riots revealed to Hungarians the existence of a wide range of alternative publics openly embracing radical political ideas and inhabiting pockets of civil society that have been hidden from the reach of mainstream media. In the following section I try to introduce some of these organizations and shed light on how they are linked to the radical right-wing party, Jobbik.

Civic Associations: Vehicles for Radical Nationalism

In Figure 8.1 I created a map that aims to visually summarize the field of radical nationalist civic associations by the type of activity that determines the dominant character of these organizations. Table 8.1 in the Appendix contains a comprehensive list of radical right-wing civic associations recently active in Hungary that provided the raw data for the diagram in Figure 8.1. Undoubtedly, most examined organizations mix

Figure 8.1: Map of radical nationalist civic associations by type of activity

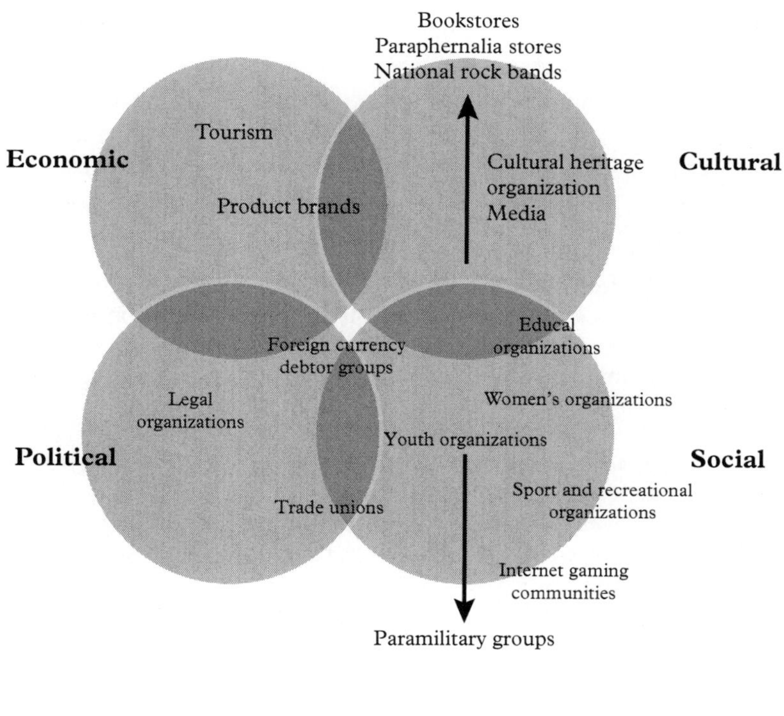

economic,[38] social, cultural and political concerns in their activities, but the relative weight of these dimensions varies across organizations. The diagram tries to classify them according their most salient trait.

As several scholars[39] have suggested, radical nationalist groups have been very adept at using online and social media to create an alternative public sphere to share and disseminate their ideas and activities. I used this insight in my empirical research to reconstruct the landscape of radical civic activism and compile the list in Table 8.1. I started with some well-known groups (Goyim riders, kuruc.info, national rock bands) and quickly discovered that their websites nearly always include a collection of links to other like-minded organizations. These are often designated as "links to our friends' websites," "links to our supporters," and it was chiefly by tracing these links that I assembled Table 8.1.[40] I do not claim the list to be exhaustive, but it provides a comprehensive sampling of existing organizations to illustrate the wide range of social and cultural activities they pursue. They include cultural associations that promote the preservation and cultivation of Hungarian "traditions" such as the learning of the Hungarian Runic alphabet that is said to be a rune-like script used in Transylvania in the 9th century; *baranta*, a Hungarian martial arts; pre-Christian pagan religious practices[41]; or the historic preservation of traditional Transylvanian village and religious architecture. There are also several sports organizations, among them a women's handball team, a motorcycle

[38] This mixing is best illustrated by economic associations because even seemingly entirely for-profit businesses, for instance, in the heritage tourism industry in Transylvania have a mission beyond just making money. The Deáky András Agrotourism Bed and Breakfast company is a case in point, as it offers "alternative history lectures" and plays an important part in local architectural heritage preservation in addition to offering a broad range of programs that aim at heritage cultivation (e.g., local culinary and folk traditions including music and dance. Zoltán Ilyés, "Az emlékezés és a turisztikai élmény nemzetiesítése," in *Nemzet a mindennapokban. Az újnacionalizmus populáris kultúrája*, ed. Margit Feischmidt et al. (Budapest: L'Harmattan, 2014), 290–341.

[39] Trencsényi, "Beyond Liminality?" Feischmidt "Nemzetdiskurzusok."

[40] The network structure of the links will be explored in a separate article.

[41] László-Attila Hubbes, "A Comparative Investigation of Romanian and Hungarian Ethno-Pagan Blogs," *Reconnect Working Papers* 2, accessed July 9, 2014, http://papers.ssrn.com/sol3/papers.cfm?abstract_id=1984597.

association, and the fan club of one of the oldest and most iconic Hungarian soccer teams, Ferencváros. The rock bands listed in the table represent a peculiar genre of political rock labeled "national rock."

These diverse groups draw on the symbolic imagery of Hungarians' historic independence struggles against Ottoman occupation in the sixteenth and seventeenth century and later against Habsburg rule; the loss of Transylvania (and parts of Northern and Southern Hungary) after World War I; as well as Hungarian popular legends about Hungarian settlers from the time of the Hungarian Conquest at the turn of the ninth and tenth centuries. They blend this medley of historical motifs into a contemporary anti-capitalist rhetoric in which Hungarian independence is lost, for instance, to foreign multinational corporations and the European Union.

There are numerous bookstores that sell nationalist and chauvinist literature, CDs of "national rock" bands and radical paraphernalia such as car stickers in the shape of pre-Trianon (i.e., pre-1920) Hungary, considered an obvious irredentist symbol, or pins and statutes of the *turul*, a huge falcon-like bird that serves as the messenger of god in Hungarian origin myths. Similarly, nearly every tattoo salon in Hungary today has a special category for these mythic nationalist motifs that can include images of Greater Hungary, the Holy Crown of St. Stephen, Runic calligraphy, or flags with the controversial red-white Árpád stripes.[42,43]

While these material objects might seem simultaneously trivial and tacky, they turn these symbols into props of everyday life, thereby domesticating and gradually legitimating them. Materiality and ready visibility render these symbols conspicuous signs that play a central role in the everyday performance of group membership and cultural kinship

42 Anett Sőrés, "A (Nagy)Asszony varrva jó? Jellegzetes tetoválások a szélsőjobboldali csoportok körében," *Művelődés-, Tudomány- és Orvostörténeti Folyóirat* 2 (2011): 115-123.

43 The flag was originally associated with the House of the Árpád, the founding dynasty of the Hungarian Kingdom that ruled Hungary from the tenth to the thirteenth century. It is part of Hungary's current coat of arms but was also used by the Hungarian Nazi party, the Arrow Cross Party in the 1930s and 1940s.

both to insiders and outsiders.[44] Even a few years ago it was rare and disturbing to see Greater Hungary stickers on cars in lieu of the nondescript letter H stickers used to designate Hungary, but by now they have become so widespread that everyone just takes them for granted.

The book and paraphernalia stores also function as focal points in organizing right-wing radical groups, as they regularly host readings and various other events bringing together related civic associations and independent sympathizers who might stumble on the right organization for them. Right-wing media sources, most of which are online news portals, are particularly important because they play a similar role in unifying, modernizing and diffusing radical cultural and political discourse.

Dominant themes shared by these organizations echo the subjects of mythical nationalism that was invented and loosely codified in the process of nineteenth century nation-state formation, and then complemented with motifs derived from the national trauma of the Treaty of Trianon rather than any explicit Nazi or neo-Nazi ideology.[45] These shared themes are essential because they connect these organizations into a larger and fairly cohesive network while offering anchors of commonality that strengthen the cultural bond among members. The relevance of mythical nationalism is also emphasized in the case of other Central and Eastern European countries, especially in Poland.[46]

Some of these civic organizations have direct links to Jobbik, the right-wing radical party. For instance, the largest bookstore is owned by a prominent member of the party. Similarly, the Hungarian Guard, the most profiled and demonized organization on the list, is a uniformed paramilitary formation that was founded by Jobbik's president. Some associations (e.g., an "independent" police trade union) have

---

44 Iddo Tavory, "Of Yarmulkes and Categories: Delegating Boundaries and the Phenomenology of Interactional Expectation." *Theory and Society* 39 (2010): 49–68.

45 *Egyezzünk ki a múlttal! Műhelybeszélgetések történelmi mítoszainkról, tévhiteinkről,* ed. László Lőrincz (Budapest: Történelemtanárok Egylete, 2010).

46 Geneviève Zubrzycki, "History and the National Sensorium: Making Sense of Polish Mythology," *Qualitative Sociology* 34 (2011): 21–57., Geneviève Zubrzycki, "Aesthetic Revolt and the Remaking of National Identity in Quebec, 1960–1969," *Theory and Society* 42 (2013): 423–475.

formed official alliances with Jobbik while most remain completely independent, beyond sharing intellectual kinship and frequenting each other's events. National rock bands, for instance, often perform at Jobbik gatherings.[47]

In the following sections I zoom in on three examples from the list of organizations in Table 8.1, presenting them as case studies that show how these civic associations are both the source and collective product of contemporary right-wing radicalism. In general there is little empirical research on these right-wing civic organizations. The handful of existing studies usually focus on single cases, principally on national rock bands, online news media, and tourism.[48] Therefore, I selected cases that reflect the range and diversity of the organizations in this field including social, economic, political and cultural associations. The case studies are in part based on data that was collected from online sources used in the first phase of the research that aimed to map the alternative public sphere created by right-wing populist groups with the help of new media (see Figure 8.1 and Appendix). I traced the online presence (websites, blogs, YouTube videos) and studied the online self-presentation of the selected organizations complementing this information with the analysis of a wide range of primary and secondary documents including local media coverage on the emergence and history of the organizations as well as content analysis of public controversies involving them (e.g., the linguistics debate regarding the name of the Goyim Riders club).

---

[47] Margit Feischmidt and Gergő Pulay, "Élmény és ideológia a nacionalista popkultúrában," in *Nemzet a mindennapokban. Az újnacionalizmus populáris kultúrája*, ed. Margit Feischmidt et al. (Budapest: L'Harmattan, 2014), 249–90.

[48] Feischmidt and Pulay, "Élmény és ideológia"; Rita Glózer, "A nemzet helyreállítása a magyarországi radikális mozgalom ellenségtematizáló diskurzusaiban," in *Nemzet a mindennapokban. Az újnacionalizmus populáris kultúrája*, ed. Margit Feischmidt et al. (Budapest: L'Harmattan, 2014); Zoltán Ilyés, "Az emlékezés és a turisztikai élmény nemzetiesítése" in *Nemzet a mindennapokban. Az újnacionalizmus populáris kultúrája*, ed. Margit Feischmidt et al. (Budapest: L'Harmattan, 2014), 290–341., András Zsuppán, "Politikai okkultizmus Magyarországon 8: Ifjú szívekben," *Magyar Narancs*, January 5, 2006, https://m.magyarnarancs.hu/belpol/politikai_okkultizmus_magyarorszagon_8_ifju_szivekben-64987.

GOYIM RIDERS

The first organization is called the *Gój Motoros Egyesület,* the "Goyim Motorcycle Association" and its members are known as the "Goyim riders." This organization aptly reflects the complex, often perplexing and counterintuitive symbolic imagery that characterizes these radical associations. It also highlights the covert and highly coded nature of the racist and chauvinist rhetoric they embrace. The group was officially registered as a non-profit civic association in 2006 but has existed informally at least since 2000. The association's stated goal is "to protect Hungarian national and Christian ideas and values, cultivate national traditions, and organize motorcycle tours to visit historical landmarks and commemorate key figures of Hungarian history."[49]

The very name of the organization has been the subject of significant controversy. It spawned, for instance, a series of philological essays in the premier weekly of the Hungarian liberal literati, *Élet és Irodalom* [Life and Literature], in which distinguished linguists debated whether the name implies social and racial exclusion.[50] Goyim, namely, is a Yiddish and Hebrew word which denotes a non-Jewish person and was commonly used in the nineteenth and twentieth centuries by Hungarian Jews to describe non-Jews. The linguistic debate revolved around trying to decide whether this term that has been used to describe an out-group is neutral or pejorative, especially in a context when a group turns the out-group definition into an in-group definition. Although the semantic incoherence of the label is confusing even for linguistic experts, the use of the term goyim does assume a high level of familiarity with Jewish culture in the Hungarian population at large; otherwise the intricate double entendre would not work.

In addition to igniting heated semantic disputes, Goyim riders have also been involved in libel suits against journalists in the liberal

---

49 http://www.gojmotorosok.hu/index.php?page=about.

50 László Kálmán, "A Gój Motorosok elnevezésről," *Élet és Irodalom,* November 23, 2007, https://www.es.hu/cikk/2007-11-25/kalman-laszlo/a-goj-motorosok-elnevezesrol.html, Tamás Gecső, "A Gój Motorosok esete a kék halakkal," *Élet és Irodalom,* January 4, 2008, https://www.es.hu/cikk/2008-01-07/dr-habil-gecso-tamas/a-goj-motorosok-esete-a-kek-halakkal.html.

media who openly called them fascists in radio and TV interviews. They actually won the most high-profile libel case, and the journalist was ordered to pay a fine for insulting the Goyim riders.

Members of the association do not fit well with the lumpenproletariat image of right-wing radicals propagated by mainstream media. The motors and the corresponding elaborate gear worn by members are costly and assume that most of them are financially well-endowed. The honorary president of the association is a relatively well-known sportsman, a former carriage driving world champion, and the owner (with his brother) of one of the largest supermarket chains in Hungary (CBA), which is the only Hungarian-owned national grocery chain. The current editor-in-chief of Hungary's second largest public radio channel, MR2 Petőfi Rádió, was also a longtime member of the organization (some claim he actually still is). Other high profile members and supporters include famous rock singers of highly popular and established rock bands as well as actors.

The group always denies accusations that it advocates anti-Semitism and fascism, but it embraces racist and chauvinist views in more subtle ways. Their logo (see http://www.gojmotorosok.hu) depicts a figure on a stylized motorcycle against the backdrop of Greater Hungary (i.e., pre-World War I, pre-Trianon Hungary), which is a "traditional" marker of irredentism despite the riders' claim that they only use it as a token of solidarity with ethnic Hungarians who live (and often suffer from cultural and social discrimination) in the regions that were taken away from Hungary in 1920. More disturbingly, Goyim riders have organized motorcycle convoys to demonstratively cruise in small towns that have been the scene of high-profile violent crimes and where rumors sprang up that the perpetrators might have been Roma citizens. They have not attacked anybody but their presence unmistakably is meant to be a signal of intimidation to local Roma populations. Goyim riders have thus been quite active in lending tangible support to the "Gypsy-crime" theory that has been invented and marketed by radical right-wing media. The case of Goyim riders illustrates how civic organizations can become, quite literally, carriers and self-appointed enforcers of exclusionary worldviews under the disguise of cultural heritage protection and sports activities.

THE HUNGARIAN GUARD PARAMILITARY ORGANIZATION

The *Magyar Gárda* (Hungarian Guard) was launched in August 2007 as an offshoot of the far-right Jobbik (Movement of a Better Hungary) party. The inauguration ceremony took place in front of the residence of the Hungarian president in Budapest's historic Castle District and was officiated by Lajos Für, Hungary's first post-communist minister of defense who was a representative of the, by now defunct, center-right party, the Hungarian Democratic Forum (MDF). The first fifty-six members of the Guard—a symbolic number chosen to recall the 1956 revolution—paraded in an outfit that was clearly intended to be a uniform: black boots, black trousers, white shirt with a black waist-coat, and black caps emblazoned with the red-white stripes of the so-called "Arpad" flag. They were holding the Hungarian flag together with the ancient "Arpad" banner of red and white stripes. The Arpad stripes form a dubious symbol because even though they are part of Hungary's official coat of arms, they are also closely associated with the Nazi Arrow Cross regime, which ruled Hungary from October 1944 to March 1945 and incorporated the stripes into its own flag.

The inauguration ceremony was also attended by three priests representing Hungary's main Christian denominations (Catholic, Calvinist and Evangelical) who blessed the Guard's flag,[51] several dozen members of an even more radical group, the Nemzeti Őrsereg, and Maria Wittner, a veteran of the 1956 revolution and member of Parliament for FIDESZ, Hungary's ruling party.[52] There was also a group of 500-1000 protestors representing various anti-fascist, leftist and Roma organizations staging a counter-demonstration where the prominent leftist philosopher and public intellectual, Gáspár Miklós Tamás declared the Guard "anti-Hungarian, anti-human, anti-national and stupid."

The second major public event, during which six hundred new members were admitted into the Guard, was held in October 2007, coinciding with the anniversary of the 1956 revolution, in Heroes'

---

51 The churches later claimed that the priests were acting in a personal capacity and not officially representing the church.

52 Adam LeBor, "Marching Back to the Future: Magyar Garda and the Resurgence of the Right in Hungary," *Dissent* Spring (2008): 34-38.

Square, one of Budapest's major public squares that can accommodate large crowds and demonstrations. The recruits marched into the square in military formations while hundreds of onlookers clapped and cheered. In the following years several thousand members were initiated into the organization in similar inauguration ceremonies in Budapest and the countryside. These events are also filmed and made available on YouTube attracting tens of thousands of viewers.

Unsurprisingly, the black uniform and military drills conjured up uneasy associations with the militia groups of the Nazis and Mussolini which Gabor Vona, the leader of Jobbik and founding member of the Guard, repeatedly denied. He explained that the Guard's uniform was nothing to be worried about as it only recalled the traditional outfit of Hungarian peasants—a testament to this is the fact that the black-pant-white-shirt-waistcoat combination topped with a black hat is a ubiquitous site in Hungarian folk-dance performances.[53] By rejecting the fascist symbolism, Vona was deliberately aiming to situate the Guard in Hungarian (folk) traditions and mainstream culture.[54]

In fact, the Guard was officially registered as a cultural heritage association and was part of a broader call on the right to "reinvent civil society."[55] Nevertheless, it was linked to Jobbik from the very start, and accordingly, the list of founders included well-known members of the party like Vona as well as journalists and actors who had been close sympathizers of Jobbik, but also some FIDESZ loyalists such as the journalist András Bencsik, the owner of an influential conservative weekly whose partner, Zsuzsa Takács designed the Guards' uniform.[56] The association's mandate included activities such as tending to soldiers' graves and memorial sites of historic battles as well as participating in disaster relief efforts, civil defense, and various forms of community service.

---

53 The design team behind the uniform also emphasized that it tried to modernize traditional peasant wear by combining it with contemporary casual clothing like cargo pants. The waistcoat that has a stretching lion embroidered in the back was actually copyrighted by the designers (VB 2007).

54 LeBor, "Marching Back."

55 Miklós A. Németh, *Kettős kereszt avagy a Gárda jelenség* (Budapest: Masszi, 2007).

56 Bencsik left the organization in 2008.

At the same time, however, the Guard was also called upon to contribute to strengthening Hungary's "national self-defense" and to the "maintenance of public order." Jobbik has always seen the Guard as the precursory base for the future establishment of a "National Guard" (*Nemzetőrség*) that would help protect Hungary in case of foreign aggression. Yet, it is against the Hungarian constitution to form an armed civic association, so despite the strong military symbolism the Hungarian Guard was never an arms carrying organization. Additionally, setting up the Guard was a reaction to the experience of the 2006 street riots, police brutality, and the breakdown of public order as well as to perceptions of deteriorating public safety, particularly in the Hungarian countryside, that the far-right has attributed to the Roma minority and labelled the problem of "Gypsy crime."

It is true that the Guard has been active in local community service, disaster relief and beautification of neglected graveyards, especially in more rural areas, but it has also engaged in openly discriminatory activities that eventually caused its demise, pushing it into illegality. Namely, besides their charity work, Guard members organized numerous demonstrative marches dubbed "health, mood and public-safety-enhancing walks" [57] in villages and small cities of Eastern and Central Hungary.

One of the marches, organized in December 2007 in Tatárszentgyörgy,[58] a small village in Pest county, south of Budapest proved decisive in the subsequent legal suit against the Guard. Uniformed members of the Hungarian Guard (joined by members of the Nemzeti Őrsereg) partook in a procession against "Gypsy crime" and for the "public safety of the countryside" demanding the racial segregation of the Roma. Tensions in the village were riding high, as the march, whose chief purpose was to intimidate the Roma population, was met by the counter-demonstration of human rights groups and Roma residents of the village. This event was treated as key evidence in the court

[57] "egészségügyi, közérzet- és közbiztonságjavító séta"

[58] Two years later in 2009, this village became the site of one of the killings in the gruesome "Gypsy murders" case. A middle-aged Roma man and his five-year old son were shot after their home was set on fire by the serial killers.

proceedings that began in 2008 and ended with a ruling that ordered the disbanding of the Guard in July 2009. It demonstrated, namely, that the activities of the Guard were in sharp conflict with its stated goals and founding deed; they aimed at invoking fear and inciting hatred against ethnic and racial minorities. Jobbik appealed the decision at the European Court of Justice arguing that it violated the basic right to freedom of assembly and association, but the case was rejected and the ban was upheld in 2013.

However, shortly after the Guard was disbanded by court order, the association was reestablished as "The New Hungarian Guard." The organization now operates illegally—which has not stopped Jobbik's president from attending some of its events—the inauguration ceremonies now take place on private property to avoid confrontation with the police. Although the Hungarian Guard is in many ways a singular and uniquely visible organization, it is embedded in a larger institutional field and a longer history of paramilitary organizations. Similar paramilitary organizations were thriving in interwar Europe, including Hungary, and one in particular, the so-called "Ragged Army" (*Rongyosgárda*), which came to life in the wake of Hungary's failed Communist revolution of 1919, has been seen by the Guard as an important historical forerunner.[59] Likewise, as Table 8.1 shows, there are several other smaller but analogous paramilitary organizations including the Highwaymen's Army (*Betyársereg*), or the Association for a Better Future (*Szebb Jövőért Mozgalom*) that have strong ties to the Guard and its successor groups constituting a closely knit network, as mapped by the Athena Institute, a Budapest-based independent think tank.[60]

---

59 Zoltán Barotányi, "A Rongyos Gárda története," *Magyar Narancs*, March 26, 2009, https://magyarnarancs.hu/belpol/a_rongyos_garda_tortenete_-_a_peldakep-71019.

60 Victoria Fomina, *Mapping the Network of Hungarian Extremist Group*. Research Report (Budapest: Athena Institute, 2013), Figure 2.

Figure 8.2: Hungarian Extremist Groups Network (strong ties),

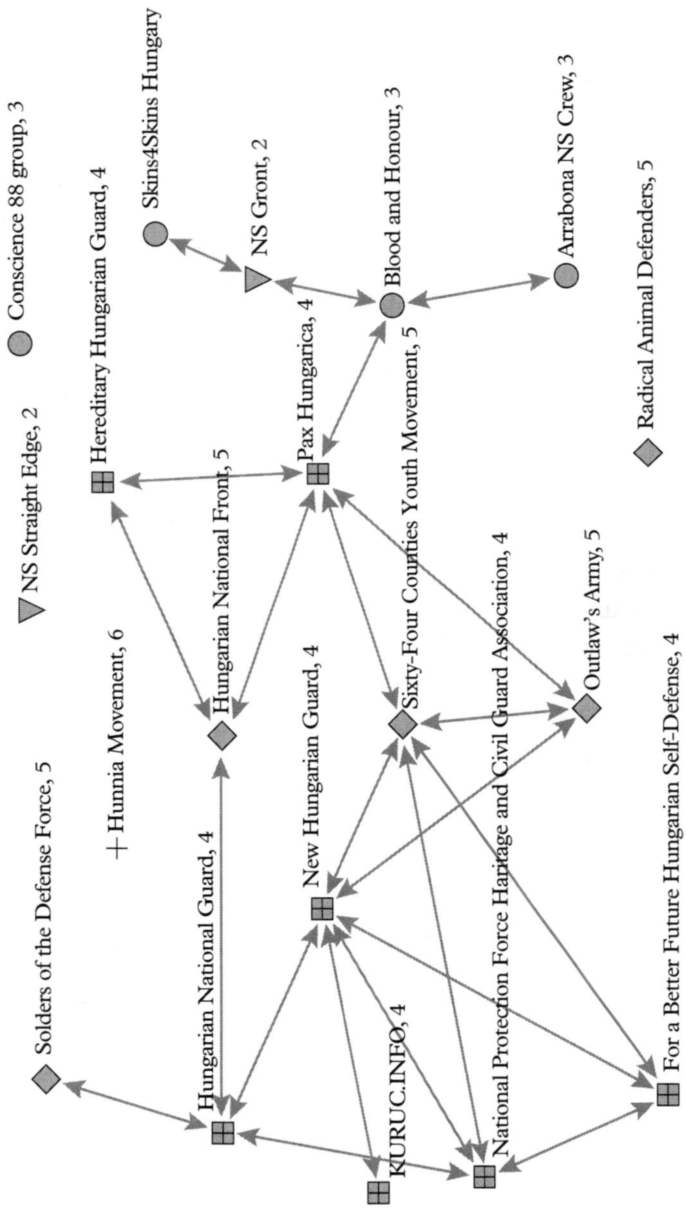

Source: Fomina (2007: 30)

Paramilitary organizations undoubtedly constitute the most radical and notorious examples of uncivil publics because they openly question the authority of the state and its monopoly over the use of legitimate force. They are a symptom of high levels of anomie and loss of faith in the existing public order. At the same time, they also highlight the centrality of violence in the symbolic repertoire of radical nationalism even if this violence is not necessarily acted out.

FOREIGN-CURRENCY DEBTOR ORGANIZATIONS

In the wake of the global financial crisis and European sovereign debt crisis, a new set of civic organizations emerged on the Hungarian scene that have attempted to mobilize and organize large segments of the Hungarian population that fell victim to the rapid expansion of foreign-currency loans and the sharp devaluation of the Hungarian local currency after 2008. The most visible and active of these organizations listed in Table 8.1 also embrace a radical populist rhetoric and symbolic imagery. This element draws attention to the importance of the anti-capitalist theme in the repertoire of radical populism in Hungary. It also highlights that the right-wing radical populist version of anti-capitalist rhetoric, which mixes anti-austerity, anti-globalization, anti-colonialization and anti-EU motifs, seems to have resonated more closely with various Hungarian publics than a leftist, liberal, or even anarchist critique of capitalism.

Foreign-currency loans are one of the chief causes behind Hungary's skyrocketing external debt. Immediately prior to EU accession, Central and East European countries embarked on liberalizing capital movements. Rapid privatization in the corporate and banking sector led to a large presence of multinationals in Hungary that had easy access to international capital markets. Local subsidiaries of Western European banks, funded at low costs by their parent banks, began to aggressively market cheap mortgage loans to Hungarian households denominated in foreign currency, primarily in Swiss francs.

Cash-strapped Hungarian households, grossly underestimating the exchange rate risk, began to indulge in foreign-currency loans, especially mortgages, and quickly built up a large unhedged foreign currency debt. The foreign currency debt-to-GDP ratio reached 30 percent by 2008 and foreign-currency debt amounted to nearly 70 percent of total household debt in Hungary.[61] While other CEE countries also introduced foreign-currency loans in the same period, the level of indebtedness never reached the alarmingly high levels of Hungary and has remained steadily around 10 percent of the GDP.[62]

The rude awakening of Hungarian households from this foreign currency binge came in 2008 as the global financial crises engulfed Hungary as well. Between September 2008 and November 2011 Hungary's local currency, the forint, depreciated against the Swiss franc by 66 percent (EAAG 2012). As a result of the drastic devaluation of the local currency, monthly mortgage payments and the total value of mortgages skyrocketed, pushing more and more families to default on their payments and risk losing their homes to foreclosures. After 2010, the new Fidesz government introduced a series of measures that were meant to ease the burden of foreign currency loans for Hungarian households. But many argue that these were half-hearted attempts that mostly served the government's populist propaganda instead of bringing actual relief to the indebted. Banks, nevertheless, remain one of the main targets of popular ire in the country given that in 2011, 41 percent of Hungarian households held some form of debt, typically a mortgage in Swiss francs.

Seeing the government's reluctance to resolve the foreign-currency loan crisis, a loose set of debtor organizations has cropped up to bring together indebted households, organize demonstrations against banks, provide legal aid to affected families, and lobby the government for more effective relief measures. Many of these debtor organizations criticize the government from the right, and although their symbolic vocabulary shows close affinities with that of Jobbik, they claim to have no direct links to Jobbik. One of the most influential of these debtor organizations is called the Koppány Group (*Koppány Csoport*). Koppány is

---

61 EEAG (European Economic Advisory Group). The EEAG Report on the European Economy, "The Hungarian Crisis," CESifo, Munich 2012, 115–30.

62 In Slovakia and the Czech Republic it was also mainly firms and not private households that borrowed in foreign currency. Poland is the only other country where a significant share of private households also became severely indebted in foreign currency. But even in the Polish case, these foreign currency loans peaked around 30% of total household debt (EEAG 2012).

an actual historical figure and a central character in the story of Hungary's conquest of the Carpathian Basin and its incorporation into Europe at the turn of the tenth and eleventh centuries. He was the uncle of St. Stephen, Hungary's first genuine Christian king, who should have succeeded his brother on the throne following his death in 997. But Koppány was against Hungary's converting to Western Christianity, and a succession struggle ensued between him and Stephen ending in his defeat.[63] Koppány has enjoyed a widespread cult in popular culture, standing in for the tribal and pagan values of ancient Magyars as well as Hungarians' defiance to Western European domination.

In a similar vein, another debtor organization that calls itself, "The homeland is not for sale," plays on the close linguistic proximity between the Hungarian words for home (*ház*) and homeland (*haza*), drawing parallels between the fight to keep one's mortgaged home from multinational banks and the country's resistance to EU-sanctioned austerity measures or to global credit agencies such as the IMF. In addition to rallying against the banks they blame for the escalation of the foreign-currency debt crisis, they also strongly protest the sale of Hungarian agricultural land to foreigners.[64]

Nationalist visual symbols, especially the Holy Crown of St. Stephen or the red-white striped Arpad flags, routinely appear on their demonstration posters, websites, T-shirts, and printed manifestos to punctuate their critique of globalization, market capitalism, and EU domination (see, for instance, the logo of the "The homeland is not for sale" movement at http://kaslerarpad.hu). Recently, they have also tried to organize themselves into a political party during the 2014 national elections and the European parliamentary elections but failed to reach the election threshold. They, thus, continue to operate as a civic organization.

The case of foreign currency debtor organizations underscores the importance of critical economic discourse made up of an eclectic mix

---

63 According to the widely disseminated legend, upon his defeat, his body was cut into four pieces and displayed on the walls of the four main strongholds of the Kingdom of Hungary as a warning to remaining rebels.

64 Zalán Zubor, "Zaklatott lázadók vezetnék a népet a devizahitelek ellen." *HVG,* August 23, 2013, https://hvg.hu/itthon/20130823_Devizahiteles_szervezetek.

of anti-globalization, anti-austerity, anti-neoliberal, anti-EU and anti-capitalist arguments. This economic dimension is pivotal though often overlooked in studies of right-wing populism at the expense of over-emphasizing the social exclusionary (racist, homophobic, xenophobic) and anti-democratic themes.

Conclusion

I have argued in this paper that contrary to the widely held view that sees the radical populist backlash as a result of a weak civil society in Eastern Europe, the growth of illiberal politics has been significantly aided by a new wave of civil society activism that began at the turn of the millennium. By no means am I suggesting that civil society is inhabited solely by right-wing radicals in Hungary today. It remains a diverse space with strong human rights groups, for instance, although these have come under increasing attack from the government that tries to extend its control over civic actors as well. I wanted to call attention to the significant role uncivil publics play in reimagining civil society and in shifting the boundary between publics and politics. In this interpretation, the problem of rising political populism does not stem from the lack of civic associationalism per se but rather from the fact that civil society has also become a hotbed of right-wing radicalism.

These civic associations are at the forefront of reinventing the symbolic vocabulary of nationalism, re-enchanting cultural membership by re-anchoring it in mythical (often "premodern") traditions, and seeking social arrangements that are governed by a charismatic type of legitimacy. In other words, they emphasize particularistic and autochtonous values as a counterpoint to economic globalization and European integration that are seen as root causes of diminishing economic and political sovereignty and the loss of cultural identity. There are, of course, additional reasons why the radical right has become the force it is today, but its firm rooting and support in civil society suggests that its political success is unlikely to be merely ephemeral.

Appendix

Table 8.1: Radical Nationalist Civic Associations[65]

Type of Civic Association	Name of Organization
Protecting and promoting cultural heritage (*hagyományörző egyesületek*)	Baranta: Baranta Hagyományos Magyar Harcművészetek Országos Szövetsége (Baranta: The National Association of Traditional Hungarian Martial Arts)
	Aranyszablya Történelmi Vívóiskola (Golden Saber Historical Fencing School)
	Magyar Huszár és Hagyományörző Szövetség (The Association for Cultivating Hungarian Hussar Traditions)
	Forrai Sándor Rovásíró Kör (Sándor Forrai* Runic Script Circle)
	Lelkiismeret '88 (Conscience '88)
	Szabó Dezső Színház (Dezső Szabó* Theatre)
	Magyar Táltos (Hungarian Shaman)
	Nemzeti Egyletek (National Guilds)
	Nemenyi.net—Amerikai polgári körök lapja (North American Civic Circles)

65 Names of these organizations often contain references to historical figures and events that are central to the nationalist canon, geographical regions that were part of pre-1918 Hungary (e.g., Délvidék) or employ turn of phrases (e.g., "public safety") that are closely associated with a right-wing nationalist vocabulary. It is not possible to elaborate the historical background of each figure here for lack of space, but feel free to contact the author for further details.

* *Names of historical figures.*

Type of Civic Association	Name of Organization
Sports and recreational clubs	Ferencvárosi Szurkolók Szövetsége (Ferencvárosi Soccer Team Fan Club)
	Gój Motorosok (Goyim Riders)
	Hunnia kézilabdacsapat (Hunnia Handball Team)
	Nemzeti Érzelmű Motorosok (National Riders)
Legal organizations	Nemzeti Jogvedő Alapítvány (National Rights Advocacy Foundation)
	Szent Korona Lovagrend (Holy Crown Chivalric Order)
	Szent Korona Országért Alapítvány (Country of the Holy Crown Foundation)
Youth organizations	64 Vármegye Mozgalom (64 Historical Counties Movement)
Internet communities	Magyar Klán (Warriors of Hungary)
	Bombagyar.hu (Bomb factory)
Educational organizations	Attila Király Népfőiskola (King Attila* Community College)
	Körösi Csoma Sándor Magyar Egyetem (Körösi Csoma Sándor *Hungarian University)
	Dobogó Mitikus Magyar Történelem (Dobogó Mythical Hungarian History)
	Örökség Népfőiskolai Szövetség (Association of Heritage Community Colleges)
	NapÚt: A természetes műveltség honlapja (SunPath: the Site of Natural Cultivation)
Popular music bands ("national rock" bands)	Hungarica (Hungarica)
	Hunnia (Hunnia—Latin name for Hungary)

Type of Civic Association	Name of Organization
Popular music bands ("national rock" bands)	Kárpátia (Carpathia—referring to the Carpathian Mountains)
	Nemzeti Front (National Front)
	Oi-kor (Oi-age)
	Romantikus Erőszak (Romantic Violence)
	Ismerős Arcok (Familiar Faces)
	Egészséges Fejbőr (Healthy Head Skin)
	Magozott Cseresznye (Pitted Cherry)
	Franka Deli [name of singer]
	Titkolt Ellenállás (Secret Resistance)
	Vádló Bitófák (Accusing Gallows)
Trade union	Tettrekész Magyar Rendőrség Szakszervezete (Ready-for -Action: Hungarian Police Union)
Women's organizations	Zrínyi Ilona Magyar Asszonyok Nemzeti Szövetsége (Ilona Zrínyi National Association of Hungarian Women)
	Lórántffy Zsuzsanna Nőegylet (Zsuzsanna Lórántffy Women's Guild)
Paramilitary organizations	Magyar Gárda (Hungarian Guard)
	Betyársereg (Highwaymen's Army)
	Hunnia Mozgalom (Hunnia Movement)
	Kárpát Haza Őrei (The Guards of the Carpathian Homeland)
	Magyarok Nyilai Nemzeti Felszabadító Hadsereg (Hungarian Arrows National Liberation Army)
	Szebb Jövőért Egyesület (Association For a Better Future)

Type of Civic Association	Name of Organization
Bookstores and Paraphernalia stores	Magyar Menedék Könyvesház (Hungarian Refuge Book House)
	Gyepű Könyvesbolt (Lawn bookstore)
	Emese álma (Emese's Dream bookstore)
	Fehérlófia Könyvesbolt (Son of the White Horse bookstore)
	Püski Kiadó és Püski-Masszi könyvesház (Püski Publishing House and Püski-Masszi Bookstore)
	Szkítia könyvesboltok (Scythia bookstores)
	Turánia Hagyományörző Áruház (Turania Heritage Department Store)
	Turul bolt (Turul shop)
	Magyaros Termékek online shop (Hungarian Goods Online Store)
Tourism	Délvidéki Portyázók Baráti Köre (Friendship Circle of the Adventurers in the Southern Territories [referring to the northern region of Serbia])
	Deáky András Agroturisztikai Panzió (Deáky András Agritourism Motel)
	Kárpáteurópa Utazási Iroda (Carpathian-Europe Travel Agency)
Product brands	Harcos (Warrior)
	Heniem [furniture brand]
Media	Kuruc.info (Kuruc.info online news portal)
	Magyar Hang nemzeti rock magazine (Hungarian Voice National Rock Magazine)
	Nemzeti Bulvár (National Tabloid)

Type of Civic Association	Name of Organization
Media	Nemzetőr napilap (National Guard daily)
	Szent Korona rádio and TV (Holy Crown TV and Radio broadcasting)
	Hunhir (Hun News)
	JobbHírek (Better News)
	Alternatív Hírportál: "A nemzeti médiafigyelő"
	Barikád: az új erő lapja. Közvédelmi hírportál (Baricade: the [online] Daily of the New Force. "Public Safety" News Portal
	Echo TV (Echo TV)
	Pro Hungaria Nemzeti Portal (Pro-Hungary National Portal)
	Pannon Rádió (Rockszerda) (Pannonia Radio Rock Wednesdays)
Foreign-Currency Mortgage Debtor Organizations	Koppány Csoport (Koppány* Group)
	Radikális Bankellenes Csoport (Radical Anti-Bank Group)
	A haza nem eladó mozgalom (The Home is Not For Sale Movement)
	Otthonvédelmi Tanács (Council for the Protection of Homes)

BIBLIOGRAPHY

Armony, Ariel C. *The Dubious Link: Civic Engagement and Democratization.* Stanford: Stanford University Press, 2004.

Barotányi, Zoltán. "A Rongyos Gárda története." *Magyar Narancs*, March 26, 2009, https://magyarnarancs.hu/belpol/a_rongyos_garda_tortenete_-_a_peldakep-71019.

Berezin, Mabel. "Politics and Culture: A Less Fissured Terrain." *Annual Review of Sociology* 23 (1997a): 361–83.

Berezin, Mabel. *Making the fascist self: The political culture of interwar Italy.* Ithaca, NY: Cornell University Press, 1997b.

Berman, Sheri. "Civil Society and the Collapse of the Weimar Republic." *World Politics* 3 (1997): 401–429.

Brubaker, Rogers M., Margit Feischmidt, Jon E. Fox, and Liana Grancea. *Nationalist Politics and Everyday Ethnicity in a Transylvanian Town.* Princeton, NJ: Princeton University Press, 2006.

Calhoun, Craig. J. *Habermas and the Public Sphere.* Cambridge, MA: MIT Press, 1992.

Chatterjee, Partha. *Politics of the Governed: Reflections on Popular Politics in Most of the World.* New York: Columbia University Press, 2004.

Cody, Francis. "Publics and Politics." *Annual Review of Anthropology* 40 (2011): 37–52.

Cohen, Jean, and Andrew Arato. *Civil Society and Political Theory.* Cambridge, MA: MIT Press, 1992.

Comaroff, John L., and Jean Comaroff, eds. *Civil Society and the Political Imagination in Africa: Critical Perspectives.* Chicago: University of Chicago Press, 1999.

Edensor, Tim. *National Identity, Popular Culture and Everyday Life.* Oxford: Berg, 2002.

Edensor, Tim. "Automobility and National Identity Representation, Geography and Driving Practice." *Theory, Culture & Society* 21 (2004): 101–120.

EEAG (European Economic Advisory Groups). 2012. The EEAG Report on the European Economy, "The Hungarian Crisis," CESifo, Munich 2012, 115–130.

Emirbayer, Mustafa, and Mimi Sheller. "Publics in History." *Theory and Society* 28 (1999): 145–197.

Feischmidt, Margit. "Nemzetdiskurzusok a mindennapokban és a nacionalizmus populáris kultúrája." In *Nemzet a mindennapokban. Az újnacionalizmus populáris kultúrája*, edited by Margit Feischmidt, Rita Glózer, Zoltán Ilyés, Veronika Katalin Kasznár, and Ildikó Zakariás, 7–51. Budapest: L'Harmattan, 2014.

Feischmidt, Margit, Rita Glózer, Zoltán Ilyés, Veronika Katalin Kasznár, and Ildikó Zakariás. *Nemzet a mindennapokban. Az újnacionalizmus populáris kultúrája.* Budapest: L'Harmattan, 2014.

Feischmidt, Margit, and Gergő Pulay. "Élmény és ideológia a nacionalista popkultúrában." In *Nemzet a mindennapokban. Az újnacionalizmus populáris kultúrája*, edited by Margit Feischmidt, Rita Glózer, Zoltán Ilyés, Veronika Katalin Kasznár, and Ildikó Zakariás, 249-90. Budapest: L'Harmattan.

Fomina, Victoria. *Mapping the Network of Hungarian Extremist Group*. Research Report. Budapest: Athena Institute, 2013.

Fox, Jon E., and Cynthia Miller-Idriss. "Everyday Nationhood." *Ethnicities* 8 (2008): 536–563.

Glózer, Rita. "A nemzet helyreállítása a magyarországi radikális mozgalom ellenségtematizáló diskurzusaiban." In *Nemzet a mindennapokban. Az újnacionalizmus populáris kultúrája*, edited by Margit Feischmidt, Rita Glózer, Zoltán Ilyés, Veronika Katalin Kasznár, and Ildikó Zakariás. Budapest: L'Harmattan, 2014.

Gecső, Tamás. "A Gój Motorosok esete a kék halakkal." *Élet és Irodalom*, January 4, 2008, https://www.es.hu/cikk/2008-01-07/dr-habil-gecso-tamas/a-goj-motorosok-esete-a-kek-halakkal.html.

Goldfarb, Jeffrey. *Reinventing Political Culture: the Power of Culture Versus the Culture of Power*. Cambridge, UK: Polity, 2012.

Gramsci, Antonio. *Selections from the Prison Notebooks*, New York: International Publishers, 1971.

Habermas, Jürgen. *The Structural Transformation of the Public Sphere: An Inquiry into a Category of Bourgeois Society*. Cambridge, MA: MIT Press, 1989.

Hall, John A. "The Nature of Civil Society." *Society* May/June (1998): 32–41.

Hann, Chris. "Nationalism and Civil Society in Central Europe: From Ruritania to the Carpathian Euroregion." In *The State of the Nation: Ernest Gellner and the Theory of Nationalism*, edited by J. A. Hal, 243–257. Cambridge, UK: Cambridge University Press, 1998.

Heller, Peter. "Civil Society and Democracy in Post-Transition South Africa." Unpublished manuscript.

Hipsher, Patricia L. "Democratic Transitions as Protest Cycles: Social Movement Dynamics in Democratizing Latin America." In *The Social Movement Society*, edited by Sidney Tarrow and David Meyer, 152–172. New York: Rowan and Littlefield, 1998.

Hubbes, László-Attila. "A Comparative Investigation of Romanian and Hungarian Ethno-Pagan Blogs." *Reconnect Working Papers* 2. Accessed July 9, 2014. http://papers.ssrn.com/sol3/papers.cfm?abstract_id=1984597.

Ikegami, Eiko. "A Sociological Theory of Publics: Identity and Culture as Emergent Properties in Networks." *Social Research* 4 (2000): 990–1029.

Ikegami, Eiko. *Bonds of Civility. Aesthetic Networks and the Political Origins of Japanese Culture*. Cambridge, UK: Cambridge University Press, 2005.

Ilyés, Zoltán. "Az emlékezés és a turisztikai élmeény nemzetiesítése." In *Nemzet a mindennapokban. Az újnacionalizmus populáris kultúrája*, edited by Margit Feischmidt, Rita Glózer, Zoltán Ilyés, Veronika Katalin Kasznár, and Ildikó Zakariás, 290–341. Budapest: L'Harmattan, 2014.

Juhász, Réka. "Látogatottsági adatok: A Kuruc.info a leglátogatottabb hírportál." Accessed July 15, 2014. http://kuruc.info/p/6/37381.

Headlines of Nation, Subtexts of Class: Working Class Populism and the Return of the Repressed in Neoliberal Europe. Edited by Don Kalb and Gábor Halmai. New York: Berghahn Books, 2011.

Kálmán, László. "A Gój Motorosok elnevezésről." *Élet és Irodalom*, November 23, 2007. https://www.es.hu/cikk/2007-11-25/kalman-laszlo/a-goj-motorosok-elnevezesrol.html.

Kovács, Mária. *Liberal Professions and Illiberal Politics: Hungary from the Habsburgs to the Holocaust.* New York: Woodrow Wilson Center and Oxford University Press, 1994.

Laitin, David D. "National Revivals and Violence." *European Journal of Sociology* 36 (1995): 3–43.

LeBor, Adam. "Marching Back to the Future: Magyar Garda and the Resurgence of the Right in Hungary." *Dissent* Spring (2008): 34–38.

Lőrincz, László, ed. *Egyezzünk ki a múlttal! Műhelybeszélgetések történelmi mítoszainkról, tévhiteinkről.* Budapest: Történelemtanárok Egylete, 2010.

Nemes, Robert. "The Politics of the Dance Floor: Culture and Civil Society in Nineteenth-century Hungary." *Slavic Review* 60 (2001): 802–823.

Nemes, Robert. *The Once and Future Budapest.* DeKalb, IL: Northern Illinois University Press, 2005.

Németh, Miklós A. *Kettős kereszt avagy a Gárda jelenség.* Budapest: Masszi, 2007.

Palonen, Emilia. "Political Polarisation and Populism in Contemporary Hungary." *Parliamentary Affairs* 62 (2009): 318–334.

Pappas, Takis S. "Populist Democracies: Post-Authoritarian Greece and Post-Communist Hungary." *Government and Opposition* 1 (2014): 1–23.

Putnam, Robert, Robert Leonardi, and Rafaella Y. Nanetti. *Making Democracy Work: Civic Traditions in Modern Italy.* Princeton: Princeton University Press, 1993.

Riley, Dylan. "Civic Associations and Authoritarian Regimes in Interwar Europe: Italy and Spain in Comparative Perspective." *American Sociological Review* 2 (2005): 288–310.

Riley, Dylan. *The Civic Foundations of Fascism in Europe: Italy, Spain, and Romania, 1870–1945.* Baltimore, MD: JHU Press, 2010.

Rupnik, Jacques. "From Democracy Fatigue to Populist Backlash." *Journal of Democracy* 4 (2007): 17–25.

Sőrés, Anett. "A (Nagy)Asszony varrva jó? Jellegzetes tetoválások a szélsőjobboldali csoportok körében." *Művelődés-, Tudomány- és Orvostörténeti Folyóirat* 2 (2011): 115–123.

Stamatov, Peter. "The Making of a 'Bad' Public: Ethnonational Mobilization in Post-communist Bulgaria." *Theory and Society* 29 (2000): 549–572.

Stewart, Michael S. *The Gypsy Menace: Populism and the New Anti-gypsy Politics.* London: Hurst & Company, 2012.

Tavory, Iddo. "Of Yarmulkes and Categories: Delegating Boundaries and the Phenomenology of Interactional Expectation." *Theory and Society* 39 (2010): 49–68.

Trencsényi, Balázs. "Beyond Liminality? The Kulturkampf of the Early 2000s in East Central Europe.' *Boundary 2* 41 (2014): 135–152.

VB. 2007. "Első kézből a Magyar Gárda outfitjéről." Accessed October 4, 2015. http://velvet.hu/trend/garda0905.

Zubor, Zalán. 'Zaklatott lázadók vezetnék a népet a devizahitelek ellen." *HVG,* August 23, 2013. https://hvg.hu/itthon/20130823_Devizahiteles_szervezetek.

Zubrzycki, Geneviève. "History and the National Sensorium: Making Sense of Polish Mythology." *Qualitative Sociology* 34 (2011): 21–57.

Zubrzycki, Geneviève. "Aesthetic Revolt and the Remaking of National Identity in Quebec, 1960–1969." *Theory and Society* 42 (2013): 423–475.

Zsuppán, András. "Politikai okkultizmus Magyarországon 8: Ifjú szívekben." *Magyar Narancs,* January 5, 2006. https://m.magyarnarancs.hu/belpol/politikai_okkultizmus_magyarorszagon_8_ifju_szivekben-64987.

What Lies Beneath the Appeal of the Radical Right to Elite Skilled Workers? The Impact of Deeply Ingrained Nationalism and Perceptions of Multiple Exploitations[1]

ESZTER BARTHA and ANDRÁS TÓTH

Introduction

One of the most enduring legacies of the 20th century mental image of blue-collar workers is that they form a homogeneous working class that harbors Marxist or at least left-wing political sympathies and supports socialist, social democratic or Communist parties. It was taken for granted that workers as a societal pillar[2] would vote for the left. Indeed, until the 1980s, established working-class neighborhoods and trade unions were considered to be the electoral basis of left-wing political

[1] The project was supported by the Hungarian Academy of Sciences within the framework of the project entitled "Társadalmi konfliktusokra adott identitáspolitikai válaszok" and the NKFIH-OTKA K 120010 Project entitled "Az iparimunkásság alakváltozása: Az 1990 utáni szakmunkásréteg társadalmi-politikai tagozódása."

[2] András Tóth distinguishes between the process of class formation (in which the workers aim to overthrow the capitalist world order) and pillarization (the creation of a web of institutions centred on trade unions and associations providing for mutual aid to the workers, which solidified as a distinct social pillar during the 19th century, facilitating their integration into the emerging new industrial society). In his view, pillarization preceded the formation of Marxist political parties, and the success of the latter depended to a large extent on their domination of the workers' pillar. For a more extensive discussion see: András Tóth, "The Birth of the Workers' Pillar and its Relationship with the Marxist Working-class Formation," (2019), accessed September 30, 2018.https://www.academia.edu/38369548/TA_Formation_of_workersdocx.pdf.

parties ranging from "moderate" social democrats to more "militant" or radical Communists. This was true, for example, in Great Britain[3] and in the Netherlands[4]; and it was also true for the Western European Communist parties in countries where they were significant, in France[5] or in Italy.[6] In the state socialist countries of the Soviet bloc, the Communist parties claimed to rule in the name of a largely idealized (and empirically at best dubious) "working class."

The last decade of the century, however, saw an increasing appeal of populist, far right-wing political parties amongst workers in many Western European countries.[7] Parallel to this political shift, the allegiance of trade unions and of workers to social-democratic parties was also weakened.[8] Authors such as Marliére[9] blamed the embracing of the so-called neoliberal policies by the Western European social democratic parties for this shift.

After a short revival of the socialist parties in Central and Eastern Europe in the mid-1990s, which were seen by many as "successor" Communist parties, a similar shift to the right in workers' vote was observed, while support for the left receded.

This article intends to broaden the explanations of why workers are attracted by right-wing populism in the former Communist coun-

---

3 Ian McAllister et al., "Class Dealignment and the Neighborhood Effect: Miller Revisited," *British Journal of Political Science* vol. 31(2001): 41–59.

4 Frans Becker and René Curperus, *Politics in a Fragmented Society. The 2010 Elections in Netherlands*, International Policy Analysis: Friedrich Ebert Stiftung, 2010.

5 François Platone, "Les structures du vote de gauche à Paris," *Revue française de science politique* 6 (1977): 820–847.

6 Geneviève Bibes and Christine Alix, "Les elections legislatives italiennes d'avril 1963," *Revue française de science politique* 4 (1963): 911–950.

7 Paul Taggart, "New Populist Parties in Western Europe," *West European Politics* 1 (1995): 34–51.

8 An influential analysis of this shift of workers' political choices is offered by Didier Eribon, *Returning to Reims* (Los Angeles: Semiotext(e), 2013). The rising importance of the topic is also shown by the fact that the journal *International Labor and Working-Class History* specifically addressed this shift of workers' political alliances at a global level in its issue No. 93. Spring 2018.

9 Philippe Marliére, "The Decline of Europe's Social Democratic Parties," *Open Democracy* (2010), accessed October 30, 2018. https://www.opendemocracy.net/philippe-marliere/decline-of-europes-social-democratic-parties).

tries, where memories of the socialist past and the experiences of the "transition" from planned to market economy have substantially impacted on the economic status and political choices of the workers and their families.

In the literature discussing this shift of workers' political orientation in East-Central Europe, David Ost argued,[10] building on his previous study of the roots of Solidarity in Poland,[11] that the liberal intelligentsia betrayed the workers and chose the road of neoliberal capitalism, which effectively impoverished many workers, who either lost their jobs or had to be content with very low wages in comparison to the earnings of the new "capitalists" (managers, successful entrepreneurs, etc.). Thus, the workers voted for the radical right in order to punish the intelligentsia and the new neoliberal elite. A variant of this theory is that in Hungary the electoral coalition between the liberal and socialist political forces led to the embracement of a neoliberal economic program by the socialist party, which disappointed many workers, who sought for a new political "shelter" in the right or the far right.[12]

Kalb and Halmai offered a somewhat different explanation for the increasing appeal of the radical right amongst workers.[13] To simplify the key thesis of the book, globalization and neoliberal capitalism disrupted traditional working-class communities, and rendered workers more dependent on the whims of capitalism. Right-wing populism offers a panacea for the insecurity of the world and the everyday struggle for a decent living. Feischmidt, following the argument of Kalb and Halmai, defined neo-nationalism as a response to the global and local crises generated by semi-peripheral capitalism.[14]

---

[10] David Ost, *The Defeat of Solidarity: Anger and Politics in Postcommunist Europe* (Ithaca, NY: Cornell University Press, 2005).

[11] David Ost, *Solidarity and the Politics of Anti-politics. Opposition and Reform in Poland 1968* (Philadelphia: Temple University Press, 1990).

[12] Zoltán Pogátsa, *Magyarország politikai gazdaságtana* (Budapest: Osiris Kiadó, 2016).

[13] *Headlines of Nation, Subtexts of Class: Working-Class Populism and the Return of the Repressed in Neoliberal Europe*, ed. Don Kalb and Gábor Halmai (New York - Oxford: Berghahn Books, 2011).

[14] *Nemzet a mindennapokban. Az újnacionalizmus populáris kultúrája*, ed. Feischmidt et al. (Budapest: L'Harmattan – MTA Társadalomtudományi Központ, 2014), 46.

These explanations take account of the fact that the transformation processes following 1989–1990 destroyed the socialist socio-economic model of "universal" (or nearly universal) employment[15] and life-time job security across the region. Indeed, in the critical anthropological literature Eastern European workers were explicitly depicted as a new "subaltern" class.[16] While subalternity was already used by Rudolf Bahro in the context of state socialism to explain workers' location at the bottom ranks of a knowledge-based division of labor in socialism,[17] this stream of literature argues that "transition" to a capitalist market economy deepened the subalternalization of labor. The fact that there was so little "native" research done on workers in post-1989 Hungary until recently[18] is in itself indicative of the loss of the symbolic capital of the "working class."

---

15 This was, of course, true for Hungary only in theory. Roma women constituted, for instance, a group, which was partly "left out" of this socialist achievement (Susan Zimmermann, "Gender Regime and Gender Struggle in Hungarian State Socialism," *Aspasia*, vol. 4 (2010):1–24.).

16 David Kideckel, "The Unmaking of an East-Central-European Working Class," in *Postsocialism: Ideals, Ideologies and Practices in Eurasia*, ed. C. M. Hann (London: Routledge, 2002), 114–132; David Kideckel, *Getting by in Postsocialist Romania: Labor, the Body and Working-Class Culture* (Bloomington: Indiana University Press, 2008); Michal Buchowski, *Rethinking Transformation: An Anthropological Perspective on Postsocialism* (Poznan: Humaniora, 2001); Don Kalb, "Conversations with a Polish Populist: Tracing Hidden Histories of Globalization, Class, and Dispossession in Postsocialism (and Beyond)," *American Ethnologist*, vol. 36 (2009): 207-223; *Headlines of Nation, Subtexts of Class: Working-Class Populism and the Return of the Repressed in Neoliberal Europe*.

17 Rudolf Bahro, *The Alternative in Eastern Europe* (London: NLB, 1977). See also György Konrád and Iván Szelényi, *The Intellectuals on the Road to Class Power* (New York: Harcourt Brace, Jovanovich, 1979). In his critique of Stalinist society, Trotsky argued already in the 1930s that the Stalinist bureaucracy became the main beneficiary of the new Soviet regime (Leon Trotsky, *The Revolution Betrayed. What is the Soviet Union and Where is It Going?* (New York: Doubleday, Doran and Co., Pathfinder Press, 1937.)).

18 "Native" interest in labor anthropology and social history is very recent (see, e.g. the academic and organizational efforts of Tibor Valuch). To support comparative anthropological research in the region, the Visegrád Anthropologists' Network (V4 Net) was launched in 2017 at the Max Planck Institute of Social Anthropology on the initiative of Chris Hann, http://www.eth.mpg.de/4638411/Visegrad_Network.

While workers in the critical literature are seen as "losers" (of the change of regimes, of transformation and global capitalism), here we turn to a different group—the elite, skilled workers of multinational companies. The inspiration comes from an earlier research of Tóth and Grajczjár.[19] They demonstrated, through the analyses of a nationally representative survey in Hungary, that radical right-wing political messages appealed not only to the "losers" of economic change, but also to those, who can be deemed the "winners" of globalization and an open European economy.

Thus, we have formulated the following research question: how can we explain the increasing appeal of right-wing political populism to elite skilled workers, who enjoy considerable job security, good working conditions and earn decent wages in comparison to the Hungarian average?

In line with this research question, we intentionally selected interview partners from a specific group, which can be described as the "elite" workforce in direct production: young or middle-aged skilled workers employed by a large multinational company in Western Hungary, in a city that attracted high flows of FDI after 1989. This multinational company has a long and well-deserved reputation of being a "good" employer, offering its employees relative job security, good working conditions, high-level company welfare provisions and good wages compared to the Hungarian average. The company also supports labor interest representation—local trade unions and workers' councils are functioning to allow employees to have a voice.

Our interview partners well represented this "elite" stratum of the blue-collar workforce of the company, most of them were elected workers' representatives, trade union shop stewards, and some were members of the workers' council. Our assumption is that these workers also act as "opinion-leaders" at the shopfloor. We interviewed only men workers, for two reasons: 1) they dominate these positions; 2) they proved to be more "accessible" interview partners than women. We mainly focused on the age group of 25–45. Altogether twelve life-history interviews were conducted in 2015, which was complemented with two focus group discussions (each with three participants). The interviews and group discussions

19 András Tóth and István Grajczjár, "Different Roads to the Siren Songs of the Extreme Right in Hungary," in *Changing Working Life and the Appeal of the Extreme Right*, edited by Jörg Flecker, 201–17 (London: Ashgate, 2007).

were recorded, with the full information and consent of the participants. Since anonymity was promised to all interview partners, we used pseudonyms for everybody. We have to list some important obstacles to the empirical work, amongst them difficulty to "enter" the field, difficulty to find interview partners and gain consent to the recorded interview and general mistrust of the researchers. One of the authors of this article has established long-term contacts with the workers, without which it would have been impossible to collect even this limited sample.

In recent years, there has been a strong political and academic interest in Hungarian right-wing radicalization.[20] But little, if any, sociological or anthropological research addressed the above described group of workers and the question of why they give "credit" to right-wing populist messages. We argue that our case study can offer a glimpse into the complex motivations that "push" workers to the far right—and not only in Hungary.

Hungarian Workers Between the Political Left and Right

As the renowned labor historian and sociologist of the interwar era, Gyula Rézler demonstrated,[21] the structure of the large industrial workforce in Hungary emerging from the mid-19th century onwards,

[20] András Tóth and István Grajczjár, "The Rise of the Radical Right in Hungary," in *The Hungarian Patient: Social Opposition to an Illiberal Democracy*, ed. Jon Van Til and Péter Krasztev (Budapest: CEU Press, 2015); Domonkos Sik, "Incubating Radicalism in Hungary—the Case of Sopron and Ózd," *Intersections, East European Journal of Society and Politics* 1, accessed February 8, 2016, http://intersections.tk.mta.hu/index.php/intersections/article/view/31; Erzsébet Szalai, *Koordinátákon kívül: Fiatal felnőttek a mai Magyarországon* (Budapest: Új Mandátum, 2011); András Körösényi, "A politikai polarizáció és következményei a demokratikus elszámoltatásra 1990–2010," *Working Papers in Political Science* 1 (2012): 1–24. Margit Feischmidt, "Mindennapi nacionalizmus és a másság cigányként való megjelölése," in *Nemzet a mindennapokban,* 401–447.; Tamás Rudas, "A Jobbik törzs szavazóiról," *Társadalmi Riport, 2010.*, ed. Tamás Kolosi and István György Tóth, 512–526 (Budapest: Tárki, 2010); Kristóf Szombati, *The Revolt of the Provinces: Anti-Gypsyism and Right-Wing Politics in Hungary* (New York - Oxford: Berghahn Books, 2018).

[21] Gyula Rézler, *A magyar nagyipari munkásosztály kialakulása 1867–1914* (Budapest: Rekord, 1938).

was hierarchical and strictly segmented on the basis of ethnicity, religion, education, training, skills, living place (urban/rural divide) and gender.[22] Following in Rézler's footsteps, the English labor historian Mark Pittaway studied the patterns of the Hungarian workers' social and political behavior in the period between 1944 and 1958 on the example of three industrial communities.[23] The first segment was the stratum of urban male skilled workers, for whom the intertwined world of trade unions and the social democratic party ensured a separate life within society. The second segment was composed of workers living in a rural environment and being embedded in a patriarchal labor culture. Their views can be characterized as predominantly conservative, right-wing and Christian nationalist (strongly influenced by religion). The third group encompassed closely knit working-class communities such as the mining colonies in Tatabánya, whose dwellers were open to radical social ideologies, both communism and fascism—the latter in the form of the Arrow Cross movement,[24] the most successful Hungarian National Socialist Party in the interwar era.

After the Second World War, and in particular after 1948, the newly established Communist regime attempted to impose on the workers "from above" a militant, radical left-wing class-consciousness tailored to the needs of the regime. The failure of this attempt was best demonstrated in 1956, when predominantly young, male workers constituted the largest group of the protesters and actually fighting revolutionaries in the capital city.[25] Workers' protests continued even after the military defeat of the revolution (mass strikes, workers' councils).[26]

---

[22] See also Tóth's argument of the workers' pillar in Hungary. András Tóth, "The Birth of the Workers' Pillar," ibid.

[23] Mark Pittaway, *The Workers State: Industrial Labor and the Making of Socialist Hungary, 1944–1958* (Pittsburgh: The University of Pittsburgh Press, 2012).

[24] For a concise history of this movement in English, see: Mark Pittaway, "Fascim in Hungary," in *The Oxford Handbook of Fascism,* ed. R. J. B. Bosworth (Oxford: Oxford University Press, 2010).

[25] The revolution spread from the capital to the countryside but the most important struggles were fought in Budapest.

[26] From recent literature on the social history of 1956 see: *Munkások '56. Az 1956-os Intézet XXII. évkönyve,* ed. János Rainer M. and Tibor Valuch (Budapest: Országos Széchényi Könyvtár 1956-os Intézet Alapítvány, 2017).

János Kádár, the leader of the newly established Communist Party called Hungarian Socialist Workers' Party (MSZMP) was therefore well motivated—apart from his personal disposition—to seek for a political and social compromise with the "working class," especially with the skilled, male, urban elite.[27]

The essence of this policy was to ensure ever-increasing standards of living, provide for proper housing and education, support workers' education and community life and enable them a certain degree of upward social and economic mobility. A new workplace policy was introduced, which restored the traditional elite positions within the hierarchy of the factory.[28]

While Kádár made important concessions to the workers' elite, in the official self-representation of the regime, the orthodox Communist ideology was preserved—at least until the 1980s. According to this, the "working class" constituted a unified, homogenous, class-conscious, revolutionary force under socialism, and in addition, it formed the real "ruling class" of the regime. This concept was central to the legitimizing ideology of all Communist regimes in Eastern Europe and the Soviet Union –with varying levels of political dissent and retaliation.

The 1960s saw major economic reform attempts within the Soviet bloc, which were accompanied by fierce political struggles within the ruling communist parties. In Hungary, many people hoped that the introduction of the New Economic Mechanism (1968) would trigger a more "liberal" political climate and a more "likeable" regime. This was the political context of the attempt of a young Hungarian intellectual, Miklós Haraszti, to "explore" the factory from within (he was in fact "sent" to the factory after being expelled from the university for his radical left-wing political views and his protest against the oppression of the Prague Spring). Haraszti was offered the chance to re-enter the socialist paradise at the price of writing a "propaganda book" (a

[27] Mark Pittaway, *From the Vanguard to the Margins: Workers in Hungary, 1939 to the Present* (Leiden: Brill, 2014), Földes György, *Hatalom és mozgalom, 1956-1989* (Budapest: Reform Könyvkiadó – Kossuth Könyvkiadó, 1989), Eszter Bartha, *Alienating Labour: Workers on the Road from Socialism to Capitalism in East Germany and Hungary* (Oxford–New York: Berghahn Books, 2013) (Series: International Studies in Social History).

[28] Pittaway, *From the Vanguard*, ibid.

so-called production novel) of the everyday life of Hungarian workers. Instead, his manuscript, which was eventually published in the West in 1978, with the title *A Worker in the Workers' State,* provoked legal proceedings against the author, who claimed no less than that workers were exploited to the same effect under "actually existing" socialism as they had been under capitalism, and that they were, in fact, fully conscious of this exploitation. The trial also served to discipline dissident Hungarian intellectuals, whose hopes for a better socialism were crushed by the oppression of the Prague Spring and the subsequent ideological triumph of the hardliner Communists in Hungary.

While Haraszti admittedly wrote "belles-lettres" or, at best, ethnography, István Kemény was a professional academic, who combined fieldwork with survey methods. His studies showed that industrial workers did not make up a homogenous "working class" under the socialist regime in Hungary, either in its social composition or in its culture, and this stratification manifested itself even in the division of labour: workers commuting from the countryside who were usually less qualified than their "native," urban counterparts, occupied lower ranks in the production hierarchy, while highly trained, skilled, or "core workers," who often came from old working-class dynasties, dominated the positions of functionaries, foremen and other key positions in production.[29]

There is a wealth of literature on industrial sociology written during the socialist period, all dealing with the role, strategies and bargaining power of workers in production. An early survey was conducted by Lajos Héthy and Csaba Makó in the Rába factory, on workers and automation.[30] This survey also included questions about the workers' trust in enterprise democracy, trade union, and even in the party itself. In several later works Makó and Héthy demonstrated that there was an informal wage bargain between the "core" workers and the management; this well demonstrated the survival of the old

[29] From recent literature on the urban/rural divide, see Zsuzsanna Varga, "Mit ér a munkás, ha paraszt (is)? A falusi munkásság és a hatalom a Kádár-korszakban," *Korall* 49 (2012): 37–57.

[30] Lajos Héthy and Csaba Makó, *Az automatizáció és a munkástudat* (Budapest: MTA Szociológiai Kutató Intézet Kiadványa, 1975).

hierarchies,[31] which the Communist authorities sought so eagerly to eliminate in the 1950s.[32]

Although she did not study workers directly, in the more "liberal" climate of the 1980s, Erzsébet Szalai already observed a growing individualization amongst workers and also amongst other strata of late Kádárian society.[33] From the end of the 1970s, the regime encountered substantial financial difficulties, and it continued to expand the private or informal sector (the so-called "second economy"), to render people more motivated to work both inside and outside of the factory, and to provide them with extra incomes (albeit often at the cost of overtime work and health damages). The consequence was a newly emerging stratification between those who had access to the private economy and those who had not, leading to an increasing individualization in the life strategies of workers. This, in turn, had a lasting impact on workers' political activity as it rendered the organization efforts of unions almost impossible after the collapse of the compulsory unionism of the socialist regime.[34]

FAMILY HISTORIES AND WORKERS' APPROACHES TO THE HUNGARIAN HISTORY OF THE 20TH CENTURY

The Kisalföld region, where our interviews were conducted, was traditionally treated with suspicion by orthodox Communists even in the Kádár era, and many party functionaries saw it as a place of "right-wing" or "petite-bourgeois" political dissent.[35] The historical roots go back to the collectivization campaigns in the short-lived Hungarian Soviet Republic (1919) and then under Rákosi in the 1950s, and even later under Kádár in the 1960s, which caused considerable suffering to

[31] Lajos Héthy and Csaba Makó, *Munkások, érdekek, érdekegyeztetés* (Budapest: Gondolat, 1978).

[32] Pittaway, *The Workers State*, ibid.

[33] Erzsébet Szalai, *Beszélgetések a gazdasági reformról* (Budapest: Pénzügykutató Intézet Kiadványai, 1986).

[34] András Tóth, "Attempts to Reform a Workers' Movement Without Mass Participation," in *Trade Unions in Europe*, ed. J. Waddington and R. Hoffman (Brissels: ETUI, 2000), 305–338.

[35] See also Eszter Bartha, *Alienating Labour;* Domonkos Sik, "Incubating radicalism."

the smallholders living in the area. The traumatic experience of these waves of collectivization was preserved in the collective memory of the respondents, many of whom came from peasant or worker-peasant families. While in the previous research[36] especially older workers, who were socialized in the Kádár regime, expressed a nostalgia for the security and calculability of life experienced back then, the 2015 interviews gave a different picture. Our interview partners (who mostly had either no or very few direct memories of the past regime) would typically prefer to speak of family grievances or outright persecution of family members suffered under "Communism," the lack of personal freedom (strict border control and limited travel opportunities) and shortage economy.[37]

One of our interview partners[38] came from a Communist "party cadre" family (as he called them) but as a young man he emigrated to the West (Switzerland). This is how he remembered the socialist regime:

> My family was privileged also at that time [the Kádár regime]. Everybody was in a high position, well-educated, etc. I was a privileged guy also under Communism [he laughs]. I went to the West

36 Eszter Bartha, "It Can't Make me Happy that Audi is Prospering: Working-class Nationalism in Hungary after 1989," in *Headlines of Nation, Subtexts of Class: Working-Class Populism and the Return of the Repressed in Neoliberal Europe*, ed. Don Kalb and Gábor Halmai (Oxford–New York: Berghahn Books, 2011), 92–112.

37 Similarly, Li Ju also found that old Chienese workers had in fact positive memories of the Communist past (community, secure living, upward social mobility). Ju Li,"How It Was/Is Told, Recorded and Remembered: The Discontinued History of the Third Front Construction," *Journal of Historical Sociology* 3 (2015): 314–341.

For an analysis of post-socialist memory, see Dominic Boyer, "Ostalgie and the Politics of Future in East Germany," *Public Culture* Spring Issue 2 (2006): 361-381. and Dominic Boyer, "From Algos to Autonomous: Nostalgic Eastern Europe as Postimperial Mania," in *Post-communist Nostalgia*, ed. Maria Todorova and Zsuzsa Gille, 17-28 (Oxford–New York: Berghahn Books, 2010), and Maria Todorova, "From Utopia to Propaganda and Back," in *Post-communist Nostalgia*, ed. Maria Todorova and Zsuzsa Gille (Oxford–New York: Berghahn Books, 2010), 1-13.

38 He was selected to be interviewed in spite of his "more mature" age because he was a political activist of the far-right wing party Jobbik at the time when we conducted the fieldwork.

> because I don't' like others telling me where the border is. No one will tell me that there is a fence here, which you cannot cross. Communism was an artificial society. Three-four men did the same job as a single Swiss worker. However, they supported working-class culture, although if you did not want to join the party or KISZ [Communist Youth Alliance], they would blackmail you.
>
> István, 54, skilled worker

One of our interview partners told us that his father had participated in the 1956 revolution and, as a consequence, a decade later our partner suffered negative discrimination at the university entrance exam and had to take up a manual job. An apparently energetic and hard-working man, he later recouped this disadvantage, and he even joined the Communist Party during the socialist regime. Today, however, he harbors staunch anti-Communist feelings (which he mainly explains by the discrimination that he experienced as a young man), and is a voter of the most radically anti-Communist, right-wing political force. On the basis of a much greater sample (more than 150 life-history interviews), Erzsébet Szalai found that many young activists of the party Jobbik[39] had grandparents who suffered repression under Communism.[40]

Religious commitment or church membership were also cited to justify the anti-Communism of the speaker and (mostly) his family. We know from archival evidence that the party leadership of the county "eagerly" and consistently fought against the influence of the church (the Roman Catholic Church was the strongest in the region), at least in rhetoric during the whole era.[41] Christian education was treated with deep suspicion and priests were seen as potential trouble-makers from the perspective of an atheist party and the Communist regime.

---

[39] Jobbik was the most successful far-right wing political party in Hungary at that time (and also in 2015).

[40] Erzsébet Szalai, *Koordinátákon kívül: Fiatal felnőttek a mai Magyarországon* (Budapest: Új Mandátum, 2011).

[41] See e.g. Eszter Bartha, *Alienating Labour: Workers on the Road from Socialism to Capitalism in East Germany and Hungary* (Oxford–New York: Berghahn Books, 2013).

> I come from a Catholic family, if I vote for the socialists that would imply my exclusion from the family. I would never ever vote for a socialist, this is something that I would never change.
>
> Mátyás, 37, skilled worker

Thus, many interview partners were responsive to political messages, which resonate with strong anti-Communism.

PERCEPTIONS OF MULTIPLE EXPLOITATIONS

It is a well-known and well-documented phenomenon that many Hungarians have been disappointed with the change of regimes, which failed to bring them the living standards and levels of consumption that they saw in advanced market economies such as West Germany or Austria.[42] This failure has nourished a deeply felt resentment against the "West."

The perception of exploitation was addressed at three different levels in the interviews. First, as we described above, many workers constructed their family history as one of exploitation by the "Communists." In this narrative, the party leaders of the reformed left, the MSZP (the Hungarian Socialist Party) appear as the successors of the old Communist party bureaucracy which, after 1989, "sold" the country to the "West." Secondly, at the level of the factory, workers strongly criticized the "unjustly high" wage differentials between the "direct" (blue-collar) and the "indirect" (engineers, managers and white-collar) employees. Károly, for instance, told us a story in which he had to teach a freshman engineer how the engine functioned. Further, the wage difference between the workers and the technocrats was also seen as a means of downgrading the very skills that were an integral part of workers' self-esteem. This further alienated them from the technocrats and high-

[42] For a review of the literature, see Tibor Valuch, *A jelenkori magyar társadalom* (Budapest: Osiris, 2014). See also, e.g. Zsuzsa Ferge, *Vágányok és vakvágányok a társadalompolitikában* (Budapest: L'Harmattan Kiadó, 2012).

János Ladányi, *Leselejtezettek: A kirekesztett népesség társadalom- és térszerkezeti elhelyezkedésének átalakulása Magyarországon a piacgazdasági átmenet időszakában* (Budapest: L'Harmattan Kiadó, 2012); Erzsébet Szalai, *Koordinátákon kívül: Fiatal felnőttek a mai Magyarországon* (Budapest: Új Mandátum, 2011).

ranking managers, who allegedly received unfair amounts of remuneration from the profits that they, the workers have produced:

> Many engineers think that they are the gods but they often lack elementary technological knowledge and culture. The working class is undervalued and the management and the engineers are greatly over-rewarded. I don't envy anyone their money but then the expectations should be equally different.
>
> Károly, 42, skilled worker

The third level at which the issue of exploitation was addressed in the interviews has an international dimension, and refers to the wage differential between the "East" and "West," the money paid to the workers in Hungary and in the "mother" country. While the interview partners stressed that their wages were higher than the Hungarian average, most would argue that the money was not enough compared to their expectations. Some told us they would even consider emigration in the hope of higher wages.

The perception of multiple exploitations contradicts the self-image of many workers, who hold work, vocation and labor efficiency and output in a high esteem:

> I believe in what I can do myself. I think that if something is wrong in my environment, then I will change it. If I am not satisfied with what I have, I will try to change it so that I can have enough. I like to be successful. Money does not interest me that much, I like to be successful in what I am doing. This is what drives me.
>
> Csaba, 37, skilled worker

This leads us to the next question: why does the political left in Hungary fail to profit from this resentment?

THE POLITICAL CONTEXT

In October 1989, MSZMP (the Hungarian Socialist Workers' Party), changed its name, dropping out the letter "M," which stood for the term "worker." The newly established MSZP became a moderate, non-Marxist, socialist party, advocating an extensive welfare state in the context of market economy and political democracy. This political agenda enabled the party to win three elections before 2010 (in 1994, 2002, and 2006). In a sometimes uneasy governmental coalition with the liberal party SZDSZ (Alliance of Free Democrats), the socialists sought to maintain the welfare state while ensuring open doors to foreign investors.

After the parliamentary elections of 2002, the triumphant socialists formed a coalition with SZDSZ, the leading liberal party of the era. During the electoral campaign, the socialists promised a "welfare system change," which was then put into practice by Prime Minister Péter Medgyessy, who substantially increased wages in the state sector, following his electoral victory. The welfare system change undoubtedly worked—the municipal elections in the autumn of 2002 brought a landslide victory for the socialists.

No wonder that the socialists sought to use the same recipe in 2006, when they promised even more welfare to the working people. After the parliamentary electoral victory, however, the government had to introduce a severe stabilization package in order to cut state budget deficit. In addition, as Prime Minister Ferenc Gyurcsány openly admitted, at a closed party meeting, that he intentionally lied in his campaign to ensure electoral victory for the socialists. The speech was leaked out, and successfully discredited not only the Prime Minister but also the political left, which failed to remove Gyurcsány from power. Moral outrage was translated into mass demonstrations and political protests, which became particularly violent at the anniversary of the 1956 revolution. All these contributed to the landslide victory of the political right led by the party FIDESZ at the municipal elections in 2006, which gave FIDESZ a strong and reliable political and social basis in the Hungarian countryside.

The 2008 credit crunch forced the socialist-led government to implement further austerity measures, which, in turn, further eroded the popularity and credibility of the party. In addition, the political right successfully appropriated the original welfare program of the socialists, promising support, protection and security to the "little man."

The recipe worked again, but this time it benefited the Hungarian political right. In the parliamentary elections of 2010, FIDESZ won a landslide victory, while Jobbik, the strongest and best-organized far right-wing party, received almost as many votes as the socialists.

NATIONALISM AND ANTI-ROMA SENTIMENTS

The claim of membership in decent, majority society was closely linked with the open expression of strong anti-Roma sentiments.[43] Indeed, many of our respondents argued that Roma people were unable to integrate into Hungarian society, and their culture rendered them markedly different from "ethnic" Hungarians in a negative sense (they are too lazy to work, they produce too many children only to get social subsidies, they steal from ethnic Hungarians, physically threaten them, etc.). These stereotypes were frequently voiced both in the group discussions and the interviews.

> I think that Jobbik and the gypsies are good friends because Jobbik would not be in Parliament if it were not for the gypsies.
>
> Zsolt, 40, skilled worker

"Gypsy criminality"—a conception that Jobbik successfully thematized—was frequently evoked to justify anti-Roma feelings and the generally held view that the Roma people cannot get integrated into the majority society because of cultural reasons. While "gypsies" were mostly seen as violators of moral and cultural norms established in the majority society, Jobbik was seen by many as the proper instrument of restoring "order" and "social justice."

> What is the good thing about Jobbik? They are young, they say what people want to hear. They bring order. Taxation equals dictatorship. The American model. I would also strengthen public safety, there is no public safety in Hungary, things have become so loose…
>
> Károly, 42, skilled worker, trade union leader

While in previous research (Eszter Bartha, "It Can't Make Me Happy"), openly racist arguments were used less frequently (and were targeted

[43] Anti-Roma biases and stereotypes have a voluminous literature in Hungary. Here we mainly build on Margit Feischmidt, "Mindennapi nacionalizmus," 401–447, who demonstrated the essential link between neo-nationalism and anti-Roma sentiments.

mainly at "Jewish" capital), in this research, anti-Roma feelings were openly discussed. Certainly, these feelings were further reinforced by the tabloid press, "Facebook culture" (social media) and the success of Jobbik in thematizing "gypsy crime" and "welfare dependence" in the "visible" and "venerable" public.[44]

Conclusion

Apart from the findings discussed in the previous subchapters, we could demonstrate that neo-nationalism as defined by Margit Feischmidt (2014) provides the workers with a language and a set of cultural codes through which they can voice their dissatisfaction with what we termed as "perceptions of multiple exploitations" (see part 2.2). The political left in Hungary failed to profit from these perceptions partly for reasons deeply embedded in 20th century Hungarian history and the fierce struggle between the radical right and left, which impacted the family histories of the interview partners, and partly for the political, tactical and organizational mistakes of the socialist party after 2006 (see part 2.3.).

While many factors that explain the political weakness (or outright failure) of the socialist party in Hungary are specific to the country (so is the complex history of the far-right political and social movements in the 20th century), we can single out some elements that have a wider East-Central European scope. Family histories, memories of suffering or persecution under "Communism," the loss of the appeal of political messages based on class identities (which started well before the actual collapse of the Communist regimes) and the perceptions of multiple exploitations all render workers conducive to anti-Communist, nationalistic and traditionalist right-wing political messages. We could also detect the strong presence of a perceived threat of the "strangers," who violate established social and moral norms—in this case the Roma minority –a "danger" that Jobbik so successfully thematized. Further conducive factors are age (they were mostly young or middle-age

---

44 For a political analysis of the rise of Jobbik see: Tóth András and Grajczjár István, "The Rise of the Radical Right in Hungary," ibid.

people, and the youth always tend to be more radical) and gender (they were all men workers). Although we did not study perceptions of masculinity in this paper, most of the interviewed workers undoubtedly held "traditionalist" views of family and gender roles.

BIBLIOGRAPHY

Bahro, Rudolf. *The Alternative in Eastern Europe*. London: NLB, 1977.

Bartha, Eszter. "Transition, Transformation, 'Postsocialism': Theorizing Systemic Change in Eastern Europe." In *After Twenty Years: Reasons and Consequences of the Transformation in Central and Eastern Europe,* edited by Krisztián Csaplár-Degovics, Miklós Mitrovits, and Csaba Zahorán, 13–34. Berlin: Terra Recognita Alapítvány, 2010.

Bartha, Eszter. "It Can't Make Me Happy that Audi is Prospering: Working-class Nationalism in Hungary after 1989." In *Headlines of Nation, Subtexts of Class: Working-Class Populism and the Return of the Repressed in Neoliberal Europe*, edited by Don Kalb and Gábor Halmai, 92-112. Oxford–New York: Berghahn Books, 2011.

Bartha, Eszter. *Alienating Labour: Workers on the Road from Socialism to Capitalism in East Germany and Hungary*. Oxford–New York: Berghahn Books, 2013. (Series: International Studies in Social History).

Becker, Frans, and René Curperus. *Politics in a Fragmented Society. The 2010 Elections in Netherlands*. International Policy Analysis: Friedrich Ebert Stiftung, 2010.

Berezin, Mabel. "Politics and Culture. A Less Fissured Terrain." *Annual Review of Sociology* vol. 23 (1997): 361-383.

Bibes, Geneviève, and Christine Alix. "Les élections législatives italiennes d'avril 1963." *Revue française de science politique* 4 (1963): 911–950.

Binder, Mátyás. "Changes in the Image of 'Gypsies' in Slovakia and Hungary After the Post-Communist Transition." In *After Twenty Years*, edited by Krisztián Csaplár-Degovics et al., 307-336. Berlin: OEZ Verlag, 2010.

Boyer, Dominic. "Ostalgie and the Politics of Future in East Germany." *Public Culture*. Spring Issue 2 (2006): 361–381.

Boyer, Dominic. "From Algos to Autonomous: Nostalgic Eastern Europe as Postimperial Mania." In *Post-communist Nostalgia*, edited by Maria Todorova and Zsuzsa Gille, 17–28. Oxford–New York: Berghahn Books, 2010.

Buchowski, Michal. *Rethinking Transformation: An Anthropological Perspective on Postsocialism*. Poznan: Humaniora, 2001.

Burawoy, Michael. *The Politics of Production: Factory Regimes under Capitalism and Socialism*. London: Verso, 1985.

Burawoy, Michael, and János Lukács. *The Radiant Past: Ideology and Reality in Hungary's Road to Capitalism*. Chicago–London: The University of Chicago Press, 1992.

Dalton, Russel L. *Citizen Politics in Western Democracies: Public Opinion and Political Parties in the United States, Great Britain, West Germany and France.* Chatham, NJ: Chatham House, 2006.

Didier, Eribon. *Returning to Reims.* Los Angeles: Semiotext(e), 2013.

Feischmidt, Margit, and Glózer, Rita, and Ilyés, Zoltán, and Kasznár Veronika Katalin, and Zakariás, Ildikó. *Nemzet a mindennapokban. Az új nacionalizmus populáris kultúrája.* Budapest: L'Harmattan – MTA Társadalomtudományi Központ, 2014.

Feischmidt, Margit. "Mindennapi nacionalizmus és a másság cigányként való megjelölése." In *Nemzet a mindennapokban,* edited by Margit Feischmidt et al., 401-447.

Feischmidt, Margit, and Peter Hervik. "Mainstreaming the Extreme: Intersecting Challenges from the Far Right in Europe." *Intersections, East European Journal of Society and Politics* 1(2015). Accessed February 11, 2016. http://intersections.tk.mta.hu/index.php/intersections/article/view/80.

Ferge, Zsuzsa. *Vágányok és vakvágányok a társadalompolitikában.* Budapest: L'Harmattan Kiadó, 2012.

Földes György. *Hatalom és mozgalom, 1956–1989.* Budapest: Reform Könyvkiadó – Kossuth Könyvkiadó, 1989.

Gorz, André. *Farewell to the Working Class. An Essay on Post-Industrial Socialism.* Boston: 1982.

Hann, Chris, ed. *Postsocialism: Ideals, Ideologies and Practices in Eurasia.* London: Routledge, 2002.

Haraszti, Miklós. *A Worker in a Worker's State.* New York: Universe Books, 1979. [*Darabbér. Egy munkás a munkásállamban.* Párizs: Magyar Füzetek Könyvei, 1979.]

Héthy, Lajos, and Csaba Makó. *Az automatizáció és a munkástudat.* Budapest: MTA Szociológiai Kutató Intézet Kiadványa, 1975.

Héthy, Lajos and Csaba Makó. *Munkások, érdekek, érdekegyeztetés.* Budapest: Gondolat, 1978.

Ignácz, Károly, and Balázs Szabó. "Választási eredmények Budapest történelmi munkásnegyedeiben 1994–2014." *Eszmélet* 104 (2014): 75–98.

Kalb, Don. "Conversations with a Polish Populist: Tracing Hidden Histories of Globalization, Class, and Dispossession in Postsocialism (and Beyond)." *American Ethnologist,* vol. 36 (2009): 207–223.

Kalb, Don, and Gábor Halmai, eds. *Headlines of Nation, Subtexts of Class: Working-Class Populism and the Return of the Repressed in Neoliberal Europe.* Oxford–New York: Berghahn Books, 2011.

Kemény, István. *Velünk nevelkedett a gép. Magyar munkások a hetvenes évek elején.* Budapest: Művelődéskutató Intézet, 1990.

Kideckel, David. "The Unmaking of an East-Central-European Working Class." In *Postsocialism: Ideals, Ideologies and Practices in Eurasia,* edited by C. M. Hann, 114-132. London: Routledge, 2002.

Kideckel, David. *Getting by in Postsocialist Romania: Labor, the Body and Working-Class Culture.* Bloomington: Indiana University Press, 2008.

Konrád, György, and Iván Szelényi. *The Intellectuals on the Road to Class Power.* New York: Harcourt Brace, Jovanovich, 1979.

Körösényi, András. "Nómenklatúra és vallás. Törésvonalak és pártrendszer Magyarországon." *Századvég* 1 (1996): 67-93.

Körösényi, András. "A politikai polarizáció és következményei a demokratikus elszámoltatásra 1990–2010." *Working Papers in Political Science* 1 (2012):1–24. Budapest: MTA TK PTI, 2012.

Krausz, Tamás. "A magyar történetírás és a marxizmus. Megjegyzések a 'kelet-európaiság' problémájához." In *Vitás kérdések a Szovjetunió és Kelet-Európa XX. századi történetében,* 219–290. Budapest: Ruszisztikai Könyvek XXXIII. Russica Pannonicana, 2011.

Ladányi, János. *Leselejtezettek: A kirekesztett népesség társadalom- és térszerkezeti elhelyezkedésének átalakulása Magyarországon a piacgazdasági átmenet időszakában.* Budapest: L'Harmattan Kiadó, 2012.

Li, Ju. "How It Was/Is Told, Recorded and Remembered: The Discontinued History of the Third Front Construction." *Journal of Historical Sociology* 3 (2015): 314-341.

Marliére, Philippe. "The Decline of Europe's Social Democratic Parties." *Open Democracy,* March 16, 2010: Accessed October 30, 2018. https://www.opendemocracy.net/philippe-marliere/decline-of-europes-social-democratic-parties.

McAllister, Iain, Ron J. Johnston, Charles J. Pattie, Helena Tunstall, Danny F. L. Dorling, and David J. Rossiter. "Class Dealignment and the Neighbourhood Effect: Miller Revisited." *British Journal of Political Science* vol. 31(2001): 41–59.

Miller, W. L. "Social Class and Party Choice in England: A New Analysis." *British Journal of Political Science* vol. 8 (1978): 257–284.

Nagy, Éva Katalin. "Munkástanácsok 1989-ben: A dolgozói tulajdonkérdése a rendszerváltás folyamatában." In *Határokon túl: Tanulmánykötet Mark Pittaway (1971–2010) emlékére,* edited by Eszter Bartha and Zsuzsanna Varga, 461–480. Budapest: L'Harmattan Kiadó, 2012.

Ost, David. *Solidarity and the Politics of Anti-politics. Opposition and Reform in Poland 1968.* Philadelphia: Temple University Press, 1990.

Ost, David. *The Defeat of Solidarity: Anger and Politics in Postcommunist Europe.* Ithaca, NY: Cornell University Press, 2005.

Pickles, John, and Adrian Smith. *Theorising Transition: The Political Economy of Postcommunist Transformations.* London: Routledge, 1998.

Pittaway, Mark. "Fascim in Hungary." In *The Oxford Handbook of Fascism,* edited by R. J. B. Bosworth, 380–397. Oxford: Oxford University Press, 2010.

Pittaway, Mark. *The Workers State: Industrial Labor and the Making of Socialist Hungary, 1944–1958.* Pittsburgh: The University of Pittsburgh Press, 2012.

Pittaway, Mark. *From the Vanguard to the Margins: Workers in Hungary, 1939 to the Present.* Leiden: Brill, 2014.

Platone, François. "Les structures du vote de gauche à Paris." *Revue française de science politique* 6 (1977): 820–847.

Pogátsa, Zoltán. *Magyarország politikai gazdaságtana*. Budapest: Osiris Kiadó, 2016.

Rainer, János M ., and Tibor Valuch, eds. *Munkások '56. Az 1956-os Intézet XXII. évkönyve*. Budapest: Országos Széchényi Könyvtár 1956-os Intézet Alapítvány, 2017.

Rézler, Gyula. *A Magyar nagyipari munkásosztály kialakulása 1867–1914*. Budapest, Rekord, 1938.

Rudas, Tamás. "A Jobbik törzsszavazóiról." In *Társadalmi Riport, 2010*, edited by Tamás Kolosi and István György Tóth, 512–526. Budapest: Tárki Budapest, 2010.

Sik, Domonkos. "Incubating Radicalism in Hungary – the Case of Sopron and Ózd." *Intersections, East European Journal of Society and Politics* 1 (2015): 101–121. Accessed February 8, 2016. http://intersections.tk.mta.hu/index.php/intersections/article/view/31.

Swidler, Ann. "Culture in Action: Symbols and Strategies." *American Sociological Review* 2 (1986): 273–286.

Szalai, Erzsébet. *Beszélgetések a gazdasági reformról.* Budapest: Pénzügykutató Intézet Kiadványai, 1986.

Szalai, Erzsébet. *A civil társadalomtól a politikai társadalomfelé. Munkástanácsok 1989–93*. Budapest: T-Twins Kiadó, 1994.

Szalai, Erzsébet. "Tulajdonviszonyok, társadalomszerkezet és munkásság." *Kritika* 9 (2004): 2–6.

Szalai, Erzsébet. *Koordinátákon kívül: Fiatal felnőttek a mai Magyarországon.* Budapest: Új Mandátum, 2011.

Szombati, Kristóf. *The Revolt of the Provinces: Anti-Gypsyism and Right-Wing Politics in Hungary*. Oxford–New York: Berghahn Books, 2018.

Taggart, Paul. "New populist parties in Western Europe." *West European Politics* 1 (1995): 34–51.

Todorova, Maria. "From Utopia to Propaganda and Back." In *Post-communist Nostalgia*, edited by Maria Todorova and Zsuzsa Gille, 1-13. Oxford–New York: Berghahn Books, 2010.

Tóth, András. "Attempts to Reform a Workers' Movement Without Mass Participation." In *Trade Unions in Europe*, edited by J. Waddington and R. Hoffman, 305–338. Brussels: ETUI, 2000.

Tóth, András. "The Failure of Socialdemocratization of the Hungarian Union Movement." In *Workers after Workers' States*, edited by Stephen Crowley and David Ost, 47–71. Oxford–New York: Rowman and Littlefield, 2002.

Tóth, András. "The Birth of the Workers' Pillar and its Relationship with the Marxist Working-class Formation." 2018. Accessed September 30, 2018. https://www.academia.edu/38369548/TA_Formation_of_workersdocx.pdf.

Tóth, András, and István Grajczjár. "Different Roads to the Siren Songs of the Extreme Right in Hungary." In *Changing Working Life and the Appeal of the Extreme Right,* edited by J. Flecker, 201–217. London: Ashgate, 2017.

Tóth, András and István Grajczjár. "Jobbik: a radikális jobboldal térnyerése Magyarországon." In *Tarka Ellenállás: Kézikönyv rebelliseknek és békéseknek,* edited by Péter Krasztev and Jon Van Til, 411–452. Budapest: Napvilág Kiadó, 2013.

Tóth, András, and István Grajczjár. "The Rise of the Radical Right in Hungary," in *The Hungarian Patient: Social Opposition to an Illiberal Democracy*, edited by Jon Van Til and Péter Krasztev. Budapest: CEU Press, 2015.
Trotsky, Leon. *The Revolution Betrayed. What is the Soviet Union and Where is It Going?* New York: Doubleday, Doran and Co., Pathfinder Press, 1937.
Valuch, Tibor. *A jelenkori magyar társadalom*. Budapest: Osiris, 2014.
Van der Linden, Marcel. *Western Marxism and the Soviet Union: A Survey of Critical Theory and Debates since 1917.* Leiden: Brill, 2007.
Van der Linden, Marcel. *Workers of the World: Essays toward a Global Labor History*. Leiden: Brill, 2008.
Varga, Zsuzsanna. "Mit ér a munkás, ha paraszt (is)? A falusi munkásság és a hatalom a Kádár-korszakban." *Korall* 49 (2012): 37-57.
Zimmermann, Susan. "Gender Regime and Gender Struggle in Hungarian State Socialism." *Aspasia*, vol. 4 (2010): 1–24.

Who Brings the Political Change? Divergent Understandings of Politics Among Politically Active Students[1]

DÁNIEL OROSS, DÁNIEL RÓNA, and ANDREA SZABÓ

Introduction

This article investigates the political activity of the Hungarian youth with special attention to college and university students. University students have played an important role in revolutionary changes throughout Hungarian history (1848, 1956). Members of this age cohort are embedded both in the traditional values of their families and in the new ideas of youth organizations, and are therefore very sensitive to societal changes. Analyzing university student's attitudes is relevant because among social institutions universities are one of the most important socialization agents for democratic education. Universities play an important role in democratic citizenship education and the training of citizens inside the university has also an impact on democracy outside the university. Therefore we aim to explore politically active college and university students and describe their political identity and motivations.

Former research suggest that although young Hungarians show indifference toward politics, if they encounter a social problem that closely affects them, then and only then do they stand up for their rights. We aim to describe political communities, groups that can mobilize, articulate the political opinion of young people at a collec-

[1] Dániel Róna's research has been supported by the Hungarian Academy of Sciences (MTA) Premium Post-Doctorate Research Program.

tive level. Therefore, we adopt a phenomenological perspective on politics, which considers passivity as a "normal state" for young people and regards political activity as something unusual, which should be understood from the perspective of their current activities. This is how the main patterns of their political participation, the process of political socialization and the main motivation behind participation (or lack of participation) can be better understood. The phenomenological approach groups students and explains along which collective identities (e.g., passive, active, loyal and rebellious students) their activity can be described. By finding those groups that can offer collective consciousness and community spirit to active young people, it becomes possible to describe adequately actual processes that characterize the political activity of university students as a distinguished group of the Hungarian youth. Our aim is to find out if there are active groups of Hungarian students and to show how numerous they are compared to the whole population of young Hungarians.

First, we will review the literature on the political activities of the Hungarian youth and clarify our approach. Then, based on a national survey sample from 2018 we describe general trends concerning ideological and attitudinal differences between the voting age population in Hungary, young people and university and college students. The next step is based on a university and college student surveys conducted in 2013 and in 2015; we use cluster-analyses to pinpoint the main political community groups of Hungarian university and college students. In order to highlight the latest trends we take a closer look at Western-oriented and liberal groups of Hungarian youth. Finally, the main findings and consequences will be discussed.

Youth and the Democratic Transition

Hungary was the first country in the East-Central European region that succeeded in building and stabilizing democratic institutions following the collapse of communism in 1989/1990. However, it was achieved through the negotiations of the elites and young people were not particularly active within the process. Student's views on democracy are primarily shaped by the contemporary institutions that play a key role in the political socialization of youth (e.g. family, school, peer group and media). Following the democratic transition of the country, these institutions had to face new challenges and had to play new roles. The specificity of the Hungarian case is that a fragmented, semi-peripheral political socialization became characteristic[2],[3] where the role of these institutions in transferring democratic values to young people is not clarified. Even though the new system is different both institutionally and functionally from the communist regime, and despite the current system being the antithesis of the previous system ideologically,[4] institutions within a fragmented, semi-peripheral political socialization are unable to prepare students for the requirements of democratic citizenship and certain patterns from the former, communist period and of earlier revolutive socialization persist.[5]

At the start of the democratic transition there appeared a myriad of new forms of political participation within the post-socialist Hungarian society. Concerning Hungary there have been few studies referring to these changes in participation patterns. In the last decade, studies focusing on youth and politics all drew on the large-sample *Ifjúság* (Youth) surveys conducted every four years.[6] The conclusion that can be drawn on the basis of these results is that Hungarian young

2 László Laki and Andrea Szabó, "Mi lehet a magyar fiatalok demokráciaszkepszise mögött?" in *Racionálisan lázadó hallgatók II.: Apátia - radikalizmus - posztmaterializmus a magyar egyetemisták és főiskolások körében,* edited by Andrea Szabó (Szeged: Belvedere Meridionale Kft, 2014), 18–40.

3 Ildikó Szabó, *Nemzet és szocializáció. A politika szerepe az identitások alakulásában Magyarországon 1867 –2006* (Budapest: L'Harmattan Kiadó, 2009).

4 Ildikó Szabó, *A pártállam gyermekei* (Budapest: Új Mandátum Könyvkiadó, 2000).

5 Adrienn Bognár and Andrea Szabó, "Politikai szocializációs modellek Magyarországon, 1990–2016," in *Csendesek vagy lázadók?—A hallgatók politikai orientációi Magyarországon (2011–2015)*, edited by Andrea Szabó and Dániel Oross (Szeged—Budapest: Belvedere-MTA TK PTI, 2015), 14-35.

6 *Ifjúság2004 Gyorsjelentés,* edited by Béla Bauer and Andrea Szabó (Budapest: Mobilitás, 2005); *Ifjúság2008 Gyorsjelentés,* ed. Béla Bauer and Andrea Szabó (Budapest: Szociálpolitikai és Munkaügyi Intézet, 2009); Dániel Oross, "Társadalmi közérzet, politikához való viszony," in *Magyar Ifjúság 2012: tanulmánykötet,* ed. Levente Székely (Budapest: Kutatópont Kft., 2013), 283–315.

people are passive and apolitical, more apolitical and more passive than their Western-European peers.[7]

For decades now Hungarian society—in international comparisons—has been noted for its apathy and low levels of civic participation and activism.[8] Regarding the level of formal organization among the Hungarian youth former studies (e.g., the *Ifjúság* studies) unanimously describe the current youth cohort as a disorganized, fragmented generation. All of the examinations showed, however, that among the youth, those in university and college form an exception to the general rule. They are the ones who are relatively more active, of whom a relatively large proportion (approximately 55% of those studying at university) have some form of organizational affiliation.[9] Recent studies have shown that interest in public life and the willingness to be politically active has grown in certain groups.[10] These groups, however, are not always committed to democratic values. In 2013, our research on college and university students found that almost three-quarters of the students surveyed were unhappy with democracy, with only 23% of respondents reporting any satisfaction.[11] Growing civil society activism is strengthening antidemocratic processes as much as democracy itself[12]. We examine this dilemma from the approach of youth groups and their unequivocal interest in the far-right, but we also consider

---

[7] Dániel Oross and Andrea Szabó, "Changing Tendencies of Youth Political Participation in Europe: Evidence from Four Different Cases," in *Values and Identities in Europe: Evidence from the European Social Survey*, ed. Michael J. Breen (Abingdon: Routledge, 2017), 160–183.

[8] Bauer and Szabó, *Ifjúság* 2005, Bauer and Szabó, *Ifjúság* 2009, Oross, "Társadalmi közérzet."

[9] Tamás Kern and Andrea Szabó, "A politikai közéleti részvétel alakulása Magyarországon, 2006-2010," in *Részvétel, Képviselet, Politikai változás*, eds. Róbert Tardos, Zsolt Enyedi and Andrea Szabó (Budapest: DKMKA, 2011).

[10] Andrea Szabó, *Exit, Voice, Loyalty and Neglect –Political Attitudes of Hungarian University and College Students* (Prague: Heinrich Böll Stiftung, 2015).

[11] Andrea Szabó, *Political Orientations, Values and Activities of Hungarian University and College Students* (Prague: Heinrich Böll Stiftung, 2013).

[12] Dániel Róna and Anett Sőrés, "A kuruc.info nemzedék. Miért népszerű a Jobbik a fiatalok között?" in *Racionálisan lázadó hallgatók. Radikalizmus, posztamterializmus, apátia a magyar egyetemisták és főiskolások körében*, ed. Andrea Szabó (Szeged: Belvedere, 2012), 113–157.

another group of active youth as well, who are situated outside the current political palette and have postmodern values.

There are examples from the Central-Eastern European region where students were active in shaping democracy. Student organizations and opposition politicians had been actively protesting against Milošević for some years. Disappointment emerged as people compared the expectations of revolution to the realities of democracy. In that context, Greenberg[13] wrote about "politics of disappointment" in students' flexible negotiation of changing meanings of youth politics where student activists were both objects of disappointment and well poised to confront the contingencies of activism as they moved between street protest and institutionally based democratic engagement and reform. Student protesters positioned themselves as altruistic representatives of the people, they refused to endorse any particular opposition party and distanced themselves from "formal" politics. Serbia became one of a handful of models of "color revolutions" that would form the basis for a new benchmark of democratization policy and scholarship.[14] Otpor was a complicated and deeply contradictory organization: creative and pragmatic, hierarchically and horizontally organized, and rooted in long-standing Serbian protest traditions and internationally supported approaches to democratic revolution. Serbian student activists co-created and popularized forms of political organizing, and they were in some ways shadowed by their own success.

Even though Hungary does not have any youth activist movements like Otpor at a national level, there are moments that call into question the statement on the apolitical and passive Hungarian youth. In the fall of 2011, in the winter of 2012, and then in the fall of 2014, university groups mobilized mass demonstrations that took place in Budapest and in the country's major cities—even in western European cities—which radically contradicted the well-known apolitical stereotypical image. Sit-ins at universities happened (similarly to events that were organized in 2009 in Vienna or in Zagreb) for the first time in Hungary in 2012 when students protested against the Hungarian Government's

[13] Jessica Greenberg, *After the Revolution: Youth, Democracy and the Politics of Disappointment in Serbia,* (Stanford: Stanford University Press, 2014), 8.

[14] Ibid., 14.

planned cuts in the state subsidies to finance college tuition in Budapest on December 10, 2012.[15]

However, the impact of these events on Hungarian college and university students cannot be detected by a participation approach, by the traditional theory of democratic political participation. There is a need to go beyond investigating young people's level of participation, to better understand the reasons of their activity and passivity. We think that a "phenomenological" approach is necessary, an internal, intrinsic approach that is able to understand the "voice" of young people. According to Williams, there is a need for an additional application of a theory and a methodology that makes it easier to understand the importance of such unique participatory forms. In the United States much research attention was drawn to culture as an area where a change of action takes place, and sociologists dealing with protests and movements became interested in the consequences of these changes.[16] American social scientists started to investigate the recruitment, retainment, motivation and mobilization of members of social movements by using theories of collective identity and the theoretical framework of symbolic interactionism. The forerunners of the US researchers' intellectual movement were the German phenomenological sociologists, Alfred Schütz who worked mainly in the 1940s, and the foraging theory of symbolic interactionism (Erving Goffman, Harold Garfinkel). These researchers, in dealing with social movements, were not simply interested in participation and they not only tested different forms of it, but rather they considered the broader

---

[15] Pál Susánszky and Márton Gerő, "A Hallgatói Hálózat (HaHa) mobilizációs jellemzői," in *Racionálisan lázadó hallgatók II.: Apátia – radikalizmus – posztmaterializmus a magyar egyetemisták és főiskolások körében,* ed. Andrea Szabó (PTI Budapest—Szeged: Belvedere Meridionale—MTA TK, 2014), 278; Dániel Oross, Tamás Kovács, and Andrea Szabó, "University Students' Democratic Values and Attitudes towards Democracy in Hungary. European Quarterly of Political Attitudes and Mentalities," *EQPAM* 1 (2018): 15-30.

[16] Rhys H. Williams, "The Cultural Contexts of Collective Action: Constraints, Opportunities, and the Symbolic Life of Social Movements," in *The Blackwell Companion to Social Movements,* ed. David A. Snow, Sarah A. Soule, and Hanspeter Kriesi (Oxford: Blackwell Publishing Ltd, 2004), 91–115.

external ("cultural environment") and the narrower internal movement conditions ("internal" dimensions) of movement culture[17] that surrounded them. Accordingly, the static structural models were replaced by the investigation of dynamic and interrelated mechanisms and processes when analyzing the transition to the new forms of participation at the millennium. The great researchers of social movements, as McAdam, Tarrow and Tilly began to test increasingly the processes, the actors/activists and their collective identities.[18] The works of Gamson represent a particularly important addition to the participatory approach highlighting three elements from understanding to the motivation to act: "injustice," "agency" and "identity." These help activists and organizers to understand the problems and dilemmas and to explore the ways in which the social grievances trigger actions.

According to Williams,[19] it is important to investigate the collective identities of young people, or more properly speaking, to examine their collective political thinking. We claim that the description of different forms of political participation is important and indispensable, but such an analysis has a rather static nature. The dynamic approach in this case means seeking and revealing the collective political communities that offer collective consciousness, identity, attachment, thinking ("collective behavior") to young people, promoting, in this way, the formation of political action (participation). Those kind of political actions have an overwhelming force at the moment of their birth but fade quickly. Those one-time events (2011, 2012, 20104) can be considered as momentary rebellion, a point at which the lurking deep dissatisfaction explodes. It is, thus, worth addressing the character of the rebellion thoroughly.

When using the term "rebellion" we first refer to what Antony Downs meant when he used the term rationality. Rationality, here, meant that an individual "moves toward his goals in a way which, to the best of his knowledge, uses the least possible input of scarce resources per unit of valued output" (1957). Downs combined the

[17] Rhys H. Williams, "Constructing the Public Good: Social Movements and Cultural Resources," *Social Problems*," 1995/42, 124–144.

[18] *Transnational Protest & Global Activism,* ed. Donatella Della Porta and Sidney Tarrow (New York: Rowman & Littlefield Publishers, INC, 2005).

[19] Williams, "The Cultural Contexts."

rationality axiom with a self-interest axiom, so that rational behavior, in his model, indicated "rational behavior directed primarily toward selfish ends" (1957, 27).

The second part of the term, rebellion, is rooted in the notion of a "postmodern riot." According to Máté Szabó, a postmodern riot is—unlike modern protests which were homogeneous, "combined issues"—characterized by one common issue and loose claims, however, participants formulate them along diverse, informal, spontaneous choices. The events have a central thread but the implementation is much more diverse than it was at any time in history. Moreover, where appropriate, the central claim is carried simultaneously by traditional movements (unions), by new social movements (feminists) and by postmodern movements (such as anarchism)[20]. The riot can be violent, of course, but violence is not the target; it is not the violence that is a characteristic feature of the term Szabó chooses, but eclecticism, diversity and coexistence are.[21] Connected to an issue—such as the anti-globalization protests in Seattle—activists with different perspectives, religions, ideologies, and languages get together, but it is likely that they never meet each other again. There is a single goal, which young people with different views and ideologies may take up from a set of sympathetic issues and claims. Once a claim is embraced, they stand up for it in proportion to their self-interest, but they never act together again.

Thirdly, we use the term rebellion as a characteristic of young Hungarians' political behavior. Although young Hungarians are passive and are interested in politics if and only if they face a political issue that affects them very much, they occasionally make their voices heard (e.g., at the end of the year 2012 when the government introduced restrictions within the higher education system). Their actions are very diverse and innovative, in some cases even loud and expressive, and they are not anti-democratic. Rebels are basically democratically-minded and approve of the capitalist market-economy, but they are critical (in some cases extremely critical) of the existing Hungarian

[20] Máté Szabó, "Globális kommunikáció, civil társadalom, tiltakozás," *Fordulat.* 1 (2008): 96–116. http://fordulat.net/pdf/1/szabo.pdf.

[21] Máté Szabó, *A tiltakozás kultúrája Magyarországon. Társadalmi és politikai tiltakozás* 2 (Budapest: Rejtjel Politológia Könyvek, 2007), 186–187.

versions of those systems. They stand up because of an issue, and after doing so, they return to their everyday lives (from which they try to exclude politics as much as possible). The notion of rebellion explains the attitudes of the Hungarian youth; it puts into context their level of political activity (or rather their lack of activity). We call these groups rational because their actions are primarily determined by self-interest. Rebellion refers to their high degree of dissatisfaction not just with the political elite but with the political system as well.

The root of this is basically a passive behavior originating from socialization mechanisms. In new and re-established democracies "automatic" transmission of democratic values from one generation to the next cannot be taken for granted.[22] In Hungary, neither the most important agent of socialization, the family, nor the most important institutional agent, school, orient young people toward participation.[23] As mentioned above, family members raised during the decades of state socialism learned passive patterns of participation, and apart from a short period of euphoric years following transition the new regime did not require particularly high levels of activity from them either. Families had permanent economic problems: poverty, mass unemployment, and social leveling. Compared to these issues, a participation-centric socialization function was not considered important. Nevertheless, the Hungarian school systems still did not manage to teach democratic civic education. Western European and especially German solutions remain un-adopted. Hungarian schools are still highly hierarchical and conservative. In terms of civic education, the educational system is inconsistent and incomplete. Since the process of the political socialization in Hungary indoctrinates passivity into young Hungarians, political passivity can be considered as a "normal state" of young people—during the last three decades there has been little change in this field.[24]

---

22 R.G. Niemi and M.A. Hepburn, "The Rebirth of Political Socialization," *Perspectives on Political Science*, 1 (1995): 9.

23 Mihály Csákó, "Állampolgárokat nevel-e az iskola?" in *Arctalan (?) nemzedék: Ifjúság 2000–2010,* ed. Béla Bauer and Andrea Szabó (Budapest: Nemzeti Család- és Szociálpolitikai Intézet, 2011), 101–114.

24 Mihály Csákó, "Ifjúság és politika," *Educatio* 4 (2004): 535–550.

Clearly, at this point, political activity and passivity, as well as political preferences, can be explained from different aspects. In the following analysis we consider results from the aspect of the phenomenological approach to rebellion.

Data and Methods

The emergence of novel forms of participation presents a theoretical challenge, prompting researchers to come up with new concepts and distinctions. These different attempts at conceptualization have engendered an emerging methodological consensus, according to which research focusing on explaining political participation should seek to group different forms of participation into statistical clusters. We draw on this analytical tool, as well as on Verba, Scholzman, and Brady's advice[25] to approach the explanation of participation through a focus on resources as key conditions of existence.

The database containing Hungarian university students was collected by Active Youth in Hungary Research Group via online and face-to-face interviews. The first survey was carried out in the spring of 2013, and the second in the spring of 2015. The first survey was conducted with a so-called hybrid technique: 1,693 persons (56%) filled out the online survey at http://www.aktivfiatalok.hu through the website, while another 1,347 persons (44%) were asked to answer questions via a face-to-face interviews. The distribution of the sample reflects the distribution of the entire student population regarding gender, level of education, and faculty affiliation. The 2015 survey used only face-to-face technique (N=800). The database contains 3,040 university and college students. The distribution of both samples reflects the distribution of the entire student population regarding gender, level of education and faculty affiliation—and the cross tabulations of these variables. Thus, for example the proportion of female BA students from the Faculty of Economics (Corvinus University) reflects the proportion of this group in the entire student population.

---

[25] S. Verba, K.L. Schlozman, and H.E. Brady, *Voice and Equality. Civic Voluntarism in American Politics* (Cambridge, MA: Harvard University Press, 1995).

National, representative survey samples, carried out by polling company Medián, were the second major data source of the paper. We pooled two Medián samples (face-to-face surveys from October and December 2018) and analyzed 2,400 respondents. We also focused on young people, respondents between the age of 18 and 30 (N=225). These national surveys served as a basis of comparison.

Results

RECENT TRENDS AMONG HUNGARIAN YOUTH

The paper will focus on Hungarian youngsters in general and university students in particular. To avoid conceptional stretching it is important to describe the units of analysis and pinpoint the ideological and attitudinal differences between them. The voting age population in Hungary (18+) is approximately 8 million people. 1.3 million of them are between the ages of 18 and 29. Finally, there are little more than 0.2 million university and college students in the country. Thus, students are just a small—but significant—part of the entire youth. As it is reflected in Figure 9.1, youngsters are less keen on conservative, religious-Christian, and leftist (social

Figure 9.1. The most important political labels among Hungarian young people (December 2018) (percentage)

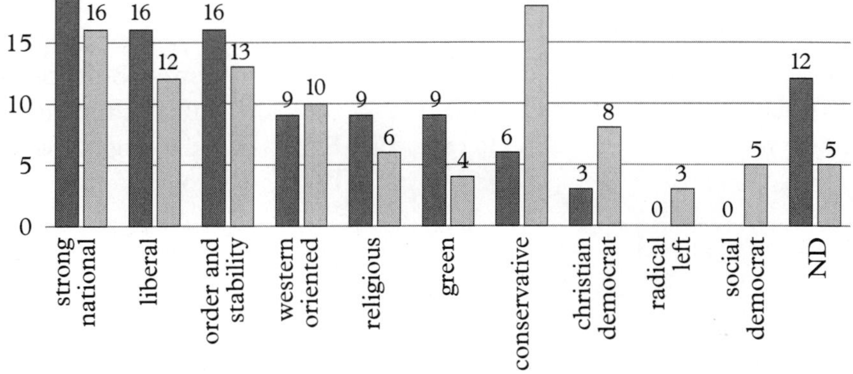

Source: Median Poll, December 2018. N=1200.

democratic) values than their older counterparts. Even more importantly, more than half of them could not choose *any* ideological label.

When they were asked to place themselves on the left–right and liberal–conservative scale, they tended to prefer the center—indicating a great deal of uncertainty and uneasiness (Figure 9.2), as opposed to older people.

Figure 9.2. Place in ideological scales among Hungarian young people (December 2018) (percentage)

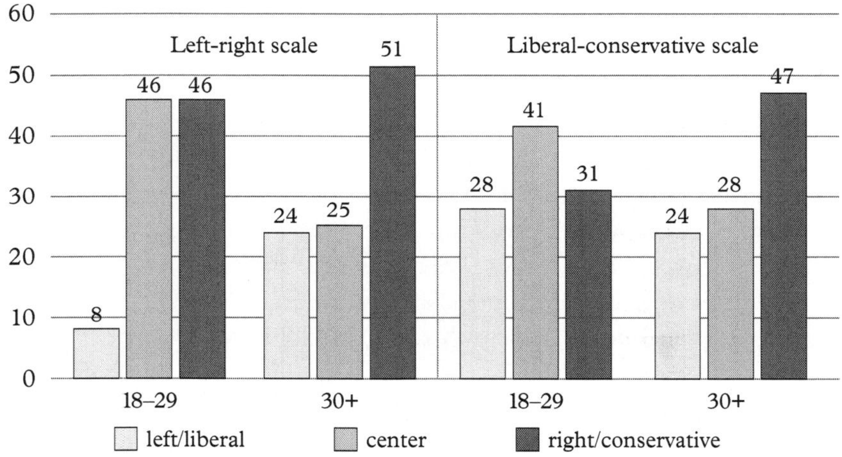

Source: Median Poll, October–December 2018. N=2400.

It is also striking that the Hungarian population at large tends to be much more conservative than liberal, more right-wing than left-wing. Almost half of the people above the age of 30 preferred the right and conservative part of the scale and would vote for Fidesz. As previous research indicates, this is a reflection of partisan choice rather than a manifestation of real value preference.[26] Even among youngsters, the

[26] Zsolt Enyedi and K. Benoit, "Kritikus választás 2010. A magyar pártrendszer átrendeződése a bal–jobb dimenzióban," ["Critical Election 2010. The Realignment of the Hungarian Party System in Left-Right Dimension,"] in *Új képlet. A 2010-es választások Magyarországon,* [The New Formula. Elections in Hungary in 2010,] ed. Z. Enyedi, R. Tardos, and A. Szabó (Budapest: DKMKA, 2011), 17–42.

proportion of liberal and conservative identifiers is almost equal. The "left" label proved to be even more unpopular among people below the age of 29 than the "liberal."

Finally, young people were almost twice less likely to choose a political party (Figure 9.3), this is the best indicator of their alienation regarding politics. *This corroborates the picture of the literature about an apolitical, passive, disaffected youth.*

Figure 9.3. Party preferences among Hungarian young people (October–December 2018)

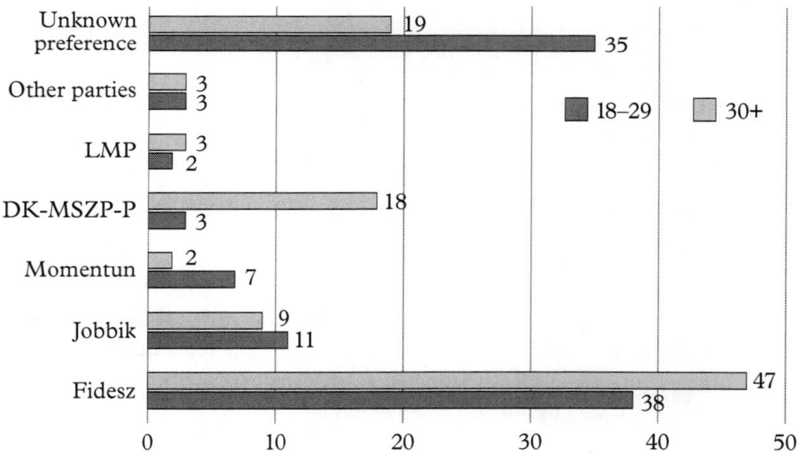

Source: Median Poll, October–December 2018. N=2400.

The Figure shows that Fidesz still dominates the political landscape among the youth—although to a lesser extent than it does among the entire population. There are three other significant camps: the apolitical, passive, undecided voters, the nationalist voters (Jobbik) and the Western-oriented, mostly liberal voters (Momentum[27]).

[27] *Momentum Movement* (Hungarian: Momentum Mozgalom) is a Hungarian political party founded on March 4, 2017 by citizens without ties to established parties. It is best known for starting off a petition against the Budapest bid for the 2024 Summer Olympics in January 2017, as a civil organization. The petition for a referendum in Budapest was successful, however, the government has cancelled the bid before a referendum could have been

As university and college form an exception to the general rule among young Hungarians, in the following section, we shall examine the above mentioned groups (and the greens as well) in our university and college student sample. As those communities are established via socialization mechanisms, we consider them to be stable over the years. The proportions might be slightly different but the picture (e.g. the salient groups) are similar among them.

CLUSTER ANALYSES AMONG HUNGARIAN STUDENTS

In order to identify active and passive university and college students we ran K-Means cluster analysis with variables that did not include any political parties, but where the activity and ideological character of the young people was clearly identifiable. We are looking for an "internal" dimensions based on Williams and Gamson that can reveal the political community, the collective consciousness that offers identity and a sense of connection for young people, frames the way they think, and promotes political participation.

Via cluster analysis we analyzed political attitudes, ideological orientations of college and university students related to different dimensions of political community. Via cluster analysis we could identify 6 groups of Hungarian university and college students (see Figure 9.4, Figure 9.5).

1. *The biggest cluster of college and university students is the cluster of Apolitical, passive (38%) students* (see in the middle of Figure 9.4 and Figure 9.5). While the other clusters have some political features, some variables that allow for further description, this cluster cannot be well characterized along political dimensions. Those who are in this cluster do not particularly care what kind of political system they live in. Additionally, they are unsure whether they want to vote in the

held. The ideology of the party is liberal—the party supports gay marriage, the decriminalization of cannabis and abortion rights. They are pro-European and anti-Putin and reject neither globalization nor capitalism. Leaders of Momentum like to compare the party to Emmanuel Macron's party, La République En Marche! claiming that Momentum seeks to transcend old divisions between left and right.

Figure 9.4.
Hungarian university and college students' cluster map on left-right (left=1, right=7) and liberal-conservative scales (liberal=1, conservative=7) (averages)

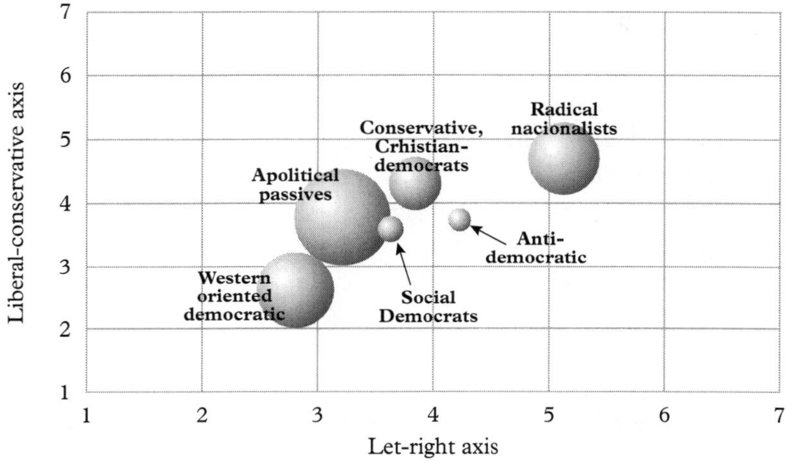

Source: Active Youth Research, 2013–2015. Own calculation.

Figure 9.5. Hungarian university and college students cluster map on moderate–radical (moderate=1, radical=7) and liberal–conservative axis (liberal=1, conservative=7) (averages)

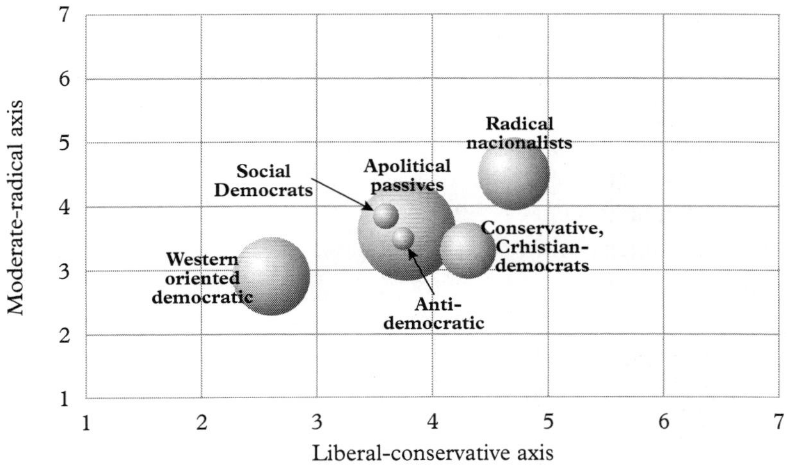

Source: Active Youth Research, 2013–2015. Own calculation.

upcoming parliamentary election and, if they do want to vote, they are uncertain about which party to vote for. The most important feature of the members of the cluster is, therefore, political passivity, which is reflected by all forms of their participation and by their relationship toward the parties—mostly by keeping their distance. One element binding those in this cluster together is their loose identification with the label "green." However, since they are completely passive and uninterested in social and political issues, this identification does not mark an ideological commitment to "green politics." It perhaps also marks a loose identification with healthy eating, organic foods, selective waste-management and other superficial elements of the "green consumerist" lifestyle that are in vogue with the youth. Because of their lack of interest in politics, these students are just drifting with the political events, and their political activity is negligible.

2. *The members of the cluster called Antidemocratic are in favor of dictatorship* (2%), order and stability, but on the other hand they would not take part in an upcoming election this Sunday (see in the middle of Figure 9.4 and Figure 9.5). This means that the members of this cluster are very skeptical of the democratic system—they do not accept and do not want to legitimate the frameworks of the democratic system by taking part in elections.
3. The cluster is very small. It has a mainstream *left-wing character* and is related to Western oriented social democrats from several aspects.
4. *The first active cluster is the so called Western-oriented democrats* (25%) (see in the left corner of Figure 9.4 and Figure 9.5). In the question that prompted respondents to choose between Hungarian and Western values, those who ended up in this cluster markedly identified themselves with the latter. They are also strongly in favor of democracy even though they are skeptical of the current democratic system. Their mindset is liberal and pro-European. They are interested in politics and in social problems. Based on their fathers' level of education, they can be characterized as coming from highly educated backgrounds, as urban dwellers and as atheists. This group is highly concentrated in Budapest and bigger cities. Their preferred method of political participation is online and the election activity. They are overrepresented among students holding master's and PhD degrees (therefore, among older students) and also among students majoring in the social sciences (economics, social science and arts).

5. *Another active cluster among full-time university students in Hungary is the cluster named Radical nationalists (20%) after the Jobbik party*[28] (see in the right corner of Figure 9.4 and Figure 9.5). Members of this group are strongly nationalistic, radical, and denounce all forms of Western ideology. On the left–right scale they strongly pull to the right. They believe "Gypsy-crime" is a fact and would, under certain circumstances, be willing to trade democracy for authoritarian rule. This is the sole cluster where gender plays an important role, given that the majority of this group consists of males. The cluster is formed by active individuals who make use of both traditional and virtual forms of political participation. They have a lower average age: members are overrepresented among students pursuing a degree under the pre-Bologna system, among students pursuing bachelor's degrees, as well as among those enrolled in computer science and engineering majors. The subjective financial situation of this group is somewhat worse. Most of them stem from families of lower or medium education (secondary or vocational school).
6. *The last active cluster being a Conservative, Christian Democrat is the best predictor of this group (12%)*, followed by three equally important traits: religion, being a Fidesz-voter,[29] and satisfaction with the current democratic system. The members of this cluster are religious, conservative, they lean right, and are mostly active in traditional forms of political participation. It is important to note, regarding this group, that while they hold traditional values, they also deem democracy the best type of system. This group is overrepresented among degrees that are not split into undergraduate and master's studies, among them religious studies majors, legal studies majors, national defense majors, education majors and students pursuing advanced theological studies. In our survey, conservative

[28] Jobbik (Jobbik Magyarországért Mozgalom, Movement for a Better Hungary) is a radical right party; founded in 2003, it entered the Hungarian political mainstream in 2009 when it achieved 15 percent of the votes in the European Parliamentary elections.

[29] Fidesz (Fiatal Demokraták Szövetsége, Alliance of Young Democrats) has been the government party of Hungary since 2010. Led by Prime Minister Viktor Orbán, Fidesz is a conservative party and a member of European People's Party.

students tended to be wealthier. Usually, their parents have university (or even doctoral) degrees. They are much more self-confident regarding their professional future and consider their career prospects to be more promising than those of other students.

THREE POLITICAL COMMUNITIES IN THE HUNGARIAN YOUTH

After the above-presented results of cluster analysis, we selected the three most politically active groups. We want to characterize their most important political features. Two of the three active groups explicitly show a "rebellious" character and both these groups define their identity against the group that is currently in power, but from a completely different angle. The third group is also active, but does not take a stance against the government, rather, they support the current government and they receive various forms of state support through pro-government youth organizations. However some signs indicate that in the event of power loss of their favorite political party (Fidesz–KDNP) they would be the most active, most rebellious group out of the three groups. This third political community is therefore currently not rebellious, but since its members are very active, this justifies the distinction.

First, we could distinguish a cluster which is based on the Conservative, Christian Democrat cluster, which we call "right wing activists."[30] This orientation consists of believers, because its members are religious, but also because they believe in the omnipotent character of elder members of the party and in their wisdom, almost unquestioningly. They identify themselves with the values of Fidesz without any criticism. This orientation is much more conformist in character than were the founders of the party; members of the cluster follow the road that has been built by the party leaders. In Debrecen,[31] for instance, several participants of our focus group pointed out the overwhelming and one-sided effect they encountered: their teachers, parents, football-coach, priest and friends are all Fidesz voters. The main difference

---

[30] Zoltán Kmetty, "Fiatal, vallásos és fideszes," in *Racionálisan lázadó hallgatók II.: Apátia—radikalizmus—posztmaterializmus a magyar egyetemisták és főiskolások körében*, edited by Andrea Szabó (Szeged—Budapest: Belvedere Meridionale—MTA TK PTI, 2014), 181–195.

[31] Major city in Eastern Hungary.

between this group and the green-left and radical rebel groups is that "right-wing activists" cannot be regarded as a movement. Besides the church—which is getting less and less popular among young people—there is no non-political (or half-political) pillar of their orientations. There are no bottom-up popular initiatives or organizations which would enhance the political values of conservatism among youngsters. Fidelitas and other Fidesz-youth platforms are top-down organizations which are not youth-oriented.

Two other young active or "rebel" groups identity can be pinpointed, which were described by the academic literature as well.[32, 33] Thus, these political communities—basically subculture groups that provide lifestyle to young people—indirectly encourage participation. These groups have a voice that is understandable to the active sections of youth society. These active political groups are able to affect the entire youth; they can influence, organize and manage them.

First "Rebel" Political Community: the Radical Rebels

In some countries, young people are more likely to support this party family,[34] but the correlation is robust only in Austria (Freedom Party of Austria, or FPÖ) and Hungary (Movement for a Better Hungary, Jobbik). Overall, there is no univocal tendency in Europe. As for qualification, according to conventional wisdom, the extreme right is more popular among the less educated, poor citizens ("modernization

---

32 Kern and Szabó, "A politikai közéleti részvétel," Róna and Sőrés, "A kuruc.info nemzedék," András Keil, "Adalékok a Critical Mass nemzedékről. Az egyetemista-főiskolás LMP szavazók jellemzése," in *Racionálisan lázadó hallgatók: Radikalizmus, posztmaterializmus, apátia*, ed. Andrea Szabó (Szeged—Budapest: Belvedere Meridionale, 2012), 278.

33 Andrea Szabó, ed., *Racionálisan lázadó hallgatók II*, 278.

34 M. Lubbers, G. Mérove, and P. Scheepers, "Extreme Right Wing Voting in Western Europe," *European Journal of Political Research* 3 (2002): 345–78; W. Van der Brug, M. Fennema, S. de Lange, and I. Baller, "Radical Right Parties: Their Voters and Their Electoral Competitors," in *Class Politics and the Radical Right,* ed. J. Rydgren (Oxon: Routledge, 2013), 62–63; Han Werts, Peer Scheepers, and Marcel Lubbers, "Euro-scepticism and Radical Right-wing Voting in Europe, 2002–2008: Social Cleavages, Socio-political Attitudes and Contextual Characteristics Determining Voting for the Radical Right," European Union Politics.

losers").[35] Recently, however, many scholars have challenged this view, pointing out that there is no correlation whatsoever between the level of education and far-right sympathy.[36]

The second rebel political community we call the "Radical rebels," as defined by Szabó and Kern[37]), since this group is exactly the same as that referred to in our K-Means cluster analysis as "Radical nationalist."[38] We consider it a special group because the subculture—and based on that, the electorate of the extremist party Jobbik—has a generational background. The Internet and the grassroots level are the two strong strains of the radical subculture—they reach out to most newcomers using these two types of communication and mobilization.

Jobbik is not only popular among the 18–29 years-old cohort. According to a national representative sample of the Medián polling company and our university and college student sample, its popularity reaches the highest peaks in the cohort of those who are under 22 years old. The younger a person is, the more likely he/she would support the far-right party. For that, the most compelling explanation is a cultural one.[39] According to this, students mainly join because they need a community that offers them identity and a distinct world view—and

---

35 Hans-Georg Betz and Stefan Immerfall, *The New Politics of the Right: Neo-Populist Parties and Movements in Established Democracies* (St. Martin's Press: New York, 1998), Herbert Kitschelt and Anthony J. McGann, *The Radical Right in Wetern Europe. A Comparative Analysis* (Ann Arbor: University of Michigan Press, 1995).

36 Van der Brug et al., "Radical Right Parties," S. Bornschier and H. Kriesi, "The Populist Radical Right, the Working Class, and the Changing Face of Class Politics," in *Class Politics and the Radical Right,* ed. J. Rydgren (Oxon: Routledge, 2013).

37 Andrea Szabó and Tamás Kern, "A magyar fiatalok politikai aktivitása," in *Arctalan (?) nemzedék,* ed. Béla Bauer and Andrea Szabó, 37–80.

38 The Hungarian name of this group is "*Kuruc.info*" group. Kuruc.info is a news portal operated from the U.S. which provides space for extremist, xenophobic voices. The portal is the most read on-line news source among supporters of Jobbik. Its reach is broader than the number of regular student readers, extending throughout the far-right subculture. Kuruc.info is the unofficially preferred media outlet of Jobbik; it amplifies every component of the party's ideology. Many far-right supporters regard it as the only source of the "truth," which broadcasts the "facts" hidden by the liberal and foreign-influenced media.

39 Róna and Sőrés, "A kuruc.info nemzedék."

in the case of many, Jobbik supplies these in unique proportion and manner. First of all, young citizens have the most freedom of availability and activity: they are preoccupied by relationships, work, or membership in civic organizations at a much smaller rate than preceding generations. This is, of course true for all young people, but—according to the data—it characterizes Jobbik supporters to a greater extent than those who are of the same age but vote for other parties.

Most respondents found Jobbik to be more active in their community than all the leftist parties combined. Jobbik puts considerable effort into addressing the youth: it organizes a variety of camps, professional events, protest and cultural programs prominently supported by "national rock" bands and other elements of the far-right subculture (for instance organizations of material arts and folk traditionalists). Symbols are very important too: many students wear badges, t-shirts, bells with Árpád-stripes, Turuls,[40] and maps of Greater Hungary. Internet sources—which are used primarily and most frequently by young people in Hungary—especially sites like kuruc.info, enhance the availability of Jobbik as well. To sum up, Jobbik offers precisely what youth voters need: world interpretation, identity, and belonging to a community.

Second "Rebel" Political Community: The Green-left Rebels

According the surveys conducted in several European countries, both highly qualified people and youths are more prone to support this party family.[41] Ecological inferences also confirm this tendency: the strongholds of green parties are in big cities, capital cities, especially the suburbs - places with a high proportion of young and educated inhab-

---

40 Árpád-stripe is a flag which symbolizes ancient Hungary for radical right voters, but leftist citizens consider this as the symbol of the fascist and Nazi past of Hungary. Turul (an eagle) similarly divides public opinion.

41 Martin Dolezal, "Exploring the Stabilization of a Political Force: The Social and Attitudinal Basis of Green Parties in the Age of Globalization," *West European Politics* 3 (2010): 534–552; Daniel Oesch and Line Rennwald, "The Class Basis of Switzerland's Cleavage between the New Left and the Populist Right," *Swiss Political Science Review* 3 (2010): 343–372; Marc Hooghe et al.,"Explaining the Green Vote: Belgian Local Elections, 1994–2006," *Environmental Politics* 6 (2010): 930–950.

itants.[42] Thus, university and colleges students are the "typical" supporter of green parties. This social group is too small to be analyzed in most survey samples; nonetheless, there are examples which corroborate this hypothesis.[43]

As for our results, the composition and characteristics of these "Western oriented democrats" perfectly coincides with the youth group called *"Green-new left rebels"*[44] by Szabó and Kern.[45] The characteristic values shared by the members of this group include: environmentalism, post-materialism, and revolt against the established elite. In accordance with European tendencies, the green movement appeals mostly to well-off young people in major cities. Members of the group tend to emanate from the ranks of those who have been called the "winners" of Hungary's democratic transition. This ideological group is detached from "traditional politics" and its members are searching for new values. According to Inglehart's framework[46] these college and university students are characterized by post-materialistic values.[47] The party preferences of the green-new left rebels—compared with those of the two other groups—are not fully formed. Its members adapt to the ever-changing nature of the Hungarian party structure, when looking for those political elites that are close to them.

The rational and heavily Western-oriented nature of their participation is clearly demonstrated in several dimensions. Concerning the political activity of the green-new left rebels the dominant element is, on the one hand, on-line participation and, on the other hand, direct forms of participation. It is a characteristic fact that its members were the largest cohort involved in protests that have been organized on the Internet (therefore on-line and direct forms of participation are linked in their case). Additionally, they get information through the on-line

42 Szabó, *Political Orientations.*
43 Dolezal, "Exploring the Stabilization."
44 The Hungarian name is Critical Mass political community. Critical Mass is the name of an urban bicycle parade that is held on the last Friday of each month worldwide in about 300 cities. In Budapest it is held in April on Earth Day and in September at the European mobility week and car-free Sunday.
45 Szabó and Kern, "A magyar fiatalok politikai aktivitása."
46 Inglehart, 1997.
47 Keil, "Adalékok a Critical Mass nemzedékről."

media. It is no coincidence that these young people are the winners of the regime change. They are able to transfer their advantageous background—a family with high cultural and financial capital—to their own "benefit." For example, they are those young people in the society of students who study abroad or work abroad and have experiences that enable them to work and even to establish themselves in the Western part of the world in the future. Another important aspect of their Western orientation is their ideological character. As noted above, green-new left rebels are ideologically atheist, open-minded, politically left or center-left oriented, with liberal and green ideology. Thus, the green-new left rebels have an anti-establishment nature in a sense that their way of life and thinking can be described as a new green-left ideology. Its members are the most tolerant toward minorities; it is the most inclusive group, having received this mentality either through multi-generational family socialization or during their studies in social sciences or humanities.

WESTERN ORIENTED YOUTH

Based on the 2018 Median poll we assume that the *Apolitical, passive* cluster may be the largest group in the entire adult population and among young people as well. We believe that the *Conservative, Christian Democrat* cluster is probably the largest politically active group. However the *Radical nationalists* may be of a similar size among young Hungarians. Finally, we assume that Western-oriented democrats may be much smaller within the whole population. But to see the latter group more clearly, we take a closer look on them by analyzing two national representative survey samples.

As our cluster analysis showed, a sizable part of the Hungarian student population considers themselves as Western-oriented and liberal. We would like to respond to the latest developments in the topic. According to Medián polling data, one-quarter of the Hungarian youth (18–29) choose these labels (Figure 9.1). After the marginalization of Együtt–PM in 2014, they lacked a viable political alternative. By the beginning of 2017, however, a group of approximately 100 youngsters initiated a referendum against the Olympic bid of Budapest—and, surprisingly, managed to collect 266,000 signatures for that. They formed a political party called Momentum and reached 3% at the 2018 national election. The party is extremely over-represented among youngsters below the age of 29: 10% of those who named a party preferred Momentum (58% chose Fidesz, 11% opted for Jobbik, Medián data, December 2018).

Due the recent emergence of the party we don't have data about its popularity among students—but we do we have some regarding the full youth population. Although the party refuse any kind of political labels (e.g. leftist, liberal), its constituency has distinct characteristics: 58% of Momentum voters regard themselves as liberal and Western-oriented, pro-European (25% of the full population choose these labels), and 65% of them strongly supports the country's EU-membership (as opposed to 31% of the full population) (Figure 9.6.).

Figure. 9.6. Do you support or oppose the country's EU-membership?

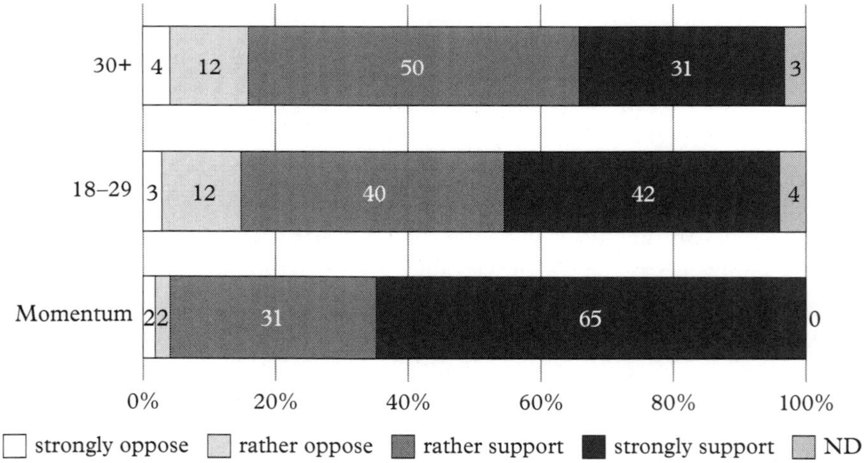

Source: Median Poll, October–December 2018. N=2400.

They are less unified in terms of left-right and liberal-conservative self-placement. 31% consider themselves leftist, 15% rightist, and 55% placed themselves in the middle of the 7-point scale. (The corresponding data of the full population: 23% left, 51% right and 26% in the middle, Figure 9.2.). 40% of Momentum voters choose the liberal part of the scale, 18% preferred the conservative part and 41% opted for the center. (The corresponding data of the full population: 25% liberal, 46% conservative and 29% in the middle, Figure 9.2). Thus, they are significantly more leftist and liberal than the Hungarian average but most of them still refuses to label themselves as such—following their party's stance. Momentum's statements are usually not ideologically motivated (although they participated at the gay-parade and expressed their pro-choice stance, for instance).

Apart from the ideological gap it managed to fill there are few other possible reasons behind Momentum's salient popularity among youngsters. Without student survey data, however, we are left with speculation.

First of all, established opposition parties failed to provide a viable alternative to the Orbán government. Thus, many people become more and more dissatisfied with the parliamentary opposition parties. Second, with the successful anti-Olympics campaign, Momentum gained an image of an active party ("do instead of talk"). This characteristic appealed many youngsters. Third, Momentum was quick to recognize that without a solid organizational background the party's success could be just temporary. It has more members and activists than other parties, and most of them are young people. Fourth, and most importantly, it has an image of a party of youngsters. All of its prominent politicians are youngsters (below the age of 32), its main messages are mostly generational. These make Momentum a possible choice for many ambitious, interested youngsters. Momentum is the third self-proclaimed generational party in Hungarian politics (after Fidesz between 1988 and 1993 and Jobbik between 1999 and 2006).

Conclusion

In our chapter we aimed to reveal new empirical data on the political activity of Hungarian youth and go beyond former claims that young Hungarians are passive. By using a phenomenological approach we tried to find active groups of students that have influence on political thinking an on mobilization of different youth communities.

Our results confirmed young Hungarian's alienation regarding politics. Similar to main findings of the literature about an apolitical, passive, disaffected youth, we found that young people were almost twice less likely to choose a political party than adults. Most indicators show that young people are not very different from the whole population. Those who are really different are really just a thin layer of the society (but the overwhelming majority of young politicians come from this layer). Our results also confirmed that among the youth, those in university and college are the ones who are relatively more active.

We could detect six clusters of students, and from them three active groups. In the cluster analysis we labeled the biggest groups as Apolitical passive (38%) students. The members of the cluster called Antidemocratic are in favor of dictatorship (2%), do not accept the democratic system, and do not want to legitimate it by taking part in elections. The third cluster is very small (3%), it has a mainstream left-wing character and is related to Western oriented social democrats from several aspects.

We identified three active groups. We found the cluster of Conservative, Christian Democrats (12%) that belongs to the "Right-wing activists" group. The cluster named Radical nationalists (20%) considered to belong to the "*Radical rebel*" political community and we gave a detailed explanation on the characteristics of students belonging to this group. A green-new left rebels ideal type consists mostly of Western-oriented democrats (25%).

Our results have proved that a sizeable part of university and college students are active. They are not only ideologically engaged but their party preferences are also expressed by their values and political sympathies. The real novelty of our research is that we found three demonstrable communities of roughly similar size. These groups show significant differences in political activity compared to the other groups. We consider these communities to be established gradually via socialization mechanisms after the regime change. They are not the results of a given political situation, rather "products" of the transition process that started in 1990. If a given student is active, individual participation takes place within the framework of these groups. They show the characteristics of different political ideologies and "organize" different forms of political activity.

Of the Hungarian political culture, a passive mentality was the most characteristic for decades. There is no evidence that suggests that "the children of democracy" have different attitudes. Change might be brought by a relatively thin layer of students who are considered to be the elite of the Hungarian youth—those who are really western oriented and democratically minded. But only future research can tell us whether that change will come or not.

BIBLIOGRAPHY

Bauer, Béla, and Andrea Szabó, eds. *Ifjúság2004 Gyorsjelentés.* Budapest: Mobilitás, 2005.

Bauer, Béla, and Andrea Szabó, eds. *Ifjúság2008 Gyorsjelentés.* Budapest: Szociálpolitikai és Munkaügyi Intézet, 2009.

Betz, Hans-Georg, and Stefan Immerfall. *The New Politics of the Right: Neo-Populist Parties and Movements in Established Democracies.* New York: St. Martin's Press, 1998.

Bíró-Nagy, András, and Dániel Róna. "Tudatos radikalizmus. A Jobbik útja a Parlamentbe, 2003–2010." In *Nemzet és radikalizmus,* edited by András Lánczi, 242–283. Századvég: Budapest, 2011.

Bognár, Adrienn, and Andrea Szabó. "Politikai szocializációs modellek Magyarországon, 1990–2016." In *Csendesek vagy lázadók?—A hallgatók politikai orientációi Magyarországon (2011–2015),* edited by Andrea Szabó and Dániel Oross, 14–35. Szeged—Budapest: Belvedere-MTA TK PTI, 2015.

Bornschier, S., and H. Kriesi. "The Populist Radical Right, the Working Class, and the Changing Face of Class Politics." In *Class Politics and the Radical Right,* edited by Jens Rydgren, 10–29. Oxon: Routledge, 2013.

Csákó, Mihály. "Ifjúság és politika." *Educatio,* 4 (2004): 535–550.

Csákó, Mihály. "Állampolgárokat nevel-e az iskola?" In *Arctalan (?) nemzedék: Ifjúság 2000-2010,* edited by Béla Bauer and Andrea Szabó, 101-114. Budapest: Nemzeti Család- és Szociálpolitikai Intézet, 2011.

Della Porta, Donatella, and Sidney Tarrow, eds. *Transnational Protest & Global Activism.* New York: Rowman & Littlefield Publishers, INC, 2005.

Dolezal, Martin. "Exploring the Stabilization of a Political Force: The Social and Attitudinal Basis of Green Parties in the Age of Globalization." *West European Politics* 3 (2010): 534-552.

Downs, A. *An Economic Theory of Democracy.* New York: Harper & Row, 1957.

Enyedi, Zsolt, and K. Benoit, "Kritikus választás 2010. A magyar pártrendszer átrendeződése a bal–jobb dimenzióban." ["Critical Election 2010. The Realignment of the Hungarian Party System in Left-Right Dimension."] In *Új képlet. A 2010-es választások Magyarországon [The New Formula. Elections in Hungary in 2010],* edited by Z. Enyedi , R. Tardos, and A. Szabó, 17-42. Budapest: DKMKA, 2011.

Greenberg, Jessica. *After the Revolution: Youth, Democracy and the Politics of Disappointment in Serbia.* Stanford: Stanford University Press, 2014.

Hooghe, Marc, Bruno Heyndels, Dimi Jottier, Tuba Bircan, and Sarah Botterman. "Explaining the Green vote: Belgian Local Elections, 1994–2006." *Environmental Politics* 6 (2010): 930–950.

Inglehart, Ronald, and Gabriela Catterberg. "Trends in Political Action: The Developmental Trend and the Post-Honeymoon Decline." *International Journal of Comparative Sociology* 43(2002): 300–316.

Keil, András. "Adalékok a Critical Mass nemzedékről. Az egyetemista-főiskolás LMP szavazók jellemzése." In *Racionálisan lázadó hallgatók: Radikaliz-*

mus, posztmaterializmus, apátia, edited by Andrea Szabó, 157–183. Szeged: Belvedere Meridionale, 2012.

Kern, Tamás, and Andrea Szabó. "A politikai közéleti részvétel alakulása Magyarországon, 2006–2010." In *Részvétel, Képviselet, Politikai változás*, edited by Róbert Tardos, Zsolt Enyedi, and Andrea Szabó, 17–56. Budapest: DKMKA, 2011.

Kitschelt, Herbert, and Anthony J. McGann. *The Radical Right in Western Europe. A Comparative Analysis*. Ann Arbor: University of Michigan Press, 1995.

Klingemann, H., and D. Fuchs, *Citizens and the State*. Oxford: Oxford University Press, 1995.

Kovács, András. "The Post-Communist Extreme Right: The Jobbik Party in Hungary." In *Right-Wing Populism in Europe*, edited by R. Wodak, M. Khosravi Nik, and B. Mral, 223–235. Bloomsbury, London: Politics and Discourse, 2013.

Kriesi, H. "Political Mobilization, Political Participation and the Power of the Vote." *West European Politics* 1 (2008): 147–168.

Laki, László, and Andrea Szabó. "Mi lehet a magyar fiatalok demokráciaszkepszise mögött?" In *Racionálisan lázadó hallgatók II.: Apátia – radikalizmus - posztmaterializmus a magyar egyetemisták és főiskolások körében*, edited by Andrea Szabó, 18–40. Szeged: Belvedere Meridionale Kft, 2014.

Lubbers, M., G. Mérove, and P. Scheepers. "Extreme Right Wing Voting in Western Europe." *European Journal of Political Research* 3 (2002): 345–78.

Mannheim, Karl. "The Problem of Generations." In *Essays on the Sociology of Knowledge by Karl Mannheim*, edited by P. Kecskemeti. New York: Routledge & Kegan Paul, 1952.

McAdam, Doug, John D. McCarth, and Mayer N. Zald. *Comparative Perspectives on Social Movements: Political Opportunities, Mobilizing Structures, and Cultural Framings*. New York: Cambridge University Press, 1996.

Medema, S.G. "Creating a Paradox: Self-Interest, Civic Duty, and the Evolution of the Theory of the Rational Voter in the Formative Era of Public Choice Analysis." *Œconomia*, 1 (2013): 61–86.

Niemi, R.G., and M.A Hepburn. "The Rebirth of Political Socialization, Perspectives on Political Science." *Perspectives on Political Science* 1 (1995): 7–21.

Norris, P. *Democratic Phoenix. Reinventing Political Activism*. Cambridge: Cambridge University Press, 2002.

Oesch, Daniel, and Line Rennwald. "The Class Basis of Switzerland's Cleavage between the New Left and the Populist Right." *Swiss Political Science Review* 3 (2010): 343–372.

Oross, Dániel. "Társadalmi közérzet, politikához való viszony" In *Magyar Ifjúság 2012: tanulmánykötet*, edited by Levente Székely, 283–315. Budapest: Kutatópont Kft., 2013.

Oross, Dániel, Tamás Kovács, and Andrea Szabó. "University Students' Democratic Values and Attitudes towards Democracy in Hungary. European Quarterly of Political Attitudes and Mentalities" EQPAM 1 (2018): 15–30.

Oross, Dániel, and Andrea Szabó. "Changing Tendencies of Youth Political Participation in Europe: Evidence from Four Different Cases." In *Values and Identities in Europe: Evidence from the European Social Survey*, edited by Michael J. Breen, 160–183. Abingdon: Routledge, 2017.

Norris, Pippa, and John Curtice. "Getting the Message Out: A Two-step Model of the Role of the Internet in Campaign Communication Flows during the 2005 British General Election." *Journal of Information Technology and Politics* 4(4): 3–13.

Róna, Dániel, and Anett Sőrés. "A kuruc.info nemzedék. Miért népszerű a Jobbik a fiatalok között?" In *Racionálisan lázadó hallgatók. Radikalizmus, posztmaterializmus, apátia a magyar egyetemisták és főiskolások körében,* edited by Andrea Szabó, 113–157. Szeged: Belvedere, 2012.

Rudas, Tamás. "A Jobbik törzsszavazóiról." In *Társadalmi Riport 2010,* edited by Tamás Kolosi and István György Tóth. Budapest: Tárki, 2010.

Szabó, Andrea, Béla Bauer, and László Laki, eds. *Ifjúság2000, Tanulmányok I. kötet.* Budapest: Nemzeti Ifjúságkutató Intézet, 2002.

Szabó, Andrea. *Political Orientations, Values and Activities of Hungarian University and College Students.* Prague: Heinrich Böll Stiftung, 2013.

Szabó, Andrea. *Exit, Voice, Loyalty and Neglect—Political Attitudes of Hungarian University and College Students.* Prague: Heinrich Böll Stiftung, 2015.

Szabó, Andrea, and Tamás Kern. "A magyar fiatalok politikai aktivitása." In *Arctalan (?) Nemzedék,* edited by Andrea Szabó and Béla Bauer, 37–80. Budapest: Nemzeti Család- és Szociálpolitikai Intézet, 2011.

Szabó, Andrea, and Dániel Oross. "A demokratikus részvétel tendenciái a magyar egyetemisták és főiskolások körében." In *Racionálisan lázadó hallgatók,* edited by Andrea Szabó, 65–110. Szeged: Belvedere Meridionale, 2012.

Szabó, Balázs. "Az új parlamenti pártok szavazóbázisának jellemzői Budapest példáján." *Politikatudományi Szemle* 3 (2013):92–116.

Szabó, Ildikó. *A pártállam gyermekei.* Budapest: Új Mandátum Könyvkiadó, 2000.

Szabó, Ildikó. *Nemzet és szocializáció. A politika szerepe az identitások alakulásában Magyarországon 1867 –2006.* Budapest: L'Harmattan Kiadó, 2009.

Szabó, Máté. *A tiltakozás kultúrája Magyarországon. Társadalmi és politikai tiltakozás 2.* Budapest: Rejtjel Politológia Könyvek, 2007.

Szabó, Máté. "Globális kommunikáció, civil társadalom, tiltakozás." *Fordulat.* 1 (2008): 96–120. http://fordulat.net/pdf/1/szabo.pdf.

Székely, Levente, and Andrea Szabó. *Ezek a mai magyar fiatalok!: A Magyar Ifjúság Kutatás 2016 első eredményei.* Budapest: Új Nemzedék Központ Nonprift Közhasznú Kft, 2017.

Susánszky, Pál, and Márton Gerő. "A Hallgatói Hálózat (HaHa) mobilizációs jellemzői." In *Racionálisan lázadó hallgatók II.: Apátia - radikalizmus - posztmaterializmus a magyar egyetemisták és főiskolások körében,* edited by Andrea Szabó, 278.

Van der Brug, W., M. Fennema, S. de Lange, and I. Baller. "Radical Right Parties: Their Voters and Their Electoral Competitors." In *Class Politics and the Radical Right,* edited by Jens Rydgren, 52–74. Oxon: Routledge, 2013.

Verba, S., K. L. Schlozman, and H. E. Brady. *Voice and Equality. Civic Voluntarism in American Politics.* Cambridge MA: Harvard University Press, 1995.

Werts, Han, Peer Scheepers, and Marcel Lubbers. "Euro-scepticism and Radical Right-wing Voting in Europe, 2002–2008: Social Cleavages, Socio-political Attitudes and Contextual Characteristics Determining Voting for the Radical Right." *European Union Politics*, 14(2): 183–205.

Williams, Rhys H. "Constructing the Public Good: Social Movements and Cultural Resources." *Social Problems*," 1995/42, 124–144.

Williams, Rhys H. "The Cultural Contexts of Collective Action: Constraints, Opportunities, and the Symbolic Life of Social Movements." In *The Blackwell Companion to Social Movements,* edited by David A. Snow, Sarah A. Soule, and Hanspeter Kriesi, 91–115. Oxford: Blackwell Publishing Ltd, 2004.

List of Contributors

ESZTER BARTHA is Associate Professor at the Faculty of Humanities of Eötvös Loránd University, Budapest, Hungary.

NÓRA CHRONOWSKI is Associate Professor at the National University of Public Service, Faculty of Law Enforcement in Budapest, Hungary, and Visiting Researcher of the Hungarian Academy of Sciences, Centre for Social Sciences, Institute for Legal Studies.

MARGIT FEISCHMIDT is Head of Research Department, Research Chair, Institute for Minority Studies at the Hungarian Academy of Sciences, Centre for Social Sciences, Budapest, Hungary; Associate Professor at University of Pécs, Institute for Media and Communication Studies.

KRISZTA KOVÁCS is Marie Curie Research Fellow 2019–2021, WZB Berlin Center for Global Constitutionalism, and Associate Professor, Eötvös Loránd University, Faculty of Social Sciences.

BALÁZS MAJTÉNYI is Researcher, Hungarian Academy of Sciences, Centre for Social Sciences, Institute for Legal Studies, and Associate Professor, Eötvös Loránd University, Faculty of Social Sciences.

GYÖRGY MAJTÉNYI is Professor at the Eszterházy Károly University of Applied Sciences, Eger, Hungary.

VIRÁG MOLNÁR is Associate Professor of Sociology, The New School for Social Research, New York.

CHRIS MOREH is Lecturer in Sociology and Criminology, School of Psychological & Social Sciences, York St John University, United Kingdom.

ZSOLT KÖRTVÉLYESI is Researcher, Hungarian Academy of Sciences, Centre for Social Sciences, Institute for Legal Studies, and Assistant Professor, Eötvös Loránd University, Faculty of Social Sciences.

DÁNIEL OROSS is Research Fellow, Hungarian Academy of Sciences, Centre for Social Sciences Institute for Political Science.

DÁNIEL RÓNA is Premium Post-doctoral Research Fellow, Hungarian Academy of Sciences; Assistant Professor, Corvinus University of Budapest.

ANDREA SZABÓ is Senior Research Fellow, Hungarian Academy of Sciences, Centre for Social Sciences Institute for Political Science; Assistant Professor, ELTE Faculty of Law, Institute of Political Sciences.

ANDRÁS TÓTH is a Senior Research Fellow of the Hungarian Academy of Sciences, Centre of Social Sciences.

Index

M

N

O

P

R

S

T

U

V

W

Y